CHARLES BOOTH'S
LONDON

A PORTRAIT OF THE POOR
AT THE TURN OF THE CENTURY
DRAWN FROM HIS
*LIFE AND LABOUR OF THE
PEOPLE IN LONDON*

SELECTED AND EDITED BY
Albert Fried and Richard M. Elman
FOREWORD BY
Raymond Williams

PENGUIN BOOKS
BY ARRANGEMENT WITH
HUTCHINSON OF LONDON

Penguin Books Ltd, Harmondsworth, Middlesex, Englan
Penguin Books Inc., 7110 Ambassador Road, Baltimore, Maryland 21207, U.S.A.
Penguin Books Australia Ltd, Ringwood, Victoria, Australia

—

First published by Hutchinson 1969
Published in Pelican Books 1971

—

Foreword copyright © Raymond Williams, 1969
Introduction copyright © Albert Fried and Richard M. Elman, 1968

—

Made and printed in Great Britain by
Richard Clay (The Chaucer Press) Limited
Bungay, Suffolk
Set in Linotype Baskerville

This book is sold subject to the condition
that it shall not, by way of trade or otherwise,
be lent, re-sold, hired out, or otherwise circulated
without the publisher's prior consent in any form of
binding or cover other than that in which it is
published and without a similar condition
including this condition being imposed
on the subsequent purchaser

*For little Margaret
and littler Benjamin...*

Contents

FOREWORD BY RAYMOND WILLIAMS	9
PREFATORY NOTE	13
INTRODUCTION	15

1. POVERTY — 47
- The School Board Visitors — 47
- The Setting — 50
- The Eight Classes — 54
- Some Examples of Class A — 72
- Poverty by Districts — 84
- Standards of Living — 92
- Household Economics — 97
- London Street by Street — 103

2. OCCUPATIONS — 161
- Sweating — 161
- Confectionery — 175
- Bread-baking — 182
- Prostitution — 189

3. THE JEWS OF LONDON — 200
- The Jewish Community — 200

4. RELIGION AND CULTURE — 227
- Religion — 227
- Habits of the People — 247
- Institutions — 290

5. ILLUSTRATIONS: RANDOM OBSERVATIONS FROM BOOTH'S NOTEBOOKS — 314

6. RECOMMENDATIONS — 368
- Economic Conditions of Life — 368
- Various Methods of Inquiry — 373
- Eliminating Poverty — 379
- Industrial Remedies — 392

The Organization of Charity	406
Housing	414
Expansion	422
Conclusion	427

BIBLIOGRAPHY 439

Foreword

BY RAYMOND WILLIAMS

THIS selection from the three editions and more than seventeen volumes of Charles Booth's *Life and Labour of the People in London* is very welcome. It makes available, in a convenient introductory form, one of the major documents of the late Victorian city, and is interesting beyond this as an example of an influential method in social inquiry, and as a sign of change in middle-class attitudes towards poverty.

Individuals are always likely to differ, in what they know or try to find out about poverty in their own place and time. We have seen this again, seventy years after Booth, in the range of contemporary attitudes to the facts of poverty, whether in our own society, in which many people are still poor in what is called a welfare state and even an affluent society, or more generally in the world, where the great majority of our fellow human beings are still desperately poor. There is a question of getting the facts, and then the more crucial question of how we respond to them. But each of these questions is held within deep underlying assumptions, learned and repeated in daily experience, about our real relations with other men. If, for example, we think that what we call other races are inferior, we may not concern ourselves with the fact that they are poor, or, if the facts are forced on our attention, we have a prepared answer: that their poverty is the consequence of their inferiority. Similar kinds of evasion and false explanation have been repeatedly used about the poverty of other social classes and groups.

And beyond even this, the idea of poverty is itself a social construction. To say that a man is poor is to make a comparison, and therefore to indicate, for acceptance or rejection, a relationship between him and others, or between him and ourselves. It is one thing to be so deprived of food, shelter and clothing that life itself cannot or can only just be maintained. Such absolute deprivation is easily recognized as poverty, but there are many stages above it for which the description as poor suggests itself: both because our ideas of what constitute adequate conditions for human life are continually changing – we indicate health and happiness, as well as mere survival; we add education, literacy, freedom, opportunity, security to our basic needs – and because, in any case, poverty is a comparative estimate, in the light of the experience of others, or of ourselves at different stages of our lives. And the range of this comparison is then crucial. The people who were called poor relations by rich Victorian families were well off by comparison with the majority of their fellow countrymen, but the range of comparison that prompted the description was within a known class, to which the poor relations, but not other poor people, belonged. Similarly, when English professional people, after the last war, began referring to themselves as the new poor, they were not seriously suggesting that they were poor in relation to the majority of other people, but rather that they were poor in relation to the habits and expectations of their own families and accustomed and expected way of life. With a different social range and perspective, growing up in the family of a railwayman on less than fifty shillings a week, I did not think of myself as poor – indeed for a time accepted as success an eventual five pounds a week, if I passed my examinations – until different experience and different comparisons came into view.

There are people now, in Britain, as poor as some of those investigated by Booth. That persistence always needs emphasis. But his inquiry was a landmark for two reasons: his attempt to establish a 'poverty line', and his accumulation of evidence on which, eventually, a change of orthodox attitudes to poverty, and then of legislation, could be based. It is significant that he set out on his inquiry to disprove what he took to be sensational radical propaganda. That kind of scepticism is as persistent as poverty itself, but few men do what Booth then did, so thoroughly over so many years. And then again, behind his scepticism, and indeed, in the end, recurring as a dogmatic belief, there was the orthodox view, on which the 1834 Poor Law and much earlier practice had been based, that poverty was not only a condition avoidable by individual effort, but was even a kind of crime (as Samuel Butler satirically observed in *Erewhon*) meriting not relief but harsh correction. It was Booth's young assistant, his cousin Beatrice Potter, who eventually, with her husband, Sidney Webb, wrote the decisive Minority Report (1909) of the Royal Commission on the Poor Laws, with an emphasis on the prevention of poverty, by social means, and the institution of social services, on which so much subsequent legislation was based. By then, there was also Seebohm Rowntree's *Poverty: A Study of Town Life* (1901), and a growing political campaign for reform.

Booth, then, was a signal for a movement which went far beyond him. He did not, of course, discover the existence of poverty. Taking only the nineteenth century, and the new problems of widespread urban poverty in an expanding industrial society, no reader of the early radicals – Wooler, Hetherington, Carlile, Owen, Place, Cobbett – no reader of Dickens or Elizabeth Gaskell or Disraeli, of Edwin Chadwick and the Mayhew brothers, of Carlyle, Ruskin, Kingsley, F. D. Maurice, Matthew Arnold, William Morris and so many others, could really be ignorant. Indeed Booth had been preceded, on his own ground, by Henry Mayhew's remarkable *London Labour and the London Poor* (1852); and Frederick Engels's *The Condition of the Working Class in England* (1845, translated 1885) and parts of Karl Marx's *Capital* (1867, translated 1887) had already provided detailed documentation.

What Booth did that was new was not only to continue the inquiry, on a large scale, but to introduce and formalize a method of impersonal inquiry (the comparison with Mayhew is very instructive here, and illuminates two different traditions) which could be associated with the impersonal remedies and the separation from political analysis which are the strengths and weaknesses of that kind of social engineering on which so much subsequent dealing with poverty has been based. As an investigator (it was sometimes different as a man), Booth is not *with* the poor, as the whole plan of his inquiry (mapping and then visiting) makes clear. But he is observing poverty, as a general phenomenon, and seeking means of organization to intervene and amend it. This is not, perhaps, in the end, either the deepest or the most practical response, but of its kind it is a monument, with a continuing influence on English social thought and inquiry. And because the objects of observation are human, in that extraordinary landscape of the late Victorian city which, following Dickens, Gissing and Wells were describing, the experience, often, breaks beyond the method, and is there in its own right and substance, to connect with our own lives.

Poverty, in the end, means nothing, unless this connection is made. We who have seen the 'poverty line' become the 'minimum standard', with restricting and inhuman effects on what was once a careful and a humane reform, need to consider being poor as a whole experience, in men and women like ourselves, and not only as a problem for investigation, classification and report. What Booth sees is important enough; the way he sees it, and how he responds, are of equal interest. For this critical and historical importance, for respect but also for response, in ourselves, Booth needs to be read and thought about, as this selection now makes more widely possible.

RAYMOND WILLIAMS

Prefatory Note

THIS collaboration dates from the time we were both employed as study directors at the Columbia University School of Social Work, under the supervision of Professor Richard Cloward. We were engaged in separate projects dealing with the work of Mobilization for Youth among the poor of the Lower East Side in New York City. In the course of our research we became acquainted with Charles Booth's writings, and were struck at once by the picture Booth drew of London poverty – and of London in general – in the 1880s and 1890s, and by the relevance of that era to the concerns of our time. Furthermore, Booth helped us to understand how Americans see the poor, for the recommendations he made then anticipated many of the programmes which are being carried out today. At the same time, he seemed to provide a first-rate model for any exhaustive inquiry into urban poverty. Consequently, we have collaborated to put together this book in the belief that others who have evinced concern about current American strategies to eliminate poverty may benefit from reading the record of Booth's investigations, at least in part.

This selection of Booth's writings is organized as a reader. It is not a systematic exposition of his ideas. Every volume of the three editions of *Life and Labour* has been consulted. The passages have been selected for their vividness, readability, and intrinsic interest. Often, they are not as symptomatic of Booth's motivating ideas as of his random curiosities. In all instances we have indicated through footnotes where the passages selected can be found in the original Booth texts. Obvious typographical errors in the original text have been corrected, and certain inconsistencies in spelling, punctuation, and style regularized. Omissions are indicated by ellipses. Bracketed editorial interpolations have been italicized to distinguish them from bracketed comments by the author.

The student of Booth may find, however, that he wishes to consult other sources. Therefore, we have concluded our book with a brief bibliography of works about Booth and about the general period, including the various general editions of his work, now all out of print.

ALBERT FRIED
RICHARD M. ELMAN

New York City

Introduction

1

21 June 1887 marked the fiftieth anniversary of Queen Victoria's accession, and Englishmen celebrated the event with feasts and public ceremonies. The middle classes had particular cause to rejoice. The past half-century had witnessed their triumphant rise to power. They were the masters of large-scale industry, of international trade and banking. They were the chief beneficiaries of the recent British expansion in Africa, the Middle East, and Asia. And they set the moral, political, and cultural tone of English life. In attaining their power, the middle classes had stamped their seal of liberalism on the nation. The doctrine of *laissez faire*, the ideal of unfettered individualism, the belief in the pursuit of self-interest as the guarantor of justice and harmony and happiness – these had become accepted British truths by the 1880s.

But there were signs that the great machine of progress was running down. The middle classes were less confident of the future than they had been fifty years before. In the early 1870s Britain suffered the worst depression in her history, and at a time when the United States and Germany were challenging her industrial supremacy and her command of the world's markets. The depression not only produced mass unemployment, it forced millions of farmers to flee the Irish and English countryside to the cities. Yet the cities were unable to support their own burgeoning populations. And to make matters still worse, waves of Eastern European Jews began streaming into the industrial centres, occupying slum neighbourhoods adjacent to those inhabited by the native-born.

A spirit of insurgency sprang up in Britain. By the 1880s, labour was displaying greater militancy than at any time since the Chartist uprisings. Union membership rose vertiginously (from around 750,000 to nearly 1,500,000), strikes grew more frequent and aggressive (notably those of the London match girls, the gas workers, and above all, the dock workers), and for the first time socialist ideas found a receptive audience among workers. Some trade union leaders finally concluded that labour could expect no redress from the existing political order, and in 1893 they formed the Independent Labour Party, the parent of the modern British Labour Party.

The party's effects were not immediately felt. Responding to the pressures from below, reform movements were developing within both major political parties. 'Tory Democracy', led by Randolph Churchill, and the Liberal Party 'Radicals', led by Joseph Chamberlain, proposed giving more help and greater home rule to the cities, enlarging aid to education, revising the poor laws – all of which violated the sacred canons of *laissez faire*. 'The state', said Chamberlain, summing up the case for government intervention, 'is justified in passing any law, or even in doing any specific act, which in its ulterior consequences adds to the sum of human happiness.' And in the course of the 1880s Parliament did pass several important reforms: it imposed a death duty, initiated a system of progressive taxation, extended the voting franchise, and allowed a considerable measure of self-government to localities. Though these laws hardly penalized the upper classes or benefited the lower, they were unmistakable portents of the future, and both the defenders and the critics of the old order saw them as such.

Meanwhile, a segment of the middle class was experiencing a *crise de conscience*. This was reflected in the enormous volume of protest literature read in the 1880s. From John Ruskin, William Morris, Thomas Carlyle, and the disciples of Henry George, the British public learned that predacious capitalists and venal landlords were destroying traditional English freedoms and that radical changes must be instituted at once to remove the vices of unearned increment and production for profit, prevent the desecration of city and country, and affirm the dignity of labour. A number of intellectuals and professionals became socialists: most of them belonged to the Fabian Society (established in 1884), which plumped for gradual reforms similar to those advanced by Tory and Liberal insurgents. Increasingly influential were the Christian Socialists, Marxists, Anarchists, and a host of tiny sects, each with its own panacea. 'The origin of the ferment', Beatrice Webb recalled in her autobiography, 'is to be discovered in a new consciousness of sin among men of intellect and men of property.... The consciousness of sin was a collective or class consciousness; a growing uneasiness, amounting to conviction, that the industrial organization, which had yielded rent, interest and profits on a stupendous scale, had failed to provide a decent livelihood and tolerable conditions for a majority of the inhabitants of Great Britain.'[1]

2

Beatrice Webb had Charles Booth in mind when she wrote about the consciousness of sin. A cousin of Booth's wife, she was very close to Booth in the 1880s, when she collaborated with him in his great investigation of the London poor. Booth's family, business associates, and personal friends were members of the Liberal, Nonconformist establishment that had grown up in the new industrial and commercial cities of nineteenth century Britain, in particular Manchester, Birmingham, Sheffield, Glasgow, and Liverpool, where Booth was born in 1840 to a prosperous Unitarian family. When he was in his early twenties, he and his brother went into the shipping business; they had little trouble finding capital. By the

1. Beatrice Webb, *My Apprenticeship* (London, Longmans, Green & Co., 1926), pp. 173-4.

1880s they had become extremely rich, thanks to their purchase of the most up-to-date steamships.

Curiously, though his business affairs gave him the opportunity to make frequent trips to the eastern United States, we have little evidence that Booth felt obliged to observe social conditions in the young, developing nation with any of the passion which he dedicated to British affairs.

For even as a young man Booth had dabbled briefly in radical theories and movements. He consorted with Benthamite Utilitarians and Comtean enthusiasts who preached 'the religion of humanity'. For a while he was involved in efforts to bring about free secular education. In 1871, he married Mary Macaulay, a niece of the historian Thomas Babington Macaulay. A year later, he suffered a physical breakdown from overwork, and gave up politics and radical causes to attend solely to his business and personal affairs.

For the next decade or so, he maintained a detached interest in public issues, keeping abreast of events through his Liberal family connections – the Macaulays, the Trevelyans, the Potters, et al. It was at this time, in the mid seventies, that his wife's cousin, then Beatrice Potter, came to know him. In her autobiography, she described the impression 'this interesting new relative' made upon her:

Nearly forty years of age, tall, abnormally thin, garments hanging as if on pegs, the complexion of a consumptive girl, and the slight stoop of the sedentary worker, a prominent aquiline nose, with moustache and pointed beard barely hiding a noticeable Adam's apple, the whole countenance dominated by a finely-moulded brow and large, observant gray eyes, Charles Booth was an attractive but distinctly queer figure of a man. One quaint sight stays in my mind: Cousin Charlie sitting through the family meals, 'like patience on a monument smiling at' – other people eating, whilst, as a concession to good manners, he occasionally picked at a potato with his fork or nibbled a dry biscuit. Fascinating was his unself-conscious manner and eager curiosity to know what you thought and why you thought it; what you knew and how you had learnt it. And there was the additional interest of trying to place this strange individual in the general scheme of things. No longer young, he had neither failed nor succeeded in life, and one was left in doubt whether the striking unconventionality betokened an initiating brain or a futile eccentricity. Observed by a stranger, he might have passed for a self-educated idealistic compositor or engineering draughtsman; or as the wayward member of an aristocratic family of the Auberon Herbert type; or as a university professor; or, clean shaven and with the appropriate collar, as an ascetic priest, Roman or Anglican; with another change of attire, he would have 'made up' as an artist in the Quartier Latin. The one vocation which seemed ruled out, alike by his appearance and by his idealistic temperament, was that of a great captain of industry pushing his way, by sheer will-power and methodical industry, hardened and sharpened by an independent attitude towards other people's intentions and views – except as circumstances which had to be wisely handled – into new countries, new processes and new business connections. And yet this kind of adventurous and, as it turned out, successful profit-making enterprise proved to be his destiny, bringing in its train the personal power and free initiative due to a large income generously spent.[2]

Booth's interest in social issues was aroused again in the early 1880s, soon after he moved to London, where he opened a branch of his business. London then epitomized the extraordinary contrasts that characterized nineteenth-century liberal England. There was bourgeois London, with its grand boulevards, its great public monuments to industry, trade, finance, and government, its affluent homes, its new parks, opera houses, and museums, its stores, richly stocked with goods from every corner of the earth. Then there was *petit-bourgeois* and working-class London, with its tidy streets, tidy shops, tidy homes,

2. ibid., pp. 212–3.

its numerous churches, its music halls and its pubs. Finally, there were the slum ghettos radiating out into the suburbs, with their unpaved streets, their disease-ridden and overcrowded tenements, their poorhouses and old age homes, their missionary sects, their pervasive dirt, prostitution, and alcoholism. These three component societies of London might have lived in different cities for all that they knew or cared about each other.

Politically and administratively, London had scarcely advanced beyond the Middle Ages. In the 1880s, with a population of over four million, it still lacked a water, sanitation, and public health system; it still suffered from periodic plagues of typhus and cholera; and its poor laws were as archaic and oppressive as ever. There was no central government to speak of. Not until 1888 was a County Council established to assume overall responsibility for education, sewage disposal, housing, and hospitals.

Booth became concerned about the problems of poverty and unemployment in London, and sedulously attended lectures and debates at Toynbee Hall and Oxford House; he spoke with socialists of all persuasions, and befriended a group of philanthropic social workers. But none of their answers satisfied him. Socialism he regarded as a pernicious intrusion upon individual rights, and philanthropy in all its forms, however well-intentioned, he thought hopelessly ineffective. The radicals and the social workers had failed to tell him what he wanted to know: exactly how the poor lived, exactly how discontented they were – how, concretely, they might be helped.

Booth already knew something about the poor from his own visits to the East End of London. He enjoyed walking through these slums – the worst, perhaps, in Britain – observing their exotic behaviour, eating in their 'coffee palaces', attending their music halls and their missions. Later, he occasionally rented a room in the home of a typically poor family. He learned to respect the integrity of the poor; he even envied them their bitter necessity and the strength they mustered to endure it. His wife thought he felt more relaxed rooming in at the East End than staying at his estate with its 'quiet and beauty'. She wrote: 'He likes the life and the people and the evening roaming – and the food! which he says agrees with him in kind and time of taking better than that of our class.'

Booth was also attracted to the East End by the terrible Darwinian struggle for mastery that went on in its streets. There the veil of hypocrisy and pretence was torn away. In his words: the

> clash of contest, man against man, and men against fate – the absorbing interest of a battle-field – a rush of human life as fascinating to watch as the current of a river.... The feeling that I have just described – this excitement of life which can accept murder as a dramatic incident, and drunkenness as the buffoonery of the stage... looked at in this way, what a drama it is!

While Booth explored the East End, the British middle classes were also growing interested in the condition of the London poor. Until the 1880s, Englishmen had learned of poverty mainly from novels, radical tracts, government blue books, and pornography. But these either dealt with poverty in passing, or appealed to only a small number of readers. A new kind of literature, consisting partly of straight *reportage* and partly of personal anecdote, arose in the 1850s with the appearance of Henry Mayhew's *London Labour and the London Poor*, and later with works such as Thomas Beames's *Rookeries of London*, James Ewing Ritchie's *Night Side of London*, and James Greenwood's *Seven Curses of London*. In 1883 the London Congregational Union, a missionary group, published a sensational best-seller, *The Bitter Cry of Outcast London*, an incredible portrait of destitution, squalor, and vice. Then in 1885 the *Pall Mall Gazette*, a popular, somewhat leftist London newspaper, serialized the results of a survey of working-class districts taken by the Marxist Social Democratic Federation. The survey showed that one out of four Londoners lived in abject poverty. This information, if true, was alarming, for it was published just when the economy had suffered another reverse, when unemployed workers were holding larger and more frequent rallies, and when talk of revolution could be faintly heard in the distance.

Booth, however, was sceptical of the reports about poverty because they conflicted with his own impressions. He thought they were inspired by religious or political ideology, or by the desire for sensationalism, rather than by a concern for the truth. Many allegedly poor people, he had found, lived decent and contented lives. But how could he prove this? How could he convince others that his views were more accurate and reliable than those of social workers, journalists, missionaries, and radicals? He decided that only a scientific inquiry, using the latest statistical and quantitative techniques, would yield objective answers to these questions. Early in 1886, Booth called on F. D. Hyndman, the wealthy autodidact who headed the Social Democratic Federation, to complain that the Federation, in its survey of the London poor, had 'grossly overstated the case'. Booth refused to believe that a million Londoners lived in 'great poverty', and he promised Hyndman that he would conduct his own survey. He would expose the palpable exaggerations of the socialists and refute their 'incendiary' statements once and for all. It took Booth seventeen years and seventeen volumes to complete the project, and in the process he was surprised to discover that, if anything, the Social Democratic Federation had erred in underestimating the extent of London poverty.

3

In setting himself the task of investigating the lives and occupations of all the inhabitants of London, Charles

Booth had no clear idea of the method he would employ or of the resources that were available to him. He found the census reports of 1881 inadequate for his purposes: they failed to give a breakdown of occupations or incomes or the distribution of wealth. Moreover, Booth had no staff to help him. In the spring of 1886, he managed to recruit several volunteers, but they quickly withdrew as soon as he elaborated his plans.

Beatrice Potter was the one volunteer who stayed on. A profound and touching friendship grew out of the collaboration between these two Victorians: the unhappy intellectual woman of twenty-seven who had recently turned down a brilliant marriage to Joseph Chamberlain because she was determined to lead a useful, independent life as a social reformer; and the paternalistic, class-conscious businessman, conservative in habits and beliefs, especially in regard to the place of women. 'We are very fond of each other,' she confided to her diary in 1887. 'A close intimate relationship between a man and a woman without sentiment (perhaps not without sentiment, but without passion or the dawning of passion). We are fellow-workers, both inspired by the same intellectual desire. Only in his life it is an etc: in my life if it becomes anything, it would become the dominating aim.'

Booth and his helper finally found a source of material for the study. Joseph Chamberlain informed them that he had discovered a great deal about the lives of the Birmingham poor – whose condition he had sought to alleviate – from records kept by local School Board visitors.[3] Following up this lead, Booth met the London School Board visitors responsible for the East End, the first area he intended to investigate. They had exactly what he was looking for: a detailed account of every family with children of school age or pre-school age. But as Booth later learned, not every poor person had a

3. See Chapter 1, pp. 47–50, where Booth discusses in detail the function of the School Board visitors.

family, and not every poor family had school-age or pre-school-age children. Accordingly, he drew on other sources, chief among them the Poor Law statistics and the police reports of registered lodging houses.

The next step was to sort out and classify the enormous mass of data. The problem confronting Booth and Beatrice Potter was whether to classify the poor by incomes or by occupations. Booth decided to combine both. He established a system of double-entry bookkeeping. One entry listed income levels and conditions of poverty under eight 'Classes', A to H, A representing the hopeless of the poor: 'occasional labourers, loafers and semi-criminals', and H representing the comfortable middle class. Booth also had expensive neighbourhood and district maps drawn up, inventing colour equivalents of the different classes: black stood for A at one end of the spectrum; yellow stood for H at the other. The second entry listed the known occupations of the East End – thirty-nine in all. Each wage earner was to be placed under the appropriate occupational rubric or 'Section'. When filled up, the two entries could be checked against each other and an exact correlation drawn between earnings, occupation, and standard of living.

With the method thus defined, at least abstractly, it became a simple though time-consuming matter for Booth – now with the help of hired assistants – to gather and classify the material. Wishing to maintain scrupulous objectivity, Booth forbade his staff to visit the streets and homes that the School Board officials or the police described to them. Not until they had recorded all the information from official sources did he permit them to interview people and add their own impressions to the data in their notebooks. Even so, the researchers continued to observe the strictest proprieties. 'With the inside of the houses and their inmates', Booth stated, 'there was no attempt to meddle. To have done so would have been an unwarrantable impertinence...'

Inevitably Booth came up against the question, What is poverty? Unless he defined the meaning of poverty with some precision, his study, for all its thoroughness, would be as arbitrary as the studies he had criticized. Accordingly, he invented a quantitative standard of measurement – a 'poverty line' of eighteen to twenty-one shillings a week for a 'moderate'-sized family. Classes C and D fell within this income range. Booth calculated that families belonging to the poverty-line classes would make ends meet if they lived frugal and rigorously self-disciplined lives, if their wants were simple and their 'vices' few – and if their luck held out. Below the poverty line was the nether world of the 'very poor', comprising classes A and B, who were 'at all times more or less in want'. Theirs was a world utterly without hope.

Booth published the results of his initial investigation in April 1889, exactly three years after he had begun it, under the title *Life and Labour of the People*. Though it was a much reduced version of his original plan – it embraced only East London – the volume was a vast compendium of charts, maps, statistics, harrowing descriptions of families, homes, streets, conditions of work, brought together under the general subject of poverty. This leviathan study was divided into three unconnected parts: 'The Classes', which included detailed surveys of the district, street by street, house by house, along with lengthy essays on the institutions and relations of the poor – all written by Booth himself; 'The Trades', of which two sections (those dealing with the docks and tailoring) were written by Beatrice Potter, and the rest (concerning bootmaking, furniture, tobacco, silk manufacturing, and women's work) by other members of Booth's team; finally, 'Special Subjects', which contained chapters on the system of labour known as sweating, by Booth; on the Jewish community (London's Jews then being concentrated in the East End), by Beatrice Potter;

and on the recent influx of population, by one of the assistants.

But in spirit, in motivating ideas, in its organic and imaginative conceptions, *Life and Labour* was Booth's work. Moreover, the organization of the book – or rather the lack of it – pointed to a serious shortcoming inherent in his method. He assumed, in the grand tradition of English empiricism, that the facts speak for themselves, that they are perceived by the senses, gathered up by an impartial mind, and formed into ever larger and more accurate generalizations. In practice, however, these generalizations tended to be mere pigeonholes, each properly labelled. There was no sense of the whole underlying and fusing the separate parts. Booth told a great deal about East London in the 1880s, but he did not show how and why the district as a whole developed into a slum, nor did he compare it with similar communities, subject to similar conditions, in Britain and elsewhere. Booth's study was detached from its context of time and place and change.

But his method also had the virtues of its limitations. The strength of English empiricism lies precisely in its openness, its willingness to allow for novelty and originality, its refusal to be imprisoned in *a priori* systems of thought. In a word, nothing must stand between the observer and the 'facts'. That is why Booth saw the world of poverty with a fresh and unbiased eye. His writings conveyed the ingenuousness, the honesty, of his perceptions. Furthermore, when Booth conducted his survey, he had no precedents to guide him except occasional reports from factory inspectors, royal commissions, the census, and other statistical surveys. There had been no inquiry into poverty in general, no breakdown of incomes and classes. The various schools of 'scientific' sociology that had arisen earlier in the nineteenth century, notably those of Comte and Marx, could not have helped him even if he had agreed with them. They were

INTRODUCTION

primarily concerned with the totality of history and with the laws of social evolution, not with particular and immediate problems revolving around the way people live. In attempting to deal with just these problems, Booth, for all the defects of his method, was a pioneer. He established his own precedent.

Booth's wanderings among the habitations of the poor on Chester, Eldon, Ferdinand, and Dutton streets, his tough-minded, empirical descriptions of housing, styles of dress, eating habits, shops, and employment, may recall George Orwell's visits nearly fifty years later among the poor of Wigan Pier. There is an openness to reality, a willingness to look at squalor without coating it over with moralistic language, and a humility before the plight of some of the poor which give the writing a literary distinctiveness truly reminiscent of Orwell's own efforts to assert decency. It is journalistic without seeming callous and sensationalistic. 'Here in Ferdinand Street', he writes of one packed block of houses, 'not an inch was lost, and the fingers of any passer-by might have tapped at any window and door as he passed along.'

In his writings about the poor, Booth uses metaphor and figurative language sparingly. There is a deliberate no-nonsense quality to the prose which may be a trifle off-putting to those accustomed to learning of poverty through the lyricism of a James Agee or the rhetorical indignation of James Baldwin. But, though Booth's primary aim was not to create literature but to describe reality, it is difficult to read his writings today without reflecting on the literary strengths of such a method. He has a remarkably good ear for common speech and an eye for telling details. One pictures him – tall, stooped, notebook in hand, intent upon his subject, asking frequent questions, at times a trifle self-deprecating, but never so aware of his posture as to lose sight of his inquiry. Booth was, apparently, courteous almost to a fault, and his prose is a perfectly unaffected vehicle for such decorum. Sometimes we are hardly conscious of the intrusion of his style. To judge from his frequently tortured letters of self-doubt to his wife and other collaborators, his control was a carefully contrived persona, yet the ease with which Booth is able to maintain the illusion is striking. And if the prose, like the thought, never manages to encompass the total reality behind London poverty, it does manage to convey strength, resilience, patience, a certain toughness of observation which seems wholly pertinent to the harsh black-and-white realities he was called upon to observe; and the humour is gentle and conversational, hardly ever censorious as one might expect of a man of his class:

To have her husband at the antipodes and to go back to her shop did not agree with Mrs. Mayson's idea of married life and she told him so when he next came home. Thus appealed to he was willing to settle down, and he took up the trade of painter, perhaps because his wife's father was or had been connected with that line of business...

At any rate he was able to obtain and keep regular employment and from that day to this has lived quietly at home with his wife.

'But one never knows,' she would say, 'a restless fit might at any time come over him,' and she added that within a year of the time when she was speaking he had, on coming home one evening, announced his intention of taking train to Liverpool, there to find a ship.

'Better wait till tomorrow,' she had said; and when tomorrow came, the idea had passed.[4]

Booth tried hard to accept the poor, to be at ease among them, but the effort never deterred him from reporting their wretchedness:

... Mrs. Pierce's husband has been dead a good many years and, besides son and brother-in-law, she has living upstairs in this house a married daughter and her husband, whose little

4. From Booth's notebook, quoted by Mary Booth in *Charles Booth, a Memoir* (London, Macmillan & Co. Ltd., 1918), p. 105.

girl it is that sits on Mr. Pierce's knee, making dangerous play with his knife when she can get it. She is three years old, but small and backward – can't talk at all beyond saying 'ta', and can barely walk, it seems, having had very bad health – one sickness after another for months together.[5]

Whether Booth's manner, which lends so much dignity to the poor without special pleading, would be as appropriate to writing about them today is worth considering. Nowadays the writer about poverty is likely to make much of his own motivations, to assert his involvement, or to agonize over it, even attempting to de-class himself, and always questioning his relatedness because of the strain of trying to relate; but Booth's prose shows none of the strains of such an engagement. No doubt he was inspired to begin his researches chiefly because – like many another Englishman of his class and era – he felt vaguely threatened by the presence of so much poverty and wished to specify the problem in hopes of finding the most decorous and appropriate solutions to it. Yet once he encountered the poor, his compassion was never tidy or priggish; it was what motivated him to keep on learning and writing. Booth did not, like some romantic solipsists of today (and of past days), attempt to render poverty in its most existential terms. Probably he would have found such efforts contemptible, for he truly believed that between himself and the poor there was an unbridgeable gap of class and culture. But by forcing himself to live among the poor, to make a confrontation with their lives, he achieved a human recognition. The prose is never so tendentious that it does not reflect such a recognition. Stripped of abstractions, except for an occasional epithet which temper or compassion provokes, it describes a reality only to be found in the streets of London. As Booth himself pointed out in a letter to his assistant Ernest Aves: 'I am afraid we are sure to shock very many good people in the conclusions – the danger

5. From Booth's notebook, ibid., p. 114.

of hurting is rather to be found in the details necessary to support these conclusions. *It cannot be entirely avoided, but must never be wanton.*' (Editor's italics)

Thus, Booth must be listed under that most misunderstood of contemporary phenomena, the middle-class reformer. Booth's study of the poor also achieved its first objective: it gave the public some idea of the dimensions and meaning of poverty in London. Never before had the middle classes been told in such harrowing detail about the effects of moral decay and destitution, about the domestic lives of the poor, about the oppression of work, the condition of women workers, the practice of sweating, about the new immigrants. Booth's dry statistical data furnished incontestable proof that the socialists had been in error; they had actually seen only a fraction of London poverty. In the *Pall Mall Gazette* of 1885, the Social Democratic Federation had contended that twenty-five per cent of the working class was poor, a statistic that Booth then condemned as shockingly high. He now found that the proportion in East London was close to thirty-five per cent; that of the 900,000 people in the district, 314,000 were poor; that of these far more than half (185,000) belonged to families earning less than eighteen shillings a week; and that more than half of these in turn (over 100,000) suffered from acute 'distress'.

Booth made a second important discovery. On the basis of information received from 4,000 poor people, he concluded that the cause of poverty in about eighty-five per cent of the cases was either 'employment' (both lack of work and low pay) or 'circumstances' (large family and sickness). 'Habit' ('idleness, drunkenness and thriftlessness') accounted for only about fifteen per cent. Booth's evidence thus demolished the middle-class myth that poverty resulted from personal failure, vice, or improvidence. Despite himself, he implicitly lent support to the socialist argument that poverty was a collective, not an individual, responsibility.

INTRODUCTION

Clearly, Booth in his role as investigator was a radical, willing to go wherever his pursuit of the truth led him. But as a man of affairs he still remained an implacable conservative. The gap between these two sides of Booth's personality emerged whenever he offered his own judgements and evaluations. He could, for example, admit that a third of the population lived in poverty and then go on blithely to assure his public that there was no cause for alarm. 'This is a serious state of things,' he wrote, 'but not visibly fraught with imminent social danger, or leading straight to revolution.' He urged patience and calm. 'That there should be so much savagery as there is, and so much abject poverty, and so many who can never raise their heads much above the level of actual want, is grave enough; but we can afford to be calm, and to give attempts at improvement the time and patience which are absolutely needed if we are to do any good at all.'

Oddly for a man who took such pride in his tough-mindedness, Booth sometimes cast a romantic glow over the poor — at least over those who had not sunk below the poverty line. He envied them their simplicity, their virtues, their innocent happiness. Though he spent much of his writing in describing the terrors of poverty, he could still say: 'I perhaps build too much on my slight experience, but I see nothing improbable in the general view that the simple natural lives of working-class people tend to their own and their children's happiness more than the artificial complicated existence of the rich.' If Booth ever bothered to ask the working-class people if *they* thought they were happy, he has left us no record of such an exchange of views.

The gap between the investigator and the man of affairs was especially manifest in Booth's recommended solution to the problem of poverty. It rested on his distinction between the more or less self-sufficient poor (classes C and D) and the hopeless poor (classes A and B). Booth came to the conclusion that the existence of classes

A and B threatened to drag down the classes directly above them, thereby unsettling the entire social structure. Accordingly, he proposed the extirpation of class B. This was to be done through the establishment of compulsory labour camps, sealed off from the rest of society, where men and women would be taught skills and work discipline while their children were raised under strict supervision. If the poor failed in their special camps, they would be sent to poorhouses and their children taken from them. If they succeeded, they would be allowed to re-enter civilization.

How could such a staunch defender of *laissez faire* liberalism wish to grant the state ruthless, plenary power over so many people? Booth believed that individualism would be strengthened, not diminished, by this extension of 'state socialism', as he called it. Socialism, in his view, was the exercise of state power over those who could not help themselves, or who constituted a danger to the community. Jails, insane asylums, workhouses, and other such institutions were examples of socialism. Under Booth's scheme, socialism would find its proper sphere in a preponderantly individualist society. 'My idea', he explained,

is to make the dual system, Socialism in the arms of Individualism, under which we already live, more efficient by extending somewhat the former and making the division of function more distinct. Our Individualism fails because our Socialism is incomplete.... Thorough interference on the part of the State with the lives of a small fraction of the population would tend to make it possible, ultimately, to dispense with any Socialistic interference in the lives of all the rest.

Booth was certain that the advantages of abolishing class B would soon be felt throughout society. The derelicts, 'semi-criminals', and so on of class A would be 'harried out of existence'. The members of classes C and D would earn more money, rise above the poverty line, and eventually 'join hands' with classes E and F – the skilled workers who belonged to trade unions and co-operatives. Some day, Booth hoped, unions and co-operatives would embrace all the people who worked for a living, not merely the élites of labour. Workers would 'build from the bottom, instead of floating, as now, on the top of their world'.

But in the long run, it was the middle class that stood to gain most from the Draconian measures Booth recommended. He reasoned that socialism as an ideology appealed primarily to the more literate, better paid, better organized workers of classes E and F – to those who had a stake in society. 'Here, rather than in the sufferings of Class A, or the starvation of Class B, or the wasted energies of Class C, or the bitter anxieties of Class D, do we find the springs of Socialism and Revolution.' By abolishing mass poverty, the state, at a single stroke, would pacify classes E and F and exorcise the threat of 'Socialism and Revolution'. Obedience and sense of duty would return to the factory. Industry would become more efficient. The 'forces of individualism and the sources of wealth' would be left 'untouched'.

Booth's judgements and recommendations constituted only a trivial part of *Life and Labour of the People*, and the press, in reviewing the book, paid little attention to them. What impressed – or terrified – his reviewers was his dissection of London's rotting interior. The readers of the book, whatever their predilections, could no longer disregard the problem of poverty nor content themselves with homilies about the humble and deserving poor.

4

As soon as *Life and Labour* was published in 1889, Booth set out to complete his survey of poverty in London. He and his assistants worked rapidly, using the same sources as before – the reports of the School Board visitors – and in two years a second volume appeared.[6] In form and method it resembled the first. It put forth an immense quantity of material under several loosely connected topics. Booth admitted that he had 'enlarged the wilderness of figures', but had not 'done much to make the path more clear'.

The second volume took in all the districts omitted from the first (Central, South, and outlying London), with a total population of three million. But if its scope was broader, it was also more superficial than the first. Booth and his co-workers avoided inquiring into the personal lives, the incomes, the expenditures of the poor. Instead, they concentrated on describing streets, neighbourhoods, and districts and on cataloguing their inhabitants under the appropriate classes, A to H. This information was simultaneously projected on to a series of detailed and very exact maps, the colours of which corresponded to the breakdown of classes; these maps were issued together as a companion volume. If Booth had done nothing else, he would deserve recognition for having had these remarkable poverty maps of London drawn up and published.

He was appalled by what he discovered in his expanded investigation. He had assumed that the rest of London was much less poor than the East End and that there existed a direct relation between poverty and density of population. But he now found that 30.7 per cent of all the people of London lived on or below his poverty line. Moreover, the poor were scattered throughout the city, even in the least crowded areas, and often in the same neighbourhoods as the middle and upper classes. Poverty was like a fungus spreading over the London landscape:

---

6. Its title was turned round to read *Labour and Life of the People*, because another author, Samuel Smiles, laid claim to the original title with his book *Life and Labour, or Characterizations of Men of Industry, Culture and Genius*, published in 1887.

the maps made that clear. But Booth held fast, refusing to modify his opinions. He still counselled patience and calm good sense.

In the interval between the publication of the two volumes, Beatrice Potter and Booth had parted ways. In the course of her work in the East End, she became convinced that poverty could not be dealt with piecemeal or through sporadic reforms but only through a change in the organization of society as a whole. She grew interested in the cooperative movement and then in socialism. 'My friendship or rather my companionship with Charlie is for the time dropped – our common work is ended', she wrote in her diary. The break was complete when she announced that she was marrying Sidney Webb, who had made a name for himself as a leader of the Fabian Society. 'You see,' Mary Booth said to her on learning of her decision, 'Charlie and I have *nothing* in common with Mr. Webb. Charlie would never go to him for help, and he would never go to Charlie, so that it would not be natural for them to see each other.' Beatrice Potter's 'Apprenticeship' – as she titled the first volume of her autobiography – was over.

But at that point, Booth had explored the life but not the labour of the people; he had carried out only half of his project. In 1892, he decided to correct this deficiency, and launched his second full-blown investigation, this one into the industrial life of the poor. 'The first Inquiry', he explained in one volume of the industry series, 'had been an attempt to describe the inhabitants of London, especially the poorer part of them, and their social conditions, as they lived, street by street, family by family, in their homes.' The aim of the industry series, he continued, 'was to review the people as they work, trade by trade, in their factories, warehouses or shops, or pursue their avocations in the streets or on the railways, in the markets or on the quays; to consider their relations to those whom they serve, whether employer or customer, and the remuneration they receive; and finally, to examine the bearing which the money earned has on the life they lead.' To accomplish this, Booth determined to list every trade in London and then classify every wage earner in the city under his particular trade. When this was done, he would collate the two master lists – incomes, already compiled, and occupations – bringing the whole project to a grand consummation.

Booth drew on a rich variety of sources for his industry series: the census reports of 1891, factory inspection notebooks, trade unions, managers or owners of businesses, and, of course, the workers themselves. The survey was complex and laborious, but Booth and his team went ahead smoothly, and after completing their research, brought out one volume after another in quick succession. By 1897, the fifth and last of the volumes of the industrial series had been published. Booth added these to a four-volume reissue of his previous study on poverty, the whole thus constituting a nine-volume second edition of *Life and Labour of the People in London*.[7]

Booth wrote only a few of the essays in the industry series. He had been occupied with other problems at the time, and had entrusted his assistants with the main responsibility for the work. This may account for the fact that these books are on the whole exceedingly dull; they lack the vivacity and feeling for detail that characterize Booth's own writings. Worse, the essays on industry departed from Booth's original intention, which was to correlate poverty and working conditions. His assistants lost themselves so completely in minutiae and technicalities that they neglected the central questions: How did the wage earners spend their money? how did they live? where did they stand on the income scale? Because they were unable to answer these questions, Booth had to

7. 'For this new edition', Booth wrote in the opening pages of the series, 'I have altered the title by adding to it the words "in London", such being the actual limitation of the subject matter.'

drop his ambitious plan. Life and labour remained separate and distinct entities.

Once again, Booth the businessman took leave of Booth the radical investigator. The investigator – or rather his staff – had spared none of the details of factory life: the oppressive working conditions, the long hours and low pay, the insecurity of the job, the reduction of men to commodities. Booth acknowledged the 'helplessness of the worker, whether unionist or non-unionist'. Yet when he evaluated the facts, Booth sang paeans of praise to the capitalist system and condemned interference with the prerogatives of entrepreneurs. Though he welcomed 'socialist' measures to eliminate poverty and regulate incomes, he insisted that they must never be applied to industry, where progress rested on the unfettered struggle for survival, where state controls of any kind dried up the springs of creativity and wealth. And while he granted the value of labour unions, he insisted that they too must not go beyond their strictly defined limits and act as a restraint on trade.

What then was to be done to reduce the 'helplessness of the worker'? Ultimately nothing, Booth maintained, but education. For only education could be depended on to form the character of the worker. Booth did not discuss the kind of education he favoured. Presumably, he meant one that would inculcate habits of self-reliance according to the canons of Manchester liberalism.

In one of the industry volumes, Booth alerted his readers to the prospect of yet another study: 'I trust in the efficacy and utility of the scientific method in throwing light upon social questions,' he wrote, 'and the work on which I am engaged is not yet finished.' In the course of his investigations, he had come to realize that there was something more to the lives of the people than work and consumption, that there was a distinct culture of poverty. He had perceived this years before in his sojourns in the back streets of Liverpool and London. Following the completion of the industry series, he prepared to probe more deeply into 'the forces for good and evil that are acting upon the condition of the people'. He wanted to know how the poor were influenced by social and political institutions, by philanthropic organizations, by government agencies, and above all, by religious bodies.

And so, for the third time, Booth and his helpers cast their nets in search of material. Interviews were conducted with nearly every religious, social, and philanthropic group in London – some 1,800 in all; publications and journals, pamphlets and circulars of every description were read; the local and district administrations of the city were carefully studied; visits were made – mostly by Booth himself – to churches, missions, chapels, and meeting-houses. In collecting the data, Booth encountered a particularly knotty problem arising from the very subject of his inquiry. How could he possibly attain scientific exactitude in a survey of something as amorphous as culture? How could he measure attitudes and influences? These questions suggested their own answers. Booth had no choice but to abandon the scientific model on which he had based his previous studies; he had to rely now on his personal impressions, on what might be called qualitative descriptions. 'Our object', he stated candidly, 'has been to obtain truthful and trustworthy impressions, which we might hope to be able to transmit to our readers, of whom, though many would know accurately some parts, few can have surveyed the whole field.'

This reliance on impressions gave the volumes of the religious series – seven in all, published in 1902 and 1903 – a unity and pointedness that the earlier series on poverty and industry lacked. For the first time, Booth's evaluations were organically related to the descriptive data instead of being superimposed upon them. The two sides of Booth – the inquisitive investigator and the cautious businessman – had finally been reconciled.

Both had hoped that religion would act as a powerful

influence on the moral and spiritual lives of the people. He sadly came to the conclusion that its influence was either negligible or pernicious. His poverty maps showed that the Anglican, or Established, churches generally were to be found in those neighbourhoods or streets coloured red and yellow (classes G and H). The Church of England, in other words, was the church of the well-to-do. Booth had mixed feelings about the various Nonconformist religions, which embraced a segment of the middle class as well as the upper reaches of the poor (mostly class D). He approved of the Quakers, the Unitarians, and the Congregationalists because they tended to regulate social behaviour and made definite ethical demands upon their followers. There were many Nonconformist religions of which he disapproved, chief among them the 'Wesleyans' (or Methodists) and Baptists. Their appeal to the emotions, their missionary activities, he regarded as 'a spiritual debauch', and their conversions he found 'exceptionally hysterical' and superficial. He compared the Salvation Army to a band of 'Ethiopian minstrels'. He especially deplored the charity work of the missionaries – their exploitation of weakness to gain their ends. 'The admixture of Gospel and giving produces an atmosphere of meanness and hypocrisy, and brings discredit on both charity and religion.'

The most interesting sections of the religious series dealt with the working class (E and F). Booth seemed to sympathize with, or at least understand, the tendency of workers to reject the Church of England and to think religion in general irrelevant when not hypocritical. They expected 'a religious man to make his life square with his opinions'. Yet it was their experience that the worst bosses were often the most devout Christians, that piety was no guarantee of justice. Booth discovered that the moral forces shaping the lives of workers were socialism and trade unionism, not religion. These new ideologies, he had to admit, saved the workers from passivity and offered them faith, hope, and dignity. And he had to admit further that the socialist administrations that had recently been voted into office in some localities were notably more dedicated and efficient than their predecessors. Under the circumstances, Booth was prepared to modify his opinions slightly about socialism, to acknowledge that it meant more than state repression and the denial of individualism. But this did not make it any more palatable to him.

Booth's verdict on the influence of religion flowed directly from the results of his survey. 'Taken as a whole', he declared, 'the efforts of religious bodies to improve the condition of life ... fail.' The upper classes observed the merest formalities; the workers were indifferent or hostile; large segments of the middle class and the poor were susceptible to meaningless evangelism; while the very poor, sunk in sloth, were beyond reach except as charity cases. And so, despite the statistics on church attendance and the number of missions and conversions, London, he found, was 'a heathen city'. The profundity of Booth's insight has become increasingly apparent with the passage of time. Today, even the façade of piety is gone, and few Englishmen have anything to do with organized religion.

Booth's friends had looked forward to the final volume of the third edition. There they had expected him to pull together the loose ends, give a sense of unity and purpose to the previous sixteen volumes, and, at last, set forth concrete recommendations for reform. Alfred Marshall, the great economist, had written to him: 'You must for the sake of all, for knowledge, for purpose, for ideals – and I will throw in, though somewhat irrelevantly, for Booth – for the sake of all you must make that volume the best thing you possibly can. The best of the kind that has been done ...' But Booth's final volume, judged even from a much lower level of expectation than Marshall's, was a disappointment. It said nothing new. It provided no synthesis or overview of the project as a whole. It merely reaffirmed Booth's faith in the redeeming power of individualism and his belief in the efficacy of 'limited socialism' – meaning the elimination of class B. He left it to others to come up with the solutions; he offered none. His closing words were sad and self-deprecating, as though he were apologizing for having let his readers down.

> Perhaps the qualities of mind which enable a man to make this inquiry are the least of all likely to give him that elevation of soul, sympathetic insight, and sublime confidence which must go to the making of a great regenerating teacher. I have made no attempt to teach; at the most I have ventured on an appeal to those whose part it is.

Booth thus concluded his seventeen-year study of the life and labour of the people of London by appealing to conscience.

During these years, Booth had been working on a cognate problem, scarcely mentioned in his volumes on poverty, industry, and religion. In the late 1880s, he discovered that an astonishingly high percentage of old people ended up in the workhouse, that in certain London districts old age was the primary cause of pauperism. Accordingly, he proposed in 1892 that the state provide weekly pensions of five shillings for men and women reaching the age of sixty-five. This too was socialism, but socialism, in his view, that promised to grant people more, not less, independence. Pensions, he stated, would introduce 'something of that security necessary to a higher standard of life, a security of position which will stimulate rather than weaken the play of individuality on which progress and prosperity depend'. Booth, then, was saying that the responsibility for maintaining a 'higher standard of life' rested on society at large, which was precisely what radicals like Joseph Chamberlain and moderate socialists like the Webbs were saying, and what has come to be the classic defence of the modern welfare state.

Year after year, Booth promoted his pension scheme, in articles and books and speeches, citing always the volumes of statistics he had collected on the relation between old age and poverty. Vigorously opposing him were the spokesmen of the charity organizations who argued that a state 'dole' was no substitute for personal guidance by social workers, that the poor simply lacked the strength to be independent. But the demand for pensions mounted, especially from the burgeoning trade union movement, and by the turn of the century, the Liberal Party had incorporated Booth's proposal into its platform. In 1908, two years after the smashing Liberal victory which ushered in the British welfare state, Parliament passed the Old Age Pensions Act. Typical of the congratulations Booth received for his part in bringing the act to fruition was the statement by the National Committee of Organized Labour:

> Old Age Pensions should be a Civil Right, Universal, non-Contributory, and free from all taint of the Poor Law. In the sphere of Principle, Our Victory is complete, and we are proud to acknowledge that Our Victory is Yours. You have supplied the Ideas, the Arguments, the convincing considerations...

But by the time these words were addressed to him, Booth's conservatism had hardened into dogma. The swelling power of trade unions, the emergence of the Independent Labour Party, the increasing radicalism of the Liberals – these were disturbing events to Booth and he reacted to them by falling back on his nineteenth-century principles. In a series of pamphlets written in 1910 and 1911, he called for the expansion of the Poor Law[8] – as opposed to the socialists and radical Liberals

---

8. The Poor Law, instituted in 1601 during the reign of Elizabeth I, forced local parishes to support the poor, who were wandering in ever greater numbers through the countryside and the cities. By the end of the eighteenth century, over 15,000 parishes were administering the law, each in its own fashion. In 1834, two years after the Reform Bill gave the affluent middle class a share of

who favoured its abolition – and for its strict enforcement against 'those whose unrestrained lives cause injury to others as well as to themselves'. And in his last work,[9] published in 1913, he deplored the new militancy of the trade unions and feared for the future of British industry unless the country adopted more restrictive labour policies.

After 1914, Booth's thoughts turned to some of the industrial and social problems that he regarded as inevitable in the postwar era. But his health, which had always been delicate, was declining rapidly. On 16 November 1916, he died in his home in Gracedieu, just outside London.

---

political power, Parliament passed the Poor Law Amendment Act, which rationalized the system in accordance with Benthamite principles of efficiency and utility. A centralized body of Commissioners was established to supervise boards of local Guardians. There were a few minor modifications of the Poor Law between 1834 and 1910-11, when Booth advocated its extension.

The governing assumption held by the authors of the Act, by the Commissioners, and especially by the Guardians, was that the poor must somehow be disciplined for their shiftlessness, or their debauchery, or their improvidence – whatever had brought about their downfall. Under the provisions of the Law, able-bodied men were condemned to the workhouse, while the aged, the infirm, orphans, mothers of young children, and others unable to care for themselves were sent to special institutions: asylums, old age homes, orphanages. But the workhouse often became the resting-place for the poor in general. Dickens, in *Oliver Twist*, gives a harrowing description of how the Poor Law was carried out, what the Guardians were like (Mr. Bumble), and what its victims thought of it.

9. *Industrial Unrest and Trade Union Policy.*

CHARLES BOOTH'S
LONDON

CHAPTER 1

POVERTY

> Booth's initial investigations of London poverty make up the bulk of this chapter. It contains his explanation of his methods, his classifications of the poor, illustrative material on their lives, case histories, and descriptions of specific streets, neighbourhoods, and sections.

The School Board Visitors[1]

THE School Board visitors perform amongst them a house-to-house visitation; every house in every street is in their books, and details are given of every family with children of school age. They begin their scheduling two or three years before the children attain school age, and a record remains in their books of children who have left school. The occupation of the head of the family is noted down. Most of the visitors have been working in the same district for several years, and thus have an extensive knowledge of the people. It is their business to re-schedule for the Board once a year, but intermediate revisions are made in addition, and it is their duty to make themselves acquainted, so far as possible, with new-comers into their districts. They are in daily contact with the people, and have a very considerable knowledge of the parents of the school children, especially of the poorest

---

1. First edition, Vol. I, pp. 5–7, 25–7. All footnote references to the volumes of *Life and Labour of the People in London* are in abbreviated form. For complete references to the editions and series of that work that have been quoted in this book, see Bibliography, p. 439.

amongst them, and of the conditions under which they live. No one can go, as I have done, over the description of the inhabitants of street after street in this huge district, taken house by house and family by family – full as it is of picturesque details noted down from the lips of the visitor to whose mind they have been recalled by the open pages of his own schedules – and doubt the genuine character of the information and its truth. . . . I am indeed embarrassed by its mass, and by my resolution to make use of no fact to which I cannot give a quantitative value. The materials for sensational stories lie plentifully in every book of our notes; but, even if I had the skill to use my material in this way – that gift of the imagination which is called 'realistic' – I should not wish to use it here. There is struggling poverty, there is destitution, there is hunger, drunkenness, brutality, and crime; no one doubts that it is so. My object has been to attempt to show the numerical relation which poverty, misery, and depravity bear to regular earnings and comparative comfort, and to describe the general conditions under which each class lives...

With regard to the disadvantages under which the poor labour, and the evils of poverty, there is a great sense of helplessness: the wage-earners are helpless to regulate their work and cannot obtain a fair equivalent for the labour they are willing to give; the manufacturer or dealer can only work within the limits of competition; the rich are helpless to relieve want without stimulating its sources...

...At the outset we shut our eyes, fearing lest any prejudice of our own should colour the information we received. It was not till the books were finished that I or my secretaries ourselves visited the streets amongst which we had been living in imagination. But later we gained confidence, and made it a rule to see each street ourselves at the time we received the visitors' account of it. With

POVERTY

the insides of the houses and their inmates there was no attempt to meddle. To have done so would have been an unwarrantable impertinence; and, besides, a contravention of our understanding with the School Board, who object, very rightly, to any abuse of the delicate machinery with which they work. Nor, for the same reason, did we ask the visitors to obtain information specially for us. We dealt solely with that which comes to them in a natural way in the discharge of their duties.

The amount of information obtained varied with the different visitors; some had not been long at the work, and amongst those who had been, there was much difference in the extent of their knowledge; some might be less trustworthy than others: but taking them as a body I cannot speak too highly of their ability and good sense.... The merit of the information so obtained, looked at statistically, lies mainly in the breadth of view obtained. It is in effect the whole population that comes under review. Other agencies usually seek out some particular class or deal with some particular condition of people. The knowledge so obtained may be more exact, but it is circumscribed and very apt to produce a distortion of judgement. For this reason, the information to be had from the School Board visitors, with all its inequalities and imperfections, is excellent as a framework for a picture of the Life and Labour of the People.

The population brought directly under schedule – viz., heads of families and school children coming under the ken of the School Board visitors, with the proportion of wives and of older or younger children all partly or wholly dependent on these heads of families and sharing their life – amounts to from one-half to two-thirds of the whole population...

The special difficulty of making an accurate picture of so shifting a scene as the low-class streets in East London present is very evident, and may easily be exaggerated. As in photographing a crowd, the details of the picture change continually, but the general effect is much the same, whatever moment is chosen. I have attempted to produce an instantaneous picture, fixing the facts on my negative as they appear at a given moment, and the imagination of my readers must add the movement, the constant changes, the whirl and turmoil of life. In many districts the people are always on the move; they shift from one part of it to another like 'fish in a river'. The School Board visitors follow them as best they may, and the transfers from one visitor's book to another's are very numerous. On the whole, however, the people usually do not go far, and often cling from generation to generation to one vicinity, almost as if the set of streets which lie there were an isolated country village.

The Setting[2]

IF London north of the Thames is considered as a semi-circle of which the City is an enlarged centre, the part with which I am about to deal forms a quadrant, having for its radii Kingsland Road running due north, and the River Thames running due east. Between these lies the Mile End Road (continued as the Bow Road to Bow), while a similar division more to the north may be made in the line of Hackney, dividing the quadrant into three equal segments, but the route to Hackney is deflected by Victoria Park, and no street exactly occupies the line. The district also includes Hoxton and De Beauvoir Town lying to the west of Kingsland Road, but is otherwise co-extensive with this quadrant. The City itself has a radius of nearly a mile, and outside of this London extends to the north and east from three to four miles. The greatest extension is at Stamford Hill, where the boundary is four-and-a-half miles from Southwark Bridge,

2. First edition, Vol. I, pp. 28–39.

and the least at Bow, where it is three-and-a-half miles from the same point. There is, however, less difference than these figures would seem to show in the actual extension of London, for from the City of Bow, the entire space is built over, whereas at Stamford Hill and Clapton there are still some open fields, and further south and east the Metropolitan boundary includes some marshy land, unbuilt on, which skirts the River Lea. A circle drawn three miles outside the City boundary practically includes the whole inhabited district; and this may be divided into two parts – an inner ring of one-and-a-half miles ending at the Regent's Canal, and an outer ring of similar width extending to Stoke Newington, Clapton, Homerton, Hackney, Old Ford, Bow, Bromley, and the East India Docks. The line of the Regent's Canal, which very closely follows the curve of the inner ring, marks a real change in the character of the district. Slight as this obstacle might be supposed to be, it yet seems to have been sufficient to gird in the swelling sides of London, and it is in itself a girdle of poverty, the banks of the canal being, along nearly its whole length, occupied by a very poor population.

The inner ring consists of most of Shoreditch, Bethnal Green (excepting the Victoria Park end), all Whitechapel and St George's, Wapping, Shadwell, and Ratcliff, with the inlying portions of Mile End, for the most part tightly packed with buildings, and crowded with inhabitants, except where occupied by business premises. Space and air are everywhere at a premium – the largest scale map shows as open spaces only a few churchyards and old burial grounds. A similar condition of things extends along the river bank, over Limehouse and Poplar proper, which lie within the outer ring, but the rest of this ring, consisting of Bow, Bromley, the outermost parts of Mile End and Bethnal Green, and the whole of Hackney, show a different character. Not only are there some large spaces open to the public – Hackney Downs, London

Fields, and Victoria Park — but the map begins everywhere to show more ground than buildings. The streets are wider; the houses have gardens of some sort; and in the houses themselves fewer people are packed. In the inner ring nearly all available space is used for building, and almost every house is filled up with families. It is easy to trace the process. One can see what were the original buildings; in many cases they are still standing, and between them, on the large gardens of a past state of things, has been built the small cottage property of today. Houses of three rooms, houses of two rooms, houses of one room — houses set back against a wall or back to back fronting it may be on to a narrow footway, with posts at each end and a gutter down the middle. Small courts contrived to utilize some space in the rear, and approached by archway under the building which fronts the street. Of such sort are the poorest class of houses. Besides the evidence of configuration, these little places are often called 'gardens', telling their story with unintended irony. But in other cases all sentiment is dropped, and another tale about their origin finds expression in the name 'So and so's rents' – not houses, nor dwellings, nor cottages, nor buildings, nor even a court or a yard, suggesting human needs, but just 'rents'.

Another sort of filling up which is very common now is the building of workshops. These need no new approach, they go with, and belong to, the houses, and access to them is had through the houses. One I know of is arranged floor by floor, communicating with the respective floors of the house in front by a system of bridges. These workshops may or may not involve more crowding in the sense of more residents to the acre, but they, in any case, occupy the ground, obstruct light, and shut out air. Many are the advantages of sufficient open space behind a house, whether it be called garden or yard, for economy, comfort, and even pleasure. Those who have seen no more, have at least obtained a sort of bird's-eye view of such places from the window of a railway carriage, passing along some viaduct raised above the chimneys of two-storeyed London. Seen from a distance, the clothes-lines are the most visible thing. Those who have not such outside accommodation must dry the clothes in the room in which they eat, and very likely also sleep; while those, more common, who have a little scrap of yard or stretch ropes across the court in front, still suffer much discomfort from the close proximity to door and window of their own and their neighbours' drying garments. From the railway may be seen, also, small rough-roofed erections, interspersed with little glass houses. These represent hobbies, pursuits of leisure hours -- plants, flowers, fowls, pigeons, and there is room to sit out, when the weather is fine enough, with friend and pipe. Such pleasures must go when the workshop invades the back yard; and it need hardly be pointed out how essential is sufficient space behind each house for sanitation.

Worse again than the interleaving of small cottage property or the addition of workshops, is the solid backward extension, whether for business premises or as tenements, or as common lodging-houses, of the buildings which front the street; and this finally culminates in quarters where house reaches back to house, and means of communication are opened through and through, for the convenience and safeguard of the inhabitants in case of pursuit by the police. The building of large blocks of dwellings, an effort to make crowding harmless, is a vast improvement, but it only substitutes one sort of crowding for another. Nor have all blocks of dwellings a good character, either from a sanitary or moral point of view.

All these methods of filling up have been, and some of them still are, at work in the inner ring. This is true throughout, but otherwise each district has its peculiar characteristics.

The area dealt with is composed of the following

unions of parishes or registration districts, containing in all about 900,000 inhabitants:

East London	
Shoreditch	124,000
Bethnal Green	130,000
Whitechapel	76,000
St George's-in-the-East	49,000
Stepney	63,000
Mile End Old Town	112,000
Poplar	169,000
Hackney	186,000
Total	909,000

The Eight Classes[3]

The eight classes into which I have divided these people are:

A. The lowest class of occasional labourers, loafers, and semi-criminals.
B. Casual earnings – 'very poor' ⎫ together the 'poor'.
C. Intermittent earnings ⎬
D. Small regular earnings
E. Regular standard earnings – above the line of poverty.
F. Higher class labour.
G. Lower middle class.
H. Upper middle class.

The divisions indicated here by 'poor' and 'very poor' are necessarily arbitrary. By the word 'poor' I mean to describe those who have a sufficiently regular though bare income, such as 18s. to 21s.[4] per week for a moderate family, and by 'very poor' those who from any cause fall much below this standard. The 'poor' are those whose

---

3. First edition, Vol. I, pp. 33–61.
4. The fluctuating purchasing power of the pound in 1888 must of course be related to the equivalent purchasing power today. – EDS.

means may be sufficient, but are barely sufficient, for decent independent life; the 'very poor' those whose means are insufficient for this according to the usual standard of life in this country. My 'poor' may be described as living under a struggle to obtain the necessaries of life and make both ends meet; while the 'very poor' live in a state of chronic want. It may be their own fault that this is so; that is another question; my first business is simply with the numbers who, from whatever cause, do live under conditions of poverty or destitution...

On the whole it will be seen that St George's-in-the-East is the poorest district, though run very hard by Bethnal Green in this unenviable race. Taking the number of 'very poor', Bethnal Green heads the list, and Stepney stands higher than St George's. Mr Jones, the able relieving officer of Stepney, disputes my conclusions here; and it must be admitted that the very high proportion of class B in Stepney, compared to the very low proportion for class C, is remarkable. The fact is that the line between casual and irregular employment at the docks and wharves and on the canal, where the men of Stepney find their living, is most difficult to draw, and it is very possible that some of those described as 'very poor' should not have been placed below the line of poverty.

Before proceeding further with comparisons of one district with another, I will describe the classes and their manner of living so far as it is known to me. And here I may say that in addition to the information obtained from the School Board visitors, for the division of the population into the eight classes, I have been glad, in describing the lives of these people, to use any available information, and have received much valuable assistance from relieving officers, rent-collectors, officers of the Charity Organization Society, and others.

[*Class A.*] The lowest class, which consists of some occasional labourers, street sellers, loafers, criminals, and semi-criminals, I put at 11,000, or one-and-a-quarter per cent of the population, but this is no more than a very rough estimate, as these people are beyond enumeration, and only a small proportion of them are on the School Board visitors' books. If I had been content to build up the total of this class from those of them who are parents of children at school in the same proportions as has been done with the other classes, the number indicated would not have greatly exceeded 3,000, but there is little regular family life among them, and the numbers given in my tables are obtained by adding in an estimated number from the inmates of common lodging-houses, and from the lowest class of streets. With these ought to be counted the homeless outcasts who on any given night take shelter where they can, and so may be supposed to be in part outside of any census. Those I have attempted to count consist mostly of casual labourers of low character, and their families, together with those in a similar way of life who pick up a living without labour of any kind. Their life is the life of savages, with vicissitudes of extreme hardship and occasional excess. Their food is of the coarsest description, and their only luxury is drink. It is not easy to say how they live; the living is picked up, and what is got is frequently shared; when they cannot find threepence for their night's lodging, unless favourably known to the deputy, they are turned out at night into the street, to return to the common kitchen in the morning. From these come the battered figures who slouch through the streets, and play the beggar or the bully, or help to foul the record of the unemployed; these are the worst class of corner men who hang round the doors of public-houses, the young men who spring forward on any chance to earn a copper, the ready materials for disorder when occasion serves. They render no useful service, they create no wealth: more often they destroy it. They degrade whatever they touch, and as individuals are perhaps incapable of improvement; they may be to some extent a necessary evil in every large city, but their numbers will be affected by the economical condition of the classes above them, and the discretion of 'the charitable world'; their way of life by the pressure of police supervision.

It is much to be desired and to be hoped that this class may become less hereditary in its character. There appears to be no doubt that it is now hereditary to a very considerable extent. The children are the street arabs, and are to be found separated from the parents in pauper or industrial schools, and in such homes as Dr Barnardo's.[5] Some are in the Board schools, and more in Ragged Schools,[6] and the remainder, who cannot be counted, and may still be numerous, are every year confined within narrowing bounds by the persistent pressure of the School Board and other agencies.

While the number of children left in charge of this class is proportionately small, the number of young persons belonging to it is not so – young men who take naturally to loafing; girls who take almost as naturally to the streets; some drift back from the pauper and industrial schools, and others drift down from the classes of casual and irregular labour. I have attempted to describe the prevailing type amongst these people, but I do not mean to say that there are not individuals of every sort to be found in the mass. Those who are able to wash the mud may find some gems in it. There are, at any rate, many very piteous cases. Whatever doubt there may be as to the exact numbers of this class, it is certain that they bear a very small proportion to the rest of the population, or even to class B with which they are mixed up, and from

5. In 1867, Dr Thomas J. Barnardo of London founded the first of a number of homes in Great Britain (and, later, throughout the Empire) for the training of destitute children, chiefly orphans. – EDS.

6. Free schools for children of the poorest classes. First established in the early nineteenth century by John Pounds, a Portsmouth shoemaker, these schools were intended as a preventive measure against juvenile delinquency. – EDS.

which it is at times difficult to separate them. The hordes of barbarians of whom we have heard, who, issuing from their slums, will one day overwhelm modern civilization, do not exist. There are barbarians, but they are a handful, a small and decreasing percentage: a disgrace but not a danger.

This class is recruited with adult men from all the others. All such recruits have been in some way unfortunate, and most, if not all, have lost their characters. Women, too, drop down, sometimes with the men, more often from the streets. A considerable number of discharged soldiers are to be found in classes A and B.

Class B – casual earnings – very poor – add up almost exactly to 100,000, or $11\frac{1}{4}$ per cent of the whole population. This number is made up of men, women, and children in about the following proportions:

Married men	17,000
Their wives	17,000
Unmarried men	7,000
Widows	6,500
Unmarried women	5,000
Young persons, 15–20	9,500
Children	38,000
	100,000

[*Booth goes on to explain that much of this class is engaged in dock-work and other forms of casual labour.*]

... In East London the largest field for casual labour is at the Docks; indeed, there is no other important field, for although a large number of men, in the aggregate, look out for work from day to day at the wharves and canals, or seek employment as porters in connection with the markets, there seems to be more regularity about the work, and perhaps less competition, or less chance of competition, between outsiders and those who, being always on the spot, are personally known to the em-

POVERTY

ployers and their foremen. Dock Labour is treated in a separate chapter. The number of those who are casually employed at the Docks does not seem large compared to the very great public concern which has been aroused, but as a test of the condition of other classes, the ebb and flow of this little sea is really important; it provides a test of the condition of trade generally, as well as of certain trades in particular – a sort of 'distress meter' – and connects itself very naturally with the question of the unemployed.

The labourers of class B do not, on the average, get as much as three days' work a week, but it is doubtful if many of them could or would work full time for long together if they had the opportunity. From whatever section class B is drawn, except the sections of poor women, there will be found many of them who from shiftlessness, helplessness, idleness, or drink, are inevitably poor. The ideal of such persons is to work when they like and play when they like; these it is who are rightly called the 'leisure class' amongst the poor – leisure bounded very closely by the pressure of want, but habitual to the extent of second nature. They cannot stand the regularity and dullness of civilized existence, and find the excitement they need in the life of the streets, or at home as spectators of or participators in some highly coloured domestic scene. There is drunkenness amongst them, especially amongst the women; but drink is not their special luxury, as with the lowest class, nor is it their passion, as with a portion of those with higher wages and irregular but severe work. The earnings of the men vary with the state of trade, and drop to a few shillings a week or nothing at all in bad times; they are never high, nor does this class make the hauls which come at times in the more hazardous lives of the class below them; when, for instance, a sensational newspaper sells by thousands in the streets for twopence to sixpence a copy. The wives in this class mostly do some work, and those who are sober, perhaps, work more steadily than the men; but their work is mostly of a rough kind, or is done for others almost as poor as themselves. It is in all cases wretchedly paid, so that if they earn the rent they do very well.

Both boys and girls get employment without much difficulty – the girls earn enough to pay their mothers four or five shillings a week if they stay at home; and if the boys do not bring in enough, they are likely to be turned adrift, being in that case apt to sink into class A; on the other hand, the more industrious or capable boys no doubt rise into classes C, D, or E.

Class B, and especially the 'labour' part of it, is not one in which men are born and live and die, so much as a deposit of those who from mental, moral, and physical reasons are incapable of better work.

Class C – intermittent earnings – numbering nearly 75,000, or about eight per cent of the population, are more than any others the victims of competition, and on them falls with particular severity the weight of recurrent depressions of trade.... In this type of work may perhaps be found the most proper field for systematic charitable assistance; provided always some evidence of thrift is made the pre-condition or consequence of assistance.

[*Class C*] consists of men who usually work by the job, who are in or out of work according to the season or the nature of their employment.[7] This irregularity of employment may show itself in the week or in the year: stevedores and waterside porters may secure only one or two days' work in a week, whereas labourers in the building trades may get only eight or nine months in the year.... The great body of the labouring class (as distinguished from the skilled workmen) have a regular steady income, such as it is.

7. In considering the status as to employment and means, a whole year has, so far as possible, been taken as the unit of time.

Some of the irregularly employed men earn very high wages, fully as high as those of the artisan class. These are men of great physical strength, working on coal or grain, or combining aptitude and practice with strength, as in handling timber. It is amongst such men, especially those carrying grain and coal, that the passion for drink is most developed. A man will very quickly earn 15s. or 20s., but at the cost of great exhaustion, and many of them eat largely and drink freely till the money is gone, taking very little of it home. Others of this class earn wages approaching to artisan rates when, as in the case of stevedores, their work requires special skill, and is protected by trade organization.... While trade is dull the absorption of surplus labour by other employment is extremely slow. There are also in this section a large number of wharf and warehouse hands, who depend on the handling of certain crops for the London market. They have full work and good work when the wool or tea sales are on, and at other times may be very slack...

Besides those whose living depends on the handling of merchandise, there are in this section all the builders' labourers, and some others whose work is regulated by the seasons. With regard to these employments the periods of good and bad work are various, one trade being on while another is off; more goods to be handled, for instance, on the whole, in winter than in summer, against the stoppage of building in cold weather. I do not think, however, that one employment is dovetailed with another to any great extent; it would not be easy to arrange it, and most of the men make no effort of the kind. They take things as they come; work when they can get it in their own line, and otherwise go without, or, if actually hard up, try, almost hopelessly, for casual work. The more enterprising ones who fill up their time in some way which ekes out their bare earnings are the exceptions.... The pressure is also very severe when there are many young children; a man and his wife by themselves can get along, improvident or not, doing on very little when work fails; the children who have left school, if they live at home, readily keep themselves, and sometimes do even more. It is in the years when the elder children have not yet left school, while the younger ones are still a care to the mother at home, that the pressure of family life is most felt.

... Provident thrift, which lays by for tomorrow, is not a very hardy plant in England, and needs the regular payment of weekly wages to take root freely. It seems strange that a quality so much needed, and so highly rewarded, should not be developed more than seems to be the case. There may, however, be more of such thrift among the irregularly employed than is generally supposed, for it is those who do not have it who come most under observation. I understand that death clubs with a weekly subscription of halfpenny to twopence per head are very commonly subscribed to, and there are instances of a system by which tradesmen are paid small sums all through the summer against the winter expenditure at their shop, receiving the money on a deposit card, and acting in fact as a sort of savings bank. But such cases are exceptional; the reverse would be the rule, credit being given in winter against repayment in summer. Most benefit societies, death clubs, goose clubs, etc., are held at public-houses, and the encouragement to thrift is doubtful. The publican is left too much in possession of the field as friend of the working man, and his friendship does not practically pay the latter, who is apt to spend more than he saves.

There will be many of the irregularly employed who could not keep a permanent job if they had it.... They are thus a somewhat helpless class, not belonging usually to any trade society, and for the most part without natural leaders or organization...

... In this class the women usually work or seek for work when the men have none; they do charing, or washing, or needlework, for very little money; they bring no particular skill or persistent effort to what they do, and the work done is of slight value. Those who work the most regularly and are the best paid are the widows...

Class D, small regular earnings, poor, are about 129,000, or nearly 14½ per cent of the population. It must not be understood that the whole of these have quite regular work; but only that the earnings are constant enough to be treated as a regular income, which is not the case with the earnings of class C. Of D and C together we have 203,000, and if this number is equally divided to represent those whose earnings are regular and irregular, which would be to place the standard of regularity a little higher than has been done in this inquiry, the result would be equal numbers of each grade of poverty – 100,000 of B or casual, 100,000 of C or intermittent, and 100,000 of D or regular earnings, out of a total population of 900,000, or one-ninth of each grade...

The men ... are the better end of the casual dock and waterside labour, those having directly or indirectly a preference for employment. It includes also a number of labourers in the gas works whose employment falls short in summer but never entirely ceases. The rest ... are the men who are in regular work all the year round at a wage not exceeding 21s. a week. These are drawn from various sources, including in their numbers factory, dock, and warehouse labourers, car-men, messengers, porters, etc.; a few of each class. Some of these are recently married men, who will, after a long period of service, rise into the next class; some are old and superannuated, semi-pensioners; but others are heads of families, and instances are to be met with (particularly among car-men) in which men have remained fifteen or twenty years at a stationary wage of 21s. or even less, being in a comparatively comfortable position at the start, but getting poorer and poorer as their family increased, and improving again as their children became able to add their quota to the family income. In such cases the loss of elder children by marriage is sometimes looked upon with jealous disfavour.

Of the whole ... none can be said to rise above poverty, unless by the earnings of the children, nor are many to be classed as very poor. What they have comes in regularly, and except in times of sickness in the family, actual want rarely presses, unless the wife drinks. As a general rule these men have a hard struggle to make ends meet, but they are, as a body, decent steady men, paying their way and bringing up their children respectably. The work they do demands little skill or intelligence.

In the whole class with which this section is identified the women work a good deal to eke out the men's earnings, and the children begin to make more than they cost when free from school: the sons go as van boys, errand boys, etc., and the daughters into daily service, or into factories, or help the mother with whatever she has in hand.

The comfort of their homes depends, even more than in other classes, on a good wife. Thrift of the 'make-the-most-of-everything' kind is what is needed, and in very many cases must be present, or it would be impossible to keep up so respectable an appearance as is done on so small an income.

Class E. Regular standard earnings.... This is by far the largest class of the population under review, adding up to 377,000, or over forty-two per cent.

[*It*] contains all, not artisans or otherwise scheduled, who earn from 22s. to 30s. per week for regular work. There are some of them who, when wages are near the lower figure, or the families are large, are not lifted above the line of poverty; but few of them are *very poor*, and the bulk of this large section can, and do, lead independent lives, and possess fairly comfortable homes.

As a rule the wives do not work, but the children all

do: the boys commonly following the father (as is everywhere the case above the lowest classes), the girls taking to local trades, or going out to service.

The men in this section are connected with almost every form of industry, and include in particular carmen, porters and messengers, warehousemen, permanent dock labourers, stevedores, and many others. Of these some, such as the market porters and stevedores, do not earn regular wages, but both classes usually make a fair average result for the week's work. . .

It may be noted that classes D and E together form the actual middle class in this district, the numbers above and below them being very fairly balanced.

The wage-earners of class E take readily any gratuities which fall in their way, and all those who constitute it will mutually give or receive friendly help without sense of patronage or degradation; but against anything which could be called charity their pride rises stiffly. This class is the recognized field of all forms of co-operation and combination, and I believe, and am glad to believe, that it holds its future in its own hands. No body of men deserves more consideration; it does not constitute a majority of the population in the East of London, nor, probably, in the whole of London, but it perhaps may do so taking England as a whole. It should be said that only in a very general way of speaking do these people form one class, and beneath this generality lie wide divergences of character, interests, and ways of life. This class owns a good deal of property in the aggregate.

Class F consists of higher class labour . . . and the best paid of the artisans, together with others of equal means and position from other sections, and amounts to 121,000, or about $13\frac{1}{2}$ per cent of the population. . . . Besides foremen are included City warehousemen of the better class, and first-hand lightermen; they are usually paid for responsibility, and are men of very good character and much intelligence.

This ... is not a large section of the people, but it is a distinct and very honourable one. These men are the non-commissioned officers of the industrial army. No doubt there are others as good in the ranks, and vacant places are readily filled with men no less honest and trustworthy; all the men so employed have been selected out of many. The part they play in industry is peculiar. They have nothing to do with the planning or direction (properly so called) of business operations; their work is confined to superintendence. They supply no initiative, and having no responsibility of this kind they do not share in profits; but their services are very valuable, and their pay enables them to live reasonably comfortable lives, and provide adequately for old age. No large business could be conducted without such men as its pillars of support, and their loyalty and devotion to those whom they serve is very noteworthy. Most employers would admit this as to their own foremen, but the relation is so peculiar and personal in its character that most employers also believe no other foremen to be equal to their own.

Their sons take place as clerks, and their daughters get employment in first-class shops or places of business; if the wives work at all, they either keep a shop, or employ girls at laundry work or at dressmaking.

There is a great difference between these men and the artisans who are counted with them as part of class F: the foreman of ordinary labour generally sees things from the employer's point of view, while the skilled artisan sees them from the point of view of the employed. Connected with this fact it is to be observed that the foremen are a more contented set of men than the most prosperous artisans...

Later on separate accounts are given of cabinet-making, boot-making, tailoring, cigar-making and silk-weaving. The rest of the artisan trades have no features peculiar to the East End, and would be better considered for the whole of London, but the following remarks may be made:

Building trades. – These show the signs of the depression of trade. The poor and very poor between them are 33·6 per cent of their numbers. The unskilled labourers employed in building operations are of course not counted amongst the artisans.

Together with furniture, etc., are grouped the shipwrights and coopers. The shipwrights have little work – a large portion of the trade is dead, and the coopers also complain. It is stated at the Docks that there is less work for the coopers because sugar and coffee are now imported in bags instead of hogsheads. On the whole, however, the coopers seem better off than most others, and are a large body of men; they are of two sorts, the wet coopers, who are highly skilled, and make good wages, and the dry coopers, some of whom are hardly coopers at all, mending barrels and boxes in a rough-and-ready fashion, and earning but little. The percentage of 'poor' is twenty-eight per cent and of very poor ten per cent in this section.

Food production, including slaughtermen, journeyman bakers, brewers' servants, sugar-refiners, fish-curers, and cigar-makers. – Of these the best paid are the slaughtermen and brewers' servants; it has, however, been difficult to distinguish between the brewers and the brewers' labourers. The distinction is not very material, as the other employments in this section are on the whole poorly paid, and rank in that respect little, if at all, above the standard of labour in which section brewers' labourers ought to be. Bakers, sugar-refiners, fish-curers, and cigar-makers, all suffer more or less from cheap immigrant labour. The sugar business has been extremely slack, and fish-curing, though prosperous, is an industry of the poor. The percentage of poor in this section is twenty-two-and-a-half per cent, and of very poor four per cent.

Following the six sections of artisans in my schedules come other wage-earners, such as railway servants, policemen, and seamen, and the classification by industry then passes from wage-earners – who, to give value to their work, have to please the wage-payers – to profit-earners, who, in order to be paid, have to please the public – a marked difference. The commonest labourer and the most skilful highly paid mechanic are alike in that whatever they do their labour will be wasted if misapplied, and that as to its application they have no responsibility: they are paid their wages equally whether they have or have not produced the value in consumption that is to be hoped for out of their work; but the master manufacturer, like the poor flower girl, or the common street acrobat, must please his public to earn anything. The distinction is no question of wealth; with the artisans, as with ordinary labour, we have seen under one denomination very varied conditions of life; and among the profit-earners also we shall again find all classes.

First come those who make their profit out of manufacture, and form the link between the wage-earners and the dealers, in so much as, while the dealers supply, and must please the public, the makers work to satisfy the dealers. Lowest in the scale are:

Home industries and small manufacturers who do not employ. – These work at home, buying the materials and selling the product. Home industries, where the whole family work together, are such as slipper-making, toy-making, firewood-cutting, etc. Those who work by themselves, but also on their own materials, are small bootmakers and tailors (making and mending), watch and clock-makers (entirely repairing), locksmiths, picture-frame makers, and many more. With them are here included sweeps and printers, who employ no one, but do not themselves work for wages. Altogether this is a considerable and rather interesting class, the last relic of an older industrial system...

POVERTY

Small employers, employing from one to ten workpeople or servants. – This class is for the most part energetic and well-to-do, but includes the much vilified 'sweaters', many of whom are only a shade better off than those whose labour they control.

The number of large employers... is not very considerable. Then follow those who deal direct with the public, beginning at the lowest point of class with:

The street trades, which consist of three main divisions: street performers, street sellers, and general dealers. They include organ-grinders and acrobats, professional beggars, those who sell penny notions from a tray in the City streets, and newspaper hawkers, with the poorest of the costermongers;[8] and (amongst the general dealers) the buyers in a small way of old boots for 'translating', old clothes for renovation, collectors of old iron, etc., whose whole business, whether in buying or selling, is conducted amongst the very poor. Many of these belong to the lowest class, and hardly a full proportion of them come naturally into the schedules.

Further contingents from the street trades pass into class B and C, in company with casual and irregular labour; these are musicians in poor or irregular employ, costermongers without capital, chair-caners, street glaziers, and struggling dealers.

The life of these people is much like that of the casual labourer.... They live from hand to mouth, and go for change of air to Margate sands, or 'hopping', in the season.

The remainder of the street sellers and general dealers are pretty well-to-do, certainly above the line of poverty, and are included in class E. They include ordinary public musicians with regular work, billiard-markers, scene-painters, and travelling photographers; costermongers with capital in stock and barrow, and perhaps a donkey;

---

8. Originally 'apple-sellers'; by Booth's time, 'barrow-boys' selling any perishable food-stuff. – EDS.

coffee-stall keepers, cats'-meat men, and successful general dealers. The section, taken altogether, is a large one in the East End of London. Certain parts of Whitechapel, including the neighbourhood of Petticoat Lane (now called Middlesex Street), serve as a market for outlying districts. To deal 'in the Lane' is a sufficient description of many we have met with.

'Dealing' and 'street selling' are distinct occupations, except at quite the bottom level. The dealer is a small itinerant merchant; the street seller is a sort of shopkeeper, whose stock is contained in a stall, a barrow, or a basket. The general dealers are nearly all Jews, and some of them buy and sell in a large way, and handle large sums of money, though their ways of life are hardly removed from those of the quite poor of their nationality. The business of a general dealer is never visible on the surface, and with some it is a mystery, to which, perhaps, the police only could furnish a key; while the street sellers, as a rule, whether in a large or small way, are most open and palpable servants of the public. Costermongers of the upper grade are a very well-to-do set; they have a valuable property in their stock, etc.; they sometimes have both stall and barrow, working as a family; and some step up into the shopkeeping class by establishing the wife in a small shop, while the man still goes round with the barrow. The street trades seem prosperous, and those who drive these trades are better off today than many skilled workmen, though of much lower social grade, and in fact a rough lot. In this employment the possession of capital is a very great power. The man who has wit to get together a little money, and resolution enough to keep his capital sacred, spending only his profits, and saving out of them against the loss of a donkey, or the need of a new barrow, will surely prosper. Those who have to borrow pay dear for the accommodation, and besides are probably the men whose character or whose necessities make saving impossible to them. There are men in the East End who make a large income by letting out barrows to this class.

Among the lower grade of costermongers are to be found labourers who take to street selling as an alternative when work is slack, but it is probably difficult to make such a combination successful. The poor among the street sellers are forty-four-and-a-quarter per cent, the very poor twenty-five per cent.

Next in order in the industrial classification are:

Small shops, or shops where no assistants are employed, a very wide class, including people in the greatest poverty attempting to pay rent and obtain a living out of the sale of things of hardly any value to customers with hardly any money, and every grade upwards to the well-to-do tradesman with a prosperous business closely looked after by wife and junior members of the family, who being sufficient in themselves need employ no one.

I have been able roughly to apportion this section to the different classes, but it is often impossible to say whether a shop is making money or not. It perhaps loses, and is closed, and at once another takes its place. It may reasonably be assumed that if they do not drop out of existence as shops, profit is on the whole to be found in the business. This, however, gives an inadequate picture of a class on whom, whether in decrease of sales or increase of bad debts, must fall much of the weight of a depressed condition of trade. It may be that the cheapened cost of what they have to sell, and the full prices, which the credit they give and the hand-to-mouth habits of their customers enable them to charge, leave a good margin: and so far they have not been seriously attacked by the co-operative system, which may some day step in between them and their profits.

It is to be noted that most of the quite small shops in the district are not included at all in this section, being kept by the wives of men otherwise employed, whose families are here scheduled according to the man's trade.

These small shops play only a subsidiary part in the family economy, and it is not to be wondered at if those who try to make an entire living out of a business so handicapped, find it very difficult...

[*Booth continues with a short description of classes G and H, the lower and upper middle classes.*]

It is to be remembered that the dividing lines between all these classes are indistinct; each has, so to speak, a fringe of those who might be placed with the next division above or below; nor are the classes, as given, homogeneous by any means. Room may be found in each for many grades of social rank.

Some Examples of Class A[9]

THE ROONEY FAMILY AND ITS CONNECTIONS

Martin Rooney, aged eighty-six, now in Bromley workhouse, married Ellen King, and this family has been prolific in paupers.

First there is Mary Rooney, the wife of Martin's brother James, who was deserted by him in 1867 and has had relief in various forms since, including residence in the sick asylum for several years. She also applied on behalf of her married daughter, Mrs Wilson, and her son Michael appears on the books; but with this branch we do not go at present beyond the second generation.

The old man Martin, who is now blind, applied for admission in 1878. His wife was then in hospital, having broken her leg when intoxicated. He had been a dock labourer, and had received twenty-one pounds from the Company in 1857 on breaking a leg. He was admitted to Poplar Workhouse. A month later his wife, who is twenty-four years his junior, came out of hospital and

9. Second edition, Vol. VIII, pp. 317–23.

POVERTY

was also admitted. The relieving officer made a note that he did not know a more drunken disreputable family than this one. He had seen the woman 'beastly drunk' at all times of the day. From this time the old man remained in the house, but the woman went out several times, and when out was more than once seen in the streets in a drunken condition. She worked sometimes at the Lead Works, sleeping occasionally with her sons, at other times in various places – in water-closets, on stairs, etc. When her son Patrick was sent to prison for two months she went into the house. In 1888 she absconded, but in March 1889, applied for readmission; she had fallen down and cut her face on the Saturday night before.

This couple had three children – Patrick, James, and Bridget. Patrick, born in 1853, by trade a stevedore, is now in Poplar Workhouse. He was living with his mother in 1886, and she made application for medical attendance for him. He was suffering from rheumatism. He became worse and was sent to the sick asylum; was discharged, but again admitted a month or two later. Next year he was sent to Bromley Workhouse. He bears a bad character, and was in prison two months in 1888, and had one month in 1889 for attempting to steal some ropes. On coming out of prison he again applied for admission to the workhouse, and was sent to Poplar. He had a bad leg. He got work on the day he was discharged from the sick asylum, injured his leg, and was readmitted to workhouse. He served fourteen or fifteen years in the Royal Marines, and was discharged in 1885 for striking a petty officer. He was for this sentenced to six months' imprisonment by court-martial.

James, the second son, is a labourer, not married. He used to live with a woman named O'Reill, but left her, or she him, and is at present living with another woman.

Bridget, the eldest, born 1847, married John Murdock, a bricklayer's labourer, eight years older than herself, and there are four children, all boys. Murdock deserted his wife several times, and has been sent to prison for it. She in turn left him in 1877, and has been living with another man since. After this he was in Bromley House with the children. The two eldest were emigrated to Canada in 1880. The man's sister married Richard Bardsley, whose mother, a widow, is living at Bromley, and whose brother and brother's wife both had relief there.

Murdock had also a brother George, a general labourer, who lived with Anna Peel, a prostitute, whose parents are now in West Ham Workhouse. This woman applied in 1878 for sick asylum or medical relief for the man, and six months later wanted an order for the sick asylum herself. The relieving officer visited her two days later, but she had gone to her father at Stratford. In 1885 she came again and was admitted, suffering from syphilis. She had been living at a brothel in James Street for three years. George Murdock is now dead.

Murdock's mother married again, and both she and the man she married, Thomas Powles, are now in Bromley House. Powles, a dock labourer, had an accident, being burnt on a barge at Gravesend in 1875. He came to London then, and was admitted to the sick asylum. In 1877 he applied for relief, saying he had been knocking about, sleeping in barges, etc. He was admitted to the house. The next record was in 1883, when he asked for medicines for his wife. She had had a fall and was very ill. The relieving officer visited and found the home (one room) clean and comfortable; medical relief was given. In 1884 the man was admitted to the asylum, having met with another accident. He had been out of work some time then. In 1886 the man was ill again. He had not worked for five weeks, and they had lived by selling their things. He became worse, and was sent to the sick asylum in April. He did not stay long, but in two months' time applied again for relief outside. He had only earned 8s. in the two months. Three days later the doctor recommended his removal to the sick asylum. Later in the same year his wife was taken ill; and finally they were both admitted to Bromley Workhouse.

We may now come to the relatives of Eliza King, Martin Rooney's wife. She had three sisters – Susan, Jane, and Sarah Anne. Of Susan we only know that she was in service at Guildford. Jane married Thomas Milward. In 1879 Milward applied for medical aid. He could not pay. Whatever money he gave his wife she spent in drink, and if he did not give her money she sold the furniture. Relieving officer made a note that he knew the woman was a notorious drunkard. On visiting he found her in the room drunk, while another woman (Mrs Harvey of Spring Street) was 'reclining on a heap of something which served as a bed', speechlessly drunk. The sick man was sitting by the fire. He always found the room thus, with no furniture, although the man earned from 30s. to 40s. a week. A month later the woman came and said her husband was dead, and that she wanted him buried by the parish. During 1880 and 1881 Mrs Milward had medical relief frequently. She went to the Lead Works, and this work and drink seemed to be telling on her. Some time in 1882 she picked up with a man named Robert Belton, a carpenter, and she lived with him at intervals until 1885. This man was in Bromley Workhouse with a bad leg in 1879, and again later, and died in the sick asylum in 1885. Mrs Milward says he was a great drunkard, which was pot calling kettle black. After Belton's death she injured her shoulder, and having sold up Belton's home and spent the money, applied for admission. She was sent to Poplar Workhouse, and since then has been in and out several times. She hurt her shoulder three times when out from the workhouse, probably through falling while drunk. On two occasions she walked to Guildford to see her sister.

Sarah Anne, the remaining sister, married Thomas Searle, who broke his neck falling downstairs when drunk. It is even said that some of his relatives threw him down in a quarrel. The family was reported as utterly disreputable and very drunken. Left a widow, she kept herself by washing, and does not seem to have had any assistance from the parish herself. She had three children – Edward, Martha, and Francis. Of Edward there is happily no record. Martha married Peter Connor, and her aunt, Mrs Milward, applied on her behalf for medical aid in 1882, she having hurt herself from falling from a ladder at the Lead Works. She had separated from her husband about three years before. He was a bus driver and lived at Notting Hill. After leaving him she lived a while at his sister's, and then went to her mother's in South London, and when her mother moved to this neighbourhood came with her. She was, however, living at the time with a dock labourer in a common lodging-house – a connection which did not last long.

Francis Searle cohabited with a woman named Augusta Hendy from 1877, he being then twenty-two, and he married her in 1885. They had three children. The woman asked for medical aid for her child Wilfrid in March 1880. The relieving officer found the room filthy, with a bed on the floor. In May of the same year the man applied on behalf of the woman. She was found to be suffering from his ill-usage, had black eyes, and had been beaten much. From this time there were frequent applications for medical aid. In July 1881, the woman was admitted to Poplar Workhouse, and was there confined of her third child Edith. In July 1882, their landlady made application, saying that Francis Searle and Augusta Hendy were ill at her house. The relieving officer visited with the doctor. The woman came downstairs without shoes or stockings, a miserable-looking creature. The man, woman, and child were sent to Poplar. After this there were no more applications till 1886, when the man came for medical aid for his child Constance. In 1887 the man applied for medicine for the children; he said he 'was married now'. During the greater part of 1888 the children were ill, and several applications were made by the parents, the last being in November 1888. This woman, Augusta Hendy, was the daughter of old Benjamin Hendy, known as 'Red Ben', who is now in the workhouse, and every one of whose family has had relief. Benjamin Hendy, the younger, age thirty, a dock labourer, not married, was sent to the sick asylum at the end of 1880, and in 1884 went into Poplar Workhouse. Margaret, another of them, was a servant. In 1879 she hurt her face while staying with Augusta, and had medical aid. In November 1883, she went into Poplar Workhouse and was confined of a male child (Robert), born in 1884. With this workhouse child we come at last to the end of the Rooney family and its connections.

THE GRANTS AND THE M'PHERSONS

ALEXANDER GRANT, aged sixty-seven, inmate of Bromley Workhouse, came in through an accident, but the whole story of the case discloses drink and pauper associations as the underlying causes. The first application for assistance was by the man's wife in 1879 for medicine for her mother. The old woman is now dead; her husband, who died in 1857, had been for twenty-seven years gate-keeper at the London Docks. Next, in April 1882 Mrs Grant asked for medicines for her husband. There are five sons and two daughters, all grown up. The eldest son, who is married and has four children, is a coal-porter, and suffers with bad eyes. Two more are in Australia. The two youngest sons and the two daughters are single, and live at home. The sons pay their mother 13s. and 10s. a week respectively. In September 1882, the youngest son was sent to the fever hospital. In October of the same year the father was knocked down by a chaise in Commercial Road, and four days afterwards, when he went to the hospital, it was found that his ribs were fractured.

He could not be kept there, and was sent to the sick asylum. In February 1883, the woman obtained medicine for the elder son. She said her husband had not worked for five months. In March she complained to the relieving officer that her husband was a drunken, good-for-nothing fellow, who spent all he could get in drink. He had taken the boots of an orphan boy who lived with them, and spent the money he got for them in drink. In April they owed £6 rent, still occupying the house where they had been since 1877. The rent was 8s. a week, and they sub-let part. In September 1883, the man asked to be admitted to Bromley Workhouse, and the wife said her children would keep her, but not their father, 'because he ill-treated her and spent his money in drink'. He was admitted to Poplar Workhouse. In April 1884, the man asked for readmission. He had just been discharged from the sick asylum. His wife was living with one of her sons. In June the wife complained that she had fallen downstairs and hurt herself, and mentioned incidentally that her niece, Charlotte M'Pherson, coming out of prison, had smashed her windows and been locked up for it. Medical aid was given to Mrs Grant, and continued till May 1885. Grant himself was transferred to Bromley (Infirm) Workhouse in June 1889.

Mrs Pardon (Charlotte M'Pherson's mother) was Mrs Grant's sister, and had two daughters – the elder one, Emma, born about 1838, lived with a man, James Fernie, and had five children by him, of whom only one was living in 1880. Mrs Grant applied for medical assistance for James Fernie in September 1880. He had been attending the London Hospital, and had not worked for nine or ten weeks. Emma had then just come out of prison, where she had served nine months for felony. Fernie was admitted to the sick asylum, and died there. Emma was in prison again in 1883, this time for three months, for stealing shirts. Of James Fernie's people we learn that he had a brother David, whose wife was at Colney Hatch in 1878, and he endeavoured by lying and other means to evade his responsibility, although he was in regular work.

The case of Mrs Grant's other niece, Charlotte M'Pherson (sometimes called Eastwood), is even worse. Her husband, M'Pherson, was a sailor, and she, both before and after her marriage, was a prostitute. She applied for relief in June 1881, four years after her marriage. The note made on her case says, 'A shocking bad character, and nearly blind. She was in the sick asylum before she was married, and then had an illegitimate child. She is so bad her husband will not live with her.' She was admitted to Poplar Workhouse. There was another application in 1883, and during the interval she had lived part of her time with her sister, Emma Fernie. In January 1884, she came again with Mrs Grant; she had been drinking and threatening everybody. In June following she was again admitted; she had been staying at a common lodging-house, where she had taken men. Another prostitute had beaten her. Charlotte had only come out of prison a few days before, having had fourteen days for breaking windows (a favourite pastime with her). In July 1884, she came to the Relief Office drunk, and the police had to remove her. She had five shillings in her pocket. From this time onward there is an almost continuous string of applications. In April 1885, she was taken to the workhouse by the police; she had been in a rescue home, but a man with whom she cohabited had taken her away. In June she was with her mother for a few days. In October she was again ejected from the Relieving Office, drunk. In 1886 she was for a while in the sick asylum. In July 1887, she applied for admission, and being told to wait, broke eight panes of glass, for which she was sentenced to seven days' hard labour. There are several other records of applications when drunk. In October 1888, she came out of Poplar Workhouse 'just for a change, not feeling well'. The last freak recorded is in April 1889, when she was again sent to prison for breaking windows at the workhouse. The full list of her admissions to, and discharges from, Poplar Workhouse between September 1886, and April 1889, is as follows:

Admitted	Discharged	Admitted	Discharged
16 Sept. 1886	11 Nov. 1886	3 Sept. 1888	3 Oct. 1888
18 Nov. 1886	31 Dec. 1886	5 Oct. 1888	10 Nov. 1888
10 Feb. 1887	21 April 1887	14 Nov. 1888	24 Dec. 1888
21 April 1887	3 June 1887	30 Dec. 1888	3 Jan. 1889
9 June 1887	14 July 1887	5 Jan. 1889	10 Jan. 1889
26 July 1887	6 Sept. 1887	11 Jan. 1889	9 Feb. 1889
9 Sept. 1887	26 Dec. 1887	10 Feb. 1889	16 Feb. 1889
29 Dec. 1887	30 Dec. 1887	19 Feb. 1889	11 Mar. 1889
19 Jan. 1888	9 May 1888	25 April 1889	29 April, to Prison
10 May 1888	30 Aug. 1888		

REUBEN GREEN AND HIS CHILDREN[10]

REUBEN GREEN, born in 1816, was a shoeblack, and seems to have needed no personal relief till 1880, when he was sixty-four. He then applied for admission, saying that he could not support himself. His wife, a year younger than himself, earned 9s. at bottle-washing. He was not admitted till the following winter, when he was in for a few months. During 1882 he had medicines, and came into the house again in November. Every winter it was the same; November saw him in the house. His wife meanwhile continued to keep herself by bottle-washing. He died about 1885. In February 1889, old Mrs Green, then seventy-two, was admitted to the sick asylum, having met with an accident, and after two months' treatment was transferred to Bromley House, where she now resides.

This old couple, harmless enough themselves, are at the root of a very flourishing pauper tree. They had five children – three girls and two boys – whose history is as follows:

Sarah, the youngest, born 1856, married George

10. Second edition, Vol. VIII, pp. 339–42.

Harper, a dust car-man, and had five children (again three girls and two boys): the second girl died at two years old, and the twins, who came last, only lived a few months. The children seem to have been continually ill, and medicine was frequently applied for. The Union buried the little girl in 1885, and the second of the twins, the father's means having been exhausted by burying the twin that died first. The man's work was uncertain till 1887, when he obtained a regular job at 20s. a week, and no further applications have been made. He is reported sober and industrious, but may have been too ready to apply to the parish. His brother, Thomas Harper, was in the sick asylum in 1881; and both his sisters, married women, are known at the Relief Office.

Eliza, born in 1855, is reported as a little 'queer in the head', and has probably never been able to do much for herself. She was living with her parents in 1878 when the record begins with an application for readmission to Poplar Workhouse, which was granted. She came out because 'she could not pick the oakum'. She had before been in the sick asylum and at Bromley, and wanted to get back to the sick asylum. She passes from one institution to another according to her state of health, spending most of her life in this way.

Reuben Green, the younger, born in 1852, was a dock labourer, and in 1886 married a woman with whom he had then lived for several years, and who had been a factory hand. They had several children, but all of them died. The man had medicine in 1884 and 1887, and the woman in 1888 and 1889. They seem to have no other relief: the man's work is irregular.

Thomas Green, born in 1850, was a tank-maker. He married early a girl whose mother was known to the Guardians, and had seven children. The first application recorded is in 1879, for medical attendance for his third child. He had been out of work two months. From that time till 1888 there were continuous applications for medical aid to wife and children. Mrs Green was attended in two confinements. The man never seems to be in regular work and the woman drinks. The Charity Organization Society rejected the case because of the woman's bad character, and that of the man. In 1886 the man and four children were admitted to the workhouse.

Mary, the eldest, born 1884,[11] is the most unsatisfactory of all. Her first appearance was in 1879, when old Reuben, her father, asked to have her admitted 'as she was dying'. She no doubt hoped for the sick asylum, but was sent to Bromley Workhouse, and immediately took her discharge. In 1881 she seems to have formed a connection with Henry Coleman, a dock labourer, eleven years older than herself, and with him she has lived off and on ever since. In 1884 she suffered from rheumatism and asked for medicine. In 1885 she had medicine, and again in 1886, and from then to the present time nearly every month there has been an application and medicine given for 'four weeks more'. Coleman himself had medical attendance in 1889, and died a few days after. He was buried by the Union – cost, £1 13s. 6d. There was a daughter, Jane, born in 1868, as to whose father nothing is said. The girl's history finishes that of the Green family, and is the connecting link with that of the Blundells, into which she married. Sam Blundell, her husband, born in 1863, was a car-man, but only earned 15s. a week. Jane's mother applied for medical attendance for her daughter in 1888, and the order was given. The relieving officer's note speaks of these people as a 'wretched lot'. There are two little children. Jane herself worked as a factory hand.

Blundell's father is in Bromley Workhouse. He was born 1828, and was a carter. His wife, born 1831, worked in the dust-yard. They had a number of children born between 1853 and 1875. The man worked for one firm as a car-man for forty-five years, receiving 15s. a week and

---

11. The dates have obviously been confused here. – EDS.

perquisites. He asked for medicine in 1882. His home was described as a most filthy place. Later he was sent to the sick asylum. His wife was in liquor when she asked for his admission. During 1864, 1865, 1866, and 1867, the man was ill at intervals. He had medical attendance, and on one occasion went into the house. He did not do much work, and the home was maintained by his wife, and his son John, who may be assumed to be the respectable member of the family, as no more is heard of him. In 1888 the old man asked to be admitted, and in the autumn he entered the house at Poplar. He was transferred to Bromley in 1889, absented himself for a week at Easter, was readmitted, and there remained when this account of him was written.

The Blundells' eldest daughter, Elizabeth, born 1853, married a dust car-man, and was a widow in 1878, with two young children. She had medicine for one of them in 1879, and herself died in 1881. The children now live with their grandmother.

The second daughter. Clara, born 1856, cohabited with, and afterwards married, Thomas Parr. A child of this couple, born before they were married, died in the Children's Hospital in 1878. The mother brought the body home, but the man refused to bury it, and for the time left her. This woman had medical attendance in 1879.

Of another daughter, Caroline, we happily know nothing except that she married. Joan, the next in order, born 1862, married James Bunting, a coal-tank filler, and had two children. In 1889 she had medicine for the baby. Her husband was looking for work. He had lost his tank-filling job through a strike four years previously, and had worked in the Docks since. Samuel, the next, is the man already described who married Mary Green's daughter; and there are two younger boys, born 1873 and 1875, employed at wood-chopping.

Even here the record does not end. The elder Blundell

had a brother, and this man's son Robert, born 1841, a dock labourer, we hear of. He had a wife and four children, and his wife asked to be admitted to the infirmary, having a breaking out under her arm. Both man and wife are dirty and drunken.

Poverty by Districts[12]

OF the population of Whitechapel $18\frac{1}{4}$ per cent appear as employed in making clothes, $6\frac{1}{2}$ per cent in cigar-making and food preparation, 8 per cent are street sellers and general dealers, and $5\frac{1}{4}$ per cent are small employers, mostly of the poor 'sweater' type. All these are employments of the Jews.

Stepney, on the other hand, has few, if any, of these — only $7\frac{1}{4}$ per cent all told against 38 per cent in Whitechapel. Stepney is essentially the abode of labour: here the casual labourers reach their maximum of nearly 11 per cent of the population, and have their homes in a mass of grimy streets and courts; and here are to be found also the largest proportion of regularly paid labour, viz., 24 per cent of the population. In all, nearly 39 per cent of the population of Stepney are counted in the five sections of labour against only about 18 per cent so counted in Whitechapel.

Midway between Whitechapel and Stepney, in character as well as geographically, comes St George's-in-the-East. Doubtless a line might be drawn which would fairly divide the population of St George's into two portions, the one side falling naturally with Stepney and the Docks, the other side with Whitechapel and the Jewish quarters. The makers of clothes, 18 per cent in Whitechapel, become $9\frac{1}{2}$ per cent in St George's, and fall away to 1 per cent in Stepney. The preparers of food and tobacco,

12. First edition, Vol. I, pp. 63–72.

$6\frac{1}{2}$ per cent in Whitechapel, become $4\frac{1}{2}$ per cent in St George's, and drop to about 2 per cent in Stepney. On the other hand, the casual labourers, who are 11 per cent in Stepney, stand at 9 per cent in St George's, and fall away to 4 per cent in Whitechapel; and so also with the other classes of labour, except those with irregular pay, who seem to bear a larger proportion to the population in St George's than anywhere else. On the whole, it may be said that St George's shares in the poor characteristics of both her neighbours, and is more entirely poverty-stricken than either.

Passing from Whitechapel to Mile End Old Town, we more quickly get rid of the foreign element, but it is to be found in the westernmost angle or tongue; while in Poplar, where dress and food preparation and general dealers added together are only 4 per cent as compared to 29 per cent in Whitechapel, there is hardly any trace of it.

Passing north and west we see the same thing – food and dress fall to 12 per cent in Bethnal Green – half of what they are in Whitechapel, to 9 per cent in Shoreditch, and to 6 per cent in Hackney.

In Bethnal Green and Shoreditch the four sections of artisans take the leading place, and amongst furniture and wood-work find here their home, accounting for 14 per cent of the population.

Thus it will be seen that Whitechapel is the dwelling-place of the Jews – tailors, bootmakers, and tobacco-workers – and the centre of trading both small and large; Stepney and St George's the district of ordinary labour; Shoreditch and Bethnal Green of the artisan; in Poplar sub-officials reach their maximum proportion, while Mile End, with a little of everything, very closely represents the average of the whole district; and finally Hackney stands apart with its well-to-do suburban population.

Each district has its character – its peculiar flavour. One seems to be conscious of it in the streets. It may be in the faces of the people, or in what they carry – perhaps a reflection is thrown in this way from the prevailing trades – or it may lie in the sounds one hears, or in the character of the buildings.

Of all the districts of that 'inner ring' which surrounds the City, St George's-in-the-East is the most desolate. The other districts have each some charm or other – a brightness not extinguished by, and even appertaining to, poverty and toil, to vice, and even to crime – a clash of contest, man against man, and men against fate – the absorbing interests of a battle-field – a rush of human life as fascinating to watch as the current of a river to which life is so often likened. But there is nothing of this in St George's, which appears to stagnate with a squalor peculiar to itself.

The feeling that I have just described – this excitement of life which can accept murder as a dramatic incident, and drunkenness as the buffoonery of the stage – is especially characteristic of Whitechapel. And looked at in this way, what a drama it is! Whitechapel is a veritable Tom Tiddler's ground, the Eldorado of the East, a gathering together of poor fortune-seekers; its streets are full of buying and selling, the poor living on the poor. Here, just outside the old City walls, have always lived the Jews, and here they are now in thousands, both old-established and new-comers, seeking their livelihood under conditions which seem to suit them on the middle ground between civilization and barbarism.

The neighbourhood of old Petticoat Lane on Sunday is one of the wonders of London, a medley of strange sights, strange sounds, and strange smells. Streets crowded so as to be thoroughfares no longer, and lined with a double or treble row of hand-barrows, set fast with empty cases, so as to assume the guise of market stalls. Here and there a cart may have been drawn in, but the horse has gone and the tilt is used as a rostrum whence the salesmen with stentorian voices cry their wares, vying with each other in introducing to the surrounding crowd their cheap garments, smart braces, sham jewellery, or patent medicines. Those who have something showy, noisily push their trade, while the modest merit of the utterly cheap makes its silent appeal from the lower stalls, on which are to be found a heterogeneous collection of such things as cotton sheeting, American cloth for furniture covers, old clothes, worn-out boots, damaged lamps, chipped china shepherdesses, rusty locks, and rubbish indescribable. Many, perhaps most, things of the 'silent cheap' sort are bought in the way of business; old clothes to renovate, old boots to translate, hinges and door-handles to be furbished up again. Such things cannot *look* too bad, for the buyer may then persuade himself that he has a bargain unsuspected by the seller. Other stalls supply daily wants – fish is sold in large quantities – vegetables and fruit – queer cakes and outlandish bread. In nearly all cases the Jew is the seller, and the Gentile the buyer; Petticoat Lane is the exchange of the Jew, but the lounge of the Christian.

Nor is this great market the only scene of the sort in the neighbourhood on Sunday morning. Where Sclater Street crosses Brick Lane, near the Great Eastern Station, is the market of the 'fancy'. Here the streets are blocked with those coming to buy, or sell, pigeons, canaries, rabbits, fowls, parrots, or guinea pigs, and with them or separately all the appurtenances of bird or pet-keeping. Through this crowd the seller of shell-fish pushes his barrow; on the outskirts of it are moveable shooting galleries, and patent Aunt Sallies,[13] while some man standing up in a dog-cart will dispose of racing tips in sealed envelopes to the East End sportsman.

Brick Lane should rightly be seen on Saturday night, though it is in almost all its length a gay and crowded

13. A carnival sport in which sticks or balls are thrown at a puppet head on a pole with a pipe in its mouth. The object of the game is to break the pipe or knock the figure down .– EDS.

scene every evening of the week, unless persistent rain drives both buyers and sellers to seek shelter. But this sight – the 'market street' – is not confined to Brick Lane, nor peculiar to Whitechapel, nor even to the East End. In every poor quarter of London it is to be met with – the flaring lights, the piles of cheap comestibles, and the urgent cries of the sellers. Everywhere, too, there is the same absolute indifference on the part of the buyer to these cries. They seem to be accepted on both sides as necessary, though entirely useless. Not infrequently the goods are sold by a sort of Dutch auction – then the prices named are usually double what the seller, and every bystander, knows to be the market price of the street and day, 'Eightpence?' 'Sevenpence?' 'Sixpence?' 'Fivepence?' – say 'Fourpence?' – well, then, 'Threepence halfpenny?' A bystander, probably a woman, nods imperceptibly; the fish or whatever it is passes from the right hand of the seller on which it has been raised to view, on to the square of newspaper, resting on his left hand, is bundled up and quick as thought takes its place in the buyer's basket in exchange for the threepence halfpenny, which finds its place in the seller's apron or on the board beside the fish – and then begins again the same routine, 'Eightpence?' 'Sevenpence?' 'Sixpence?' etc.

Lying between Middlesex Street and Brick Lane are to be found most of the common lodging-houses, and in the immediate neighbourhood, lower still in reputation, there are streets of 'furnished' houses, and houses where stairways and corners are occupied nightly by those without any other shelter. So lurid and intense is the light which has lately been thrown on these quarters,[14] that the grey tones of the ordinary picture become invisible.

As to the registered Lodging-houses, it must be said

14. Booth is referring to some of the sensational contemporary journalistic exposés of the London poor. See Introduction, pages 21–2. – EDS.

and remembered that they did, and do, mark a great improvement. However bad their inmates may be, these houses undoubtedly represent the principles of order, cleanliness, and decency. It is useless to demand impossibilities from them. Those who frequent them come under some sort of regulation, and are under the eye of the deputy, who in his turn is under the eye of the police. Even in the worst of these houses there is a great mixture – strange bedfellows whom misfortune has brought together – and amongst the houses there are many grades. The worst are horrible dens, but the horror lies really in their inmates, who are incapable of any better way of living.

The plan of all alike is to have a common kitchen, with large hospitable fire, and dormitories above. The quarters for single men consist of large rooms packed close with dark-brown truckle beds – room to move between bed and bed, and that is all – the women's rooms are, I believe, the same, while the quarters for the 'married' are boxed off by partitions. There are some who are really married, many whose relations though illegal are of long standing, and others again who use the accommodation as a convenience in their way of life.

The registered Lodging-houses are, as I have said, better than the unregistered 'furnished apartments', and so long as the low class exists at all, it must evidently lodge somewhere. This class tends (very naturally) to herd together; it is this tendency which must be combated, for by herding together, they – both the quarters they occupy, and their denizens – tend to get worse. When this comes about destruction is the only cure, and in this neighbourhood there has been of late years a great change brought about by the demolition of bad property. If much remains to do, still much has been done in the clearing away of vile spots, which contained dwellings unfit for human use, and matched only by the people who inhabited them. The railways have cleared some parts, the Board of Works other parts. The transformation goes slowly on, business premises or great blocks of model dwellings covering the old sites. Meanwhile the inhabitants of the slums have been scattered, and though they must carry contamination with them wherever they go, it seems certain that such hotbeds of vice, misery, and disease as those from which they have been ousted are not again created. Many people must have altogether left the district, as the population showed a decrease of 5,000 between 1871 and 1881; but with the completion of the new buildings the numbers have again reached the level of 1871. Probably few of those who leave return; but it may be doubted whether those whose houses are pulled down are the ones to leave the neighbourhood. It is not easy to say exactly how an ebb and flow of population works. It may be the expression in large of much individual hardship: but I am more inclined to suppose that pulling down Smith's house drives him into Brown's quarters, and that Brown goes elsewhere, to his great benefit; when the new buildings are ready they do not attract Brown back again, but draw their occupants from the surrounding streets – men of the stamp of Smith or Brown, according to the accommodation they offer; the vacant places are then taken by quite new comers (in Whitechapel mostly poor foreigners) or by the natural increase in the population. The clearances have been principally confined to Whitechapel and St George's, the rebuilding almost entirely to Whitechapel.

Stepney is rendered interesting by its length of river frontage (about two miles, including all Wapping), and it is besides intersected by the Regent's Canal. It, like Whitechapel, has its foreign element, its haunts of crime, and strange picturesqueness. It, too, has been greatly changed in recent years. Ratcliff Highway hardly knows itself as St George's Street; the policeman and the School Board visitor have 'put a light in the darkness', and have begun to 'make straight the way' here, as well as elsewhere in East London.

Mile End Old Town – commonly denoted by the seeming strange letters M.E.O.T. – lies between the inner and outer ring, and looks very clean and new in spite of its name. Its streets, even the narrowest, look comparatively wide; the air is fresh and the squares and other small spaces are frequent.[15]

Poplar, a huge district, consists of the subdivisions of Bow and Bromley as well as Poplar proper. Bow includes Old Ford, and Poplar itself includes the Isle of Dogs – transformed now into an Isle of Docks. In all it is a vast township, built, much of it, on low marshy land, bounded on the east by the River Lea, and on the south by a great bend in the Thames. In North Bow and other outlying parts there is a great deal of jerry-building: desolate-looking streets spring into existence, and fall into decay with startling rapidity, and are only made habitable by successive waves of occupation; anything will do so that the house be run up; any tenant will do, who will give the house a start by burning a little coal in it; the first tenants come and go, till one by one the houses find permanent occupants, the streets settle down to respectability and rents rise: or a street may go wrong and get into such a position that no course short of entire destruction seems possible. Among the early troubles of these streets are fevers, resulting it is said from the foul rubbish with which the hollow land has become levelled. This district has had many such troubles, and is steadily living them down.

In Bethnal Green are found the old weavers' houses, with large upper room, now usually partitioned off to make two or three rooms or accommodate two families. In some cases the houses had originally only one room on each floor; and each floor, partitioned, now accom-

15. Mile End is, however, remarkable for the number of brothels to be found amongst its otherwise respectable streets.

modates its family. In several cases a family (not weavers) have taken such a room, and while living in it themselves, let a weaver stand his loom or looms in it, getting rent for each loom. Weaving still lingers, but other trades have for the most part taken its place.

Of Shoreditch, or rather Hoxton, which is the most characteristic part of Shoreditch, I am tempted to recall a description by Mr Besant, which will be remembered by all who have read *The Children of Gibeon*. There is, he says, nothing beautiful, or picturesque, or romantic in the place, there is only the romance of life in it, sixty thousand lives in Hoxton, every one with its own story to tell. Its people quiet and industrious, folk who ask for nothing but steady work and fair wages. Everybody quite poor; yet, he says, and says truly, the place has a cheerful look. There may be misery, but it is not apparent; the people in the streets seem well fed, and are as rosy as London smoke and fog will allow.

On the other hand the northern and western part of Hackney, divided from Hoxton only by the canal, is almost entirely a middle-class district. The old streets of De Beauvoir Town, or the new ones of Dalston and Upper Clapton, are alike of this kind, and in the old roads running through the new districts large and small houses are pulled down, and those of medium size erected.

Standards of Living[16]

... OMITTING class A, which rather involves the question of disorder, we have in classes B, C, and D the problem of poverty. In the population under review the 100,000 of 'very poor' (class B) are at all times more or less 'in want'. They are ill-nourished and poorly clad. But of them only a percentage – and not, I think, a large

16. First edition, Vol. I, pp. 131–9.

percentage — would be said by themselves, or by anyone else, to be 'in distress'. From day to day and from hand to mouth they get along; sometimes suffering, sometimes helped, but not always unfortunate, and very ready to enjoy any good luck that may come in their way. They are, very likely, improvident, spending what they make as they make it; but the 'improvidence of the poor has its bright side. Life would indeed be intolerable were they always contemplating the gulf of destitution on whose brink they hang'.[17] Some may be semi-paupers, going into the 'house' at certain seasons, and some few receive outdoor relief, but on the whole they manage to avoid the workhouse. On the other hand, the 200,000 of 'poor' (classes C and D), though they would be much the better for more of everything, are not 'in want'. They are neither ill-nourished nor ill-clad, according to any standard that can reasonably be used. Their lives are an unending struggle, and lack comfort, but I do not know that they lack happiness.[18]

By 'want' is here meant an aggravated form of poverty, and by 'distress' an aggravated form of 'want'. There is to my mind a degree of poverty that does not amount to want and a degree of want that does not amount to distress.

The first table on page 94 divides classes B, C, and D approximately, according to age, sex, etc.

In order to show exactly what I mean by poverty, want, and distress, and thus attach some positive value to the definition of 'poor' and 'very poor', I have attempted to investigate and analyze, in the second table on page 94, the expenditure usually current in classes B,

17. *A Village Tragedy* by Mrs Woods.
18. An analysis of the elements of happiness would hardly be in place here, but it may be remarked that neither poverty nor wealth have much part in it. The main conditions of human happiness I believe to be work and affection, and he who works for those he loves fulfils these conditions most easily.

C, D, and E, and have included a few examples from F. The figures are from genuine and, I believe, trustworthy accounts, and relate to 30 families, of whom 6 are 'very poor', 10 are 'poor', and 14 are above the line of poverty. This method cannot, however, be employed to reach the lowest level, and the imagination must be drawn upon to complete the picture of class B.

	Very poor	Poor		
	B	C	D	TOTAL
Married men	16,705	12,822	23,110	52,637
Their wives	16,682	12,760	22,990	52,432
Unmarried men	7,195	5,505	9,955	22,655
Widows	6,495	4,119	5,776	16,390
Unmarried women	5,191	3,986	6,749	15,926
Young persons, male	4,812	3,565	6,164	14,541
Young persons, female	4,623	3,363	5,833	13,819
Children	29,000	20,880	36,032	85,912
Infants	9,359	7,247	12,278	28,884
	100,062	74,247	128,887	303,196

To facilitate comparison, every family has been reduced to an equivalent in 'male adults' – allowing three-fourths for a woman and in proportion for children, and the whole 30 have been arranged in order according to their standard of life. On food, No. 1 spent 2s. 4½d. per male adult per week; No. 30 spent 10s. 1½d. On rent, fire, light, and insurance, No. 1 spent 2s. 2d.; No. 30 spent 4s. 7½d. On medicine and clothes (very uncertain items), No. 1 spent nothing; No. 30 spent 2s. 8d. Between these extremes lies my scale. The averages for each class are:

	B		C & D		E		F		
	s.	d.	s.	d.	s.	d.	s.	d.	
On Food	3	6½	4	1½	5	4½	8	8	per male
,, Rent, etc.	2	3½	2	10½	3	8½	5	7	adult
,, Clothes, etc.		1		4	1	1	2	2	per week.
	5	11	7	4	10	2	16	5	

The true average of B will be somewhat lower than

this, and if we put it at 5s. we get roughly 5s., 7s. 6d., and 10s. for the average weekly expenditure per 'male adult' below, on, and just above the line of poverty. Translated into families of father, mother, and three children of, say, eleven, eight, and six, we get as the average expenditure for such a family in each class 15s., 22s. 6d., and 30s. per week; and this, or something very like this, is the truth.

It is to be remembered that the whole income of class B is absorbed by necessary expenditure. If exceptional hauls are made they are matched by times of scarcity, when work fails. It is only by evading the payment of rent, or going short of food, that clothes or household things can be bought; and the same is very nearly true with class D. How else can any unusual call be met, or any indulgence which costs money? The poor are very generous, but out of what fund, except the exchequer of the belly, is generosity to be indulged?...

Income It will be noted that in almost all the poorer cases the admitted expenditure exceeds the supposed income. The same peculiarity attaches to other investigations of the expenditure of the poor I have met with. The explanation may be (1) the understating of the regular earnings or (2) the use of credit, met either by final evasion of indebtedness or by some windfall outside of the regular earnings.

Expenditure Food – The amount spent by class B on meat... varies from 3s. to 5s. per male adult for five weeks; the amount spent in class D varies from 3s. to 8s., and in class E from 3s. 6d. to 10s. The minimum amount in each class is about the same, being 1d. per day for each male adult, or 1d. for men, $\frac{3}{4}$d. for women, and from $\frac{1}{4}$d. to $\frac{3}{4}$d. for children. The maximum in these classes may be called 1s., 1s. 6d., and 2s. per male adult per week, and the average 9d., 1s. 1d., and 1s. 7d. The amount spent on potatoes varies considerably family by family, but the average for each class is not very different. The same may be said of butter. Fish, the food of those who cannot afford meat, stands higher with classes B and D than with E. Of bread, class D eat the most. The greater proportion of children in the examples of class B may account for a greater amount of milk and sugar consumed by this class. Tea varies as little as anything. On the whole the evident fact is that the three classes live much in the same way, only with increasing liberality, especially as to meat, green vegetables, and cheese. The figures are affected by the 'meals out', which pay a much larger part in the economy of class B than D or E.[19]

Prices of Articles

	B	C & D	E	F
Meat:				
highest	8d. per lb.	8d. per lb.	9d. per lb.	9d. per lb.
lowest	4d. per lb.	6d. per lb.	5½d. per lb.	6d. per lb.
average	6d. per lb.	7¼d. per lb.	7d. per lb.	8d. per lb.
Potatoes:				
average	½d. per lb.	½d. per lb.	½d. per lb.	¾d. per lb.
Bacon:				
highest	8d. per lb.	10d. per lb.	9d. per lb.	1s. per lb.
lowest	6d. per lb.	5d. per lb.	5d. per lb.	5½d. per lb.
average	7¾d. per lb.	7¼d. per lb.	7¼d. per lb.	8d. per lb.
Eggs:				
average	1d. each	¾d. each	1d. each	1d. each
Cheese:				
highest	—	10d. per lb.	9d. per lb.	—
lowest	—	5d. per lb.	6d. per lb.	—
average	7d. per lb.	7¼d. per lb.	8d. per lb.	8d. per lb.
Milk:				
average	4d. quart	4d. quart	4d. quart	4d. quart
Coffee:				
average	1s. 2d. per lb.	1s. 2d. per lb.	1s. per lb.	1s. 4d. per lb.

19. *Meals out.* – This item consists of twopence or threepence a day taken by daughter, son, or husband, and spent. Bread, or bread and butter, are usually taken from home, and the money goes to provide a cup of cocoa and a 'relish'.

Insurance and Club Money Out of the thirty families only five spent nothing, and these exceptions to the general rule are found in all classes. The amounts paid in B, D, and E, vary from 3½d. to 2s. 3d. per week, or from 1½ per cent to 11½ per cent of the whole expenditure.

Prices Those given are such as might be expected to vary class with class. In a note [*see table above*] I give others by which the quantities of the article consumed can be calculated if desired.

Number of purchases of tea made in 5 weeks varies in all from 72 at most to 3 at least. On the average, there were in the 5 weeks 23 journeys to the shop in class B, 10 in D, and 6 in E.

Household Economics[20]

[*After classifying some thirty families according to class, income, and occupation, Booth expatiated at some length, with illustrative materials, upon the families on his list.*]

NO. 1. This is the poorest case on my list, but is typical of a great many others. The man, Michael H—, is a casual dock labourer aged thirty-eight, in poor health, fresh from the infirmary. His wife of forty-three is consumptive. A son of eighteen, who earns 8s. regular wages as car-man's boy, and two girls of eight and six, complete the family. Their house has four rooms but they let two. Father and son dine from home; the son takes 2d.[21] a day for this. The neighbouring clergy send soup two or three times a week, and practically no meat is bought. It figures

---

20. First edition, Vol. I, pp. 140–6.
21. In the American edition of this selection the purchasing power of the pound was related to that of the American cent: an interesting if tricky computation as regards 1888. – EDS.

the first Sunday only: '3 lb. of meat at 4d.' Beyond the dinners out, and the soup at home, the food consists principally of bread, margarine, tea, and sugar. Of these the quantities are pretty large. No rice is used nor any oatmeal; there is no sign of any but the most primitive cookery, but there is every sign of unshrinking economy; there are no superfluities, and the prices are the lowest possible – 3½d. per quartern for bread, 6d. per lb. for so-called butter, 1s. 4d. for tea, and 1d. for sugar. I suppose the two rooms in which the family live will be those on the ground floor – bedroom (used sometimes as parlour) to the front, kitchen, where they eat and sit, to the back. In the kitchen the son will sleep, his parents and sisters occupying the front room. Neither of these rooms will exceed ten ft square; both, I am told (for I have not seen them), are patterns of tidiness and cleanness, which with class B is not very common. This accommodation costs about 17s. a month. On firing, etc., the H—s spent 10s. 4d. in the five weeks—as much as, and more than, many with double the means; but warmth may make up for lack of food, and invalids depend on it for their lives. Allowing as well as I can for the meals out, and the charitable soup, I make the meals provided by Mrs H— for her family to cost 1d. per meal per person (counting the two little girls as one person). A penny a meal is very little, but expended chiefly in cheap bread, cheap butter, cheap tea, and cheap sugar, it is perhaps as much as would be taken, providing rather more than half lb. of bread, and half oz. of butter, besides tea, milk, and sugar. This diet (which, if strictly adhered to, would be unendurable) is somewhat varied, so as to bring in some fish, a little bacon, and a few eggs, besides the charitable soup.

These people are, undoubtedly, 'very poor', an example of great poverty as it appears when accompanied by respectability and sobriety, and protected from distress by charitable assistance. Imagine the man a drunkard, or the woman a slattern, or take away the boy who earns half the income and put in his place a child of ten or twelve, who earns nothing and must be fed, and it is easy to realize that extremer form of want when distress is felt, or complete pauperism supervenes. From the poor living of the family there is no room to subtract anything; but class B, none the less, contains numbers who are worse off than this family.

No. 2 furnishes another example of what I mean by 'very poor'. Mr R—, the father, is old and blind, and has a weekly pension of 5s. 6d.; his wife only earns money at 'hopping' or 'fruiting'. She keeps the house clean, and both she and her husband are reputed to be quite sober. There are five daughters, but one is married and gone away. The eldest at home, a rough girl, who ruined her health at the Lead Works, does sack-making or bottle-washing, but (in March) had only earned 2s. since Christmas. The second girl works in a seed factory and gives her mother 6s. a week. The third, similarly employed, gives from 5s. to 6s. 6d., making the family house-money about 17s. 6d. a week. The fourth girl is a child at school.

This family live, to the greatest possible extent, from hand to mouth. Not only do they buy almost everything on credit from one shop, but if the weeks tested are a fair sample of the year, they every week put in and take out of pawn the *same set of garments*, on which the broker every time advances 16s., charging the, no doubt, reasonable sum of fourpence for the accommodation. Fourpence a week, or 17s. 4d. a year, for the comfort of having a week's income in advance! On the other hand, even on credit they buy nothing till actually needed. They go to their shop as an ordinary housewife to her canisters: twice a day they buy tea, or three times if they make it so often; in thirty-five days they made seventy-two purchases of tea, amounting in all to 5s. 2¾d., and all most carefully noted down. The 'pinch of tea' costs ¾d. (no doubt this is ½ oz. at 2s. per lb.). Of sugar there are seventy-seven purchases in the same time.

The R—s are a large family, the seven members counting as 4·5 male adults. Their expenditure comes to 5s. 2¼d. per 'male adult' per week. They pay about the same rent, and no doubt get much the same for it as the H—s. On firing and light they spend 14s. 8d.; this large amount may be explained by the age and infirmity of the man, but I am rather disposed to think that bad management has most to do with the excess shown in these items, as compared to other accounts. On washing materials they spend about the same as the H—s, but their insurance payments amount to 10d. a week, every member of the family being in a burial club. The girls who work at the seed factory dine away, taking 2d. a day each in money, and most likely a provision of bread and butter. Counting the family as equal to five adults to feed – that is counting the three younger girls as equal to two adults – the meals in the house seem to cost about 3d. a head for Sunday dinner, 2d. a head for dinner on other days, and 1½d. a head for the other meals.

No. 4. This family run largely on credit, and are evidently used to better things. They pay a large amount of club money, and the baby's milk and biscuits cost a good deal. The expenditure is considerably more than the acknowledged income, and poverty must be very much felt by them. The man (a bricklayer) gets something as caretaker, very little by his trade. The wife works as dressmaker, and has to put out the washing. There are six children (aged thirteen, eleven, nine-and-a-half, three-and-a-half, two, and four months).

No. 5 is the case of a widow, herself earning 7s. a week, with two grown-up children: a daughter of twenty-three, an envelope-folder, making from 9s. to 15s. a week, and a son of twenty-one 'out of work', earning casually 2s. 6d. to 5s. Altogether they do pretty well, the joint income reaching about 20s. a week, but they would certainly be classed in B in my tables. Their meals cost, on the average, 1¾d. a head. The living is very bare, the only luxury (?) an occasional bottle of ginger beer...

In No. 6 we have a case fairly representing the line between B and C or D. Thomas B— is a wharf labourer with irregular work, earning 20s. to 21s. per week. He has five children under ten years of age at home, and a girl at service who still receives both money and clothes from home. His wife, besides looking after all these children, occasionally earns money by needlework, and 3s. 6d. appears to have been received from this source one week. Irregular earnings such as these would, on a *prima facie* view of the case, place this family in class B, though by steadiness on the man's part, and good management on the part of the wife, they live as well as many families in class D. Comparing the B—s with the H—s (No. 1), we notice that although Mrs B— does much more cooking, she spends only half as much for fire and light...; on rent and cleaning they spend the same. Putting the items together, the H—s spend fully as much as the B—s on everything, except meat and drink; but on these the difference is great – 76s. as compared to 40s. – and for a smaller family counted in adults. Mr B— has all his meals at home; he may probably take something to eat with him to the wharf, and perhaps buys beer to drink with it; but the work is usually over early, and he will take his chief meal when he gets home. In the five weeks he and his wife and their young children used 40 lb. of meat at 5d., 25 lb. of fish at 3d., 150 lb. of potatoes, 172 lb. of bread, 15 lb. of flour, 6 or 7 lb. of butter, and 36 lb. of sugar, besides minor matters. This may not be choice fare, but there is something like plenty about it. The cost per meal, counting the family of husband, wife, and five small children as four persons, is 2d., or just double that of the H—s' meals.

No. 7 are just a shade better off than No. 6, and probably spend rather more than is put down, especially on food. The remarkable feature is the rent at 6s. a week. The husband pays for his own clothes, giving his wife 20s. out of 22s. 6d.

No. 8. The husband takes 4s. a day for his dinner. Wife and children do not eat much.

Nos. 9 and 10. Income acknowledged is greater than expenditure; the money, I suppose, does not come home.

No. 11. Husband keeps back 4s. a week, but pays for boys' boots and such things.

No. 12. Man, wife, and three sons; eldest son out of work. Are spending more than is coming in. Are not used to poverty – pay for cats' meat and put out washing. 'Terribly behindhand.'

No. 13. 'Father out of work, but as we had a trifle saved up before, it helps us to live for a little while, until he gets something to do.'

No. 14. Widow and three children, practically supported by daughter of seventeen, who earns 17s. 6d., keeping 6d. pocket-money. The boy of thirteen earns 4s. 6d., and keeps 3d. pocket-money.

No. 17. Much more variety in diet and better housekeeping.

No. 18. Man, wife, and wife's mother – caretakers, earning a little by odd jobs. Spend largely for medicine and medical comforts for the mother, an invalid.

No. 19. Regular wages 21s. per week. Man, wife, and one young child. . . . 'The club money is paid once a quarter, so we put it away every week.' Expenses on one Sunday were: 'Newspaper, 1d. Give my two cousins 2d. Winkles, 2d. Milk, 1d. Sweets, $\frac{1}{2}$d.' Another day we find: '$2\frac{3}{4}$d. spent on something and not put down.' Husband dines at home, but only 8s. is spent on meat in five weeks.

No. 20. Large expenditure on meat for man and wife and five children under eight; 9 lb. a week at about 8d. a lb. Total number of articles of food drops to fourteen. Very primitive housekeeping. Education deficient;

spelling remarkable: 'insharin 8d.', 'arstone 1d.', 'meet 2s.'.

No. 22. Husband earns 24s. and gives his wife 21s. She earns 4s. 6d. to 5s. Housekeeping money 25s. 6d. a week; actual earnings 28s. 6d. The heavy amount for clothes, etc. (32s. 8d.) includes 6s. 6d. for furniture and 8s. 5d. repayment of debt for funeral expenses.

No. 25. 'Man, carriage liner, has worked since childhood for same firm, wages 30s., gives wife 27s., and keeps 3s.; has meals at home at irregular hours. Extras done in evening provide "Hearts of Oak" Club money. Wife gets charge of a house in autumn, and a very few chance days' work from a friend. What she earns provides clothes and pays 20s. for children's country visit in August – two weeks, 5s. each child. Boys save prize money and choir money for clothes. Parents have no savings.'

This is the wife's own account of their position.

No. 26. Young couple – policeman and his wife. Wife gets 20s., and the husband keeps the rest of his wages, which goes to pay for the furniture on the hire system.

No. 28. Mother and son. Income under 30s. a week. Eat good meat and plenty of it, spending 1s. a day on meat.

No. 30. Husband a carpenter, makes in five weeks 237 hours at 8s. 6d., longest hours 56, shortest 36, in a week; average, $47\frac{1}{2}$, or 33s. 8d. a week.

London Street by Street[22]

THE inhabitants of every street, and court, and block of buildings in the whole of London, have been estimated in proportion to the numbers of the children, and arranged in classes according to the known position and condition of the parents of these children. The streets

22. Second edition, Vol. II, pp. 20–3.

have been grouped together according to the School Board subdivisions or 'blocks', and for each of these blocks full particulars are given in the tables of the Appendix. The numbers included in each block vary from less than 2,000 to more than 30,000, and to make a more satisfactory unit of comparison I have arranged them in contiguous groups, two, three, or four together, so as to make areas having each about 30,000 inhabitants, these areas adding up into the large divisions of the School Board administration. The population is then classified by Registration districts, which are likewise grouped into School Board divisions, each method finally leading up to the total for all London.

The classes into which the population of each of these blocks and districts is divided are the same as were used in describing East London, only somewhat simplified...

The description of these classes given already as to East London, may be taken as applying with equal force to the whole population. Much might be added to make the description more complete, but nothing need be taken away. The numbers of the lowest class (A), it is admitted, are given at a very rough estimate; they are hardly to be counted by families and so partly escape the meshes of our School Board net. They are to be found in the common lodging-houses and in the lowest streets, and a very full description of their lives and habits is given in the special chapters which treat of these subjects. Class B is fairly counted, and of what it consists, many examples are given in the description of specimen streets, but neither it nor any of the working classes, C, D, E, or F, can be dealt with properly apart from their trades or employments, as the conditions under which these people live depend mainly upon the conditions under which they work or fail to find work. An account of the life of each of the several classes that are grouped under the letters G and H would be very interesting, but is beyond the scope of this book. I am, however, able to make a division in the figures which answers pretty closely, though not quite exactly, to that between upper and lower middle class. This division is provided by the line of rental value, beyond which the School Board do not go in making their schedules. Out of the 750,000 people included in classes G and H, as nearly as possible 250,000 live in scheduled and 500,000 in unscheduled houses. These figures may be counted as representing roughly the lower and upper middle classes respectively. The wealthy classes are included with the upper middle class.[23]

Assuming that these figures are accepted as approximately correct, the view that is taken of them will depend partly upon what may have been presupposed. I imagine that bad as is the state of things they disclose it is better than was commonly imagined previous to the publication of the figures obtained for East London. On the other hand they are probably worse, especially in regard to the numbers of classes C and D, than may have been anticipated by those who have studied and accepted the East End figures.

That is to say, the poverty of the rest of London as compared to East London is perhaps greater than most people have supposed. For myself it was so. In 1888 I made an estimate based on the facts as to East London, and the comparative density of population in other parts, on the theory that density would probably coincide with the degree of poverty. The result was to show a probable 25 per cent of poor for all London, or nearly 6% less than we now get. South London and the district about Holborn are mainly responsible for the difference.

The 100,000 people counted in institutions belong

23. The unscheduled population has been estimated in proportion to the number of houses in some cases, and assumed by way of remainder in other cases, and in every instance the assumed number of servants has been added to classes E, F, to which by position they may be taken to belong.

rather to the whole of London than to the particular district in which they are found. They may be divided under four heads:

1. Indoor paupers — 45,963
2. Inmates of hospitals, asylums, homes, etc., supported mainly by charitable donations, past or present — 38,714
3. Inmates of prisons — 5,833
4. Troops in barracks, etc. — 9,320

Total 99,830

ON THE ORDINARY LONDON HOUSE[24]

THERE are houses in London having one room, but they are accidental curiosities. Of houses with but two rooms – 'one up and the other down', as it is said – there are plenty. Rows, and indeed whole streets of these independent little homes exist, and specimens may be found among the samples which follow. In some, the outer door gives direct upon the living-room, from which steep steps rise to the sleeping-room above. In others, the entrance is through a tiny hall, containing the stairs to the room above. There may sometimes be a back yard, but more often the 'back yard is in front', or oftener still these little houses form the sides of a court, across which hang the clothes-lines, while the end of it is occupied by the closets and a dustbin. In very many, but not in all cases, besides the two rooms there is a washhouse; the washhouse usually extends forward and is sometimes detached. When the washhouse is also a kitchen, the house becomes a three-roomed house, but such are comparatively rare. The next acknowledged type is the four-roomed house. These houses have no basement or cellar, but rise from the level of the street. The front door opens on to a passage which, after giving access to the front parlour, a room ten to twelve ft square, leads to a

24. Second edition, Vol. II, pp. 234–5.

kitchen hardly so large, being often cramped to accommodate the stairs. Overhead a room the same size as the kitchen looks back into a yard, while to the front is the best room of the house with two windows occupying the whole frontage. This room is often let unfurnished. If there is a back yard there is probably a small washhouse in it; and, as before, we are led on to the extra comfort of a five-roomed house, where the backward extension becomes kitchen and washhouse combined, or kitchen alone with a separate washhouse beyond. Some of these little four- and five-roomed houses stand back from the line of the street within the railings of a nominal garden, which will vary from one to three yards wide. In some quiet nooks this space is made really a garden, filled with carefully tended plants and decorated with rockery or 'grotto' of shining stones and shells – in other places the hard beaten earth is without ornament and puts forth no green life. Whether the space be large or small, planted or not, it is useful in giving some privacy to the front room, the window of which is otherwise too close to the eyes and hands of every passer-by. An old-fashioned six-roomed house usually rises from the basement; that is, has two of its rooms below the level of the street. In such a house, the stairs at the end of the passage turn down as well as up, and the kitchen parlour, looking front, occupies, like the first floor room, the whole width of the house. There is usually a back kitchen, combining washhouse and scullery, and used for the dirty work. Such a house is eminently suited for letting. The people of the house may only use the two kitchens and let both floors above, or may themselves use the upper floor as well as kitchen, or one room in it. The rooms will be let furnished or unfurnished according to the position of the occupant – the better off furnish their rooms. This is a very common type of house, and a very pleasant one if the basement rooms are not more than half sunk below the level of the street, and if a wide area helps to make the lower rooms light. The ordinary eight-roomed house is the same thing slightly larger with a storey added, and it is hardly necessary to take our descriptions further. These are the old types. New combinations such as six rooms on two floors, or nine rooms on three floors, designed specially for letting in separate tenements are now in vogue, and it may be that the old types will gradually disappear.

STREETS COLOURED BLACK[25]

SHELTON STREET

... Shelton Street was just wide enough for a vehicle to pass either way, with room between curb-stone and houses for one foot-passenger to walk; but vehicles would pass seldom, and foot-passengers would prefer the roadway to the risk of tearing their clothes against projecting nails. The houses, about forty in number, contained cellars, parlours, and first, second, and third floors, mostly two rooms on a floor, and few of the 200 families who lived here occupied more than one room. In little rooms no more than eight ft. square, would be found living father, mother, and several children. Some of the rooms, from the peculiar build of the houses (shallow houses with double frontage) would be fairly large and have a recess six ft. wide for the bed, which in rare instances would be curtained off. If there was no curtain, anyone lying on the bed would perhaps be covered up and hidden, head and all, when a visitor was admitted, or perhaps no shyness would be felt. Most of the people described are Irish Roman Catholics getting a living as market porters, or by selling flowers, fruit, fowls, or vegetables in the streets, but as to not a few it is a mystery how they live. Drunkenness and dirt and bad language prevailed, and violence was common, reaching at times

25. Second edition, Vol. II, pp. 46–82.

even to murder. Fifteen rooms out of twenty were filthy to the last degree, and the furniture in none of these would be worth twenty shillings, in some cases not five shillings. Not a room would be free from vermin, and in many life at night was unbearable. Several occupants have said that in hot weather they don't go to bed, but sit in their clothes in the least infested part of the room. What good is it, they said, to go to bed when you can't get a wink of sleep for bugs and fleas? A visitor in these rooms was fortunate indeed if he carried nothing of the kind away with him. The passage from the street to the back door would be scarcely ever swept, to say nothing of being scrubbed. Most of the doors stood open all night as well as all day, and the passage and stairs gave shelter to many who were altogether homeless. Here the mother could stand with her baby, or sit with it on the stairs, or companions would huddle together in cold weather. The little yard at the back was only sufficient for dustbin and closet and water-tap, serving for six or seven families. The water would be drawn from cisterns which were receptacles for refuse, and perhaps occasionally a dead cat. At one time the street was fever-stricken; the mortality was high, and the authorities interfered with good effect so that the sanitary condition of the street just before it was destroyed was better than it had been formerly. The houses looked ready to fall, many of them being out of the perpendicular. Gambling was the amusement of the street. Sentries would be posted, and if the police made a rush the offenders would slip into the open houses and hide until danger was past. Sunday afternoon and evening was the hey-day time for this street. Every doorstep would be crowded by those who sat or stood with pipe and jug of beer, while lads lounged about, and the gutters would find amusement for not a few children with bare feet, their faces and hands besmeared while the mud oozed through between their toes. Add to this a group of fifteen or twenty young men gambling in the middle of the street and you complete the general picture. House by house the story is as follows:

No. 2 Shelton Street. The ground floor was last occupied by Mr Mulvaney and his wife, without children at home. He was a shrewd Irishman and stepped in when it was known the houses were coming down – fitting up a small shop with a view to compensation. He is one to make money and stick to it. He collected the rents from other occupiers. The shop was on one side of the door and there was a small room opposite in which the Mulvaneys lived. At back there was a very small yard with water-tap, etc., below was a basement, which seems not to have been occupied. On the first floor, living in one large room (there being no division) were a man and wife with one daughter almost grown up. These people, like the Mulvaneys, were Irish Roman Catholics and not very friendly to English or Protestants. Were inclined to drink but were tidier than some, and before Mulvaney's time the man acted as deputy in collecting the rents. In the second floor room lived some time since a widow and her three children, who made a fair living as a costermonger. Very clean and careful, and though a superstitious Irish Catholic, very friendly and kindly disposed towards the Protestant English missionary. After their mother's death the children opened a small greengrocer's shop in Drury Lane, and since that various people have occupied the room, coming and going and leaving no record behind. The third floor was divided into two rooms, very small in size, with roofs sloping to the floor, and here to the one side lived a Covent Garden porter with his wife and three young children, and on the other side two women. All these were Irish Roman Catholics. The market porter, though of the roughest, was disposed to be friendly, and the wife a good-humoured woman, though feckless. He had been a great drunkard, signing the pledge from time to time and after a while breaking out again. He would earn a little in the morning but would spend nearly all of it in drink before he came home, would then swear and knock his wife about. The room this family occupied, besides being very small, was destitute of comfort and as dirty as could be, and full of vermin, yet the walls were covered with little pictures. One of the children, a boy of five years, fell ill, and being taken to the hospital died on the way there in his mother's arms, arriving at the hospital past help. The parents had neither money nor goods, but borrowed sufficient for the wax candles to burn near the body and light the poor little soul to paradise. The two women in the adjoining room lived together for economy, sharing the rent which would be 2s. 6d. or 2s. 3d. They bore the appearance of widows, and got their living by begging or picking up odds and ends in the street. Their room was almost destitute – all it contained would not fetch 2s. – and dirty to the last degree. Both these women were fond of drink. One of them claimed to be an officer's widow, or rather that he had deserted her and she did not know whether he was living or dead. She was of French origin and was always called 'Madame'. She spoke beautiful English and her appearance justified her tale to some extent. Such is the story of No. 2...

No. 4 Shelton Street. In one of the ground floor rooms lived Mr and Mrs Shane and their four children, the eldest of whom was fourteen at the end of the seven years during which my informant was acquainted with the family. Like so many more in this neighbourhood they were Irish and Catholics and costermongers. The man took cold from exposure and was groaning in bed for nearly nine months with pain in head as well as limbs, and finally died. During his illness and since his death Mrs Shane obtained a living for them all by selling watercresses. This family was rather tidier than some, though the woman was given to drink at times and said she 'believed in it when she could get it'. An older boy 'got into trouble' and coming out of prison was not long before he was re-committed. For the opposite room on the ground floor there are no particulars. The first floor consisted again of one large room and in it another family of Irish Roman Catholic costermongers. These were less friendly and would only open their door wide enough to afford a glimpse of wall covered with pictures and shut it again. The costermongers of this neighbourhood, it may be here observed, usually hire their barrows and borrow the money to purchase stock. They buy in the early morning at Covent Garden, bring home what they buy, sort it over, and then turn out to sell; work very hard early and late and for the most part drink hard. A risky trade, sometimes making, sometimes losing. Used to make more at it than now, it is said because there are too many at it. They often go far afield into the outskirts of London to sell.

On the second floor of No. 4 Shelton Street, there was, six months before the house was pulled down, a very sad case – a woman with four small children whose husband had gone to America. The children were without boots or food, and their mother had to lock them in the room while she went to sell oranges in the streets. On the third floor, in two small rooms, lived a family whose record goes back eleven years, – father, mother, and two children now grown up. A powerfully-built man, but, in consequence of drink, smitten four years ago with paralysis, helpless and almost speechless. He said he had been 'a bad 'un', but he went to Mass now and hoped to reach heaven. His wife was very friendly. After his father's paralysis the son, who was in a bakery in Camden Town, kept the family. The daughter had a child. Her husband, or the man with whom she lived, died soon after and the child died also. The rooms of this family were filthy, and the occupants lived like pigs. Both sights and smells were sickening.

Of the ground floor at *No. 6 Shelton Street*, and also

of the first and second floors, there is nothing particular to note; families came and went, usually costers, almost always Irish Roman Catholics, living in dirt, fond of drink, alike shiftless, shifty, and shifting. At the top, on the third floor, there lived for five years Mr and Mrs Casson and their four children, all in one small attic. The father earned little, but most of this he spent in drink; the mother was very clean and industrious, and careful, but the children were at times without food. In the adjoining room there lived also for some five years a man by the name of Smith, a car-man at about 20s. a week, and the woman with whom he lived. They were not married; the banns were once published, but on the morning when the marriage should have been solemnized the two fell out and he blackened her eye, so the ceremony had to be postponed, and, the man dying suddenly, it never came off. He was an Army Reserve man, and would drink, but in spite of all was not a bad fellow, and the woman, who had been married before, was also a nice person.

So far as we have gone it will be thought that 'black is not so very black', but we have just begun. I fear that I may tax the patience of my readers, but my aim is to show the street and its inhabitants as it existed – not selected cases, nor the mere resultant of an average, however carefully drawn out.

At *No. 8 Shelton Street*, in the parlour on the ground floor, lived Mrs McConnell and her son, now a lad of eighteen, but only half that age when they came to the house. Since her husband's death Mrs McConnell had used the parlour as a little general shop which, with occasional charing, afforded her a very scanty living. She was Irish and a Romanist, but more steady and clean than most of her neighbours, and would say of them that they were the worst people out and would rob anybody. If she gave credit she doubtless found it difficult to collect her debts. The adjoining room was occupied by a family anything but clean and respectable. In this house each floor had two rooms, and each room, though some were hardly over eight ft square, contained a family. On the first floor there was for six years a Mrs Varney and her daughter – a respectable woman, but now dead; she obtained a living by selling fowls. The adjoining room was occupied by another Irish coster family of the usual type. On the floor above in one room of the larger size lived Mrs Rooney, a quiet and harmless old lady often short of bread or a cup of tea, but never complaining. In the same room was her daughter and three sickly children. No husband appeared, but there lodged with these women and children a man of about fifty – all living together. The old lady earned two pounds at hopping three years ago, and had it taken from her on the way home. In the small room adjoining lived a mother with her daughter who gains a living for both as a prostitute. The mother is a notorious drunkard, very violent in her cups, often in trouble with the police, and struck the Protestant missionary in the face in defence of her holy mother of God, backing this up with oaths and foul language. The third floor was occupied by more Irish, and one of these, a powerful woman, took an active part in the attack on the missionary, driving him downstairs into the shelter of Mrs McConnell's shop.

In the parlour at No. 8 a man one day told the visitor that, although a Catholic, he did not believe in anything but beer. A month later he wanted some beer and, according to common report, offered a pocket-knife for fourpence; unable to sell it he, in a rage, said somebody should soon have it. Leaving Drury Lane he returned to Shelton Street, picked a quarrel with a relative and stabbed him in the heart, killing him on the spot. He escaped hanging, but got ten years, of which he has completed the greater part.

At *No. 10*, on the ground floor, we find more Irish costers coming and going. On the floor above were a man and wife: he a martyr to rheumatism, worn out with pain, and scarcely able to leave the house, and quite dependent on what she earns charing or nursing. Clean and steady people, the woman most industrious and careful, but, notwithstanding, they were often without the poorest meal. Of the second floor in this house we have no particulars. On the third floor there were, for several years, a man and woman living unmarried, of whom the woman showed a desire for marriage; but it proved that the man had a wife living, the woman a husband. This man, when sober, was most hard-working and kind, but when drunk would beat the poor woman unmercifully. At last she left him, and in a few weeks her place was taken by another of sad and sullen appearance, but content it seemed to take the position the other had vacated, as this is now five years since, and they were living together up to the time the houses were pulled down, and, in all probability, are doing so still.

In the adjoining room on the third floor lived a man of fifty with a woman of about the same age. He was a market porter and drank the larger part of his earnings. Most of what came home to the woman went also immediately to the public house. The man was never to be seen sober, but came rolling and roaring upstairs into his room. This couple lived like demons one with another, and made of their room a little hell on earth, and yet for years they lived together in this way.

As to *No. 12 Shelton Street*, we have no particular information, families coming and going, spending their money on drink and shifting their quarters to evade the rent. A trying house to visit. This applies also to the ground floor of No. 14. On the first floor, however, there lived a mother and two daughters, all very pious Roman Catholics. Both daughters worked in the City, and when one of them died the neighbours showed their respect by covering the coffin and almost filling the one room in which these women lived with costly wreaths and quantities of beautiful flowers. Mr and Mrs Carpenter, on the second floor, had been there for many years. He was at home all day. A shrewd-looking fellow, however he may get his living; she is very quiet, clean, and respectable. On the third floor were the Sulivans – man, wife, and four children – for four years. He brought home but little money, and it was all the woman could do to keep her children from nakedness and starvation. Room fairly clean. The eldest boy, now eighteen, is in prison, committed for several years. The woman deserves a better husband and son. How the man gains his living does not appear...

No. 18 Shelton Street has eight rooms. The parlours and the first floor have been occupied by a shifting set, usually a low class of costers whose wives and children sell watercresses or flowers in the streets. On the second floor lived Mr and Mrs Park with five children, and were there for at least eight years. The Parks were English Protestants; the man, now about forty-eight years old, served in India as a soldier, and was discharged in ill-health suffering from pains in the head and loss of memory due to fracture of the skull and sunstroke. His drinking habits also stand in his way. He does house-painting when he can get it, which is rare. The mother works hard for her children and attends every mothers' meeting she can, as well as every mission-hall if possible. This brings her soup three or four times a week and sometimes a loaf of bread, and so the poor woman keeps her little room, and the children with bread. At Christmas she may contrive to get two or three Christmas dinners from different places. The room here was full of rubbish – all in it would not fetch 10s.; the dirty walls covered with little pictures never taken down; vermin abounded and the stench was awful. These people have had seven children, but about eight years ago two of them, aged nine and eleven, going to school in the morning, have never been heard of since.

The rooms on the third floor were not easy of access – not that the doors offered much obstacle, as the panels were often broken in some drunken spree, and patch on patch was the result here and in many other rooms in this street. The only converse with the inhabitants would be, ' say, governor, ain't you going to give us something afore you go?' followed by 'We'll break your — neck if don't.' It was not easy to learn anything about these people. A man might be husband, or brother, or lodger; and to whom the children belonged it was impossible to say. Of such there would be many cases in the street.

No. 20 Shelton Street. In one of the parlours lived Burton, a man sixty years of age, very quiet and steady, who dragged on with his work (scavenger to Board of Works, a martyr to asthma. The woman with whom he lived drank. They had not a chair to sit on, and the room was most offensive, swarming with vermin. The missionary's visits produced some effect here, the result being seen in cleanliness and steadiness of behaviour, but the man died shortly before the house was pulled down, and since then the woman wanders here and there getting a crust where she can.

The other parlour was occupied by the usual Irish costers. On the first floor lived Mr and Mrs Parker (who, like Burton, were English). Parker rented the whole house and lived in it for eleven years, also collected rents for three or four other houses in the street. A very decent man who had formerly been a pugilist, a hard hitter and hard drinker, as his battered face testified; now an abstainer and very respectable. His tenants took advantage of his kindness. On the second floor lived a Covent Garden porter, a widower of sixty, with a grown-up daughter. They had two small rooms but possessed only one bed. Above them lived a young woman of quiet manners and doubtful character, working occasionally at charing.

No. 22 Shelton Street. In one of the parlours lived the Draytons. Father, mother, son of nineteen, and daughters of sixteen and thirteen. They occupied this room for several years. The man was a repairer of old furniture; his bench stood in the window covered with tools, bottles, and bits of furniture. The middle of the room was filled with old tables, desks, old chests of drawers, on or amongst which the meals were taken in some way, while at the back was one rude bed. The mother did nursing occasionally, the son and eldest daughter were at work and brought in something, the youngest daughter was delicate. The man had bad health and could not earn much. A quiet and sober though rather shiftless man, he had apparently lost all heart, and only wished to be gone from a world of suffering. These people my informant knew for seven years.

In the other room on the ground floor lived poor old Mrs Berry, a widow, paralysed so as to be almost speechless. Still she pushed a barrow and sold mussels in the street, and would sometimes be out many hours and travel many miles to take a few pence. At other times she would do better. A quiet and contented woman, who kept her room tidy, and although Irish was anxious to pay her rent. The rest of the house was filled with Irish costers, no different from those already described.

No. 24 Shelton Street. In the parlour to the left lived a man, wife, and two children. He was a labourer, apparently hard-working. She strong, and clean in room and person. Both drank at times, and when in drink the woman was desperate with fist and tongue. Known for about six years. To the right lived Mrs O'Brien and her two boys, eleven and eighteen years of age. She formerly lived on the third floor of No. 2. The husband was then, as he still is, in the infirmary, leaving his wife and the children (then young) in great poverty. She sold lights in the street, exciting pity with her suffering children. Nothing in the house when first known but a market basket, reversed to serve as table at which the children would kneel, and a bundle of something in the corner to serve for a bed. Out of this low state, eight years has seen this woman rise under good influence till at last her room is comfortable, and its inmates contented and happy. The boy now sells newspapers and makes his mother anxious by playing pitch-and-toss with the coppers.

The story of the first floor in this house is one of the utmost horror. A man whose name I will not even pretend to give, by trade a sweep, having three grown-up sons, lived with and abused a woman to her death. She was an orphan brought up in an industrial school and had lived with him at least eleven years, having one child by him. She was good to the other children, as well as to her own child, and kind to the man. Wife and mother in every sense, except legally. But he so knocked her about that she was never free from bruises. The sons as they grew up followed suit and her own child died. The man had regular pay – 25s. a week – and would spend nearly all in drink. He would swear at her, and kicks and blows would follow. One year she went hopping, taking one of the boys, and brought back £3 10s., only to find the rent in arrears and bills run up for her to meet. She was got into a refuge, but he coaxed her back with fair words, with what result? My witness saw her as the end was drawing near. She was but just back from hospital, her head bound up, her arms black and blue. He warned the man, not for the first time, to be careful lest he should be guilty of murder. A few weeks later the poor woman lay on her bed unconscious, with blackened eye and face all bruised. She was dying. Her sister sought the priest and secured some holy water with which she was sprinkled, and so passed away. There was no prosecution, the neighbours shielded the man, and he too is now dead. The tie which bound together this man and woman till death – and this her death at his hands – was, though voluntary, strangely strong.

Of the second and third floors in this house nothing new can be said. They were occupied by Irish Roman Catholics unwilling to open their doors to a Protestant missionary, and ready to insult and abuse any others in the house who were willing to speak to him.

At *No. 26*, it is much the same kind of thing till we mount to the third floor. Here there lived for about four years a man and woman about twenty-six years old, who earned their living by making toys in the form of mice, which are contrived to run round a wooden plate by the manipulation of a wire beneath. He making, and she for the most part selling, they might earn two shillings a day. The man, strongly built and healthy, very intelligent in speech and speaking good English, though unable, so he said, to read or write – civil but cautious, and rather suspicious lest the visitor should be prying into trade secrets – room fairly clean, but one of the smallest; the roof sloping from the side walls at 2 ft. 6 in. from the floor. No bedstead but a bundle rolled in the corner to sleep upon. One rude chair and a dilapidated table at which they worked and ate. In this way these people lived year after year.

At *No. 28*, the parlours and first floor yield no record. On the second floor lived a widow with a son and two daughters – Irish Roman Catholics. The widow sold flowers and watercresses and had a stand somewhere at the West End, where she obtained coal, bread, and soup tickets from sympathetic ladies. Some of these tickets are only for those with a family of children, and the widow counted in her grown-up daughters. She was not visited, the distance being too great. A quiet woman, getting all she could, going without if she must and making no complaint, only that trade was bad. In her room (a fairly large one) lived besides herself her grown-up son, two daughters, and two or three children of one of these daughters. No husband was to be seen. Above on the third floor of this house lived a market porter, his wife and

POVERTY

four children; this man, an Irish Catholic, was trained as a schoolmaster, became a great drunkard soon after his marriage, but was a powerful man earning good money in the market, of which his wife, a quiet and steady person, saw little. The cupboard often bare, the grate fireless, and the children without shoes or stockings; sometimes almost naked. The woman said she had lost all heart, and consequently the room was dirty as well as empty. The panels of the door told their story of drunken violence. The man belonged to a club in Clare Market (which no longer exists) called the 'Guzzlers' Club', where for so much a week members could call for what they liked.

At *No. 26*, or *28*, in the parlour there lived at one time a man by the name of Martin, with wife and three children. The wife died, no doubt of cold and hunger accelerated by the brutal treatment of her husband, who bore a dreadful character for drunkenness. The eldest girl at the age of sixteen, soon after the mother's death, give birth to a child.

At *No. 30* the occupants of ground and first floors leave no record. On the second floor there lived Mrs Hannaford, left a widow about twelve years since with five sons and daughters. One of the daughters is wife of the market porter just described as living at No. 28, and her unhappy marriage has been a source of much sorrow to the mother, who worked hard to bring up her children, and has been a quiet, sober woman. Mrs Hannaford occupies one room; her children are all out in the world except a son, who lives at home, getting but little work. The other room on this floor was tenanted by Irish Romanists, who do not care to be visited. On the third floor lived Mr O'Neill, a mender of shoes, an Irishman, a Catholic, and a very clever talker; knowing a little Latin and some Greek, and writing shorthand; a steady man, with whom the missionary has been acquainted for eleven years. He lived formerly on the third floor of No. 6. In the smaller room on this floor lived a very poor English family, father, mother, and four children. During the six years recorded these people have been 'writhing' in poverty, the woman and children sickly from want of common necessaries; the woman apparently steady; the man earns a sixpence where he can.

At *No. 32*, in the lower rooms, were the usual shifting class of people. At the top, on the third floor, Mrs Makin, a widow, lived for two years. She gained her living by shelling peas, &c., in Covent Garden. A tidy person, very industrious and wretchedly poor, frequently without food or fire; would try to do her washing, and not know how to dry the things in winter. In the other room on this floor lived a market porter with a woman who sold oranges. About ten years they had lived so when, by the visitor's influence, they were married. The man, a pensioner, spends nearly all his pension in drink when he takes the money, and then is cruel to the woman, who does most to support the home.

At *No. 34* there are eight rooms, and during the eleven years of the missionary's visits never can he remember finding a family in any one of them that could be called decent in person, room, or behaviour. Dirt, drink, and swearing prevailed with all.

The north side of Shelton Street contained houses and people of similar character.

Nos. 1 and *3 Shelton Street*, were let in tenements, 'ready furnished'. They had eight rooms, as had most of the houses on this side of the street; rooms too small for a full-sized bed except in one direction; stairs very dark, with no light save from the rooms. The people who came here to live would stay only a few days or weeks at longest, and then others would come, so that in course of a year there would have been twenty or thirty families. As a rule they had no children, and were of doubtful character.

Nos. 5 and *7* were taken by the Middlesex Music Hall

POVERTY

(the main entrance of which is in Drury Lane) to provide an extra exit. One family only lived in them.

Nos. 9 and *11* were eight-roomed houses, occupied by rough Irish costers – one family to each room, for the most part. Quarrels and noise were everyday affairs. The Irish make the most of a funeral or a wedding. A wedding at No. 11 led to a row which lasted several days, the friends of bride and bridegroom having come to blows, while the police interfered in vain.

At *No. 13*, in the parlour, lived Mrs Grant, a Protestant, who took up the rents of the other rooms. All the rest in the house were Roman Catholics, constantly on the move.

One floor of *No. 15* was occupied for twenty or thirty years by a Welshman, his wife and family, moral and industrious people. The children attended the Ragged Schools in Macklin Street (then Charles Street) for many years, and their prize-cards hung still on the walls. It is difficult to understand how quiet, decent people should be content to live and bring up their children in such surroundings.

Higher up in No. 15 lived a Protestant family, by name King, and above again some Catholics named Burke, of whom there are no particulars.

Nos. 17 to *19* were filled with Irish frequently shifting.

The parlour at *No. 21* was kept as a shop for some time, but never succeeded. Money was so hard to get from the customers. On the second floor of this house lived Mr Land, who was a resident of over thirty years' standing in the street, having lived in different houses. A man who liked a drop of drink.

Of *No. 23* there are no recorded particulars.

At *No. 25* lived a big man who was employed at one of the music halls. A useful man in case of a row to 'chuck out' the offenders. This man's house and family have been all along the ideal of the drunkard's home. On the second floor lived a well-known character, one Welsh, who sold shell-fish in the neighbouring streets and drank all he made. This man's home was even worse than that of the music-hall servant.

No. 27 was occupied by families of whom the missionary has no particulars.

No. 29 was tried as a common lodging-house for some years and failed, and was then taken by Miss Cons for a Coffee Palace and Club for young men, the first 'Coffee Palace' established in London. It passed into other hands and failed, was then turned to some other purpose, and finally the house was shut up.

At *No. 31* were private families of whom we have no records.

No. 33 the missionary remembers well. An Irishman tried to throw him downstairs, but desisted when the disturbance drew others from their rooms. At this house lived a Mrs McCormick, who sold watercresses. Her husband drank himself to death, but she having brought up her children well, has followed them to Canada, where they are doing well.

At *No. 35*, on the top floor, lived Mr Warner, a shoe doctor; he would buy old shoes and make them up with paper and paste and polish, and when necessary with leather, for sale in Dudley Street, where they might be bought for less than a shilling a pair, 'warranted'. Given fine weather they would stand a few weeks' wear, but go to pieces on the first wet day.

No. 37 was full of Irish Catholics.

No. 39, the last house on the north side, was the largest house in the street – occupied generally by Roman Catholics.

PARKER STREET

THIS street differs in some respects from Shelton Street, and, bad as Shelton Street is, Parker Street touches a little lower level. In Shelton Street the rooms were not taken by the night, but by the week. In Parker Street it was not unusual to let by the night, so that any man and woman who had met could find accommodation. Besides this there were six common lodging-houses – three for men and three for women, and both men and women would be of the most abandoned character. Over one hundred men and about eighty women were sheltered, and these were so frequently under the influence of drink that at times these places, which at their best were but sinks of iniquity, became real hells upon earth. For these places no better title can be found than thieves' or prostitutes' kitchens, but they afford shelter also for beggars. With these exceptions the inhabitants are much the same as those of Shelton Street. The street itself is, however, wider, and much of one side has been pulled down, the warehouses only being left on the north.

No. 2 Parker Street has two entrances, the one being numbered at 159 Drury Lane. One of the parlour floors is used for the sale of coal and coke, and the room over for living in.... in one of those rooms there was at one time a Mrs Carter, a woman with a fiery temper, almost fit to commit murder, and her husband has been in prison for ill-using her. She was, however, a clean, hard-working woman. These people were at times very poor. On the second floor to the right there were a man and woman (English) who had lived unmarried for fourteen years. There were no children; the room clean, with a few comforts. In the other room lived another pair in the same fashion; the woman very unhappy, brutally treated by the man, whom she says she would leave if she knew how else to get a living. Such cases are not uncommon. The man was a drunkard. On the third floor lived an old woman and her son, Irish, who declined to be visited by a Protestant missionary.

No. 4 Parker Street contained only four rooms of good size, one on each floor. In the parlour was living till lately a woman of about thirty, but who looked nearer fifty, and who went by the name of Annie Chapman. She had been living for five years with a man, but in truth she got her living on the streets, and this room was the rendezvous of other fallen women. These women, when not in drink, would tell sad stories, and without exception had been under the influence of managers of rescue homes only to return to their old haunts, and those who knew them best looked on them as quite irreclaimable. What furniture there was in the room belonged to the landlord. The first floor room was generally occupied by prostitutes and was difficult for a man to visit. One of these girls, though only twenty-one, was remembered as having been many times in prison for shorter or longer periods. The second floor bore the same character. With these women lived men partly supported by the women and acting as 'bully' when required. On the third floor there have been couples bearing the appearance of husband and wife, of clean and respectable demeanour, and the word husband has been used or a young man spoken of as son – a rare thing at this end of Parker Street.

No. 6 Parker Street had seven rooms, and was formerly a lodging-house for men of lowest type with few exceptions. It has since been let off furnished to couples, of whom not one in seven is married. In the parlour one day there was a sickly young woman with a child in her arms and shortly expecting another. She told a story of seduction and abandonment, and said she was ashamed to appeal to friends. She made a trifle by allowing other unfortunates to use her room.

In the first floor front lived a big Irish woman with two children, and with them a young woman of about twenty-seven years, whose life was that of a fallen woman – in the room all day and out at night. Six years ago this woman, who then lived in Neal Street, was lying helpless in bed suffering from the kick of a disappointed policeman, who was tried and got nine months for the offence. The room was very dirty, and the Irish woman drank and swore. In the back room there was, as a rule, an unmarried couple or two or three fallen women living together. These people were frequently on the move. When occupied by the women the room would be open to all comers. About eighteen months since, a poor woman was one morning found dead just behind the door. She was discovered when the collector went for the rent, which he did every morning. Whether she died a natural death or not was never known and little troubled about. The staircase from the passage to the first floor is in almost total darkness at midday. The furniture let with the rooms is dilapidated and swarming with vermin...

No. 8 is a lodging-house for women. An underground room, reached by stairs from the entrance passage, serves as the common kitchen and is about 11 ft by 13 ft. In this room is a large red-hot coke fire, and round about are rough tables and benches. Here at times may be seen about twenty women with matted hair, and face and hands most filthy, whose ragged clothing is stiff with accumulations of beer and dirt, their underclothing, if they have any at all, swarming with vermin. Many of them are often drunk. These women are thieves, beggars, and prostitutes. If any woman from the country is unfortunate enough to come amongst them she will surely be robbed of all that can be taken from her, and then, unfit for anything else, may fall to the level of the rest. Bad as this house is here described, it was worse in the days of the famous or infamous Mrs Collins, a gigantic woman profusely bedecked with rings, who grew enormously fat and died weighing nearly thirty stone. She made her money it was said by combining the role of lodging-house keeper with that of procuress.

No. 10 Parker Street is arranged at the back as another lodging-house for women, kept by the same people who keep No. 8 and for the same class of inmates. If a visitor go among them he is sure to be asked for money, which, if given, would as surely go to the public-house. Perhaps a quarrel will begin, and in a minute one woman has knocked another down, while a third will seize the apparent victor by the hair and with the other hand fetch heavy blows on the face; others join the fray and the whole are swearing, foaming and fighting, while the cry of murder fills the air, and some of the more timid will crouch in corners afraid to move, mingling cries with prayers. A crowd gathers near the entrance, a policeman or two are attracted and after a time will succeed in putting down the row, perhaps hailing the worst offenders off to Bow Street. The front parlour of No. 10 is used in connection with the lodging-house, but the back parlour is let to a couple with a child who look more tidy and respectable than could be expected. On the first floor lives the keeper of the two lodging-houses just described, with her children, a son of twenty and a daughter of about fifteen. On the second floor are two rooms let at about a shilling a night and occupied in the usual way. So also with the third floor for the most part, but about a year ago there lived on this floor a Mrs Claxton with a grown-up son and daughter. This woman had an appearance of having been once in a respectable position, and claimed to be the granddaughter of a clergyman; the son was a coarse-looking fellow and the daughter had not the best of reputations. They lived for nine years in the street supported to a great extent by charity.

At *No. 12* the ground floor is the stable and coachhouse of some neighbouring butcher. This house has lately been done up and is more respectably occupied than others in the street. On the first floor lives a Covent Garden porter and his wife, fond of drink and quarrelsome, but have their room in good condition comparatively. So, too, on the second floor there were till lately a father and son, bill-posters, of good character. The man is a notorious Atheist, one who holds forth on behalf of his creed under railway arches, saying that if there be a God he must be a monster to permit such misery as exists. This man suffers from heart disease, and the doctor tells him that some day in his excitement he will drop down dead. His room is full of Freethought publications. On the third floor, and in the other rooms below, there lived people of orderly habits, the landlord being particular about his tenants...

Between *Nos. 14* and *18* are workshops for box-making, etc. No. 18 was formerly an eight-roomed house. A very bad house. In the front parlour there lived for two years an Irish woman whose eye had been nearly kicked out by her husband. A quiet-mannered woman, but too much at the door to keep her room tidy and rather given to drink. In the back room lived people scarce ever at home. The first floor front was usually occupied by prostitutes and their bullies. Some years ago a man flashily dressed was decoyed into this room, and soon found himself robbed of money and watch, while those who had robbed him slipped away. He ran into the street with an open knife in his hand and wild with rage, and stabbed the first person he met, a big lad from a lodging-house near by, in two places; the deputy of the lodging-house rushed out to take the lad's part and was himself stabbed in the back; both the wounded men were taken to King's College hospital. Their assailant proved to be a man of some means, and twenty pounds was accepted as compensation by those he stabbed. The men and women who robbed him were never discovered, and did not return, and consequently the room stood empty for some days. On the second floor previous to the repairs there were for some months a tidy woman and three children who were very poor. The third floor front was mostly occupied by Irish costers or porters. There was one day a family, father, mother, and four children in this room without food or fire, or scarce any clothing, and not five shillings worth of furniture. The husband a drunkard, the wife lost all heart. The room unbearable for dirt and stench. In the back room there has been a poor widow frequently without food. She gained her living at the market. We have been describing No. 18 as it was. It has undergone great alterations after standing empty a long time. It has been built out over the stabling next door, and may now have double as many rooms. These are let furnished, not, it must be feared, to people of any better character than elsewhere in the street...

No. 24 is let in furnished apartments. It was in the occupation of a Mr Holden, a quiet man who died about a year ago, and his widow carries on the business. The characters occupying the rooms are very low indeed; one of them, a girl of eighteen, mentioned that she had been confirmed by a Bishop but had been a b— sight worse since. About two or three years ago a woman was found dead in the parlour of this house; she appeared to have been strangled...

No. 1 on the north side, at the corner of Drury Lane, does not really belong to Parker Street at all. The shop entrance is in Drury Lane, the house only enters from Parker Street, and with its inhabitants, who in position and appearance are much above the dwellers in Parker Street, we need not concern ourselves. Nos. 3 to 5 are warehouses. No. 7 has been pulled down.... The whole house for eleven years past was noted for poverty, dirt, and drink, and deaths were at one time so frequent in it that it got a bad name for 'ill luck'.

No. 9 Parker Street The last occupants of the parlours were two Salvation Army 'Slum Sisters' who stayed for about six months. These girls had a hard struggle and so far as could be seen did not succeed – at any rate they went elsewhere. The first floor for the last two years was occupied by people making but a short stay. Previously there lived here a stonemason and his wife and two daughters – Irish Roman Catholics. The man hardworking, the woman a great drunkard; the husband would trust her with no money. For several nights at a time she slept on the stairs, and through getting cold had to attend the hospital. On the second floor at the back, in a small room with window and door both broken, lived a family of Irish street sellers; father, mother, and three little children. One could see the room through the broken panel of the door, and the children would be either lying alone through the day, crying one against another, or with a dejected Irish woman who for a penny or a little bread would take charge of them. The room without a fire, the children without food. Mother either out selling or in a public-house. The father not visible at all. The mother would sometimes be lying on the bed apparently unconscious from drink. On the third floor to the front lived a widow aged sixty, an English Protestant, who gained her living by weaving carriage lace on an old loom. She was paid 1½d. a yard and could earn 9d. for a full day's work. Sitting to her loom had so cramped her that she was bowed together and could not lift herself up. She was sometimes without food or a cup of tea. She took both rooms on this floor, paying 4s. or 4s. 6d., and let the back room to another poor woman. Had lived here for seven years and been a widow for five. The room in a most dilapidated condition and the fire (like many in this street) smoked badly. In the third floor back was another widow who did a little needlework when she could get it. This was a small room with leaky, rattling window, and walls which did not appear to have been touched with a brush for a long time. This neglect sometimes arises from persons staying long and not liking to be disturbed. This poor woman had a dejected appearance and was often without fire or food and barely clad. She was brought up in a convent. Since her husband's death she has been in great depths of poverty, partly through shiftlessness. Has a trifle allowed her by a lady for rent and gets along as best she can.

No. 11 Parker Street Here before the clearance lived in the parlours Mrs Jackson, with a blind sister and sister's son. These people were English Protestants. Mr Jackson was a cabman, and after his death, four years ago, the widow, who was seventy-three years old, lived here and supported herself and the rest by washing and mangling. Though clean people, their rooms, they complained, swarmed with bugs. These houses were not fit to exist. Close by the back parlour window was the closet, making the room most offensive, and the dustbin and tap were close neighbours with the smallest space between them and the back door. On the first floor to the front lived Mrs McNeill and five children under eight years of age. She was deserted by her husband about a year and a half ago, and had to get her living by selling oranges, etc., in the street. She was latterly allowed to live rent free, after the property was bought by the Board of Works. The husband was in America. The children were often locked in during the day crying, perhaps, while the mother was out trying to earn bread for them. No fire, often no food, almost naked, and hardly two shillings worth of furniture. The woman (an Irish Catholic) seems quiet and sober and tries hard. In the back room were people in bad condition. On the second floor to the back lived another Irish widow, but without children, who got her living by selling oranges, etc. She had been here for six years, on the whole steady, though she may occasionally take a drop too much. The front room occupied as a rule by Irish. On the third floor lived another widow without children – this was an English Protestant who made kettle and iron-holders. This was one of the worst rooms in the street, from the dirty habits of the woman, who had been here for many years. There was in the room an old bed, a small table and one chair, with another table and chair falling to pieces. The woman would pick up odds and ends in the street and bring them home thinking they would be useful some day – old rags, bits of cloth, string, dirty paper, an odd boot, an old hat, or some bones – or perhaps with the idea of selling them.

These would be under the bed or on the bed, or under the table or on it, or in the cupboard or hanging on the walls, affording everywhere encouragement to vermin.... On the third floor lived a widow with two sons of fifteen and twenty. She sold flowers in the street. A robust and hard-working woman but a heavy drinker at times. The boys are a trial to her – have taken to gambling and ill-treat her. When they fall out and the mother is under the influence of drink there is hell upon earth in this room.

No. 15 was a common lodging-house kept by the same people as Nos. 8 and 10. This one was for men, and accommodated about twenty-six, mostly of the very lowest type. Some get their living by selling newspapers, or penny novelties, others as market porters, the rest are thieves or beggars. The newsvendors are thieves when they get the chance; a bad lot almost without exception. Many of these men would be without a shirt and sometimes without boots...

At *No. 19* on the ground floor there was a woman with two grown-up daughters, all looking hardened in sin. They would beg for a bread ticket as though they had not broken fast for days, but if refused the face would alter to fiendish grin and the most fearful language would follow, the strength of voice and expression leaving no doubt as to absence of food or ill-health. In the first floor front lived the Neals. The man had been a soldier and now earns his living as a market porter; his wife was fast breaking up and the son, a tall young fellow of twenty-two, appeared to be in rapid consumption; the daughter, also grown up, sold flowers in the street. All four lived and slept in this room. In the back room lived a family consisting of mother, a son of twenty, a daughter of twelve, and an old grandmother who looked eighty – a spare but tough old woman – who gets her living as a crossing-sweeper and gets a lot of food and coal tickets given. The mother sells in the streets but suffers from asthma, and the son a few months ago was at the point of death from the same complaint. The girl also looked very ill. Their room was in wretched condition – patches of plaster protruding where the walls had been roughly mended, windows stuffed with rags or mended with paper – vermin everywhere. The rest of the house filled with people of the usual type, unwilling as a rule to converse with the visitor. At the back of No. 19 was a cottage with four rooms, occupied on the ground and first floors by a clay-pipe maker and his wife, or at least the woman who lived with him, and a small child. This man had lived here for nearly two years. The basement was fitted up with a kiln for baking the pipes, and in the parlour the pipes were made. Here, too, the woman sewed and they took their meals, sleeping only in the room above. The pipe trade, it is said, has gone down of late years and is now chiefly with the public-houses. To sell them a shilling's worth the maker of the pipes is expected to spend threepence in drink, and so drink becomes the danger. This man was a decent and very intelligent man, and, talking of his neighbours, would give them a dreadful character, saying that what he had witnessed in the street would never be believed. Just in front of his windows was a dustbin and above it the window of the first floor back, and from this window he could see good food thrown away.... When short of coal for his kiln he could generally get enough out of the same receptacle – large cinders and small coal being recklessly thrown away by the old woman who lived on charity...

No. 21 Parker Street was a lodging-house for men and had been so for above eleven years. It accommodated fifty to sixty men who were of the same description as those at No. 15. The entrance to the kitchen was through a narrow passage down stone steps from a back yard into a rough kind of cavern, and then through a door into the kitchen, which was more like a dungeon than anything else, and was only lighted by a small window from Shelton Street. This window has to be left open in summer in order to get a breath of air, and one evening while the visitor was there a bucket of water was thrown in, spoiling the food and tea of those who were at table. The men, bad as they are, and ready to fight amongst themselves, were respectful to the missionary, who was permitted to hold a religious service in the room on Sunday evening, and this service seemed to be appreciated and to have a beneficial effect.

No. 23 had been a lodging for women for eleven years, and no doubt many years previously. No crime under heaven can have escaped being committed in this place at one time or another. The kitchen and its occupants were much as has already been described at No. 8. In this house the visitor has seen many girls under sixteen living as prostitutes, and known a mother living on the earnings of her young daughter. Of late years the authorities have done much to prevent such young people living in these places, and, considering that these places exist, they have been well looked after of late by the police. About nine years ago a woman was killed in this house. She had discharged herself from St Giles's Workhouse, and returning to this house, where she had been before, she chose a certain bed that was vacant, but another woman present wanted the same bed, and in a quarrel that ensued the woman from the workhouse, knocked down, fell against the iron bedstead and death instantly ensued. The woman who struck the blow was arrested and taken to Bow Street, where the very next day in the cell she gave birth to a child. She was sentenced to twelve months' imprisonment. When the missionary called on the following Sunday, he was told by the 'deputy' and others that no one could sleep in the corner where the death had happened because of the fearful noises which were heard, and he was begged to offer prayer against this infliction. He did so, using the occasion to give solemn warning to those present, and on the Sunday next succeeding heard that since the prayers had been offered in the room nobody had been disturbed. This will serve to show the superstition of these people.

No. 27 was a public-house, the keeper of which was also the keeper of the lodging-house just described, and of Nos. 6 and 14, which were let furnished, and this house for the sale of drink nicely rounded off his interests in the street, a suitable helper to the other houses; for whatever those who lodged had, after paying 4d. for their bed, or 1s. for their room, went mostly to the public-house. It was commonly believed also that this man was in the habit of receiving the goods dishonestly obtained by his lodgers, but as to this there is no certainty. He was always most respectful to the missionary, and gave free access to his houses, of which (except the public-house) full use was made.

No 29 Parker Street was a workshop and is still standing. At *No. 31* (as it was) in the parlours, occupying both rooms, there lived Mr and Mrs Dormer with three children, who had been there over eleven years. Mr Dormer, who sold shell-fish, died nine months since from the effect of drink. He had always spent nearly all he took in drink. The widow is fond of drink also, but has to work very hard to get a living for herself and the younger girl; the elder girl and the boy now get their own living. She does odd jobs. On the first floor in the one room there had lived, also for over eleven years, a bill-poster and his wife, without children. A sober, steady man, very clean in his person, but very ailing and could not earn much, not more than 9s. a week on an average. His wife, a dirty woman, eked this out by picking up what she could in the street. Pay 3s. or 3s. 3d. rent. Room very untidy. In the front room there lived all the time a widower who spent his money in drink and tobacco. On the second floor also, the tenants of the front room had been there for over eleven years. They were a widow and her children, two sons now aged fourteen and twenty-five. She worked as a charwoman. The elder son helped a little; the younger is covered with sores so loathsome as to be hardly fit to be seen, so he can neither go to school nor to work. The mother, a decent woman, goes to church regularly. In the back room lived an old woman and her grandson. She, too, was a charwoman. The grandson, twenty years of age, was turned adrift by his stepfather, and under his grandmother's care has done well; is well-dressed and kind to the old lady. Room very clean and fairly furnished compared with others. The old woman is very clean, sober, industrious, and honest – a rare specimen in this neighbourhood. In the third floor front lived Mr and Mrs Martin and three children under thirteen. These people also were fixed residents and had been here over eleven years. Martin was a dog fancier and dog doctor. On the landing there was generally a dog chained to its kennel. The dogs varied; sometimes of the smallest and sometimes of the largest kind. Cleanliness not being a strong point with Mrs Martin, the smell may be imagined. The man looked after himself for food and drink, and the woman seemed too ignorant to realize his unkind treatment or feel her poverty. She had scarcely anything to wear, and the little child of five years would run about the house in daytime almost naked, and frequently without food. In the smallest back room no one seemed to stay long. Behind this house was a workshop where skins were manufactured.

No. 33 was the last house on the north side of Parker Street, and here in place of parlour there was a house for a gig or cart. On first floor there were families both back and front not accessible of late years within the door of their rooms. They however seemed of better class than usual, with a fair amount of furniture and cleanliness. The last occupant of the back room was a widower, scavenger to Board of Works, a man who would not believe in hell or heaven. On the second floor lived the

Pearsons, man, wife, and daughter of sixteen. They had lived in the house, one room or another, for seven years. The man according to report had deserted from the army and was given to drink. He was a labourer. The woman bore a sad appearance, the girl was sickly and very deaf, but quiet and inoffensive, and had worked at waistcoat-making for a few months. Room of good size, fairly clean and comfortable.

The occupants of the back room on the floor have been shifting people – room small. On the third floor front lived another labourer, a widower, of the name of Fay. His wife who died four years ago was one of the most wretched-looking women ever seen, and complained that her husband would give her no money and drove her to sleep on the floor. The reason was that she spent all she got in drink instead of food, and no one would willingly be within five yards of her, so offensive was her breath...

MACKLIN STREET

THIS street used to be called Charles Street, and is full of common lodging-houses and houses let in furnished apartments...

No. 2 was a Ragged School. Nos. 4 and 6 were a common lodging-house, one of several held by a committee of which the late Lord Shaftesbury was chairman. Being superior to the other lodging-houses in the street, it was always full, and was used by the better class of board or sandwich-men, who tried to get in and stay there. Nos. 8 to 10, a lodging-house was known as 'Pinkerton's'. This house was of the smaller kind; the parlours formed the kitchen, instead of a kitchen being built out to the back, and below the parlours were the places for washing. Next to Pinkerton's there was a workshop, which is still standing; and beyond it, at No. 12, in the parlour lived for some years a very little woman and her deformed son, who sold bread and eatables to the lodgers. Both mother and son died a short time before the houses were pulled down. Over the parlours lived girls and women who were on the streets. There were very many of this class of women in Charles Street when the missionary first knew it, but they were gradually driven out by rebuilding, and had to seek lodgings elsewhere.

No. 14 was another common lodging-house kept by a man who had several in this street and still keeps two there. No. 16 was a large double house containing fourteen rooms, and every room would probably be let separately. This house, like the lodging-house at Nos. 8 and 10, was known as 'Pinkerton's', and for nearly thirty years was always let out 'ready furnished' as 'private rooms'; that is, girls and women on the street occupied it, men living with them who would be often interchanged. The women called them their 'husband' or their 'old man'. Rows and quarrelling were common – sad lives and sad deaths! If anyone was ill at these houses, or at the lodging-houses, word was sent to the workhouse, and the person was at once removed; hence to die here was not common. If anyone did die it would be suddenly. Beyond a gateway, leading to a yard, were Nos. 18, 20, and 22, each eight-roomed houses, let in the same way, but not belonging to Pinkerton's. The girls would move from No. 16 into one of these, and vice versa as occasion served. Beyond No. 22 were and are the Roman Catholic Schools, and beyond these again stood three common lodging-houses, Nos. 30, 32, and 34 – No. 30 being for women only, No. 32 for men, while No. 34 was for men and women together. These were three ordinary houses, and at one time, it was said, offered convenience for escape from pursuit by the police by practicable intercommunication.... In these houses the missionary for years held religious meetings, and has seen men affected to tears, so that you might well think 'there is hope of that man'; but let him get to a public-house with a few pence in his pocket, and he would soon be affected in a different way.

No. 1, on the north side, belongs to Drury Lane. Nos. 3, 5, and 7 are common lodging-houses, all for men. These still stand and are constructed in the same way as were those just described, excepting that, there being no back yards on this side, the kitchens could not be built separate, so the parlours were converted for this purpose, doors leading from one to another. Nos. 9 and 11 provide sixteen rooms and are let by the night to 'married couples'. Where now stands Staffordshire Buildings, was a court, and facing the street a common lodging-house... whence on one occasion a Frenchman, whose very clothes had been robbed from him, had to be taken by the police to Bow Street in a cab. Among the things taken from this man was a watch, and the woman who had taken it had it stolen in turn from her, and the last thief having sold it took a holiday in the country with the proceeds. All this passed as common talk in the street at the time. In this room, too, there was an inquest on a woman who died rather suddenly. She had shared a room with a man and woman, themselves living together unmarried, whom she paid for the use of the room and the bed when at liberty, and in this bed, which was so dirty that it had to be destroyed, she died. So the story was told at the inquest, where it also came out that the deceased was married and that her husband occupied a good position at the West End. She had 25s. a week from him, besides occasional presents of money. Of course she drank it all. When men or women fall from better positions and are found in these houses it is generally through drink, and such are to be found – clerks in holy orders, educated men, school teachers, merchants, reduced to the lowest condition.

No. 19, another common lodging-house for women, was a desperate place. The lowest of those for men would be preferable...

Beyond 19 and 21 is a place occupied by theatrical scene-painting, and then there is the mortuary at the corner of the side entrance to Goldsmith Street (formerly called the Coal Yard). Beyond this as far as Newton Street are now the casual wards and stone-yard. Here, at one time, there was a house with cow-sheds adjoining and a court with about six houses of three rooms each, and about six more houses to the front in Macklin Street – these houses, both in street and court, used to be full of loose women and girls. Such was Macklin Street.

GOLDSMITH STREET

This street, formerly 'The Coal Yard', lies parallel to Macklin Street, opening out of Drury Lane, but instead of reaching through to Newton Street it turns at right angles and debouches in Macklin Street. At the corner in Macklin Street stands, as already mentioned, the mortuary, and behind it reaching back some distance with blank wall to Goldsmith Street are some parish almshouses, of which the entrance is in Macklin Street, between Nos. 17 and 19. The building now used for these almshouses was originally St Giles's Round-house, an old detached fabric built, as its name imports, in a cylindrical form, but it had undergone from time to time so many alterations that its symmetry was destroyed and its walls bulging made it resemble an enormous cask, a resemblance which was increased by the small circular aperture which served for a door pierced like a bunghole in its side at some distance from the ground. This was approached by a flight of wooden steps. The prison was two storeys high, with a flat roof surmounted by a gilt vane fashioned like a key. There was considerable accommodation inside, and it had in its day accommodated many thousands of disorderly persons. In this Roundhouse it is said that Jonathan Wild and Jack Sheppard[26]

---

26. Eighteenth-century criminals. – EDS.

were in their turn locked up, and from it they succeeded in escaping. The building, which was erected in 1790, was finally given to the Almshouse authorities of St Giles's-in-the-Fields and St George's, Bloomsbury, for the residence of twenty poor women of these parishes, and was rebuilt in 1885. The rest of this portion of Goldsmith Street, occupied now by business premises, was formerly the site of Barley Court and always full of girls and base women who could do any diabolical work. Once they threw a man out of window and killed him. Just at the back of this court stood the matron's house of the new almshouses, and in the midst of such vice and wretchedness the poor old ladies lived. Of the same character were four houses of three rooms each which stood at the corner where the street turns towards Drury Lane. They too are gone, and business premises stand in their place. Proceeding along Goldsmith Street towards Drury Lane one crosses Smart's Buildings, and on the south side, where now stands the Board School, there was a peculiar place called the Galleries. Some houses two storeys high occupied by bad women faced the street, but at back was a large space of ground. This was built round and a single door was the only entrance. The ground floors of these buildings were used for stabling costers' donkeys, and above were rooms in which dwelt a rough, desperate class of Irish costers and others. One of these visited by my informant was a rat-catcher, his room full of boxes of ferrets and surly dogs. The man was as surly as his dogs and as sharp as his ferrets, and as rough a customer as any rat; his wife, a meek quiet woman, lived to do his bidding and kept the place as clean as it might be.

At the Drury Lane end on the south side of Goldsmith Street are a carpenter's shop and dairy, and beyond the dairy are the cow-sheds. The dairyman lives at the dairy, but no one now resides at the carpenter's shop. Opposite on the north corner stand 'Goldsmith's Build-

POVERTY

ings', a model block accommodating thirty families, mostly costers too newly come for individual details to be given; they are mostly second-class costers, employed by others to hawk round cheap commodities. Onward the houses bear regular numbers from 3 upwards. Nos. 3 and 5 are occupied by a family who have prospered wonderfully. Its members divide, some going into the country, where they collect moss, ferns, etc., or buy flowers, which are sent home by train and sold in Covent Garden market. Others do this on a smaller scale and single-handed, going out a few miles from London by train or tramping on foot if they have no money, to collect groundsell or chickweed for birds, or creeping-Jenny and sprays of ivy, which, coming back next day, they sell in the streets.

At *No.* 7 lives a car-man in broken-down health. He fell off his cart and being run over broke his leg. On the floor above is a very poor old lady living on charity, but a happy soul expectant of heaven...

Nos. 11, 13, and *15* contain each nine or ten families, mostly fond of drink and poor. Many of these belong to the coster class.... No. 23, the corner of Smart's Buildings, is occupied by a prosperous Irishman who deals in fish and fowls. Beyond Smart's Buildings there is a smithy and foundry occupying Nos. 25 and 27. No. 29 is a double house where lived and died an old man who had saved enough to own some of these houses, but his heirs have sold them and spent the money, and now live at top of No. 30, where also lives on the lower floor a poor coster. No. 31 is a stable with rooms over it, occupied by caretaker to parish stone-yard. Where the street turned there was a double house pulled down to make the entrance to the stone-yard, which, with the casual wards, reaches to Macklin Street.

It remains to describe Smart's Buildings. On the east side there are seven houses, each containing six rooms and cellar, and at back of each in the yard has been built a cottage of two rooms, one over the other. All these, houses and cottages alike, are occupied by very poor people, most of them occupying only one room. No. 7, next Goldsmith Street, is a shop of varieties. The woman married an Irishman and they had no children, but one day a boy was left on the doorstep and she took him in and kept him twelve months, when one day he was taken off and a little girl (his sister) left in his place. A man who came to live at a common lodging-house in Short's Gardens (close by), whose wife had left him, found out that the children were his, and that his wife had left them. The father died in hospital, and the girl stayed on and still lives with her adopted mother, who is now a widow. To No. 5 there came once a wretched family who occupied a room but paid no rent, and having notice to quit pleaded they had the fever, upon which three or four weeks were given them, and before this was up they obtained from the police an extension of three weeks more. Very likely a hard case for these people, but hard also for the poor person who, taking the whole house, looked to getting part of the rent by sub-letting. No. 4 contains seven families, among them one which for twenty years has given trouble to the police through drink, and all the time has lived in wretchedness...

It will be readily understood that I have no proof to offer for the accuracy of the foregoing statements. I have no means of checking them or any of the descriptions which will follow. The greatest care however was taken to make the account of each street complete, and I am satisfied that none of my informants had any wish but to tell their stories truthfully.

I should have been glad if I could have given as full an account of some black streets elsewhere in London, but such localities do not lend themselves satisfactorily to parochial visitation, and the material is scarce. There is moreover much uniformity. Certain types cover all the black streets, and these types are all represented in the central London group we have described. Streets filled with common lodging-houses – streets of furnished apartments occupied by prostitutes – streets of small houses, the homes of thieves. None will be all bad together. Everywhere mixed in with the rest are to be found the victims of drink or folly or misfortune, and the description of some mixed streets in which poverty rather than vice prevails may serve, with a slight allowance, as illustrations of worse places.

There is sometimes more 'house-pride' to be seen in the black than in the dark blue streets. However the money may be got, the people are not quite so poor, and I have seen great efforts made to bring the appearance of doorstep and window up to the desired standard on a Saturday afternoon, beyond anything to be met with in the dark blue streets. The houses have at times a furtive secret look, but the evil character of the black streets is rather to be seen on the faces of the people – men, women, and children are all stamped with it.

To the foregoing I will only add from my notes a description of Little Clarendon Street (black):

This street, long and narrow, presents a very unattractive vista to anyone passing along the main street and looking up. Its length is relieved by only one break where a small street crosses. Walking along it, most of the houses appear poverty-stricken and all have a grimy look. It is the same with the people. Some of them can be counted above the line of poverty, and their poverty seems to be of a dismal, vicious type. All the same their amusement is catered for. A crowd had gathered at the further end of the street round two performers, each of whom in turn did feats of skill and strength while his companion turned the handle of the piano. The crowd consisted of the inhabitants who, it being Saturday afternoon, were hanging about – young and old, male and female. Of passers-by there would be few besides myself.

In addition to the circle in the street and to women standing in the doorways, upper windows were opened and heads craned out to see the show. Ha'pence were thrown into the performer's hat, and one lady giving a penny received back a halfpenny change.

Near by, but not in this street itself, there was at about the same time another gathering. It was round a drunken man lying wounded and bleeding in the gutter near a public-house. His friends carried him off into their or his house, and another drunken man, his assailant, I suppose, but evidently sorry, tried in vain to make his thick tongue explain what had happened. A little later, when I passed again, the crowd had dwindled to a few children intent upon a little pool of blood.

DARK BLUE STREETS[27]

SUMMER GARDENS

THIS place lies at the back of Fount Street. The particulars given apply to the inhabitants of Summer Gardens, but for the purpose of description it will be convenient to describe Fount Street as well, and even to touch upon Baxter Street, the leading business street to which the other two in some sense pertain. Fount Street and Summer Gardens are both coloured dark blue. Baxter Street is black, the houses which are interspersed with the business premises having a bad character. The three together are part of one of the poorest districts in all London, a district where poverty is almost solid.

Summer Gardens is a narrow street, all dwelling-houses. Fount Street is mostly dwellings, but has some places of business, and a mission-house. Baxter Street seems full of business – cheap cabinet-work, furniture, and chairs. Cart and barrow loads of roughly shaped wood or sawn boards are in the roadway, and men pass

27. Second edition, Vol. II, pp. 94–9.

POVERTY

about with great bundles of chair backs or legs. In the centre of this street are the large church mission-buildings. There was soup going at the mission-house in Fount Street, a very large old house with wooden front, the boards overlapping like the sides of a boat. At each of its two doors a group was gathered; one, of women with jugs, the other of children who brought no jugs and would doubtless carry away the soup in a more simple manner when it could be given them. Both groups had to wait. I passed several times and still the same women, and I think the same children, stood waiting in the freezing air. The children looked well enough, more common than wretched. The women looked exceedingly cold, and no wonder, for they seemed to have run over from their houses without throwing on either bonnet or shawl, in their working aprons, bare-armed as well as bare-headed, dangling their jug and gossiping till their turn might come. At the corner as I passed along two boys met. "ad dinner?' said one. 'Yes.' 'What did you 'ave?' 'Soup.' 'Was it good?' I put in, and the answer came promptly, 'No.'. . .

Many of the houses in these streets have been formerly occupied by weavers, and have the usual large upper windows and spacious rooms (as originally built) needed for the looms. Now these large rooms are partitioned up into small ones. With these old houses are mixed others of different type. The new buildings are principally missions or schools. In Summer Gardens there live some costermongers, and in Fount Street also, empty barrows stood about and one or two baked-potato vans, ready to turn out at night. Before one door stood two barrows well loaded with oranges ready for a start (12.30); the man may have returned to dinner, but more likely his hours begin and end late. Summer Place, the next street to Summer Gardens, is more completely in the occupation of costers. Here, and still more in the yet smaller courts round about, the roads are much littered with paper unwrapped from the fruit. Amongst the scraps of paper and garbage and frozen dirt there is as usual a great quantity of bread strewn about (surest sign of extreme poverty all over London). The streets are all covered and the gutters filled with frozen dirt; harmless in its present condition and impossible for any vestry to deal with, but more or less it would be there at all times.

In one street is the body of a dead dog and near by two dead cats, which lie as though they had slain each other. All three have been crushed flat by the traffic which has gone over them, and they, like everything else, are frozen and harmless. The houses in Baxter Street and Fount Street are interspersed with little shops. Except the old-clothes shops, every shop, whatever else it deals in, sells sweets, and with most of them the sweets seem the 'leading article'. They differ only in what else they offer. With some it is toys; with others oranges and onions; with others dripping, cheese, and ham; with others again loaves of bread or temperance drinks. In almost every case cakes of some kind are sold, or little open tarts.

The particulars given below are for part of one side of Summer Gardens, compiled from the notes of one who knows the street and its people very well.

On the ground floor of No. 2 lives Mutton, a builder's labourer; he had had no work for a month, and his wife was just confined. There were four children. Came from Weymouth. The wife gave up attending the mothers' meeting connected with the church because of the bad language of other members. Above is the office of the landlord. The man in charge, a pleasant little fellow, lives elsewhere. Complained of difficulty in collecting his rents; some tenants owe thirteen weeks and have no goods worth distraining. There is also a room occupied by man and wife. The man a dirty, disreputable-looking old fellow with a sharp wit. Not at all religious. Said his brother had served the Lord till seventy-four years old and 'then He thought fit to choke him'. The old man's trade is doll-making, but having no dolls to make is in the meantime a shoeblack. He 'should be busy when the Germans were all dead'. Imported dolls came cheaper than they could be made in England. He was born not far away and had always lived in the neighbourhood. His father (a toy-maker) employed eighteen men and rented four houses. Our old man inherited the business, but failed, and is now very poor. He is over sixty. His wife does a little charing.

No. 4. On the ground floor lives a hawker with eight children; the eldest, a girl of seventeen, and a quiet gentle creature, was at home with the two youngest. She makes boot boxes. Wife was out doing half a day's work. A grown-up son lives in Fount Street. The first floor is occupied by Green, a dock labourer, with wife and four children. They subscribe to a clothing club connected with the church. At the top lives Marston, a chair-maker, with wife and four children. They also are in the clothing club. The wife makes match-boxes. She has just been confined, but the baby is dead.

No. 6. On the ground floor live Mr and Mrs Meek. Meek is a hatter and was engaged in dyeing children's hats in a portable boiler. A cheery little man. With the help of his wife he dyes, re-blocks, and trims old hats, which they sell in the streets at 3d. each. Wife had been selling them in New Cut. Had taken 6d. – last night 3d. – so she said. There are six children. Rent 6s. for two rooms; had to shift from another house where they owed rent. One of the rooms now occupied should be a shop, but the shutters are up on account of broken glass. Get free breakfast tickets and other help from church. On the first floor lives a widow who does washing. She had two sons at home out of work. The second floor is occupied by the Martins; the man was in the infirmary and his wife was away at work, leaving only the daughter at home. On the top, in one room, lives Burge, a bricklayer's labourer. Had only had one week's work since Christmas. He has a wife and five children, of whom one earns 4s. a week. Rent 3s. Helped by church. In the other room lives Grantly, a costermonger, with three young children. The wife gets four days a week at a laundry. Seem very respectable.

No. 8. This is an eighteen-room house. On the ground floor two rooms are occupied by the Robsons, a young couple with two children. The man is a coster, but was out snow-sweeping. The wife makes boxes. Decent industrious people. At the back lives Mrs Helmot, whose husband, formerly an optician, is now at Hanwell suffering from suicidal melancholia. The woman has lost several children and supports herself by washing and charing. She has charge of two children belonging to one of her daughters. Of these she takes home the youngest every evening, but the eldest (being by a former husband) stays altogether with the grandmother. This child had not been to school lately, having no boots, and only came out from behind the table when told that 'it was not the School Board man'. In the kitchen to the right, sub-let by the Robsons at 1s. 6d., lives Mrs Thomas and Mrs Flanaghan, two miserable-looking widows, who share the rent. Mrs T. sells fruit or flowers in Paternoster Row, but had this day (in February) taken nothing and got very wet-footed. Mrs F. does washing and charing occasionally. On the walls of the room hung a portrait and two other prints. Mrs T. had just pawned two aprons and a pocket handkerchief to pay the rent. She wore a pair of odd boots – bought one at a time; don't keep the wet out. Was at church last three Sundays and doubtless hoped a reward in this world as well as the next. Could only afford, she said, 'Just a cup of tea sometimes'. Mrs F. does not go to church. 'Has got no Sunday clothes.' Good clothes all pledged. Rent 7s. 6d. in arrear. Born in Hatton Garden. Had been here two years. Her father was in good circumstances, a tailor employing over sixty hands, working for a large retail house. She had married against her father's wish and been discarded. The father has been dead now sixteen years. Mrs Thomas was also born in London – at Snow Hill.

On the front floor at back was Mrs Brandon, formerly and better known as Smith. Her husband (Brandon), a Frenchpolisher, and great drunkard, deserted her on Christmas Day, and is now living with a girl at a low lodging-house. His wife still had the remains of a black eye and two cuts on the forehead by which to remember him, but does not herself bear a very good character. Living at home with her was a boy of fourteen who went out with a bookstall man. Doing nothing now because of bad weather. There was also a married daughter with an infant who pays her mother 10s. a week. This young woman's husband enlisted on the day she was confined, being then only sixteen and a half and she barely eighteen. He had signed for seven years and was at Malta. Mrs Brandon had worked in the kitchen of a City restaurant.

No. 10 has also eighteen rooms. On ground floor to right Boffin, a cabinet-maker, working on what-nots; complained of the way his work was 'sweated'. Has a wife and five children, all young. These people are very poor. To the left Hulett, a slipper-maker, with wife and four children, one (aged eight) ill. He makes a dozen in a day and a half and gets 3s. for them. In the second room on left hand lives Mrs Carden, a widow of doubtful character. Part of the first floor is occupied by Mr and Mrs Caird, both of whom drink heavily; a very rough lot. She makes boxes. Upstairs there is Mrs Wilson, a widow, who is said to go out to work. Dr Barnardo has two of her girls. There is a one-eyed boy of eleven at home. The other rooms are empty – tenants ejected for not paying their rent.

No. 12. On ground floor lives Sanderson, a cabinet-maker. He is an elderly man, a widower for five-and-twenty years, and lives here with his son, a single man of twenty-eight. They rent a workshop elsewhere, paying 3s. 6d. a week for it. The first floor is to let. Above there is a man in the building line, out of work for four months. His wife makes the insides of match-boxes for her daughter at a penny per gross (this daughter has been twice married and is separated from her second husband; has four children). There is a son aged seventeen who earns 7s. 6d. a week, and four younger children, one in very bad health with bronchitis. The children want boots. Very poor, and very little to eat. Rent 3s. 6d.

No. 14 is a shop kept by Mrs Richards, who has lived in the neighbourhood for twenty-nine years and in this house for fifteen years, and is known by everybody. She saved little by little enough to start in business, and afterwards to enlarge it. Has living with her a daughter of about nineteen, and a son who is a bus driver; and she also maintains a niece. The daughter is also thrifty, and belongs to the National Penny Bank. She was educated at St Andrew's. The son did not go to school, and went to work at nine. He was in Commissariat Transport Corps in Egyptian campaign, and might have been a sergeant if he had been better educated. Over the shop lives Mrs Campbell, a widow, with one little boy.

STREETS COLOURED PURPLE[28]

WE find in these streets a very wide range of character. All may be represented in the samples to be given, but we cannot say exactly in what proportion the various kinds exist. In some the mixture of poverty is to be found almost in every house, lying very commonly, though not always, floor by floor, in strata. In other streets it goes by houses and then is more easily distinguished. In others, one whole side of the street is better off than the other.

28. Second edition, Vol. II, pp. 172–9.

In some again, there is one special bit poorer than the rest, perhaps because of bad building, more often from the contaminating influence of other poor property lying near by at the affected point. Finally, we have streets which are poor only at one end, with some of which we have been able to deal on the map. Thus Lady Street, described among the dark blue streets, changes its colour, becoming first purple, and finally pink before the eastern end of it is reached.

The greatest difference in type lies in the size of the houses, especially as regards the number of floors, and this distinction is much enforced when, as is often the case, the larger kind of house has been built for people of larger means than those who now inhabit them, and a dwelling intended for one family is arranged as best may be for two or three families, or even more. Distinctions arising from the number of floors, and from the character of the original design, apply to the light and dark blue streets, and even in some instances to the pink streets, but it is to the purple streets that they apply most.

CUTTER'S ROW

THIS street is partly filled by business premises. It has some sawmills and places where wood is sold to the cabinet trades, and one side consists almost entirely of the backs of the large shops in the High Street. It has also a cats'-meat shop, a dried-fish shop, and a fried-fish shop in close proximity; also two or three sweet-shops. It is a street with plenty of life of its own.

No. 18. Fishmonger's shop, kept by Bloxham, who employs a youth as assistant. Mr and Mrs Bloxham live on the first floor above the shop; have one boy at school. On the top floor, front room, lives Mrs Grantly, a widow, who makes toy whips at a penny each, or 5s. 6d. and 6s. 6d. a gross. Busy about Christmas, when publicans take a lot to give away to the children as presents, just as they give sweets on Sundays at some of the public-houses. The husband has been dead six years. Mrs Grantly has four children married, one of whom allows her 1s. weekly Another son lives with her, and sells papers near the railway station. Rent 2s. 6d. In the back room lives Halhead and his wife. He is an 'out-of-work'. Used to be cigar-box maker, but trade declined, owing to use of paper packets – women's work. Has lately been working at the docks. They have a girl at service. In the second floor front room lives Pantin, a marble mason, out of work. His wife gets four days a week as laundress; looks thin and wan. Grandmother looks after the two children when their mother is at work. Seem respectable, but have only been here six months.

No. 20. Entrance to large wood-yard occupies the ground floor. On top floor lives Peel, a bill-poster, who has been out of work for twelve months, but is now doing a little. There is a wife, but no children. They owe four months' rent, and have had to sell a bedstead. Were burning old boots for fuel when visitors called. Peel drinks...

No. 24. A toy-shop. The man Brown hawks toy whips. Trade is bad. His wife and he are elderly people, very decent and struggling.

No. 26. Public house, changed hands lately, which has been an improvement.

No. 28. Baker's shop, kept by Stein and his wife; they have a grown-up daughter and some young children, and have been here for years. Stein worked for his predecessor. Very respectable people.

No. 30. Second-hand boot-shop, kept by Shaw, an elderly man. There is his wife and one daughter at home, and he has three sons married. Lived here many years. No lodgers.

No. 32. Haberdasher's shop, kept by Bird. The wife and daughter do dressmaking, as well as mind shop. The man goes out to work. Very respectable.

No. 34. Ground floor, occupied by Grind, a looking-glass frame-maker, as shop. He lives at the back, and has a sick wife and five children, one, a girl, at service, and four at home. Very friendly. He sometimes works to order, but more frequently on own account, and then takes his wares round. Works sixteen hours a day, and earns 25s. to 30s. a week. The first floor of this house is occupied by the Steads. Stead himself is a waterside labourer, but acts also as scene-shifter at the Royal Theatre. His wife used to be a pew-opener. They have two children, a girl, who is mantle-maker, but now out of work and a boy, who is at home. The wife's mother lives with them. She is widow of a Freeman (Clothworkers' Company), and receives 6s. a week pension. She sells lights at the corner of a street in the City, where she had a stall for thirty-four years. The daughter was educated at Cripplegate School. On the top floor there was a dock labourer, with wife and twins, both very poorly. These people are badly off. The man, when last visited, had been out on strike four weeks.

No. 36. The ground floor is occupied by Hilton, a fishmonger and greengrocer, who has his shop next door, and does a fair trade. Has wife and children, of whom two are at work. Very nice man; abstainer. He complained of the number of loafers about in the street. The first floor front was to let, and the occupant of the back-room out. On the top floor lives Appleby, a shoemaker, busy now, but had no work for five weeks previously. His wife makes match-boxes. They have one girl at home. Rent, 4s.; owe two weeks. Mrs Appleby attends church.

No. 15 is a lodging-house, kept by Baker and his wife, helped by their son. It is said to be respectably managed. Service held here every Sunday by a missionary.

No. 13. Public house.

No. 11. Large dwelling-house. On the ground floor lives Kerr, a general labourer, who is out of work. He worked twenty-one years for a wholesale chemist, and cannot now find employment because of his age (fifty-six), although well and hearty. Seems a respectable man. Has a wife and one child. There are three other families in the house (Jews).

No. 9A. Lower part stables. On the first floor, Park, a printer's labourer, with wife and baby. Attend church. Pay 3s. for room and small kitchen. At the top lives Gardner, a dealer in sawdust. His wife is an Irish Roman Catholic. She goes out cleaning. They have one girl at service and three children at home. The husband drinks.

No. 9. Barton and his wife live here. Mrs Park, who lives next door, is their daughter, and they have another daughter, who lives at home, and works with her mother, mending up second-hand clothes for a tailor in Virginia Row. No information as to Barton himself. The Bartons have lived twenty-five years in the neighbourhood. On the top floor lives Slattery, a shunter on the railway. Both Barton and Slattery are Roman Catholics.

No. 7. Mr and Mrs Penrose live here. Mrs Penrose was another daughter of Mrs Barton. Respectable people.

No. 5. The Mayfields occupy both floors of this house. They have seven children. Have been here about twelve months, having come from Spitalfields. Said they had been very poor, but were doing better now. Accept the occasional teas offered to those who join mothers' meetings or attend mission services, as 'of course'. Seem very respectable...

Altogether there are twenty-five houses in this street.

CARVER STREET

THIS is a dull-looking street, rather wide in proportion to its length. There is a baker's shop at the corner, and a public house in the middle of the street, accommodated in an ordinary house with part of the next added. Licensed houses of this description are quiet and comfortable, and may be either the most or least respectable. The windows of Carver Street speak the mixed character

POVERTY

of its inhabitants. It looks what it is, a typical mixed street of a crowded district, tending towards poverty rather than the reverse; it has one sweet-shop; the children do not run in the street much, and altogether there are few signs of life in it at any time compared to poorer streets. The following description of part of its inhabitants tells the story of the street very well. There are forty-four houses in all.

No. 1 is occupied by Herbert, a compositor, whose wife has just been locked up for drinking. She wears the blue ribbon for a little time, and then breaks out. There are five children, two being at work. The man has regular work, and might be comfortable but for the drink. He drinks as well as his wife. In one room upstairs lives Toogood, a labourer, with wife and child. The wife goes out charing, and puts out her child, paying a weekly sum for its care.

No. 2 is occupied downstairs (two rooms) by an elderly couple without children. The man works at road-repairing for the parish. He used to drink, but has recently become an abstainer. They are quite comfortable. The upper rooms are occupied by the married daughter of this old couple, with her husband, an engineer, and two children of school age. The engineer is in regular work, but is lazy and indifferent, and will at times leave his wife dependent on her parents. She is a very respectable young woman.

No. 3 is occupied by George, a labourer at the electric light works, in fair work. Mrs George does a little sewing, and two girls are at a factory. The other children are young. They are not very poor, and use three rooms. The remaining room is occupied by a piano-tuner, in regular work, and his wife, who drinks, or they might be comfortable. They have no children.

No. 4 is occupied on the ground floor by Masters, a labourer, with wife and four small children, three being at school. The man is in regular work. Respectable poor.

Above, in one room, is Grainger, dustman, in regular work, with wife and three children; and in the other room is Mrs Hope, a widow, who has parish relief, and does a little sewing. A blunt, outspoken old woman.

No. 5 is a larger house, with a shop and two rooms at the back, and an attic. The shop (sweet stuff) is kept by Mrs Topping. Her husband is a porter at Covent Garden, and they have five small children. They just get along. The widowed mother of Mrs Topping lives with them, and helps with the shop and children. The three upper rooms are occupied by a dustman in regular work, with wife and one child, young people; a labourer, with wife only, getting a fair amount of work; and another labourer, with wife and two children. These people are not very poor.

No. 6 has five rooms. Two are occupied by Grandy, an outside porter in regular work, with wife and three children. One by a widow, with two children, who goes out to work. Another by a dustman in regular work, with wife and one child; and the last by Plucking, a shoemaker, with wife and three children. He goes mad with drink at times, and they are very poor indeed. Have no furniture.

No. 7 is occupied downstairs (two rooms) by Wardle, a labourer at the flour mill, in regular work. He has a wife and five children; one boy goes to work; a steady couple, not very poor. Upstairs there lives King, a labourer, in irregular employ, with wife and two children. Rather respectable young people. Poor.

No. 8. Below, in two rooms, there is Street, a regularly employed labourer, with wife and four children, all at school. Very respectable people. On the upper floor lives Upton, who works at the flour mills. He has a wife and four children. Very respectable people. There is a young man lodger occupying a fifth room in this house.

No. 30. Here two rooms are occupied by Harrington, a plasterer, with wife and seven children, all going to school. The man is out of work in winter. The rest of the house is occupied room by room. In one is a labourer, in uncertain work, with wife and one child. Seeming to be very poor. In another a costermonger, selling fruit from a barrow. He has a wife but no children. Decent people. In a third room there is a widow who has parish relief, and does a little sewing and charing. She is as deaf as a post. Finally the fourth single room (formerly the wash-house) is occupied by a begging widow; one of the best beggars in the district. She, too, has parish relief, and does a little charing.

No. 31 includes a small general shop and is occupied by Tincombe and his wife with three children. The wife attends the shop. Tincombe himself is a shoemaker, and has a little shop to work in at the end of the street. They are fairly comfortable. One room in this house is occupied by Brook, a labourer, in irregular work, with wife and one child. Very poor people; and there are some empty rooms.

No. 32 is occupied by Mr and Mrs Prentice. Elderly people who have brought up a large family, all now married and gone. Mr Prentice is working in the country at present. He is a carpenter. One or two rooms are occupied by Mrs Hand, the widowed daughter of Mrs Prentice. Her husband was employed in the post office, and died leaving her with four children, one of whom has since died. The mother goes to the pickle works, and while she is gone the grandmother takes charge of the children. In another room lives a labourer in fairly regular work, with wife and one child; not very poor, and in another a porter and wife, without children.

No. 33. Two rooms are occupied by Dodgson, a labourer in regular work, with wife and five children, one at work and four at school; the man has bad health in the winter, suffering from chest disease. Very steady, respectable people. In one room lives a labourer and his wife, no children and a fair amount of work. In another a boatman and his wife; middle-aged people; pretty comfortable. And in a third a widow woman, who is poor.

No. 34 is occupied by the widow of a boatman. He committed suicide and left her with eleven children. Some have died, and she has five here now, two of whom go to work, and three to school. She makes sailor jackets, but is nearly blind. Struggles hard for her children. There are also living in this house, in one room, Coleman and his wife, and two children. Coleman was a porter but does nothing, preferring to smoke his pipe. His wife takes in washing and keeps him. In another room there lives Brough, a maker of dolls, working for his father who keeps a shop in Drumlow Road. He has a wife and two children. A third room is occupied by Owen, a labourer, often out of work, with wife and three children. They are nearly starving. The children are always ill.

CHAPTER 2

OCCUPATIONS

In one of the volumes of the first series, and in every volume of the second – which dealt with the industrial conditions of London – Booth presented profiles of the various trades and skills of the poor. We have here included only material from Booth's own pen, along with a lengthy description of prostitution from the third series.

Sweating[1]

THE word 'sweating' seems to have been originally used by journeymen tailors, among themselves, to describe contemptuously the action of those of their number who worked at home, out of hours. Aided, at first in the way of overtime only, by their wives and daughters, these men gradually found it convenient to do all their work at home, and thus introduced a complete system of homework. Finally, employing others besides members of their own family, many of them became sweaters in the second meaning of the word: that is, those who make others sweat.

The word as a picturesque nickname soon spread to other trades. Among bootmakers, who early took the word from the tailors, it is still used to mean the journeyman, while the small master (the present 'sweater' of the tailoring trade) is more appropriately called the 'chamber' or 'garret' master. Cabinet-makers followed later in using the word, the small master being called indiscriminately 'sweater' and 'garret master'. In other trades it is the

1. First edition, Vol. I, pp. 481–97.

sub-contractor or middleman who is termed the sweater; and by the general public the word has been readily accepted as meaning any employer whose workpeople are badly paid, harshly used, or ill-provided with accommodation, or any sub-contractor or middleman who squeezes a profit out of the labour of the poor.

As used in the trades themselves, unless pointed by some opprobrious adjective, the word is scarcely a term of reproach, being applied to good and bad alike. To the public mind, however, it usually implies something definitely bad; with the result that, as all alike bear it, all alike are branded by it. The functions of chambermaster, sub-contractor, and middleman, which are really distinct, become confused; every sweater passes for a middleman, and sub-contract is supposed to be an essential feature of the 'sweating system', as this medley of ideas is called. In fine, every hardship and every horror in the lives of the suffering workpeople of East London has been attributed to the iniquitous action of some peculiar industrial system. At least, public opinion insisted on inquiry; a committee of the House of Lords took the question up, much evidence has been heard, thousands of pages of evidence bearing witness to the searching ability and unexampled patience of the questioners have been printed, and we now await the report.

Failing the report, the confused nature of the popular ideas about sweating has been a serious drawback to any thorough comprehension of the value of the various kinds of evidence taken before this committee. Their Lordships have received information as to unpunctual payments, discounts off cheques, tips to foremen, bad language, and high-handed manners. Wealthy firms have been accused of taking advantage of the position of the poor seller of made-up goods who cannot afford to lie out of his money, and parts with his work at a loss rather than face immediate ruin; while now and then some poor worker, in his simple answers, has unconsciously told a sad tale of gradually blighted hopes and narrowing existence, too surely the lot of the helpless who, in these pushing days, are passed in the race by more competent or fresher workers. All this has been deeply interesting, and in many cases deeply pathetic, and although it is unlikely that all the stories told have been literally true, yet, after we have made due allowance for passion, personal pique, and race antipathy, enough remains to fill us with pity and horror at the thought that such lives can be led, such hardships endured by our fellow men.

Meanwhile, in such manner as has been possible for a private inquirer, I, too, have sought the truth, and am able to assert without hesitation that there is no industrial system coextensive with the evils complained of, although there is unfortunately no doubt at all that very serious evils exist. It is not one but many systems with which we have to deal, each having its special faults. First there is the form of sweating which is practised in the clothing trades, where wholesale manufacturers find it convenient to abdicate the position of employer, and instead of hiring workpeople themselves, make a contract with someone who does, the materials needed being nevertheless provided and prepared by the wholesale house. This may be described as *employment at second-hand*. It is not sub-contract, but is based upon a partition of the function of manufacturer between the wholesale house and the sweater, and without doubt facilitates a very acute form of competition. Again, when the wholesale house, in place of dealing directly with the workers, employs a go-between, who distributes and collects the work and perhaps performs some part of it, we have a practice, not indeed confined to industries which are said to be sweated, but definite enough. This is the sweating system as it applies more particularly to female home-workers. It is one only too well adapted to take advantage of the necessities of the very poor. Or if the wholesale house, instead of ordering what it wants beforehand, stands ready to buy from those who, having no other work to do, put their labour on to materials, trusting to sell labour and materials together, we have the sweating system as it applies to cabinet-making. This last plan, which has been called 'sub-purchase', may be made a terribly efficient engine of oppression. Or, to take quite another field, if the chamber-master is able to obtain a constant supply of learners (usually poor foreigners) who, as 'greeners', will work long hours in return for bare keep, and so reduce the cost of production, the result is to aggravate competition and depress regular wages. This is the sweating system as it applies to foreign immigration; perhaps its most intense form. Or finally, if systematic deductions are made from men's earnings by labour masters, who can thus pocket any difference that may exist between the authorized pay and the lowest competition value of the work, we have sweating as it applies to the Docks. There may be other systems of employment which fall under the general head of sweating, but these are the principal ones; and it does not concern me to make the list complete, as it is rather with the evils, however caused, that we have to do, than with industrial organizations, in which they are by no means always present...

We are now able to put forward this general proposition: That the production of certain results is an essential part of any practical definition of sweating, and hence we may abandon all talk of this or that system, and, beginning with the evils, work back to the causes.

We thus reach the third meaning which may be attached to the word sweating. Passing by, as incomplete or misleading, the prevalent conceptions of certain systems or their consequences, we may finally accept 'sweating' as expressing in a general way all the evils which the workers in certain trades or under certain conditions suffer. Thus an examination of the sweating system resolves itself into an inquiry into the conditions under which occupations recognized as 'sweated industries' are worked, and into the causes, whatever they may be, of the evils which are suffered. This is the conclusion to which I have been led, and the method which I have accepted. The facts remain the same, but the aspect under which they must be regarded is greatly changed by ruling out the all-pervading but imaginary system which has been supposed to be their cause. Some of these evils may be due to one method and some to another, but many, or perhaps most of them, are not due in any way to the manner of employment. Their roots lie deep in human nature. They are, alas! not the less real because no trade or place has a monopoly of them, and must be considered as part of the general troubles of poverty. The accounts which have been given on preceding pages in this book of dock work, tailoring, bootmaking, cabinet-making and the employments of women, describe all the sweated industries, and from these, as well as from the schedules of Vol. I, it may be seen that the majority of the workers are above the level at which there is any call for official inquiry or State interference. But in each, working under exactly the same system of employment as their more successful comrades, are large numbers of impoverished and more or less suffering people. Each has its percentage of very poor as well as of poor, and each its fringe of abject misery. In each we find poor struggling people leading painful lives, small earnings irregularly received, every kind of misfortune and every kind of incapacity. In all we are conscious of the oppression of the weak. Such troubles have not, on the whole, much to do with any system of employment; they are part of the general inequalities of life, inequalities of capacity, prudence and temper, of perseverance, of strength, of health, and good luck, as well as of birth or wealth. 'Any trade does very well if you are pretty good at it,' said a boot-finisher to me, and the reverse is, unfortunately, no less true. But, allowing that many of the troubles attributed to sweating are not industrial at all, and admitting that those which are industrial are neither essentially connected with any system of employment nor to be attributed to unhumanity, still, the trades of East London undoubtedly present a serious case of economic disease, with painful and alarming symptoms.

This disease is closely connected with the multiplication of small masters (of which there is evidence) in all the sweated industries. Of the tendencies common to all industry – on the one hand, towards the increase of successful enterprises at the expense of unsuccessful ones; on the other, towards disintegration and fresh beginnings in a small way – it is the second which has prevailed. The quite small workshop, which is, in truth, no workshop at all, but an ordinary room of an ordinary house, lived in as well as worked in, stands at some advantage over the properly appointed workshop of a larger size. The capital needed for a start is very small. A few pounds will suffice, and the man becomes a master. It is a natural ambition, and one that appeals with peculiar force to the Jews. The evils which follow are patent. Men are content, at least for a while, to make less as masters than they would receive in wages as journeymen. The wholesale houses can take advantage of the competition which arises, and prices are reduced, to the immediate loss of the sweaters and the ultimate detriment of those whom they employ.

It is this state of things which really leads to the sweating evils of long hours, low pay, and unsanitary conditions. As to *long hours*, with small employers, it is the master who sets the time. He himself is ready to work any hours, why not those he employs? They must, and they do. Long hours are a natural concomitant of irregularity of employment, which, though not usually counted as one of the evils due to sweating, is closely inter-connected with those evils. Irregularity of work is by far the most serious trial under which the people of London suffer, and results naturally from the industrial position of small workshops and home-work. The smaller the capital involved and the less the permanent fixed charge of working in business, the better suited is it for irregular employment. High organization makes for regularity: low organization leads itself to the opposite. A large factory cannot stop at all without serious loss; a full-sized workshop will make great efforts to keep going; but the man who employs only two or three others in his own house can, if work fails, send them all adrift to pick up a living as best they can. In regard to *low pay*, it is connected with poor work that we find it. What is called cheap work, but is in truth bad work, is likely to be undertaken by small men commencing as masters. These men themselves supply all the skill and use the cheapest available assistance, such as the almost unpaid labour of 'greeners'. Moreover, there is ample evidence to show that the largest shops supply the most regular work. The terms of employment in the larger and better shops, though no doubt susceptible of improvement, can hardly be accounted grievous.

Turning to the general question of wages and hours of work, we find that, compared with any standard in England, or still more on the Continent, London rates of wages are high. This is one of the attractions of the metropolis. Hours of labour must be taken in connection with employment by seasons. The best paid artisans in trades which are extraordinarily active in certain seasons, adapting themselves to this condition, work hard when employment is good and take their holidays when there is nothing to do. Such men look to make full time one week with another, and, with them, the push of work at certain seasons is not accounted a grievance. If a grievance at all, it is common to well- and ill-paid alike. The ill-paid do not, as a rule, work longer hours than the well-paid when the push is greatest, but they have more enforced idleness.[2]

It should be said that the very long hours, carrying work far into the night or beginning it very early in the morning, are in home industry frequently connected with the intermixture of domestic concerns – the baby, the dinner, the washing, if not neighbourly gossip, occupying time which must be made up. It is a hardship to have to work full-time in such cases, but rather a hardship of life than of industry, and to speak of the work as sixteen or eighteen hours a day is incorrect. Long and late hours are also often due to loss of time going to shop and waiting for work. There is in the giving out of work much reckless want of consideration on the part of the employers. This is a very real grievance, and one which is not beyond remedy, hardly perhaps by legislation, but it may be reached either by a quickened sense of responsibility on the part of the employer or by a growth of independence and conscious power on the part of the employed, which may enable them to insist on more reasonable treatment.[3]

2. In all shops alike, large or small, the wages paid are according to the skill of the operator, and according therefore to the class of work undertaken. There is a curious compensation in favour of 'cheap work' by reason of the pace at which it may be done. Speed is another kind of skill, and the two kinds are not interchangeable. Put a first-class workman on to common work and he is as helpless to earn 'fair wages' at it as the rapid low-class workman would be if good work were demanded, like the well-known fable of the Fox and the Crane.

3. East London does not get up early. It says with Burns, 'Up in the morning's na for me, up in the morning early.' Any observer whose restless spirit takes him into the streets between 6 and 8 a.m. finds every blind down. The few stragglers then going to their work shut the door on sleeping women and children, and seek their breakfast at some early coffee-stall. Between 8 and 9 the tide of life begins to flow. In sympathy with this, the evening hours are late. Work and cleaning up usually run till 8 or 9, and pleasure till about 12, and these hours apply especially to the industries we are discussing. The trades which still begin and end at 6 are unimpor-

Passing now to consider the third evil of the sweating system, *unsanitary conditions,* it is at once evident that the smaller the workshop the less likely it is that sanitation will be cared for. Inspection hardly reaches such places, and the standard of requirement of both employer and employed is very low; but with large workshops the case is different. In this respect we have in fact a sliding scale from the factory to the larger workshop, and thence downwards through the small workshop to the home. In proportion as inspection becomes possible, the evil becomes manageable. Overcrowding, again, which exists in a more dangerous form in the home than in the workshop, assuming its worst shape when home and workshop are combined, is not present in any serious way in large workshops and vanishes altogether with factories.

All this being so – the bigger workshop being comparatively innocent of evil – it is remarkable that the larger type of sweating master should have been seized upon by the public imagination as the central figure of a monstrous system. It is difficult, not to say impossible, to prove a negative – to prove that the monster sweating master of the comic papers has no existence. I can only say that I have sought diligently and have not found. If a specimen exists, he has at any rate nothing to do with the troubles we are investigating. Among the larger employers there are hard men, but the necessary conditions of their business compel them to keep on regularly a staff of competent workpeople: who must have fair wages, and can and do protect themselves from oppression. The sweating master I *have* found, and who is connected with the troubles under investigation, works hard, makes often but little more, and at times somewhat less, than his most

---

tant compared to the mass of work which does not begin till 8 or 9. Home workshops and home-work most readily fall in with these conditions, but the same hours are also accepted by factories in many instances.

skilled and best paid hands. He is seldom on bad terms, and often on very kindly terms, with those who work under him. There is here no class division between employer and employed – both in fact belong to the same class, and talk freely together; social amenities of all kinds going on naturally and easily between master and man. Or if they quarrel it is with that happy equality of tongue which leaves no sentiment to rankle unexpressed; mutual abuse and oaths clear the air, and friendly relations may be promptly renewed. In this state of things we find nothing that is monstrous, much that is very human. The proprietor of a model factory, who has employed a skilled engineer to arrange a model system of ventilation throughout his spacious premises, certainly provides better security for the health of his workpeople than the sweating master in his crowded and stifling room, but he is less likely than the poor sweating master to be sympathetic with the individual who has a cold in his head and feels the draught, and after all sympathy does more than the best of sanitary appliances to sweeten human relations and make life worth living. But all this may look like special pleading in favour of an evil state of things. Why should not the large employer be kind, too? Doubtless he may be, and continually is; but it is not he, but the sweating master, who has been the object of a strangely excited attack, an attack promoted by indignation at the hardships suffered by the poor, and seeking a victim on which to vent its anger, but at times compounded largely of lower motives. On this account I have thought it just to recall my own experience of the much-abused sweating master.

I have said that the trades of East London present a clear case of economic disease, and I have pointed to the multiplication of small masters as the tap-root of this disease. There are, however, other special causes of mischief affecting East London which should be considered: all of them are forms of competition. There is the competition of provincial England in manufacture, or in effect that of the factory with the workshop; and there is the competition of women's work, which is really a contest between the workshop and the home. Then we have that resulting from the influx into London of vigorous countrymen; and, finally, foreign competition of two sorts – (1) that which by importation of goods makes use of cheap labour abroad, and (2) that which owing to foreign immigration can make use of equally cheap labour at home. The former is in effect the competition of the Germans; the latter that of the Jews.

The unfortunate East End worker, struggling to support his family and keep the wolf from the door, has to contend with all these forms of competition. He is met and vanquished by the Jew fresh from Poland or Russia, accustomed to a lower standard of life, and above all of food, than would be possible to a native of these islands; less skilled and perhaps less strong, but in his way more fit – pliant, adaptable, patient, adroit. Or he has to contend with cheap importations, and curses the blessings of free trade; or he is pushed on one side by the physical strength of the man whose life has hitherto been spent among green fields. Or again, women are his rivals, working to support fatherless children, or to eke out their husbands' or their children's earnings or even to earn a little pocket-money to be spent on pleasure or dress. And beyond all these, outside London, but now, owing to the perfection of railway and telegraphic communication, at our very door, the vast strength of provincial England enters the field.

In the provinces factories can be managed more successfully than in London, and work suitable for them is apt to leave the metropolis; and it is to be noted that the competition of the provincial factory is doubly pernicious to London, as it can be better withstood by the socially bad but economically advantageous small workshop than by a metropolitan factory. It thus not only depresses London labour, but depresses it in its best form, and favours its worst features. For, while a trade leaves, the people stay, and form the unemployed or partially employed class, who with their striving women provide the mass of cheap labour and the facilities for irregular work in which small masters and small middlemen find their opportunity. The small workshop and home-work thus obtain a better chance, and a very vicious equilibrium is reached, which the attractiveness of London, Circe among cities compared to dull towns and duller country, helps to maintain.

As a weapon of competition, the influx into London is double-edged. He who comes brings usually fresh powers of body or mind, and finding employment – or more often coming up to employment already found – displaces some Londoner, or at least takes the position some Londoner would have held. This is the forward cut of the weapon, but the backward cut is even worse, for the displaced Londoner, and probably his wife too, can only join the sad throng who go hunting for work and find it not, or if they succeed, it is some other who goes to swell the host of those who are irregularly employed or not employed at all. This would be different if trade were not leaving London: but I fear it is doing so. On the other hand, the transfer of manufactures from London to the provinces cannot be regretted; and one must rather hope that population will gradually adjust itself to the facts, and that compensation for the passing misery in London will be found in the growth of healthy manufacturing communities such as we now see planting themselves in the Midland and Northern counties, and indeed in all parts of England where conveniences of rail or river are found.

From these considerations it will be seen that the strength of the small masters' position lies in the economic merits of the evils they encourage or produce, and that these evils stand forth as the bulwarks of London trade –

a point which must be borne in mind when remedies are considered.

Again, as to foreign importations, it is of little use to tell the East End worker who feels the grievance that all trade is an exchange, and that someone else in England, or in greater Britain, or in that greatest Britain which is subject to British capital, will benefit as much and even something more than he may lose. The argument does not interest him, and it is not surprising that those directly affected by this competition, whatever their political colour, are against free trade.

Finally, as to the Jews; I can add nothing to what appears in another chapter as to the peculiar character of their competition, but I may particularly point out that the *force* of this competition depends on a continual stream of newcomers. Let this stop, and it at once changes its character. For a time it tends to reduce wages and so lower the standard of life, but, apart from a constant influx, this is not its permanent effect. In the long run it is a competition of greater industry and greater skill. We may desire to exclude further arrivals of poor refugees; to do so, if practicable, would be very reasonable, and as popular with the Jews themselves – those who *are* here – as with our own people. But we can only do it on the ground of 'England for the English'; we cannot do it on the cry of no admittance to paupers. From top to bottom, old-established or newcomers, the Jews are a hardworking and very capable set of people, who readily learn to keep themselves, and usually get on in the world.

To summarize the position I have taken up: we have seen first that an inquiry into the Sweating system must be an inquiry into certain evils which, though having no special connection with any particular system of employment or caused by any particular form of tyranny, are none the less present and intense. These evils, so far as they are industrial at all, I attribute mainly to the multiplication of small masters and their tendency still further to increase, owing to the smallness of the capital needed for commencing business in the so-called 'sweated' industries.

Secondly, we note that present in all these industries are to be found overcrowding, irregular hours, low pay; periods of terrible strain, overtaxing the powers and exhausting the vital forces; periods of slack employment or absolute want of work, discouraging and slowly undermining the persistent energies and bread-winning determination of the worker not possessed of heroic elevation of character. These terrible evils are not, unless I am entirely mistaken in my reading of the facts which have been under my notice, necessarily connected with any of the systems with which they have been coupled in the public imagination. They are not due to 'employment at second-hand', as in tailoring and bootmaking, for we find this system in company with regular work and high pay. They are not due to the intervention of the middleman, for while the middleman throve they were less conspicuous than now; where he has been driven out they still remain, and where he has never stepped in the evils often appear in a very intense form. The same may be said with regard to sub-contract. Sub-contract may 'go hand-in-hand with plenty', providing good pay and regular employment. Nor are the evils necessarily connected with the manufacture of goods on speculation, as in cabinet-making, which we have called 'sub-purchase', though this system is doubtless most pernicious to those who have neither knowledge to forecast nor capital to await their market. In further proof of these assertions I need only refer again to the accounts given in preceding chapters of the several trades.

These, however, are the evils which, if they do not necessarily belong to the system of small masters and small middlemen prevalent in East London, at least coexist with it very extensively, and are aggravated by the atmosphere of competition in which the trades so handled are compelled to fight for an existence.

Coming now to the consideration of remedial proposals, I may say at the outset that my expectations of rapid and certain remedy are not high. For that large proportion of the misfortunes of poor workers which they encounter, not because they are workers, but because they are poor, our hope, if we decline the solution of socialism, must rest on the prospect of a gradual raising of the standard of life, upon which efforts of many kinds and from many directions must be concentrated if success is to be achieved. For the larger trade troubles which I have mapped out – the troubles due to various forms of competition – some remedies are suggested: protection of native manufacture; State-aided emigration, which shall seize hold of the stalwart countryman before he enters London; the exclusion of 'pauper' immigrants; the regulation of home industry, or even its suppression. For my part, I cannot support any of these. They appear to me either impracticable or not less dangerous than the disease – on these points I see no safe policy but *'laissez faire'*. The road is long and steep, but it is the only one that we can safely follow...

Confectionery[4]

MAKERS of sweetmeats, cakes, pastry, etc., are of two classes, those who perform their work in a bakehouse, and those who are employed in a factory. When engaged in a bakehouse, the confectioner works principally in sugar, and must, in theory at any rate, be distinguished not only from the pastrycook, who makes all kinds of biscuits, pastry, and cakes, but also from the cook who does nothing but 'stove' as contrasted with 'oven' work. A cook

4. Second edition, Vol. VII, pp. 160–6.

and confectioner holds himself forth as capable of dealing with the whole business of the 'shop trade' (as distinct, that is, from factory work), but 'pastrycook and confectioner' is a more modest appellation, denoting a narrower sphere of capacity. In London there are fully six pastrycooks and confectioners to one cook and confectioner; but a man who knows a little of everything is most likely to find employment. No man calls himself (and, probably, no man is) strictly a confectioner, and nothing more.

Under the second head (factory workers), come those who are engaged in the manufacture of all kinds of jams and sweets, including jellies, bottled and candied fruits, chocolate, jujubes, gelatine, lozenges, liquorice, boiled sugar and 'pan-goods', as a certain class of sweets are called, with such specialities as cosaques, crackers, surprise packets, the garnishing for wedding cakes, and other forms of 'ornamental confectionery'.

The confectioner who works in a bakehouse is regarded there as a privileged individual. When the bread is all made the confectioner comes in, and the 'solid' heat left in the oven usually suffices for his operation. His work is not so laborious as that of the baker, and is, moreover, all performed in the daytime. Working hours in this division of the industry are usually from seven a.m. to seven p.m., with intervals of half an hour for breakfast, dinner, and tea; and the average wages are, for foremen, £2 2s.; for second hands, £1 10s.; and for third hands, £1 5s. per week; but in ornamental confectionery, which is considered the highest branch of the trade, a first-class specialist in cake and icework will be paid £2 10s., or even £3 a week. Many Italians, French, and Swiss are employed as 'ornamentalists', and for long held the field, but Englishmen are rapidly becoming highly proficient in this department. Of Germans, very few are employed in this way, though there are so many engaged in bread-baking.

Taking it all round, this section of the confectionery trade seems to be fairly prosperous and contented. The season lasts from October till the middle of July. In the slack period very little is done, and men take their holidays then in turn, a week at a time. There is not much organization. The 'Amalgamated Union of Operative Bakers and Confectioners' contains only a very few genuine confectioners. Some, however, join the 'United Biscuit Bakers' and Pastrycooks' Society', a sort of friendly body, with burial and sick benefits.

In wholesale confectionery, by far the greater number of employees are women and girls. The census counts 4,310 female 'confectioners', but in this, as in other trades, many do not declare their occupations, for there are a much larger number to be found in East and South London factories alone. To the male hands are entrusted the mixing of the various ingredients, and the principal operations performed over the fire. We find them employed as sugar-grinders, jam-boilers, preservers, and plain and fancy confectioners. Others are packers and loaders; and in each factory are to be found engineers, stokers, coopers, carpenters, car-men, store-keepers, and ordinary labourers; while a superior class of foremen supervise the work of both men and women in the different departments. Lads are employed by some firms, but there is a tendency to replace them with women and girls.

The men are fairly well paid, and their wages sometimes touch a high figure. They range in one factory, of which we have seen the pay-sheets, from 42s. to 23s. Considerable skill and experience are needed in many of the processes, and the employment is usually permanent. But the work done by women and girls, demanding little skill, is very poorly remunerated, and is, moreover, extremely irregular and intermittent, by reason of the seasonal character of the trade. There is but little change noticeable since it was described in the chapter on 'Women's Work' in East London in a previous volume. South and East London factories show similar results. In both districts there are 'good' and 'bad' firms, and wages vary accordingly. Many regular hands in firms that are not 'good' take a remuneration ranging from 5s. to 9s. a week. Even lower figures are reported, but as such firms do not show their pay-sheets, the statements of the workers and their friends are the only evidence procurable. Work for Christmas confectionery pays the best; at it, a quick hand, even at the low rates prevailing, will make 16s. a week, but this is not for more than three months at the outside, and during the rest of the year, girls from sixteen to twenty-five years of age will only take 3s. to 6s. a week, and are lucky if they are kept on at all. The irregularly employed hands are in a still worse plight financially, but do not usually display either desire or capacity for fixed employment, being generally quite content with casual work.

Apart from those who do not aim at permanent service, there are many hard-working women and girls who are either put on short time, or thrown out altogether by reason of the fluctuations prevalent throughout the trade. In the chocolate department work is brought to a standstill in the heat of summer, and piece-workers sometimes wait all day without employment, and without pay, on the chance of the temperature falling. Or at the end of December, when Christmas stocks are completed, there may be no work in the bon-bon department for two months or more. Then there is the jam session – the time for summer fruits, or for oranges and lemons. It is to be observed that these various seasons overlap, but it does not follow that many kinds of work are done in the same factory, or that where this is so, a girl will pass from one department to another; it is more likely, perhaps, that she will not do so. Most of the work can be learnt in a week or a fortnight, and the numbers of those who, from outside, continually seek the work is great. There are, however, certain operations where considerable dexterity is called into play, as in shaping lozenges or making chocolate creams, which afford better pay and a more secure tenure.

To describe all the processes involved would be impracticable, but an attempt may be made as regards the leading features of the work, and the parts played by those engaged in it. Beginning, for instance, with fruit, lemons may be taken as a good example, the season for this fruit commencing before Christmas and lasting till the middle of April. The lemons, of which the best come from Sicily, are first squeezed by lads or girls in machines worked by hand. The juice is used in many departments, and the 'cases' are ejected into buckets to be dealt with by women, who by hand, or with the use of a machine, clean out the pulp, which is thrown away, leaving the rind intact. This may be candied whole or in large pieces. The boiling is men's work, and is a delicate process, requiring experience and judgement to obtain the right consistency before the boiled fruit passes on to the cooling-room. Some lemons are stripped of the outer part of the rind before the juice is extracted. So perfect is the machinery used for this operation that the rind of one lemon may be cut into an unbroken thread-like coil as much as twenty feet long. Fragments of the peel so cut are sometimes mixed with orange marmalade to flavour it.

In sugar-work, what are called 'boiled goods' are made by men over open furnaces, where the heat is regulated by thermometers; when the boiling liquid is poured on to the cooling tray, skilled artificers work it with their fingers till it acquires a certain consistency. The most careful manipulation is necessary lest the film that first forms over the sugar be broken, and the hot liquid spurt out and scald the operative. So, too, the preparing of 'pan-goods' is men's work. In this case a centre, usually an almond, is coated with sugar. The almonds and sugar are thrown into heated pans, and the coating takes place as these pans, jacketed with steam, turn and revolve in all directions. In the manufacture of peppermint and other lozenges, though men prepare and roll out the material, the punching is done by girls in small machines or by hand. The hand-work in this department is highly skilled, and more effective than any machine in giving a good shape to the lozenge. A clever hand-worker uses her punch with wonderful rapidity, never wasting material by deviating from the line, while she cuts and stamps her seductive lozenges. 'Boiled' and 'pan' goods together do not exhaust human ingenuity in the manufacture of sweets, although the greater part fall under one or the other heading. American confectionery – 'candy' as it is called – is a speciality for which most English factories have now a department. The products are very attractive in their combinations of colour, and in the piquancy and delicacy of their flavouring, and bear fantastic names of transatlantic origin.

The manufacture of cocoa and chocolate gives employment to many men, women and girls, the lighter portions falling to the female workers. The beans are roasted and cracked and winnowed to remove the shell and leave the nib. This last is ground between granite rollers, and, for some purposes, sugar is added during the grinding; or, to make a fine pure cocoa, the powder is subjected to great pressure to get rid of the oil which the bean contains. For chocolate creams a centre of pure boiled sugar is taken (this is the 'cream') and coated with chocolate. This process is the work of girls, and requires practice and delicacy of touch.

The most wholesale business of all, that of jam-making, is ordinarily the work of men as regards mixing and boiling, and the work of women for filling, covering, and labelling the pots; in some factories women are employed to attend to the boiling, the work being made possible for them by the use of steam.

The male operatives in the whole trade appear to be

contented, but the women and girls, as might be expected in an overcrowded and fluctuating industry, are full of complaints. The chief trouble undoubtedly springs from the low average rate of wages. Other complaints regard fines inflicted for petty causes, and overbearing conduct of foremen and forewomen; or, under another count, speak of the lack of proper accommodation for meals, and failure to clear out the 'pulp holes', which, if neglected, become very offensive and injurious to health, and especially obnoxious when meals are eaten in the workroom. Into the justification of these complaints it is not possible for us to enter deeply. As they are not made against all alike, it would seem to be certain that some factories are more considerate than others, and it may certainly be assumed that some fall very much below a proper standard of excellence.

In jam factories women and girls are often badly burnt, either from the bursting of a jar whilst it is being filled with the boiling liquid, or owing to a slip when conveying heavy loads of scalding jam from the furnace to the cooling-room. This dangerous practice is avoided at the best workshops by the use of a barrel on wheels. Accidents, too, occur from the bursting of bottles in the mineral-water department, face and hands being in this way not infrequently gashed; but mineral-water manufacture is not included in the present section, though the work is, in some instances, combined with the confectioner's business under one management. In addition to these causes of mishap, there are also allegations of illness occurring owing to the dust arising from common starch, which is often used to make the moulds, and is reported to be very injurious to the lungs.

Bread-baking[5]

IN London, and also in many provincial towns, the baker of bread turns night into day. He works for long hours in an almost tropical temperature, and inhales the gas-laden air of a bakehouse, often, though not always, small and ill-ventilated, and very generally placed below the level of the ground. The work of biscuit-makers and confectioners, on the other hand, generally falls in the daytime. Their hours are, as a rule, shorter, and their surroundings more spacious, the bulk of the trade being carried on in factories. Thus, although some bread bakeries are models of construction, and some confectionery is made in old-fashioned premises, there is a very real distinction between the two branches of the trade, and the remarks which now follow will refer only to the baking of bread.

Journeymen bakers, finding the conditions under which they work very hard, and having, as it seems, great difficulty in amending them by combination amongst themselves, turn to the legislature for assistance. They demand the stringent inspection of all bakehouses, and the closing of those which are below the level of the ground. They also ask for the abolition of night-work and Sunday work, and for the establishment by law of an eight-hours' working day. They ask this in the interest of consumers as well as workers, on the ground that bread made in unhealthy conditions is itself unhealthy, but in these demands it is manifestly more particularly the workers who are considered. Legislative interference with this trade in the interest of the *consumer* is no new thing. The comparative absence of it is, indeed, a quite modern innovation. No other trade has been subjected to so many ordinances, regulations and enactments. An 'assize of bread' was

---

5. Second edition, Vol. VII, pp. 144–50.

established in the time of King John; and from that period till the eighth year of the reign of Queen Anne the cost of bread was regulated through the assize, first, according to the price of wheat, and later, according to that of flour. The *weight* of the loaf was increased or diminished as the price of wheat and flour fell or rose, while the *price* remained constant at one penny for the loaf, or one half-penny for the half loaf, of a certain quality of bread, or the baker might keep the weight constant and vary the price, but he could not adopt both plans at once. Nor was it till 1822 that the assize was done away with. It, however, fell gradually into bad odour, both with the trade and with the public; the one being of opinion that the assize acted as an instrument of oppression against fair tradesmen, and the other dissatisfied because they found, or thought, that the price of bread, instead of being kept at a fair rate, was in fact raised by interference.

During the earlier period of the assize, special bread of the very finest flour, called 'demesne bread' or *panis domenicus*, and stamped with an effigy of the Saviour, was sold at double the regular price. The ordinary loaves had also their marks, and throughout a long series of enactments the duty of impressing distinctive marks to indicate the quality or origin of the bread was always imposed on the baker. As the old nursery rhyme has it:

> Pit-a-cake, pat-a-cake, baker's man,
> Bake me a cake as fast as you can,
> Prick it and cross it and mark it with T
> And put it in the oven for Tommy and me.

The very acts that abolished the assize of bread contain clauses rendering it obligatory to impress the letter M on all loaves made of mixed flour; indeed, penalties might even now be enforced for any infringement of the law in this respect, though they do not assume the precise form of chastisement prescribed in the time of the early

Edwards (1291–1307) when, it seems, the offending baker was drawn upon a hurdle from the Guildhall to his own house 'through the great streets where there may be most people assembled, and through those that are most dirty', with the faulty loaf hanging from his neck. Practically in our day the protection of the public is confined to the question of weight. All household bread must be sold by weight. Every customer has a right to see the loaf weighed in his presence, and if it does not turn the scale the baker or purveyor of bread is bound to add a slice from another loaf to make up the deficiency.[6]

It will be seen that there is plenty of precedent for legislative interference in this trade; or, to put it another way, many legislative experiments in this direction have been tried and have failed. But most, if not all of these, have been made in the supposed interest of the consumer as against the rapacity of the master bakers, and not at all in the interest of the men as opposed to that of their employers. What we have now to consider are the grievances of the men, and these may be divided under two heads: (1) those concerning hours of work and night-work; (2) those concerning unsanitary premises. Each of these will be dealt with in turn, but it will be convenient to give first some account of the manner in which the work is performed.

---

6. The absolute fixing of the weight of an ordinary household loaf has sometimes a curious and not altogether desirable effect on its quality. Quantity being rigid, and price incapable of fine gradation (as in the poorest districts it can only move by farthings and elsewhere usually goes by halfpence), it follows that small alterations in the value of the loaf must be provided by changes in quality. When flour becomes cheaper, the bakers who compete for the custom of the poor are ready enough to placard their windows with the reduced figure, but when the price of wheat rises, they may find it to their interest to sell a worse article rather than change the price – using inferior flour or employing adulteration of some kind, or, what is still more objectionable, contriving by slack baking to increase the proportion of water left in the bread.

Process of Manufacture – There are many descriptions of bread, each being the result of some variation in the methods pursued. Besides the English methods, which differ amongst themselves to some extent, we have, in London, Scotch, German, Austrian, and French bakeries, all of which make the bread rise by the use of yeast in some form, and there is also the special system from which the Aërated Bread Company takes its name. Besides various plans of fermentation there are ovens of different shapes and different natures, having each their special arrangements for heating or retaining the heat. In a general way it may be said that the longest and most important process is the making of the 'sponge'. A small quantity of the active yeast is mixed with flour, water, and a little salt, and the paste or dough allowed to stand till it is permeated by the rapid growth of the yeast plant, and expanded into a spongy mass by the gaseous emanation of this remarkable growth. The mass works and rises, and, discharging a portion of the gas, falls back, only to rise again. Then, at the proper moment, additional flour, salt, and water are added, and by mixing and kneading the true dough is made. This in turn must have time given it, so that once more the ferment may work and the gas be once more formed to leaven the mass. Again, at the proper moment, the loaves have to be shaped, and then forthwith plunged into the heat of the oven, which must be intense enough and sufficiently prolonged to penetrate the loaf, stop the action of the yeast, and cook the bread. The first process – that of starting the ferment, including mixing – may take from eight to twelve hours, according to the weather or other conditions: the second stage, including the kneading, may occupy three or four hours, and the baking itself from half an hour to one and a half hours, as is demanded by the character of the bread – mainly, that is, according to the proportion of water mixed with the flour, but also according to the size of the loaves and also whether they are closely packed in the oven or placed in open order. There are differences of method — some Scotch bakers introduce a middle stage, making the first a rather stiff sponge and afterwards reducing this to a liquid paste to complete the fermentation before adding the mass of the flour — but in the essential facts, where fermentation is employed, one process is very much like another. As to the ovens, the object in every case is to retain the heat and steam as far as possible, and so make it feasible to deal with successive batches of bread without much delay. The Scotch ovens have a thick stone floor and a high crown, both being calculated to reduce radiation, and serve as reservoirs to retain the heat, and are provided with a small coke furnace which can be readily blown up or damped down as required. On the Vienna system the actual baking is done by the introduction of super-heated live steam into a small oven, surrounded by hot air. The newer English ovens are heated entirely from outside; the older-fashioned ones, low in the crown with the fire set in the thickness of the wall, being superseded because of the time lost in re-heating between the batches. They, however, are themselves a vast improvement on those common in the country, and still to be found in London, in which the fire is made of wood in the very oven itself, and the embers raked out through the large door, leaving a still glowing cavern which must cool a great deal before the loaves can be safely consigned to it. Such changes come slowly — London bakers, in common with all Englishmen, hardly ever take properly to a new thing till it is, in fact, no longer new. Moreover, ovens are expensive, and although old styles may be inconvenient they are a little the cheaper, and when once built it would be expensive to replace them.

Whatever be the design of the ovens, the placing of the loaves in them is work of great dexterity and is highly paid. Each loaf of those baked singly, or each pair of loaves, when such that the loaves stick together in the baking, is placed on the end of a long flat wooden shovel or 'peel', and being pushed forward is deposited by a turn of the wrist exactly where it should be, either adjoining but apart from, or in actual contact with, the other loaves. To remove the loaves when baked, a stronger and broader instrument of the same character is used.

Such is the ordinary method of baking by hand. The work, as we have said, begins at night, and early in the morning the first batches, consisting probably of rolls or something small in size, are ready for the ovens, which from that time till about noon are continually filled and refilled till all the bread is ready and the work ends. In some small establishments the men who bake are also employed to sell. If the preceding hours have not been too long, or if this work itself be not too long continued, this may be rather an advantage than otherwise.

The methods employed in the factories differ mainly in the introduction of machinery, and in the scale on which the work is done. At a model factory, all the operations are conducted above ground, and all the rooms are thoroughly ventilated. At the top of the building the flour is stored, and as it starts on its way to become bread, passes through ingenious machinery which weighs and mixes the various qualities in certain proportions. It then passes to the cylinders below, in which revolving arms perform the work of mixing and kneading before and after fermentation has taken place. The moulding or shaping of the loaves, except it be of a rather rough description, is hand-work. In certain cases the dough, mixed and kneaded by machinery, is forced through the nozzle of an otherwise closed vessel and cut into uniform lengths by a chopper working automatically on a board sprinkled with rice-flour; but loaves prepared in this way are lacking in individual charm. When moulded the loaves go forward to the ovens, which, in the establishment here described, are various in character, English, Scotch, or Viennese, according to the style of bread it is desired to produce.

Hours of Work – The average hours in London are seventy or eighty per week, but some men are employed for fully ninety or even one hundred hours. In most bakeries of ordinary character, work commences at 11 or 12 at night (in factories, as a rule, the hours are rather shorter), and the men continue working ten, twelve, or fourteen hours, and sometimes even longer. On Friday especially, in order to supply bread for two days (Sunday's bread being purchased on Saturday afternoon or evening), the work, besides beginning earlier, is prolonged into Saturday, and even in first-class bakeries men work for seventeen or eighteen hours. This long spell, beginning on Friday evening and lasting it may be till Saturday afternoon, is followed by a rest till Sunday at midnight, when work commences again. In some poor districts the ovens may be heated for the cooking of Sunday dinners, but this work does not to any great extent fall to the lot of the journeyman baker in London.

The principal victims of inordinate hours are to be found amongst the foreign element settled here. In one case we were told – and the statement was strongly supported – that the master, a German baker, worked his men from 110 to 112 hours per week. All his employees are themselves German, and from Friday into Saturday are said to work twenty-four hours. Men go to this bakehouse fresh from the immigrant ship at very low wages. The Polish Jew bakers, who are located chiefly in St George's-in-the-East, are employed for fourteen hours a day, and the time is lengthened to eighteen or twenty on Friday night in preparation for the Sabbath. Master and man work these hours alike, and when visited after they had already been employed for sixteen hours looked, it must be said, none the worse for their protracted toil in an underground and ill-ventilated workshop.

OCCUPATIONS

Prostitution[7]

In the course of our inquiry we have obtained a great amount of information regarding the scarcely disguised practice of sexual immorality, in which prostitutes play their professional part. For the vast majority of these women some degree of publicity is almost essential. Facilities are requisite, and the men they would attract must know them for what they are. To such experienced onlookers as the police, the women who carry on this business become personally well known, and the most ordinary observer would rarely make a mistake in judging them. Even if for the moment they desire to hide their character, something in walk or manner is apt to betray them. Their places of resort and their hours are perfectly well known, and the houses they use can be brought under observation. The traffic is thus entirely open to both legislative and philanthropic interference; both Law and Gospel are unhesitating in their condemnation of it; and yet the practice continues unchecked, and in some of its manifestations is a positive scandal.

This, however, does not imply supineness on the part of either the authorities or the public; so far from this being the case, the amount of effort made to suppress the traffic and rescue the women is very great, even astonishingly so considering the unsatisfactory results attained, as has been told in a preceding volume; and I would now return to the subject in order to give those of my readers who choose to follow me particulars of the various shapes which the evil assumes; for only so can we appreciate the real nature of the task of holding it in check.

It needs to be borne in mind that the immorality involved is entirely different, in character and even in origin, from ordinary loose conduct between the sexes. Its sole aim is the satisfaction of male sexual passion, without

7. Third edition, *Final Volume*, pp. 121–31.

the responsibilities of marriage or anything that can be called a social relationship. The female share in the matter is strictly professional. The woman's passions are hardly involved at all, she is moved neither by excitement nor by pleasure; all question of 'fall' is past; as we find her, she merely seeks her living in the easiest way open to her, or is induced to follow this course of life by the desire for fine clothes and luxuries not otherwise attainable.

The women thus employed are of every class; or, to speak more exactly, men of every class are served, and the women may be classified accordingly; and in every class we find the same main distinction between the women who take the men to their own homes or are visited there by them, and those who seek the accommodation needed elsewhere. The difference is one of the utmost importance.

The terms 'brothel', 'house of accommodation', and 'disorderly house' are often used indiscriminately, but do really give expression to this radical divergence. A 'brothel' is a house in which prostitutes live, to which they bring men, and where they are at home to those who visit them. 'A house of accommodation' is one to which the women, and sometimes the men, know that they can resort as required. Both are technically 'disorderly', but 'brothel' always implies a house where several of these women ply their trade together, and yet another arrangement is therefore possible, for prostitutes may live alone and bring men home to their lodgings or be visited by them there. All these methods are found in each class socially.

In every case the women need protection and in nearly every case it is secured. Thus in the brothel, besides the house mistress, who is usually a forcible, middle-aged woman, there is always a man in reserve who can act as 'chucker-out' if required; and a house of accommodation takes care to be equally well provided; while those women who habitually bring strangers to their own private rooms must exercise a good deal of prudence, and excepting as regards women of a rather superior class, do in fact rarely live alone, being usually associated with a man who shares their earnings, and in case of need can take their part. These men are known as 'bullies', and the word may describe equally their position towards the woman or her clients. The relations between prostitute and protector in this unhallowed association have, it would seem, something of the character of a marriage – the tie a lasting one, and the woman often devoted to the man even though very roughly treated. Indeed it is said the rougher the man the more devoted the woman, his roughness, perhaps, making him the better protector. The only utterly exposed class are the low women, who, under cover of darkness, make use of back streets and open spaces, and whose unprotected state gave rise to the horrible tragedies of a few years back.[8]

In describing this social evil, I cannot avoid going into some detail. At the top of the scale, there are the fashionable brothels. In these the younger women are carefully secluded; when they walk out they are accompanied; they do not solicit; they merely show themselves. They are protected even from themselves. I do not suppose that if they wished to do so, they could very easily escape. The men who frequent such houses are rich. They are not robbed; they are merely plundered. Brothels of this high class avoid publicity, and by discretion seek to escape prosecution. There are not many of them, and they are located where they are least likely to be noticed as a nuisance. Their clientele is private and personal; those who seek them know where to find them. They are solely West End institutions. In this mode of life they represent fashion.

From these high-class houses some of the women frequent public places, such as music halls, and between

---

8. Presumably Booth is referring here to Jack the Ripper, who murdered and mutilated a number of women in the East End of London in 1888–9. – EDS.

them and kept women who lead independent lives there is some interchange, and occasionally some confusion of role. If living as kept women, they do not come within the law, and are almost unapproachable for rescue purposes.

Below these are a large number of less fashionable but still mostly West End houses, well known to the police, those who keep them being frequently prosecuted and the brothels closed. This does not seriously affect them. The house is cleared, the fines paid, and a fresh start promptly made somewhere near. In some cases the same proprietors keep more than one house, and can transfer the inmates; in others a friendly understanding between two proprietors serves the same end. The girls from these houses walk the streets or frequent public places, and a slight change of locality for the brothel does not matter. Thus not much is gained by such prosecutions. A local authority or an active vigilance committee can clear the district they control, but the mischief is simply moved elsewhere. If action is only taken when the neighbours complain, it results in the concentration of such houses in certain streets, which lose their character entirely. The police never interfere unless complaints are made.

Though activity is maintained by the frequenting of public places in the evening and until late at night, each house has also its regular connection, and while some of the inmates are out, others stay at home to receive their visitors. These girls are not so closely looked after as those in the class above, and except that they are often in debt, and perhaps purposely kept in debt to the house mistress, they have practically full liberty. If dissatisfied with the results of the associated household, there is nothing to prevent them from joining some rival establishment, or from striking out on an independent course, as is done by many of those whom they meet nightly in the streets, competing in various ways for the same class of patronage. Even the trammels of debt could hardly stop them, for although it would be difficult, if not impossible, for them

OCCUPATIONS

to get any respectable employment, in their own walk in life they are free agents; and moreover the rescue ladies are everywhere watching for an opportunity, and always ready to help.

As regards the finance of the business, a heavy charge for board and lodging usually represents the share of the house, together with a large profit on the wine which it is customary to order. The girls themselves keep their fees, and from night to night or week to week may meet very varying fortune. Some can and do save, but as a rule whatever they have after paying for their board is spent on dress.

Girls of this class are found also among those who live quietly in lodgings and use the houses of accommodation. They often 'chum' with a companion, the two sharing a room. Their way of life is almost certainly known to the people of the house in which they reside, by the hours kept, but nothing occurs which need shock the neighbours. It is said that the ladies' public lavatories and dressing-rooms in Central London are used for putting on and (before going home) washing off, the customary paint.

From this level there is a descending scale, in which the organized brothel plays a decreasing part, and the use of houses of accommodation an increasing one. Falling lower still, the bully protector or 'ponce' becomes a common factor, and takes us on to the lowest grade of all, when robbery is the object in view and drunken men the prey. But over a very large part of this traffic a drunken man might probably suffer robbery, and, under such circumstances, few men are prepared to prosecute.

The descending scale is represented by locality, and again by the class of women employed, as also by their age, and each locality, each class, and each age presents special difficulties to the reformer.

Mingled with the more regular members of this varied group of women, there are in each class some who take to the life occasionally when circumstances compel: tailoresses or dressmakers, for example, who return to their trade in busy times; girls from low neighbourhoods who eke out a living in this way; or poor women, neglected wives, or widows, under pressure of poverty; or, worst of all, such as are driven to this course by a bad husband or a bad father. Some jealousy is felt, by those who are more strictly professional, of incursions into the field occupied.

The professional character of the part played by the women is very much against rescue work, and all our informers agree in saying that the professional element is growing stronger. This is particularly the case with foreign girls, many of whom, it is said, lay by their money, looking forward to a return to their native land, and a reputable future. In such a case we may safely assume that there is no self-condemnation.

But, as a rule, it is rare to find any sense of sin, and if it can be aroused at all, it is very precarious. When quite new to the life, the memories of home may have power, or if a baby is born, the maternal instinct may make rescue possible. Otherwise, there is little to stimulate the conscience. There being no strong passion involved, there is little reaction to be laid hold of, perhaps nothing more poignant than a dull sense of degradation.

A girl's first slip may have been due to passion (sometimes), or to sexual softness (more often), or to wantonness (more often still); with man ordinarily though not always as seducer, and with other members of the community – parents, employers, and companions – sharing the responsibility in a hundred ways; but, however it may have been brought about, it is almost invariably accompanied by a feeling of shame and loss, if not of sin. The sliding down into professional prostitution, which is happily comparatively rare, is a fall of an entirely different character, in which need for money, whether due to the pressure of want or of extravagance, is the principal factor. The impulse may arise from love of ease or as a counsel of despair, or from a recklessness that lies between the two. Sometimes the life is entered upon quite coldly. 'Others do it', is the usual formula whether of persuasion or excuse. Self-condemnation hardly comes in; conscience is burked.

However adopted, very few are happy in the life. Most would say they wished to quit it; there may even be a strong feeling of disgust; but it is seldom that those who have become accustomed to this evil mode of living care to take the only road of escape and seek refuge in a rescue home, or who, if they take this step, can stand the hard work and discipline that follow. As to this the facts are undeniable; the evidence is overwhelming.

If, however, the professional character on which I have laid stress militates strongly against successful rescue work, as has been shown in a previous volume, it may perhaps help to facilitate regulation.

The object of vigilance committees is to check or suppress the open practice of vice by putting the law in motion, and stimulating the police and local authorities to take independent action. Disorderly houses can be closed whether they be brothels or houses of accommodation, and the keepers of them fined. Public-houses, dancing saloons, music halls, theatres, and other licensed places of amusement, may lose their licence if they 'harbour' prostitutes in pursuit of their calling. Nor can the streets legally be used as a rendezvous. Solicitation is an offence punishable by law. Finally, under a recent act, any man who lives on the earnings of a prostitute is liable to six months' hard labour. Each committee – besides putting in motion, wherever it is possible, the machinery of the law – makes great efforts to stir up public opinion, and social pressure is brought to bear upon the owners of houses put to improper uses.

The result has been rather to show the irrepressible character of the evil than to cure or even diminish it. It can be shifted from place to place and forced to change its shape, but it continues to exist none the less, and this being recognized, it becomes more and more difficult to get any action taken at all. Enthusiasm finds the road blocked and begins to despair. And then the voices of those who cry for regulation by the State are heard. It is, they claim, the 'only way'; but for my part I do not think such a step necessary, or, if taken, likely to be efficacious. It may, however, be wise to accept the existence of the evil as in some form inevitable, and to turn our attention to forcing it to take the least objectionable and most manageable shapes.

The organization of the brothel, and public solicitation in the streets are much the most objectionable features, and these it would be possible to suppress entirely, if at the same time the severity of pressure was removed as regards houses of accommodation and some habitual places of resort. I do not propose that either of these should be legalized or encouraged, but merely that their existence and uses should not, as a matter of practical administration, lead to prosecution, so long as decency and order were observed.

Most of the premises naturally used for one or other of these purposes – hotels and coffee-houses, or certain places of amusement – require a licence to carry on their legitimate trades, and the police already have the right of entry. Consequently in these cases it is comparatively easy to enforce a standard of decency and order; whilst even the lowest night-house or dancing saloon can be made responsible for the maintenance of order.

It happens that some of the less socially objectionable developments are precisely those in which it is often most difficult to draw the line between the actually moral and immoral, the legitimate and illegitimate, or between actions that can be or which practically cannot be interfered with. For instance, it is not possible to hold a hotel responsible for the legality of the sexual relations of its guests, and if it were possible it would be an intolerable interference with personal liberty of action, while as regards those who frequent places of amusement a censorship of morals is equally out of the question, and all that can be insisted on is outward decorum of behaviour.

If brothels of every class were persistently hunted out and prosecuted all over London while houses of accommodation were only watched, there would soon be no more of the former. The distinction between the two is clear enough. In the one case the girls live on the premises and receive the men there; in the other they come as to a hotel. Brothels represent the worst forms of organized and associated vice, and one great advantage that would tend at once to follow from their abolition would be the collapse of the trade in girls, which is by far the most iniquitous feature of prostitution.

It may be said that it would be impossible to prosecute a girl who chose to bring men for immoral purposes to the rooms in which she lived, and that it would be difficult to say what number of girls, two, three, four, or more, living together, would constitute a brothel. It seems to me, however, that any association of girls for this purpose would be considered illegal, although unless neighbours complained, it is probable that small combinations would escape notice, and to the extent that this happened they would be comparatively innocuous.

If it were less difficult to find the accommodation they require away from their own homes it is probable that the homes would be used much less for the purpose. This in itself would be a great improvement. The character of the house frequented and the fact that it would be under observation and always liable to prosecution, would provide reasonable security against violence on the one hand and robbery on the other; the prostitutes would no longer need special protection, and the odious figure of the bully might pass with that of the procuress into limbo.

Every possible course has disadvantages, and I do not pretend that the one proposed is without them. I put it forward as tending to amend the most serious developments of a moral difficulty, with the hope that if successful, it might step by step be carried further.

If other places of resort were not closed to these women, the enforcement of the law against open solicitation in the streets would at any rate be much more possible. In this respect it is probable that the position of London is exceptional, not only on account of its size, but also because it contains so many irresponsible male visitors seeking an evening's amusement. The streets of most of our provincial towns are quiet and orderly; in them there are no scenes comparable to the flaunting display of vice in London, where, since the 'Endacott-Cass' case, the police rarely interfere. Some fresh effort is needed to put an end to a public scandal which undoubtedly conduces greatly to immorality.

The actual use of dark back streets, and courts, and quiet out-of-the-way squares, by the lowest class of women, can only be checked by better lighting and patrolling, but the process of enforcing decency would be greatly facilitated if (as is perfectly possible) even this class had their houses of accommodation. The evil would be less.

The use of open spaces for immoral purposes is by no means limited to professional vice. So far as used in this way, it is by a low class of middle-aged women and young lads. As with the back streets, better lighting and constant patrolling, or the railing in and closing of such spaces at night, are the only ways to check this evil. Their adoption is even more necessary as regards the unprofessional than the professional side of immorality. Boys and girls wander off out of sight, and mischief ensues which might otherwise have been avoided; and young men and women who are keeping company deliberately make use of such opportunities.

The proposals I have made do not touch the connection of prostitution with disease, nor do I think that this can be dealt with by Contagious Diseases regulations, except as regards a body of men under discipline, confined within moderate bounds, as in a garrison town; but, in these cases, the special licensing of houses of accommodation open only to certificated women and those accompanying them may not be desirable.

CHAPTER 3

THE JEWS OF LONDON

This chapter is the work of Beatrice Potter. It is the only exhaustive description of an ethnic group in Booth's study. The Jews had recently come to London in large numbers and settled in the East End. They were the 'exotics' of their day, and this is clearly conveyed by Miss Potter's sympathetic but critical account of their community. The only other sizable ethnic group – the Irish – are not treated separately but are duly noted as such throughout the seventeen volumes.

The material in this chapter is taken from Volume I of the first edition, pp. 566–90.

The Jewish Community[1]

IN the midst of the chaotic elements of East London, the Jewish settlement stands out as possessing a distinct religious and social life, and a definite history of its own.

Over 200 years ago a small body of well-to-do Spanish and Portuguese Jews from Amsterdam settled in the neighbourhood of Houndsditch.[2] They were permitted to erect the first English synagogue immediately outside the eastern boundary of the City, and they were allotted a field in the Mile End waste wherein to bury their dead. From that time onward the Jewish community of the

1. I am indebted to the Rev. Herman Adler (Delegate Chief Rabbi) for information concerning the religion and charitable organization of the East End Jewish Settlement.
2. The Jews were banished from England in the reign of Edward I. Oliver Cromwell was induced by Manasseh ben Israel to allow a few Dutch and Portuguese Jews to settle in London; but the Jewish settlement had no legal status until the reign of Charles II.

East End increased in numbers and gradually changed in character.

With the slow decay of the unwritten law of social prejudice, whereby the children of Israel had been confined to one district of the metropolis, the aristocratic and cultured Sephardic Jews – direct descendants of the financiers, merchant princes, and learned doctors of Spain and Portugal – moved westward, and were replaced in their old homes by a multitude of down-trodden, poor, and bigotted brethren of the Ashkenazite, or German, branch of the Hebrew race. Thus towards the middle of last century the East End settlement ceased to be the nucleus of a small and select congregation of the chosen people, and became a reservoir for the incoming stream of poverty-stricken foreigners.

For a time the old settlers held aloof from the newcomers, and regarded them as a lower caste, fit only to receive alms. But with the growth of an educated and comparatively wealthy class from out of the ranks of the Ashkenazite congregations, the contemptuous feelings of the Sephardim declined. In 1760, the whole of the Jewish people resident in England (numbering some 8,000 souls) were organized under the secular leadership of the *London Committee of Deputies of British Jews*, a committee consisting of representatives from all the metropolitan and provincial congregations. And whilst the Jews were regarded as aliens by the English law, and while they laboured under manifold industrial and political disabilities, the Board of Deputies was fully recognized by the Imperial Government as a representative body, and possessed very real powers within its own community. The annals of this Board are interesting, for they illustrate the skill, the tenacity, and above all, the admirable temper with which our Hebrew fellow-countrymen have insinuated themselves into the life of the nation, without forsaking the faith of their forefathers or sacrificing as a community the purity of their race. As an organization the Board of Deputies is still retained, but its importance has naturally declined with the fulfilment of the main object of its existence.

Whilst the Board of Deputies has watched over the interests of its constituents as they have been affected by the Gentile world, the Beth Din (court of judgement) has administered ecclesiastical law within the Jewish community. For the origin of this venerable institution we must seek far back into primitive Hebrew history – into the annals of Biblical Judaism. In more modern times, during the wanderings of Israel among the Western nations and the separation of the tribes into small communities, these courts have served a twofold purpose: they have introduced order and discipline within the several communities of the chosen people, and they have obviated the scandal of Jew fighting Jew in the Gentile courts of law.

In England at the present time the Beth Din consists of the Chief Rabbi and two assessors; the court sits twice every week throughout the year. We say that its jurisdiction is ecclesiastical, because justice is administered by a priest, and according to the laws of the Jewish religion. But we must not fail to remember that with the followers of the Law of Moses the term 'ecclesiastical' covers the whole ground of moral duties as well as the minutiae of religious ceremony – includes practical obedience to the ten commandments, as well as conformity to traditional observances. In fact, religion with the orthodox Jew is not simply, or even primarily, a key whereby to unlock existence in a future world; it is a law of life on this earth, sanctioned by the rewards and punishments of this world – peace or distraction, health or disease. Hence it is impossible to define the exact jurisdiction of the Beth Din. On the one hand, the Chief Rabbi and the two assessors regulate the details of religious observance and control the machinery whereby the sanitary and dietary regulations are enforced; on the other hand, they sit as a permanent board of arbitration to all those who are, or feel themselves, aggrieved by another son or daughter of Israel. Family quarrels, trade and labour disputes, matrimonial differences, wife desertions, even reckless engagements, and breach of promise cases – in short, all the thousand and one disputes, entanglements, defaults, and mistakes of everyday life are brought before the Beth Din to be settled or unravelled by the mingled lights of the Pentateuch, the Talmud, and the native shrewdness of the Hebrew judge.

Akin to the jurisdiction of the Beth Din is the religious registration of all marriages. No Jew can enter into the married state without first obtaining the consent of the Chief Rabbi. In the case of native Jews this permission may be considered as formal; but with immigrants from distant homes, sufficient testimony is required that the parties concerned have not already contracted with other mates the bonds and ties of wedlock.

These institutions are common to the Anglo-Jewish community throughout England.[3] They are based on a representative system of a somewhat restricted character. Each seat-holder in a recognized synagogue takes part in the election of the Rabbi, wardens, and other officers of the congregation to which he belongs; every synagogue contributing to the communal fund has a right to vote for the Chief Rabbi, the central committee of synagogues, and indirectly for the Board of Deputies.

The Jewish settlement at the East End, however, stands outside the communal life, so far as voting power is concerned – partly on account of its extreme poverty, and partly because of the foreign habits and customs of the vast majority of East End Jews.

For the East End Jews of the working class rarely attend the larger synagogues (except on the Day of Atonement),

3. The Board of Deputies represents all British Jews; but the Sephardic and Ashkenazite communities have each a distinct religious organization and a separate Chief Rabbi.

and most assuredly they are not seat-holders. For the most part the religious-minded form themselves into associations (Chevras), which combine the functions of a benefit club for death, sickness, and the solemn rites of mourning with that of public worship and the study of the Talmud. Thirty or forty of these Chevras are scattered throughout the Jewish quarters; they are of varying size as congregations, of different degrees of solvency as friendly societies, and of doubtful comfort and sanitation as places of public worship. Usually each Chevras is named after the town or district in Russia or Poland from which the majority of its members have emigrated: it is, in fact, from old associations – from ties of relationship or friendship, or, at least, from the memory of a common home – that the new association springs.

Here, early in the morning, or late at night, the devout members meet to recite the morning and evening prayers, or to decipher the sacred books of the Talmud. And it is a curious and touching sight to enter one of the poorer and more wretched of these places on a Sabbath morning. Probably the one you choose will be situated in a small alley or narrow court, or it may be built out in a back yard. To reach the entrance you stumble over broken pavement and household débris; possibly you pick your way over the rickety bridge connecting it with the cottage property fronting the street. From the outside it appears a long wooden building surmounted by a skylight, very similar in construction to the ordinary sweater's workshop. You enter; the heat and odour convince you that the skylight is not used for ventilation. From behind the trellis of the 'ladies' gallery' you see at the far end of the room the richly curtained Ark of the Covenant, wherein are laid, attired in gorgeous vestments, the sacred scrolls of the Law. Slightly elevated on a platform in the midst of the congregation, stands the reader or minister, surrounded by the seven who are called up to the reading of the Law from among the congregation. Scarves of white cashmere or silk, softly bordered and fringed, are thrown across the shoulders of the men, and relieve the dusty hue and disguise the Western cut of the clothes they wear. A low, monotonous, but musical-toned recital of Hebrew prayers, each man praying for himself to the God of his fathers, rises from the congregation, whilst the reader intones, with a somewhat louder voice, the recognized portion of the Pentateuch. Add to this rhythmical cadence of numerous voices, the swaying to and fro of the bodies of the worshippers – expressive of the words of personal adoration: 'All my bones exclaim, Oh! Lord, who is like unto Thee!' – and you may imagine yourself in a far-off Eastern land. But you are roused from your dreams. Your eye wanders from the men, who form the congregation, to the small body of women who watch behind the trellis. Here, certainly, you have the Western world, in the bright-coloured ostrich feathers, large bustles, and tight-fitting coats of cotton velvet or brocaded satinette. At last you step out, stifled by the heat and dazed by the strange contrast of the old-world memories of a majestic religion and the squalid vulgarity of an East End slum.

And, perchance, if it were permissible to stay after Divine service is over, and if you could follow the quick-spoken Jüdisch,[4] you would be still more bewildered by these 'destitute foreigners', whose condition, according to Mr Arnold White, 'resembles that of animals'. The women have left; the men are scattered over the benches (maybe there are several who are still muttering their prayers), or they are gathered together in knots, sharpening their intellects with the ingenious points and subtle logic of the Talmudical argument, refreshing their minds from the rich stores of Talmudical wit, or listening with ready helpfulness to the tale of distress of a newcomer from the foreign home.

These Chevras supply the social and religious needs of

---

4. Yiddish. – EDS.

some 12,000 to 15,000 foreign Jews. Up to late years their status within the Jewish community has been very similar to that of dissenting bodies in face of a State Church, always excepting nonconformity of creed. No marriages could be celebrated within their precincts, and they were in no way represented on the central council of the Ashkenazite organization of the United Synagogues. And owing to the unsanitary and overcrowded state of the poorest Chevras, some among the leaders of the Anglo-Jewish community have thought to discourage the spontaneous multiplication of these small bodies, and to erect a large East End synagogue endowed by the charity of the West. I venture to think that wiser counsels have prevailed. The evils of bad sanitation and overcrowding are easily noted, and still more frequently exaggerated. Philanthropists are apt to forget that different degrees of sanitation and space, like all the other conditions of human existence, are good, bad, or indifferent relatively to the habits and constitutions of those who submit to them. The close and odorous atmosphere of the ordinary Chevras is clearly a matter of choice; there is not even the ghost of a 'sweater' to enforce it. In truth, the family occupying one room, the presser or machinist at work day and night close to a coke fire, would find, in all probability, a palace to worship in draughty and uncomfortable, and out of all harmony and proportion with the rest of existence. On the other hand, it is easy to overlook the unseen influence for good of self-creating, self-supporting, and self-governing communities; small enough to generate public opinion and the practical supervision of private morals, and large enough to stimulate charity, worship, and study by communion and example. These and other arguments have led to the federation of minor synagogues and their partial recognition by the communal authorities. And probably it is only a question of time before the East End Chevras are admitted to full representation in the religious organization of the Ashkenazite community in return for a more responsible attitude with regard to the safety and sanitation of the premises they occupy.

The large City and East End Synagogues meet the religious wants of the middle and lower middle class of East End Jews; the Chevras connect a certain number of the more pious and independent-minded of the foreign settlers with the communal life; but there remains some 20,000 to 30,000 Jews – men, women, and children – too poor or too indifferent to attend regularly a place of worship, but who nevertheless cling with an almost superstitious tenacity to the habits and customs of their race. This poorest section of the Jewish community is composed, with few exceptions, of foreigners or the children of foreigners. Individuals are constantly rising out of it into other classes, or leaving England for America; but their places are quickly taken by newcomers from Poland and Russia. It forms, therefore, a permanent layer of poverty verging on destitution. Now this class is united to the Jewish middle and upper class by a downward stream of charity and personal service, a benevolence at once so widespread and so thorough-going, that it fully justifies the saying, 'All Israel are brethren.'[5] Of the many educational and charitable institutions connected with the East End Jewish life, I have only space to mention one – the most talked of and the least understood – the Jewish Board of Guardians.

The title of this institution has been unfortunate, for it has led to a serious misunderstanding. The Christian world has considered the 'Jewish Board of Guardians' as analogous in function to an English parochial body; the relief it administers has been treated as official or State relief, and therefore by a simple process of deduction, its clients have been regarded as belonging to the ordinary pauper class. On the basis of this misleading analogy a

---

5. . . . The 'Free School', the largest public school in England, is a striking example of the admirable organization peculiar to Jewish charity.

calculation has been made of the percentage of the pauper class within the Jewish community; and the communal authorities have been charged with a wholesale pauperization of the Jewish poor.[6] A slight sketch of the origin of the Jewish Board of Guardians and of the actual nature of its activity will, I think, suffice to destroy the groundwork of this unmerited accusation.

From the first years of the Jewish settlement in England the influx of poverty-stricken co-religionists has been one of the central problems of Anglo-Jewish life. In 1753 the Great Synagogue tried to check immigration by refusing relief to those who had left their country without due cause. But persecution and social ostracism abroad, increasing liberty and consideration in England, combined with the warm-hearted benevolence of the more fortunate children of Israel for their poorer brethren, were social forces too strong to be curbed by the negative resolution of an official body. Charities increased on all sides, but in a chaotic state, giving rise to the worst forms of pauperism and professional begging. And those who have some experience of the present system of almsgiving practised by Christians of all denominations within the metropolis, and who are able to imagine the effect of that system intensified by a steady influx of destitute foreigners, and by the very practical view the Jews take of the religious precept of charity, will readily conceive the hopelessly demoralized condition of the Jewish poor for the first fifty

[6]. This charge was based on the Report of the Jewish Board of Guardians for 1886; and an alarmist article on the extent of Jewish pauperism appeared in the *Spectator*, April 22nd, 1887. Besides the relief administered by the Jewish Board of Guardians, free funerals were cited as indicative of pauperism. Those who understand the peculiar solemnity of mourning and funeral rites among Jews, and who appreciate the direct and indirect costliness of these, will perceive that a 'free funeral' is no more a token of pauperism than a free mass among Catholics or a free sermon among Protestants. The same may be said for the free distribution of the articles of diet needed for the celebration of religious feasts.

years of the century. To put an end to this confusing of good and evil, the three City Ashkenazite congregations instituted, in 1858, the Jewish Board of Guardians. It became the Charity Organization Society of the private benevolence of Hebrew philanthropists; only, from the first, it received generous and loyal support from the whole Jewish community.

Again, if we turn from the origin of the Jewish Board of Guardians to the nature of its work, we shall see that a large proportion of its charitable expenditure is not in any way analogous to the relief administered by a parochial Board. Of the £13,000 to £14,000 expended annually by the Jewish Board in actual relief, only £2,000 a year is given away in a form similar to out-door relief, viz., in fixed allowances, and in tickets for the necessaries of life; £3,000 a year is lent for trade and business purposes; £1,000 a year is expended in emigration; another £500 in the sanitary inspection of the homes of the poor and in the provision of a workroom for girls. Of the remainder more than 50 per cent may be considered given in the form of business capital of one kind or another, enabling the recipients to raise themselves permanently from the ranks of those who depend on charity for subsistence. Indeed, the practical effect of the relief administered by the Jewish Board, in so far as it affects individuals, is conclusively proved by the striking fact that of the 3,313 cases dealt with in the year 1887, only 268 were known to the Board as applicants prior to the year 1886. If we remember the many thousands of cases treated during the Board's existence, we can hardly, in the face of these statistics, describe those relieved by the Jewish Board of Guardians as belonging to the chronically parasitic class of 'paupers'.

Hence if we mean by the word pauper, 'a person supported by State provision', there are no paupers within the Jewish community, except a few isolated individuals chargeable to the English parochial authorities. If, on the other hand, we choose a wider definition – 'a person so indigent as to depend on charity for maintenance' – it is impossible to measure the relative extent of pauperism among Christians and Jews of the same class. For the statistics of Jewish charitable relief are, comparatively speaking, definite and complete; but owing to the disorganized state of Christian charity, and owing to the fact that our indigent parasites are to a great extent maintained by the silent aid of the class immediately above them, we can by no possible means arrive at an approximate estimate of the number of persons in our midst who depend on charitable assistance for their livelihood. Who, for instance, would undertake to calculate the number of paupers (in this wider sense of the term) among the population surrounding the Docks? Moreover, while all groundwork for the charge of pauperization is absent, we have conclusive evidence that either from the character of those who take, or from the method of those who give, Jewish charity does not tend to the demoralization of individual recipients.

But though the accusation of wholesale pauperism brought against the Jewish community cannot be maintained, there is doubtless, from the standpoint of industrial health, a grave objection to the form of relief administered by the Jewish Board of Guardians. Money lent or given for trade purposes fosters the artificial multiplication of small masters, and is one of the direct causes of the sweating system; efficient assistance to the mechanic out of work enables him to exist on reduced or irregular earnings, and thereby lowers the general condition of his class. In truth there seems no escape from the tragic dilemma of charitable relief. If we help a man to exist without work, we demoralize the individual and encourage the growth of a parasitic or pauper class. If, on the other hand, we raise the recipient permanently from the condition of penury, and enable him to begin again the struggle for existence, we save him at the cost of all those who compete with him (whether they be small masters or wage-earners, Jews or Gentiles) for the custom of the manufacturer, the trader, or the consumer; in other words, we increase that very dislocation of industry, the result of which we attempt to mitigate in special instances. Judged by its effect on the industrial development of the whole nation, we are tempted to echo sorrowfully the words of Louise Michel, '*La Philanthropie, c'est une mensonge*'.

Before I leave the question of charity and pauperism within the Jewish community, it is needful to notice certain institutions which indirectly have a most pauperizing effect, and which would assuredly achieve the utter demoralization of the Jewish poor if the work they accomplished equalled to any degree the sum of their expenditure – I mean the Christian conversionist societies. Among these the London Society for Promoting Christianity among the Jews is the largest and most influential.

This society enjoys an income of £35,000 a year. On the magnificent premises of Palestine Place (Bethnal Green) it provides a chapel, a Hebrew missionary training institute, and a Hebrew operatives' home. During the last year twelve Jews were baptized in its chapel, forty children (more than fifty per cent of whom were the children of Christian mothers) were maintained in the school, and twelve Jewish converts supported in the operatives' home. The process of conversion is very simple: board and lodging at a specially provided house during the inquiry stage, constant charitable assistance after conversion, and the free education and free maintenance of Jewish children brought up in the Christian faith. In the eloquent words of the Report:

'The present inmates (Operative Jewish Converts' Institution) appear fully to realize the contrast between their former friendless condition and their present life, in which a comfortable home, wholesome food, respectable clothing, instruction in trade, and reward-money for attention and industry accumulates till they leave the institution.'

The society has, however, one complaint against its converts. Inspired by the Jewish spirit of competing with former masters, and anxious to turn to some account their newly-acquired 'talent' of Christianity, the youthful proselytes set up in business on their own account, collecting and spending the subscriptions of zealous Christians, with no respect to the monetary claims or superior authority of the mother society. Hence the East End is sprinkled with small missions, between which and Palestine Place a certain number of professional converts wander in search of the temporal blessings of Christianity. Imagine the temptation to the poverty-stricken inhabitants of the crowded alleys of the Jewish slum! And yet, in spite of comfortable maintenance in the present and brilliant prospects in the future, the number of converts is infinitesimal, a fact that throws an interesting sidelight on the moral tenacity of the Jewish race.

The movement, however, has produced a mischievous reaction within the community. Pious-minded Jews have thought starvation or baptism a too terrible alternative to offer the utterly destitute, and a certain amount of unorganized and pauperizing relief is undoubtedly dispensed throughout the East End as a counter-blast to missionary enterprise. Moreover, Jewish philanthropists have tried to protect the friendless immigrant (without hope or chance of immediate employment) from the allurements of the Christian missionary by the same means through which they have attempted to save him from the extortions of the professional 'runner'. They have erected a 'Poor Jews' Temporary Shelter', an institution which last year provided board and lodging for a period of from one to fourteen days to 1,322 homeless immigrants. Rightly or wrongly, this institution has been looked upon with disfavour by Christians, and to some extent by Jews (notably by the Jewish Board of Guardians) as likely to attract to England pauper foreigners of the Hebrew race.

I have sketched the principal religious and charitable institutions affecting for good or evil Jewish life at the East End. A far more difficult task lies before me: to give the reader some general idea of the manners and customs of this people; to represent to some slight extent their home and outdoor life, and finally to estimate, however imperfectly, their character and capacity as members of our social and industrial state.

I think I may begin with two statements of a general character: the majority of East End Jews are either foreigners or children of foreigners; and the dominant nationality is Polish or Russian.

With regard to the preponderance of foreigners, I hardly think it will be denied by anyone who has studied the available statistics, or who has any personal experience of East End Jewish life.

For statistical material I refer the reader to Mr Llewellyn Smith's careful and elaborate calculations in the preceding chapter. He estimates that out of a total Jewish population of from 60,000 to 70,000 persons, 30,000 were actually born abroad.

At least one-half of the remainder must be of foreign parentage. But if the reader distrusts statistics, I would advise him to wander through the Jewish quarter, and listen to the language of the streets; to frequent the sweaters' dens, the gambling clubs, and the Chevras; or, if he desires a more graphic experience, to attend a meeting of working-class Jews, and try to make himself understood in his native tongue.

The Polish or Russian nationality of the vast majority of these foreigners is an equally undisputed fact and a natural consequence of the recent outbreak of Judenhetze in Russian Poland and the adjoining territories. It is, moreover, a fact of great significance in any consideration of the East End Jewish question. For we are accustomed to think, with the old German proverb, 'Every country has the Jew it deserves', a saying, in our case, inapt, since we receive our Jews ready-made – passed on to us by a foreign nation with a domestic policy diametrically opposed to our own. Before, therefore, we are able to appreciate the present characteristics and future prospects of this stream of Jewish life flowing continuously with more or less rapidity into the great reservoir of the East End Jewish settlement, we must gain some slight idea of the political, industrial, and social conditions governing the source from which it springs.

Alone among the great nations of Europe, Russia has resolutely refused political and industrial freedom to her Jewish subjects. Under the Russian Government oppression and restriction have assumed every conceivable form. No Jew may own land; in some places he may not even rent it; in one part he is not admitted into the learned professions; in another state he may not enter an industrial establishment or take part in a Government contract; while in whole districts of Russia the children of Israel have no right of domicile, and live and trade by the bought connivance of the police authorities, and in daily terror of the petty tyranny of a capricious governor. Deprived of the rights and privileges of citizens, they are subject to the full strain of military conscription, intensified by social insult and religious persecution. And yet, in spite of this systematic oppression, the children of Israel have, up to late years, multiplied in the land of their enemies and prospered exceedingly, until they may be numbered by their millions throughout the Russian Empire; absorbing the more profitable trading, and crowding every profession, mechanical and intellectual, open to Jewish competition. Once again in the history of the world penal legislation has proved a powerless weapon against the superior mental equipment of the

Jew; and it has simply forced the untiring energies of the Hebrew race into low channels of parasitic activity, undermining the morality and well-being of their Christian fellow-subjects. The Russian Government and the Russian people have slowly grasped this fact, and unwilling to adopt the policy of complete emancipation, they have changed their method of attack. The central authorities, supported by the public opinion of the injured classes, have deliberately encouraged mob-violence of a brutal and revolting character as a costless but efficient means of expulsion. Robbed, outraged, in fear of death and physical torture, the chosen people have swarmed across the Russian frontier, bearing with them, nor borrowed 'jewels of silver, and jewels of gold, and raiment',[7] but a capacity for the silent evasion of the law, a faculty for secretive and illicit dealing, and mingled feelings of contempt and fear for the Christians amongst whom they have dwelt and under whose government they have lived for successive generations.

These have been the outward circumstances forming the Polish or Russian Jew. The inner life of the small Hebrew communities bound together by common suffering and mutual helpfulness has developed other qualities, but has also tended in its own way to destroy all friendly and honourable intercourse with surrounding peoples. Social isolation has perfected home life; persecution has intensified religious fervour; an existence of unremitting toil, and a rigid observance of the moral precepts and sanitary and dietary regulations of the Jewish religion have favoured the growth of sobriety, personal purity, and a consequent power of physical endurance. But living among a half-civilized people, and carefully preserved by the Government from the advantages of secular instruction, the Polish and Russian Jews have centred their thoughts and feelings in the literature of their race

---

7. Exodus xii. 35.

– in the Old Testament, with its magnificent promises of universal dominion; in the Talmud, with its minute instructions as to the means of gaining it. The child, on its mother's lap, lisps passages from the Talmud; the old man, tottering to the grave, is still searching for the secret of life in 'that stupendous labyrinth of fact, thought, and fancy'. For in those ten volumes of Talmudical lore the orthodox Polish Jew finds not only a store-house of information and a training-ground for his intellectual and emotional faculties, but the key to all the varied perplexities and manifold troubles of his daily existence. To quote the words of Deutsch, the Talmud, besides comprising the poetry and the science of the people, is 'emphatically a *Corpus Juris*: an encyclopaedia of law, civil and penal, ecclesiastical and international, human and divine'. Beyond this law the pious Israelite recognizes no obligations; the laws and customs of the Christians are so many regulations to be obeyed, evaded, set at naught, or used according to the possibilities and expediencies of the hour.

In these facts of past training we see an explanation of the present mental and physical qualities of the majority of East End Jews. The Polish or Russian Jew represents to some extent the concentrated essence of Jewish virtue and Jewish vice; for he has, in his individual experience, epitomized the history of his race in the Christian world. But he can in no sense be considered a fair sample of Jews who have enjoyed the freedom, the culture, and the public spirit of English life. I should wish it therefore to be distinctly understood that I do not offer the slight description in the following pages of the manners, customs, and industrial characteristics of East End Jews as a picture of the Jewish community throughout England.

Let us imagine ourselves on board a Hamburg boat steaming slowly up the Thames in the early hours of the morning. In the stern of the vessel we see a mixed crowd of men, women, and children – Polish and Russian Jews, some sitting on their baskets, others with bundles tied up in bright-coloured kerchiefs. For the most part they are men between twenty and forty years of age, of slight and stooping stature, of sallow and pinched countenance, with low foreheads, high cheek-bones and protruding lips. They wear uncouth and dirt-bespattered garments, they mutter to each other in a strange tongue. Scattered among them a few women (their shapely figures and soft skins compare favourably with the sickly appearance of the men), in peasant frocks with shawls thrown lightly over their heads; and here and there a child, with prematurely set features, bright eyes, and agile movements. Stamped on the countenance and bearing of the men is a look of stubborn patience; in their eyes an indescribable expression of hunted, suffering animals, lit up now and again by tenderness for the young wife or little child, or sharpened into a quick and furtive perception of surrounding circumstances. You address them kindly, they gaze on you with silent suspicion; a coarse German sailor pushes his way amongst them with oaths and curses; they simply move apart without a murmur, and judging from their expression, without a resentful feeling; whilst the women pick up their ragged bundles from out of the way of the intruder with an air of deprecating gentleness.

The steamer is at rest, the captain awaits the visit of the Custom House officials. All eyes are strained, searching through the shifting mist and dense forest of masts for the first glimpse of the eagerly hoped-for relations and friends, for the first sight of the long-dreamt-of city of freedom and prosperity. Presently a boat rows briskly to the side of the vessel; seated in it a young woman with mock sealskin coat, vandyke hat slashed up with blue satin, and surmounted with a yellow ostrich feather, and long six-buttoned gloves. She is chaffing the boatman in broken English, and shouts words of welcome and encouragement to the simple bewildered peasant who peers over the side of the vessel with two little ones clasped in either hand. Yes! that smartly dressed young lady is her daughter. Three years ago the father and the elder child left the quiet Polish village: a long interval of suspense, then a letter telling of an almost hopeless struggle, at last passage-money, and here today the daughter with her bright, warm clothes and cheery self-confidence – in a few hours the comfortably furnished home of a small wholesale orange-dealer in Mitre Street, near to Petticoat Lane.

Seated by the side of the young woman a bearded man, his face furrowed and shoulders bent with work. He is comfortably clothed and wears a large watch-chain hanging ostentatiously outside his coat. Evidently he is not the father of the girl, for his hands are clenched nervously as he fails to catch sight of the long-expected form; he is simply the presser from the sweater's next door to the orange-dealer; and he also can afford the 1s. fee to board the steamer and meet his wife. Ah! there she is! and a gentle-faced woman, beaming with heightened colour, pushes her way to the side of the vessel, holding up the youngest child with triumphant pride. The elder boy, a lad of ten, fastens his eyes fixedly on his father's watch-chain, tries in vain to pierce the pocket and weigh and measure the watch, calculates quickly the probable value, wonders whether gilded articles are cheaper or dearer in London than in Poland, and registers a silent vow that he will not rest day nor night until he is handling with a possessor's pride a gold chain and watch, similar or superior to that adorning his father's person. Then he prepares with religious reverence to receive his father's blessing.

The scenes at the landing-stage are less idyllic. There are a few relations and friends awaiting the arrival of the small boats filled with immigrants: but the crowd gathered in and about the gin-shop overlooking the narrow entrance of the landing-stage are dock loungers of the lowest type and professional 'runners'. These latter individuals, usually of the Hebrew race, are among the most repulsive of East London parasites; boat after boat touches the landing-stage, they push forward, seize hold of the bundles or baskets of the newcomers, offer bogus tickets to those who wish to travel forward to America, promise guidance and free lodging to those who hold in their hands addresses of acquaintances in Whitechapel, or who are absolutely friendless. A little man with an official badge (Hebrew Ladies' Protective Society) fights valiantly in their midst for the conduct of unprotected females, and shouts or whispers to the others to go to the Poor Jews' Temporary Shelter in Leman Street. For a few moments it is a scene of indescribable confusion: cries and counter-cries; the hoarse laughter of the dock loungers at the strange garb and broken accent of the poverty-stricken foreigners; the rough swearing of the boatmen at passengers unable to pay the fee for landing. In another ten minutes eighty of the hundred newcomers are dispersed in the back slums of Whitechapel; in another few days, the majority of these, robbed of the little they possess, are turned out of the 'free lodgings' destitute and friendless.

If we were able to follow the 'greener' into the next scene of his adventures we should find him existing on the charity of a co-religionist or toiling day and night for a small labour-contractor in return for a shake-down, a cup of black coffee, and a hunch of brown bread. This state of dependence, however, does not last. For a time the man works as if he were a slave under the lash, silently, without complaint. But in a few months (in the busy season in a few weeks) the master enters his workshop and the man is not at his place. He has left without warning – silently – as he worked without pay. He has learnt his trade and can sell his skill in the open market at the corner of Commercial Street; or possibly a neighbouring sweater, pressed with work, has offered him better terms. A year hence he has joined a Chevras, or has become a *habitué* of a gambling club. And unless he falls a victim to the Jewish passion for gambling, he employs the enforced leisure of the slack season in some form of petty dealing. He is soon in a fair way to become a tiny capitalist – a maker of profit as well as an earner of wage. He has moved out of the back court in which his fellow-countrymen are herded together like animals, and is comfortably installed in a model dwelling; the walls of his parlour are decked with prints of Hebrew worthies, or with portraits of prize-fighters and race-horses; his wife wears jewellery and furs on the Sabbath; for their Sunday dinner they eat poultry. He treats his wife with courtesy and tenderness, and they discuss constantly the future of the children. He is never to be seen at the public-house round the corner; but he enjoys a quiet glass of 'rum and shrub' and a game of cards with a few friends on the Saturday or Sunday evening; and he thinks seriously of season tickets for the People's Palace. He remembers the starvation fare and the long hours of his first place: he remembers, too, the name and address of the wholesale house served by his first master; and presently he appears at the counter and offers to take the work at a lower figure, or secures it through a tip to the foreman. But he no longer kisses the hand of Singer's agent and begs with fawning words for another sewing-machine; neither does he flit to other lodgings in the dead of night at the first threat of the broker. In short, he has become a law-abiding and self-respecting citizen of our great metropolis, and feels himself the equal of a Montefiore or a Rothschild.

The foregoing sketch is typical of the lives of the majority of Polish and Russian Jews from their first appearance in the port of London. Usually they bring with them no ready-made skill of a marketable character. They are set down in an already over-stocked and demoralized labour market; they are surrounded by the drunkenness, immorality, and gambling of the East End streets; they are, in fact, placed in the midst of the very refuse of our civilization, and yet (to quote from a former chapter), whether they become bootmakers, tailors, cabinet-makers, glaziers, or dealers, the Jewish inhabitants of East London rise in the social scale; 'as a mass they shift upwards, leaving to the newcomers from foreign lands and to the small section of habitual gamblers the worst-paid work, the most dilapidated workshops, and the dirtiest lodgings'. But this is not all. Originally engaged in the most unskilled branch of the lowest section of each trade, Jewish mechanics (whether we regard them individually or as a class) slowly but surely invade the higher provinces of production, bringing in their train a system of employment and a method of dealing with masters, men, and fellow-workers which arouses the antagonism of English workmen. The East End Jewish problem therefore resolves itself into two central questions: (1) What are the reasons of the Jews' success? (2) Why is that success resented by that part of the Christian community with whom the Jew comes in daily contact? I venture to end this chapter with a few suggestions touching this double-faced enigma of Jewish life.

First we must realize (in comparing the Polish Jew with the English labourer) that the poorest Jew has inherited through the medium of his religion a trained intellect. For within the Judaic Theocracy there are no sharp lines dividing the people into distinct classes with definite economic characteristics such as exist in most Christian nations: viz. a leisure class of landowners, a capitalist class of brain-workers, and a mass of labouring people who up to late years have been considered a lower order, fit only for manual work.

The children of Israel are a nation of priests. Each male child, rich or poor, is a student of the literature of his race. In his earliest childhood he is taught by picturesque rites and ceremonies the history, the laws, and the poetry of his people; in boyhood he masters long passages in an ancient tongue; and in the more pious and rigid communities of Russian Poland the full-grown man spends his leisure in striving to interpret the subtle reasoning and strange fantasies of that great classic of the Hebrews, the Talmud. I do not wish to imply that the bigotted Jew is a 'cultured' being, if we mean by culture a wide experience of the thoughts and feelings of other times and other races. Far from it. The intellectual vision and the emotional sympathies of the great majority of Polish Jews are narrowed down to the past history and present prospects of their own race. But the mechanical faculties of the intellect – memory, the power of sustained reasoning, and the capacity for elaborate calculation – have been persistently cultivated (in orthodox communities) among all classes, and there has resulted a striking equality, and a high though narrow level of intellectual training.

This oneness of type and uniformity of chances, originating in the influence of a unique religion, have been strengthened and maintained by the industrial and political disabilities under which the Jews have laboured through the greater part of the Christian era, and which still exist in Russian Poland. The brutal persecution of the Middle Ages weeded out the inapt and incompetent. Injustice and social isolation, pressing on poor and rich alike, sharpened and narrowed the intellect of Israel, regarded as a whole, to an instrument for grasping by mental agility the good things withheld from them by the brute force of the Christian peoples.

In the Jewish inhabitants of East London we see therefore a race of brain-workers competing with a class of manual labourers. The Polish Jew regards manual work[8]

8. It is a mistake to suppose that the Jew is physically unfit for manual work. On the contrary, he is better fitted than the Anglo-Saxon for those trades which require quickness of perception rather than artistic skill, and he will compete successfully with the Englishman in forms of manual labour needing physical endurance, and not actual strength of muscle. Hence the Jew's success in the machine-made coat and boot and shoe trades.

as the first rung of the social ladder, to be superseded or supplanted on the first opportunity by the estimates of the profit-maker, the transactions of the dealer, or the calculations of the money-lender; and he is only tempted from a life of continual acquisition by that vice of the intellect, gambling.

Besides the possession of a trained intellect, admirably adapted to commerce and finance, there is another, and I am inclined to think a more important factor in the Jew's success. From birth upwards, the pious Israelite (male and female) is subjected to a moral and physical regimen, which, while it favours the full development of the bodily organs, protects them from abuse and disease, and stimulates the growth of physical self-control and mental endurance.[9] For the rites and regulations of the Mosaic law and the more detailed instructions of tradition are in no way similar to the ascetic exercises of the Christian or Buddhist saint seeking spiritual exaltation through the mortification or annihilation of physical instinct. On the contrary, the religious ordinances and sanitary laws of the Jewish religion accentuate the physical aspect of life; they are (as M. Rénan has observed) not a preparation for another world, but a course of training adapted to prolong the life of the individual and to multiply the number of his descendants.

Moreover, the moral precepts of Judaism are centered in the perfection of family life, in obedience towards parents, in self-devotion for children, in the chastity of the girl, in the support and protection of the wife. The poorest Jew cherishes as sacred the maternity of the woman, and seldom degrades her to the position of a

---

9. From a psychological as well as from an ethical point of view, a detailed study of the sanitary observances of the Jewish religion (more especially those relative to sexual functions) would be extremely interesting. The musical talent which distinguishes the Hebrew race has been ascribed by psychologists to the effect of these observances on successive generations.

worker upon whose exertions he depends for subsistence. Thus Jewish morality, instead of diverting feeling from the service of the body, combines with physical training to develop exclusively that side of man's emotional nature which is inextricably interwoven with the healthful and pleasurable exercise of physical instinct. Hence in the rigidly conforming Jew we have a being at once moral and sensual; a creature endowed with the power of physical endurance, but gifted with a highly-trained and well-regulated appetite for sensuous enjoyment. And with the emotions directed into the well-regulated channels of domestic feeling, the mind remains passionless. Anger, pride, and selfconsciousness, with their counterparts of indignation, personal dignity, and sensitiveness, play a small part in the character of the Polish Jew. He suffers oppression and bears ridicule with imperturbable good humour; in the face of insult and abuse he remains silent. For why resent when your object is to overcome? Why bluster and fight when you may manipulate or control in secret?

The result is twofold. As an industrial competitor the Polish Jew is fettered by no definite standard of life; it rises and falls with his opportunities; he is not depressed by penury, and he is not demoralized by gain. As a citizen of our many-sided metropolis he is unmoved by those gusts of passion which lead to drunkenness and crime; whilst on the other hand he pursues the main purposes of personal existence, undistracted by the humours, illusions, and aspirations arising from the unsatisfied emotions of our more complicated and less disciplined natures. Is it surprising, therefore, that in this nineteenth century, with its ideal of physical health, intellectual acquisition, and material prosperity, the chosen people, with three thousand years of training, should in some instances realize the promise made by Moses to their forefathers: 'Thou shalt drive out nations mightier than thyself, and thou shalt take their land as an inheritance'?

Such, I imagine, are the chief causes of the Jew's success. We need not seek far for the origin of the antagonistic feelings with which the Gentile inhabitants of East London regard Jewish labour and Jewish trade. For the reader will have already perceived that the immigrant Jew, though possessed of many first-class virtues, is deficient in that highest and latest development of human sentiment – social morality.

I do not wish to imply by this that East End Jews resist the laws and defy the conventions of social and commercial life. On the contrary, no one will deny that the children of Israel are the most law-abiding inhabitants of East London. They keep the peace, they pay their debts, and they abide by their contracts; practices in which they are undoubtedly superior to the English and Irish casual labourers among whom they dwell. For the Jew is quick to perceive that 'law and order' and the 'sanctity of contract' are the *sine qua non* of a full and free competition in the open market. And it is by competition, and by competition alone, that the Jew seeks success. But in the case of the foreign Jews, it is a competition unrestricted by the personal dignity of a definite standard of life, and unchecked by the social feelings of class loyalty and trade integrity. The small manufacturer injures the trade through which he rises to the rank of a capitalist by bad and dishonest production. The petty dealer or small money-lender, imbued with the economic precept of buying in the cheapest and selling in the dearest market, suits his wares and his terms to the weakness, the ignorance, and the vice of his customers; the mechanic, indifferent to the interests of the class to which he temporarily belongs, and intent only on becoming a small master, acknowledges no limit to the process of under-bidding fellow-workers, except the exhaustion of his own strength. In short, the foreign Jew totally ignores all social obligations other than keeping the law of the land, the maintenance of his own family, and the charitable relief of co-religionists.

Thus the immigrant Jew, fresh from the sorrowful experiences typical of the history of his race, seems to justify by his existence those strange assumptions which figured for *man* in the political economy of Ricardo – an Always Enlightened Selfishness, seeking employment or profit with an absolute mobility of body and mind, without pride, without preference, without interests outside the struggle for the existence and welfare of the individual and the family. We see these assumptions verified in the Jewish inhabitants of Whitechapel; and in the Jewish East End trades we may watch the prophetic deduction of the Hebrew economist actually fulfilled – in a perpetually recurring bare subsistence wage for the great majority of manual workers.

CHAPTER 4

RELIGION AND CULTURE

> Booth attempted, especially in the third series, to correlate the social, cultural, and religious life of the poor to incomes and economic status. There was little order or system to his observations. We have divided the material into three general topics: religion, 'habits of the people', and 'institutions', the latter consisting primarily of descriptions of local clubs.

Religion

EAST AND WEST[1]

WHEN Prince Gautama passed from his palace into the world, he became suddenly impressed by the realities of disease and decay, old age and death, to which all flesh is heir. His imagination penetrated, in a single moment of inspiraton, to the heart of things, and what he found he accepted. Recognizing and submitting to suffering and sorrow as bound up with life, he patiently sought a way of escape for mankind, and found it in a revolution of the soul, through which man might put himself beyond life's passions. His doctrine was that if the outlook of the soul were changed, everything would be changed thereby. Such was his message to mankind.

Our Western way is different. Distressed by the miseries of existence, by the horrors of disease, the breakdown of old age and the pressure of death (just as he was), we appoint Royal Commissions, we form associations, we conduct inquiries, we collect evidence, we enact fresh

---

1. Third edition, *Final Volume*, pp. 38-40.

laws, we stimulate discontent and denounce wrongdoers; and the very last thing that would occur to any one of us would be to go forth into the wilderness, to spend years in hunger and patient meditation on the innermost spiritual structure of a woeful world, and seek in this way solace for the troubles of mankind. The Eastern method is to transfer the struggle of life from the arena of the world to that of the soul, and quell it there; the Western, to drown the tumult of the soul in action. Their ideal is a passionless nirvana of individual extinction, while we accept life as an incessant struggle with evil, a combat which, even if success seems hopeless, must still be maintained.

What religion has to offer in the West as in the East, is a revolution of the soul; a change within, which will itself change everything; but which, instead of ending life's activities, renders them, with the heightening of conscience, even more acute and perhaps more complicated. There arises contest within contest; with ourselves and with our passions; with others and with their passions, and each effort made has its fore-runner and its sequel. Like wrestlers we strive wrist to wrist before the decisive throw. And no throw is final. Fresh adversaries spring up. Our emotions and passions prove the dragon's teeth of the fable. The very idea of repose is banished to another life. In this one we do not desire it.

THE ROMAN CATHOLICS[2]

THERE are six Catholic mission churches in this part of London, one of which is, indeed, situated in Limehouse, a little to the east of the limits laid down, but the district it serves includes the notorious London Street in Ratcliff, and it shares with the other churches on the river front the religious care of the rough Irish who work at the

2. Third edition, third series, Vol. II, pp. 38-42.

docks and wharves. The ministrations of these churches touch the poorest, and to give freely in charity is the rule of their religion, yet it is these poor people whose contributions support the church. A penny is paid on Sunday by those who attend Mass, which it is the duty of all to do. The priests make it their business to look up such as fail in this duty, and all have the opportunity given them of subscribing to the schools and other church expenses. Except the priests' stipends, which are of the smallest, the charges are mainly borne by the congregation. At the Limehouse mission there is an organized school collection from house to house every Sunday afternoon. Six men undertake this, having each a district, and the priest accompanies each in turn to stir up any who are backward.

The church of ss. Mary and Michael in Commercial Road was the original mission church in East London, and the population still left to it includes eight or nine thousand Catholics. The schools are endowed, but the church is supported by its people, who are mostly poor Irish labourers. This church has a powerful organization. The regular paid staff consists of five priests, but there are generally two young priests in addition who come here to learn their work; and a large number of Sisters undertake teaching, nursing and visiting. These belong to two convents. There is also a small settlement of ladies from the West End who come here to work. At these churches 10 o'clock Mass is the most crowded, and is attended by the poorest people. The priests complain of irregularity at Mass and of indifference to religious duties, but no one passing from Protestant churches to theirs would take that view. They have a higher standard. Moreover, the attendance is unmistakeably due to genuine religious feeling and a belief in the divine authority of the Church and its priesthood. Of support purchased by ordinary material benefits there is no trace. The children come to the schools and the schools are full, although the attendance leaves, it is said, something to be desired. 'Deplorable lack of parental authority' is referred to as the cause.

St Patrick's Roman Catholic Church in Wapping serves a similar class of people. The priest in charge has been there for many years, and reports an increase of crowding and poverty due to the pressure of the Jews, who are driving poor Christians out of St George's. He has a Roman Catholic population of 2,500; all are Irish or of Irish descent, with the exception of a small colony of Italians who work at Gatti's ice wharf. There are nearly six hundred children on the school register, but otherwise, save a small club for girls, nothing is done outside of the services and sacraments of the Church. The church has no money to spend, being poor and heavily in debt for its schools. It has no visitors to work for it, but the priest knows all his people, and is able to visit them himself, living, as they do, within so small an area. Nothing is given. The contrast in this respect with St Peter's, their High Church neighbour, is great.

The fourth of these riverside churches is that of the English Martyrs in Great Prescott Street. It is architecturally a rather remarkable building, and offers also the attraction of beautiful music. The bulk of the Catholic population still are poor dock labourers, but there are also tailors and other tradesmen; and here a branch of the Catholic Social Union, with the Dowager Duchess of Newcastle at its head, works in cooperation with the priests. The church itself 'gives nothing' and claims the greater influence thereby, but it is not likely that this can be said of the members of the Social Union. Against them complaints of religious bribery are made.

The priests all refer to the difficulty experienced in retaining the young men. Girls' clubs are successful, but boys after school age cannot be controlled and are apt to drift into indifference. They may, perhaps, be picked up again at marriage, but if a man marries a Protestant he may be entirely lost. Hence the great danger, from the

Catholic point of view, of mixed marriages, which otherwise might rather tend to strengthen the Church. The poor Irish, who form the bulk of the Catholic population, are careless, but are naturally devout. They are rough-people are greatly helped by their connection with the police at times, and they drink a good deal. It is not possible to trace any persistent improvement, either moral or material, in their lives, and if a religion which does not secure improvement fails, then success cannot be claimed for these churches. But, from day to day, these poor people are greatly helped by their connexion with the Church; restrained, controlled and blessed in their rough lives by its care.

The German Catholics have a special church in Union Street, near St Mary's, Whitechapel, which is filled every Sunday morning and evening with a very devout congregation, drawn largely from the working classes. The remarkable feature of this church is the bachelors' club which is connected with it, or with which it is connected, for the backbone of the mission seems to be the club. The full members are all unmarried men, mostly young. A married man only be an honorary member; a rule made to avoid all chance of petticoat government. The club, which adjoins the church, is open every evening, but its activities are greatest on Sunday. On that day it opens at 10 a.m., closing at 11 o'clock for Mass; and after the service the members enjoy a glass of Munich beer. Then some dine at the club, but the greater part go home. At 4 o'clock, when the priest gives a short address to the members, the club is again full, and amusements, billiards, etc., fill the time till 7, when the club again closes for the evening service. Afterwards ladies are admitted. The entertainments of the club include lectures, concerts, and dramatic performances. The priest is its president. Perfect order is maintained. It is not a solitary institution, but to be found, we are told, wherever there are many German Catholics. More than a thousand of such clubs exist in various parts of the globe, affiliated in such fashion that to be a member of one is to be welcome at any other, wherever it may be. Amongst the members there is, no doubt, something of that mixture of class which seems to be always practicable under Catholicism.

There is also a church of this faith to serve the Irish Colony of Mile End Old Town. The Irish there are giving place to Jews, but the church still gathers a considerable congregation.

On the whole, among the various religious elements of this district, Roman Catholicism plays an important and satisfactory part. It makes no attempt at proselytizing. 'We have', said one of the priests, 'more than enough to do in looking after our own people.'

MIDDLE-CLASS RELIGIOUS DEVELOPMENT[3]

THE northern part of the district,[4] from Highgate to Stamford Hill and from Holloway to Balls Pond and Canonbury, provides the best example of London middle-class life and of the religious and social influences to which it is subject. Amongst this population Nonconformity is strong, and amongst Nonconformists the Congregational Church is the most typical religious organization. It will be seen as we go on, that each leading sect seems to have its special milieu. The Congregationalist, Baptist, and Wesleyan each in turn come to the front, as do also the various divisions of the Church of England, and, hardly less than the Scotch Presbyterians or the Roman Catholics, find a natural place in meeting the special wants of special sections of the people. In addition, beyond making provision for the spiritual needs of its people, each sect attacks, after its own fashion, the general problems of poverty and spiritual destitution presented by this or that district.

3. Third edition, third series, Vol. I, pp. 119–32.
4. North London. – EDS.

In their working methods the sects frequently take hints from each other, and under similar circumstances often adopt similar courses. The Church of England is by no means entirely outside of this form of concurrent action. In North London her methods become more Congregationalist in character; her adherents being won and held very much as in the Free Churches, while her efforts among the poor, falling in with the facts of the situation and the character of the surrounding population, tend to concentrate in special mission districts.

These methods seem exactly to suit the middle-class North Londoner, and while there is in them much that is out of harmony with the parochial system of a national Church, and not quite in keeping even with the Wesleyan organization or with the character of the ideals and methods of the Baptist community, there is nothing in them that is other than quite natural to the Congregationalists.

With them the pulpit is practically the centre round which everything turns. Each church is self-governed and owes no outside allegiance. There is a working organization of deacons for financial and disciplinary purposes, and an inner circle of members forms the Church. The members choose their pastor, but are not necessarily united with any strictness in the bond of a common doctrine. The congregation, those who are reached by the voice of the pastor, are a larger body, including many who, for one reason or another, remain outside, or perhaps because of their youth, have not yet taken up membership; but the whole assembly, members and non-members alike, is simply the spontaneous expression of a Christian sentiment seeking leadership, mutual support, exercise, discipline, and work. On the one hand there are the Church members with whom all ultimate power lies, and on the other stands the man chosen by them as pastor, with whom rests the absolute leadership of all those who gather round him.

Of such great Congregational pulpit centres there are ten in this district, as well as two belonging to the English Presbyterian body, working on almost exactly similar lines, and there are four more in the northern portion of Hackney. There are also some others of a smaller kind. The sixteen large churches accommodate about twenty thousand worshippers, and are well filled, and in some cases crowded, both morning and evening on Sunday. They provide for the congregations a host of interests, religious and otherwise, throughout the week. Nearly all of them have established a mission church, and several have two, or even three, of such enterprises, planted not necessarily in their own immediate neighbourhood, but wherever the need seems greatest.

Their congregations are almost entirely of the middle class. There are not many wealthy members; and very few who keep carriages; but on the other hand of what are called the 'poor', there are none save at the mission churches, and excepting a few old members who have seen better days and whose needs are cared for out of the Communion offerings. Nor are there any considerable number of the regular working classes, who are for the most part untouched either by the churches themselves or by their missions. But within the wide limits of the 'middle class' they have their range; a range to be found usually in each congregation, but noticeable also in a general way between one congregation and another. Money is not lacking. These congregations pay their pastors liberally. The church buildings are kept in perfect order and the missions are well supported. When new buildings are required a special effort is made, and bazaars are a common expedient for raising money. They do not beg from outsiders, nor do they borrow systematically. With them a debt is something that has to be paid. Though not people of large incomes they are for the most part prosperous.

With them prosperity and religion go hand in hand.

This they readily recognize, thanking God for His good gifts, and praying that they may use them rightly for their own advantage and that of others. There is no trace of sourness or severity in their theories of life. Pleasure is not tabooed. The young are trusted and encouraged. Happiness is directly aimed at, but is associated with the performance of duty: duty to themselves, and to each other, and in various ways to the world around. Their pastors preach this ideal and boldly act up to it. They use their churches without hesitation for any purpose which is not actually irreligious. Concerts, popular lectures, debates on social or political questions; all find a place. Even on Sunday, in special services, they do not hesitate to combine the mundane with the spiritual. All may be done to the glory of God; but the immediate object is the brightening and deepening and widening of human lives. It is not by individual units according to High Church methods, nor as a concourse of strangers as with the large Evangelical Mission services, but in the main as families that their people are handled and held. Such work may be thought to fail, if the saving of souls by the preaching of Christ be the ultimate aim, but it is undoubtedly a wholesome and lasting influence for good...

The work of the Baptists in this district differs not very much from that of the Congregationalists. They draw their adherents from practically the same classes, but with a larger admixture of working men. They, too, have in most cases their literary societies and clubs for cricket, football, cycling, and lawn tennis, but there is a more definitely religious tone about all they do. On the other hand, they undertake less missionary work. Of their churches there are about ten in the part of the North London district we are now describing, with seating room for as many thousand, but not more than half filled at any ordinary service.

The Wesleyans have also about ten churches in this

district. They are linked in the usual circuits, and the poorer churches become practically missions run by the richer. They all seem rather to lack life, and at any rate present no especially noteworthy features. They have no share in the remarkable missionary enterprise that has been developed by this body in recent years, of which, more particularly in Central and Eastern London, I shall have occasion to speak later.

In this district there is nothing special to be said of the strict Baptists or of the minor Methodist Churches. The Brethren have a large church in Upper Clapton, with several off-shoots beyond the London boundary in Wood Green, Tottenham, and Walthamstow. They are a body of very earnest and sincere Christians. The Agapemonites have a church near Clapton Common, noticeable for the elaborate symbolic carved stonework of the building, while near Highbury Station is found the solitary example of a congregation of the Sandemanians, split into two sections. In the same district the Swedenborgians undertake an active propaganda amongst those who are dissatisfied with the teachings of other sects. They have lectures and class meetings as well as Sunday and weekday services, and social gatherings amongst their own congregation with occasional concerts and dances, got up by the young people, 'who are given free scope in this matter, it being desired to make the church in every way attractive to them'. In fact this church falls in completely with the *genius loci*.

The Unitarians also have an interesting and successful organization, which deserves notice. The church is on Highgate Hill, and is a considerable centre of social and educational work. The most remarkable feature in their organization is a reading-room used by all classes, with a library of seven thousand volumes. Of the fifteen hundred families who take out books only eleven are Unitarians. 'Our people', it was explained, 'have books at home.' The reading-room is crowded. It is open nightly, except Monday and Thursday, when the room (which is also the school-room) is needed for other purposes. No charge is made, and small indeed are the sums that are voluntarily placed in the box. Yet its success is due to the fact that neither trouble nor money is spared. The leading magazines, religious periodicals of all shades of opinion (a line of literature which no free library supplies), ladies' papers, literary papers, and illustrated journals, as well as the daily press, all find a place. And the range of printed matter offered is reflected in the persons using the place, who are of every class. The library, too, is kept well supplied with important new books; their cost being defrayed by the fines imposed when books are kept too long – a very perfect instance of indirect taxation. Otherwise the use of the library is a gift, freely made and, it would seem, freely received. Besides the reading-room and library there is, connected with this church, a social institute, with a membership of about two hundred, of whom one-fourth are their own people, and lantern lectures, concerts, etc., are given. There are also University Extension lectures, 'only second to those at Gresham College for numbers', for which text-books are furnished by the library, and the regular educational classes include drawing, painting, and music. In addition to all this there is, as usual, a Sunday school and Band of Hope. More classrooms are projected; and, meanwhile, the Sunday school overflows into the church.

The Roman Catholics have on Highgate Hill a great propagandist establishment called the Retreat of St Joseph, with a domed church that is almost a cathedral. It is the headquarters of the Passionist Fathers. They undertake parochial duties over a large district lying mostly outside of London, but their main work, and the main object for which the order was established in England, is that of conversion. Like the Swedenborgians, they seek those who are not satisfied with the religion they have rather than those who have none. In this matter it is said they have been very successful, and that more than half their regular congregation are converts, while those who fill the church in the evening, many of whom are drawn by the fame of its music, are to a large extent non-Catholics. They attract the middle and upper middle class. Such as there are of lower middle and working class, or of the poor, who attend, would be, as a rule, Catholics by birth. It is a favourite church, and for its sake Catholics come to live in the neighbourhood.

The total number of Roman Catholics in North London is not large and they are dispersed over the entire area. Two of their churches in Hackney I have passed without mention, together with the Retreat of St Scholastica (which does no propagandist work), and besides that belonging to the Passionist Fathers there are three churches in the district we are now dealing with, but none of them are of any importance. They shepherd their scattered flocks as well as they can and take a modest part in the conversion of England.

The church of England under middle-class auspices is active and successful.

Out of thirty-five parish churches which may be counted in the northern part of the district, there are eleven which, whether nominally High or Low, do actually in their efforts to attract, to hold, and to employ their people, follow pretty closely the methods of the Congregationalists, and adopt similar plans for fulfilling their duty to the neighbouring poor. The others are made up of eight old-fashioned Evangelical churches, eight again in which the ritual is High, and eight of which the organization is strictly and successfully parochial. All, or nearly all, have good congregations drawn almost entirely from the middle classes. They pay their way, being many of them without endowment.

The churches of each type are to be found together in groups, suggesting some relation to the character of the population they serve. Of those of Congregationalist type, the best example is All Saints', Upper Holloway. The attendance here is strictly middle class, the church always full and even crammed, and the proportion of men who come large. 'You can always' (the vicar claims) 'get men if you cater for them.' 'You must do away with silly hymns and with platitudes from the pulpit.' There is a popular service once a month, when some question of social, political, or intellectual interest is dealt with; and congregational life is fostered by a literary and debating society, by tennis and recreation clubs, and soirées. In one of his addresses, the vicar says.

I never tire of telling you, for it is what I believe with my whole heart, that everything that is done for the benefit of our fellows, whether it be what men call secular or religious, may be for the glory of God. All work that tends to the common good is work for the King. All work is Divine work if it be for the comfort, the well-being, the educating, the helping, and the uplifting of the race.

Besides the church itself there is a mission church, together with two mission-halls and two club-rooms, and of his congregation 220 are counted as doing work of some kind for the church. So, too, St James's, Holloway, is a great middle-class preaching centre. The poor never come, but have their special services (which they do not attend) at the mission building. It is the same with others. Of one of the clergy it is critically said, 'He makes his work too much a business, run for success'; but the success is achieved and the results are good.

In these cases personalities are strongly marked. This is shown in our notes. It can be observed in the description given of the men. Pulpit appearance is of great importance. For example, we read: 'Fine head and great shock of hair'; 'Plain, bright, humorous face'; 'Frank, almost jovial tone'; 'Good presence, muscular, attractive'; 'Massive, grey-haired man'; and with more than one a non-clerical appearance is mentioned. Or as to the character of the eloquence, 'Emotional, succeeds as a preacher', is said of one. 'Easy capacity, impressive', of another. Though frequently said of Nonconformist ministers, it is not often that such things as these are considered and come to be reported of the clergy of the Church of England.

The methods adopted are not always approved by the more old-fashioned. One of these clergy, an old man, whose own preaching has ceased to attract the worshippers who formerly filled his beautiful church, speaks with genuine detestation of the combination of 'attractions' with religion: 'A *missa cantata* and a seven-minute sermon'. Worse still in his eyes is the use of such auxiliaries as 'cards, smoking, dancing, dramatic performances, and entertainments of all kinds', culminating in the abomination of 'taking a Bible-class to the theatre for a treat'. 'You may get people to church, but not by these means will they be made Christians.' It is no doubt a somewhat jaundiced view, but serves well to indicate, by the channel of adverse criticism, what seems to me the peculiar character of this phase of happy, successful, middle-class religious development...

Of the regular working class in this district we hear little. One or two Nonconformist churches claim to have won their support to some extent; but with it seem to have lost that of the class above. It is very difficult to combine the two. Almost the only successful attempt is found in the parish of St Peter's, Highgate Hill, of which Mr Osborne is vicar. This was the scene of Mr Ditchfield's first men's services, which have been maintained by his successors. There is in the same parish a primitive Methodist congregation, composed almost entirely of working men, with a homely man of the people for their minister. Between this body and the church very friendly relations are maintained. A few others there are, not particularly successful, in which religion has largely given way to political propaganda; but on the whole the regular working classes are untouched.

The failure of the religious side of the work of all these churches and chapels amongst the poor is also admitted on all hands, great though the efforts are, and much is said of the demoralizing results of the ways in which charitable relief is given, and of competition in treats and entertainments. 'The poor remain outside, but come for help'; 'they come in hope of charitable relief'. 'We cannot visit without giving. The mission is the recognized channel for the charity of the well-to-do, and relief is expected.' 'The poor', says one, 'are great cadgers and quite indifferent to religion, unless wanting something. They are not hostile, they merely "can't be bothered".' The overlapping of 'every conceivable religious influence' is spoken of. Some abandon the attempt. 'We have never seen an opportunity to start a mission without interfering with some already at work', says one. In another case there is no mothers' meeting, and, it is added, 'these institutions are abused'. They are often spoken of as 'miserable work'; and the mothers as 'a hardened set', managing to attend two or three meetings. Finally a Scotch Presbyterian minister, one of the wisest, is altogether sceptical of the results of the free provision of mission services. 'The people', he thinks, 'should take the burden on themselves.'

The work attempted, of which the results are so unsatisfactory and disheartening, extends in some cases to the southern portion of the district, but, for the most part, the poor who are its object live in the poor parts of the north. The southern parishes have difficulties of their own.

EVANGELICAL WORK AND METHODS[5]

ROUGHLY speaking, the North London Railway forms the dividing line between North and South, as here

5. Third edition, third series, Vol. I, pp. 133–6.

adopted. On the border line there are five parishes – St Jude, St Paul, St Mary Magdalene, St Clement, and St Matthias, Barnsbury. The two last-named I have included in the southern portion of the district, in which I count eighteen parishes. Of these fourteen are Evangelical and three are High Church, while one, which is neither High nor Low, assumes successfully a simply parochial position. Of the fourteen Evangelical churches eleven are practically empty and for the most part inactive. Of the three that are fairly successful, two, St Mary and St Stephen, lie near together, a little to the north of most of this dead district; and the third, St Peter, by the canal, only succeeds, if it is to be counted success, by the employment of very sensational methods; while the incumbent of one of the other parishes near, himself a very vigorous man, described his parish as perfectly dead: 'the place an iceberg; the people as hard as nails': 'officers, choir, and congregation could all have got into one omnibus'. In like manner, of the three High churches two are practically empty, while the one that is fairly filled relies on an eclectic congregation drawn from outside the parish. The Church of England is here at a low ebb. Its only successful work is with the children. Many of the elementary day-schools belong to the churches and all of them have large Sunday-schools.

The generally Evangelical character of these churches is traced to the facts that the patronage is largely in the hands of the vicar of Islington, and that this living is itself in the hands of an Evangelical Trust, the members of which are renewed by co-optation. But except in so far as change might bring some more life, and variety some healthy rivalry, there is little real ground for the natural assumption that the churches fail because they preach Evangelical doctrine. The failure is mainly due to the class of residents. The middle class has gone, replaced by a non-churchgoing working class, and the poor are no more easy to deal with here than elsewhere.

The Nonconformists are not a whit more successful than the Church. They, too, maintain large Sunday-schools, but their regular chapels are all empty, and the result of their mission work is small. Several of the chapels, that prospered here 'while the shopkeepers still lived over their shops' (i.e. before the middle class left) have been entirely closed. Their place is taken by special missions, connected, in most cases, with an active church elsewhere. With these missions the regular working class will have nothing to do. The poor and the degraded are sought, and for them 'a great deal is done with small results.' We hear of kind-hearted ladies, without discretion, constantly imposed upon. And there are mutual recriminations. One of the clergy complains of those who corrupt the people with teas, and another, the numbers of whose congregation are sustained in the same way, speaks of Mildmay Deaconesses as 'overdoing their bribery'. The poor 'will only go where they are helped', and that the religious agencies have practically no influence upon them is confirmed by many.

The minister of a chapel belonging to the Methodist New Connexion, whose own little congregation consists of decent and prosperous working-class people, not two of whom he says could 'give half a sovereign without thinking very carefully about it', undertook, with the assistance of his workers, to visit from house to house among the working-class people of the neighbourhood. He reports that they were very well received. The people like to be called on, 'not because they hope to get something by it, but because they like to know that somebody cares about their welfare'. They, however, will not put themselves out in the least to come to church, but 'spend their Sunday lazily'. Pure indifference is the characteristic; and nowhere else, neither among the colliers of Stafford nor the dockers of Hull, has he found its equal.

Visiting was also extensively tried in this locality by a Congregational minister, who, succeeding to an almost dead cause, believes that the church is to be saved by this method. He and his helpers visited every house and tenement within a quarter-mile radius, with the result of raising the congregation from twenty-four to fifty-two in the morning, and from fifty-two to one hundred and fourteen in the evening.

The Free Methodists, too, have a church, now worked as the 'King's Cross Mission', which to some extent touches the working class. The minister and his wife have devoted themselves body and soul to the work. They were determined to fill the church on week-days as well as Sundays, and found good concerts the most successful means of doing this. They give secular music, but open with prayer; and in the same spirit they combine pastoral visiting with the distribution of cheap and good literature. The old congregation had all gone, and in these ways they sought and have found a new one. But the work is not self-supporting and tends to be less so, and to become more and more a mission to the poor, which the working class will then surely avoid. Besides good music and cheap literature, it now offers cheap food. Penny tickets representing a pennyworth of food are freely distributed, and the requisite funds are supplied from outside by the Free Methodist Connection.

Thus is the seemingly hopeless task of Evangelizing the masses shared between the Church and the Nonconformists. The methods employed are usually the same in every case. The mothers' meeting and its adjuncts; the Sunday-school and all that goes with it; these form the staple work of every mission, whatever the denomination, and there is a good deal of overlapping; for where the poor are, there the missions are crowded together. We meet here the first specimen of an independent 'Medical Mission', though there are branches of this work connected with several of the larger Missions in East London. Those who seek medical advice have first to sit through a half-hour's religious service. They make no objection to this. It is very kindly meant and is doubtless better than sitting in sadness and silence as they might have to do anywhere else, but I conceive it to be absolutely futile as a means of 'spreading the Gospel'.

THE SALVATION ARMY[6]

THE Salvation Army, originated in the East of London in 1865, claims (Christmas 1888) to have 7,107 officers, 2,587 corps, and 653 outposts, established in 33 countries or colonies; and so rapid is its growth, that 1,423 officers and 325 corps have been added in the past twelve months. Of this grand total a full proportion are situated in our district, where they have services and marches every week. In their slum work and in the provision of 'food and shelter for the homeless and starving poor' the needs of East London are specially considered, and in East London is to be found one of the homes established by the Army in connection with their rescue work. Of the slum officers it is said that 'they live amongst the people in the darkest and most wretched courts and alleys. They nurse the sick, care for the dying, visit the lodging-houses, hold meetings continually, and by their self-sacrificing lives win hundreds of poor outcasts for Christ.'

No one who has attended the services, studied the faces, and listened to the spoken words, can doubt the earnest and genuine character of the enthusiasm which finds in them its expression. The Army claims to be, and is, 'a force of converted men and women, who intend to make all men yield or at least listen to the claims of God to their love and service'. Its members hold in single faith, and with a very passionate conviction, what are known as the truths of Christianity, and desire that all men should be forced to hear of Salvation. They carry on their flag the motto 'Blood and Fire', which is explained to mean

6. First edition, Vol. I, pp. 124–7.

'the precious Blood of Christ's atonement by which only we are saved, and the Holy Spirit who sanctifies, energizes, and comforts the true soldiers of God'. It is pointed out that the doctrines they preach are 'just those which are deemed essential by all orthodox people of God. Utter ruin through the fall; Salvation *alone* from first to last, through the atonement of Christ by the Holy Spirit; the Great Day of Judgement, with its reward of Heaven for ever for the righteous, and Hell for ever for the wicked.' And they add to this a belief that 'it is possible for God to create in man a clean heart', granting him thus a sort of present and earthly Salvation. To these doctrines and principles the orthodox can have no objection. Those who give an objective value at all to the 'truths of Christianity', can hardly find fault with the very vivid language which is only a consequence of very vivid belief. Nor will those who seek mental peace in every shade of subjective value which can be attached to the same ideas, recognize anything unfavourable to the Salvation Army in the simplicity with which the orthodox doctrines are expressed. So far the Army occupies a very strong position. Justified as to its faith, is it also justified by its work?

If the student of these matters turns his eyes from those conducting the service to those for whom it is conducted, he sees for the most part blank indifference. Some may 'come to scoff and stay to pray', but scoffers are in truth more hopeful than those – and they are the great bulk of every audience of which I have ever made one – who look in to see what is going on; enjoying the hymns perhaps, but taking the whole service as a diversion. I have said that I do not think the people of East London irreligious in spirit, and also that doctrinal discussion is almost a passion with them; but I do not think the Salvation Army supplies what they want in either one direction or the other. The design of the Army to 'make all men yield, or at least listen', will be disappointed in East London. On the other hand, they will find recruits there, as everywhere else in England, to swell the comparatively small band of men and women who form the actual Army of General Booth, and who may find their own salvation while seeking vainly to bring salvation to others. Not by this road (if I am right) will religion be brought to the mass of the English people.

In rescue work I should suppose that the methods pursued would touch many, but I should need better evidence than any I have seen to convince me that of those touched many would be permanently affected by the heightened emotions and excitement which are so unsparingly used. On the other hand, something more than their own salvation must result from lives of devotion such as are in truth led by these modern soldiers of the cross.

The ultimate results of providing food and shelter at uncommercial prices can hardly be other than evil, but even this is mitigated by the evident honesty of the effort and the naïve desire shown to make it as little demoralizing as possible. Much of the same sort of thing is being done broadcast amongst the poor of the East End by many agencies; and the more of it, the more solid and sodden will the poverty become with which we have to deal.

Habits of the People[7]

MARRIAGE AND MORALITY

During the course of my inquiry into 'religious influences', which occupied the years 1897–1900, many points of interest regarding the habits of the people were noted, which, even if of small importance in themselves, and providing no complete account, have yet seemed to me worthy of collection, and may serve to reflect some light

---

7. Third edition, *Final Volume*, pp. 41–91.

on the subjects treated in the preceding volumes. I shall begin by quoting remarks on various phases of home life, and trust to be able to indicate with sufficient clearness the section of the people referred to and, when needed, the character of the authority.

Legal marriage is the general rule, even among the roughest class, at any rate at the outset in life; but later, among those who come together in maturer years, non-legalized cohabitation is far from uncommon, and this irregular relationship is commented upon not always to its disadvantage. It is even said of rough labourers that they behave best if not married to the women with whom they live. 'The difficulty' (said one of the clergy) 'is that these people manage to live together fairly peaceably so long as they are not married, but if they marry it always seems to lead to blows and rows.' They do not trust each other sufficiently to marry. A missionary mentioned the case of an old couple, whose real relationship transpired when the man was ill, who had lived together unmarried for forty years. 'He would have married me again and again' (said the woman) 'but I never could see the good of it.' On the other side it is remarked that 'marriage lines' are valued by some of the less independent poor, for the sake of the charitable relief which the respectability thus vouched for helps them to secure.

In many cases, too, a legal union is impossible, owing to a prior marriage of one or both parties. Wife desertion is described as common, and it follows naturally that the men and women pair off again, when 'as a rule, the parties are faithful to each other'. Such re-arrangements constitute in effect a form of divorce without the assistance of the Court. Many widows also drift into a similar equivocal position, either with a lodger or by accepting the position of looking after a man's house and his children.

Whether the couples are or are not married, their homes are often neglected. Of the wives it is complained that 'instead of cooking, women stand gossiping all the morning and then send out to the ham and beef shop'. 'Many are sluggards, and their unpunctuality causes quarrelling', says one witness, and adds, 'It is not surprising that they come in for blows sometimes, with their lazy, drunken habits.' In other cases it is the man who is lazy, idle, and good for nothing, content to live on the woman's earnings.

But if the family tie is not strong, neither is it exclusive. However they may have been begotten, the children are almost equally accepted as sent by Heaven, and adoption is common. There are no doubt terrible cases of neglect and cruelty, but on the whole kindness and affection reign, though it may be careless kindness and ill-regulated affection. But it is not surprising that there should be little parental control. 'The father renounces, and the mother acts capriciously.' There is often a complete absence of discipline, due, perhaps, to the absence of any accepted principle of management, the children, it is said, being sometimes 'bribed to do today what they may be beaten for doing tomorrow'. The influence of the Society for the Prevention of Cruelty to Children is undoubtedly salutary as a check on neglect and cruelty, though it may occasionally react harmfully on the attitude of parents when children threaten to appeal to it, as we are told they sometimes do. On the whole, however, the efforts, both direct and indirect, of this society, are spoken of as highly beneficial.

'The great loss of the last twenty years' is asserted to be 'the weakening of the family ties between parents and children. Children don't look after their old people according to their means. The fault lies in the fact that the tie is broken so early. As soon as a boy earns ten shillings a week he can obtain board and lodging in some family other than his own, and he goes away because he has in this way greater liberty.' Still the influence of the home is very great: 'A bad boy may come from a good home, but wherever you find a superior kind of boy you know his home must be good.'

The growing independence on the part of children is frequently spoken of. At bottom it springs from the comparative ease with which they secure employment, and this has its good as well as its bad side.

Financial independence and freedom from parental restraint bring about an early escape from the discomforts of home. As boys and girls, and as young men and young women, the sexes meet and keep company together. About this there is little that is vicious, and there is even a good deal of virtuous restraint, although the rules are not strict, at any rate in the lower ranks of labour. The mischievous results of Bank Holiday outings are frequently noted in our evidence. On the whole it may be accepted as a correct opinion that 'immoral relations before marriage among the lower classes are not unusual, and are indulgently regarded. Girls of this class do not lose caste because of an illegitimate child. A young mother bringing an illegitimate child to be registered will be accompanied by two or three companions.' 'Practically no stigma attaches', when the pair are keeping company with a view to marriage. But usually marriage, 'when needed', is expected to follow, and does follow closely on the indiscretions of the young. It may, perhaps, itself be accounted one of them. To previous relations and their results, early marriages are thus, often, immediately due. With the upper classes illicit relations tend to postpone the age of marriage; it is not so with the poor.

In some cases, especially if there are no children, there may be, amongst those who commence thus loosely, regular domesticated cohabitation unaccompanied by marriage; but this is comparatively rare. More usually the natural consequences of loose relations are regarded as leading properly to marriage, and until then domestic relations do not result. If these consequences happen, marriage is recognized as the girl's right and the young man's responsibility. Family life is thus given a fair start, and worse would be thought of any who evaded this rule, than of those whose married life, after trial, proved to be a failure; and who, having parted without ceremony, by and by form new, and perhaps more permanent, though irregular ties.

A few more quotations from our evidence may be given: 'The chief cause of early marriage is the intolerable discomfort of the home in the evening; boys' and girls' clubs have the effect of postponing marriage'; so says one of the clergy. 'They begin to walk out so early and marry very young', says another, who bears witness to the sense of honour shown – to the chivalry and faithfulness. A third thinks that 'as a rule the girls are good', and that 'if they get into trouble they marry'. 'Early marriage for pressing reasons' is very commonly reported, but it is generally added that marriage was always intended, and only 'anticipated'. From rather lower districts we hear, 'marriage very early, scarcely any till obliged to'; and again, 'forced marriages almost universal: the more respectable people six months, and others just before the child is born', and a story is told of the postponement of the ceremony on the report of the doctor that there was 'no hurry for a day or two'. 'Most young men are bounced into marriage,' says a doctor, while a schoolmaster puts it that 'if the man is a decent fellow he accepts his duty of his own accord, and if he is unwilling is often worried into marriage by his own or the girl's parents'. A clergyman vouches for the information that 'it is almost always the woman who puts up the banns'.

Of a somewhat higher class we hear that 'cohabitation is exceptional and forced marriages not common, there being a strong opinion in favour of proper relationships', and I conceive that there is no surer test of divergence of standard among the working classes themselves than the way in which this question is regarded. There are those to whom a fall from virtue in a daughter or a sister is a terrible thing, hardly to be condoned; but the more usual division is between those by whom slips of this kind are spoken of freely, and although condemned, regarded almost as a matter of course, and those who pass over with as little notice as possible a subject that it is polite to ignore. On the other hand, the classes in which there is the greatest amount of this kind of licence are for the most part free from the evils of prostitution.

It is said that as regards child-bearing, preventive checks are being increasingly used. Those who would themselves think it wrong, allude to the adoption of the practice by others. This does not apply much to the poor, who in these matters are influenced by superstition of the same character as that which brings the poorest kind of women to be churched, 'because they don't want a miscarriage next time'. But the objectionable and ill-omened practice is stated to be 'filtering down'. So, too, it is not so much amongst the poor as in the artisan class that marriages take place before the registrar. The poor think it unlucky to be without the support of the Church. But among them some give expression to the view that there is much less fuss in being married at the registrar's offices, especially in the matter of dress, bridal attire being *de rigueur* at church, and from one cause or another civil marriage are on the increase.

Among the poor marriage is hardly regarded as a responsibility. A man who is out of work and in debt needs the comfort of a wife, and takes advantage of his leisure to secure one. In a general way, the better off men are, the later they marry, but no consensus of opinion can be quoted against a rather early age for working-class marriages. Boy and girl marriages are indeed strongly condemned, but of these there are not very many, and the number is decreasing. As the result of various causes, there seems to be no doubt that the age of marriage is rising. Clubs and wider interests generally are certainly exercising a good effect in this direction. At twenty-five for men, and between twenty-one and twenty-four for the other sex, marriages are to be encouraged. A Congregationalist minister describes such marriages as 'permanent moralities'.

SUNDAYS, HOLIDAYS, AND AMUSEMENTS

MANY accounts have been given us concerning life on Sunday, both in the streets and in the homes. 'The day', says one, speaking of his own poor neighbourhood,

is comparatively quiet but for the costers shouting all day long in the poor streets. The shops, with few exceptions, are shut or only partly open. In the homes the men lie abed all the morning, mend rabbit hutches and pigeon lofts in the afternoon, and go for a walk in the evening. Their objection to going to church,

this witness adds, 'is stronger than ever'. 'Those of a rather better stamp take the "kids" for a ride on the tram'; and for these and some of a rather higher class too, a picture is drawn of the man in bed with his paper on Sunday morning and his wife cooking the dinner. A deacon of a Congregational church gives the following description of the people in his neighbourhood:

They get up at nine or ten, and as he passes to his chapel he sees them sitting at breakfast half-dressed or lounging in the window reading *Lloyd's Weekly Newspaper*. After they are washed and dressed the men wait about until the public-houses open, and then stay within their doors till three o'clock, when they go home to dinner, which meanwhile the women have been preparing. At half-past twelve, as he returns from chapel after the morning service, the minister often meets women laden with baskets of provisions from the street market near by, on their way home to cook the dinner. After dinner the men, if they have drunk much, may go to bed, but the better sort take a stroll. In the evening the young people pair off for walking out, while the elders may perhaps go to a concert or Sunday League lecture.

Here is another more summary description: 'The church bell, they say, wakes them: they get up, adjourn to the public house from one to three, dine soon after three, sleep, and either go again to the public house in the evening or to the Park.' This comes from Mile End, but is echoed almost exactly from Stockwell (*vis-à-vis* on the map): 'Up at twelve to be ready for the "pubs", which open at one; dinner any time between two and four, then sleep, and then off with wife and children to hear the band on the Common.'

By way of contrast I may add the account given by a Baptist minister in South London of the church-goers' Sunday:

The evening service is best attended; families come then. In the morning the man often comes without the wife, leaving her at home to cook the dinner. Sunday dinner, the meal of the week with his people, for which all the family are gathered together, takes place between 1 and 2.30. Some children are late for Sunday-school at three because dinner lasts so long. After dinner, when the children go to school, the men sleep, though this has been broken into to some extent by the men's P.S.A.[8] meeting lately inaugurated, to which fifty to seventy come, over a hundred being on the books. [The P.S.A. is an Evangelistic service, with instrumental and vocal music, hymns, solos, and a short address.] Tea at five, and then the evening service, which all attend.

Secular amusements on Sunday are said to have increased to such an extent as to have become a nuisance to those who like a quiet rest on that day. The brakes that drive past laden with pleasure-seekers have generally each their cornet-player, and this custom has gone so far that some suburban local authorities are making by-laws to check it.

The decent occupations, interests, and pleasures encouraged, or provided, by the efforts of the 'Sunday Society' are even more directly aimed at the improvement

8. Pleasant Sunday Afternoon.

RELIGION AND CULTURE

of the uses to be made of the Sunday holiday than are the efforts of the religious bodies, and they have been rewarded with considerable success. The victory won over the narrower Sabbatarian has been attested by the success of the Society in securing the opening of public museums on Sunday afternoons. Crowded audiences of respectable non-church-going people welcome the Sunday concerts and other entertainments offered by the National Sunday League; whilst the Sunday Lecture Society's meetings are well attended, as are also the Ethical Society's lectures and concerts. The concerts given at the Albert Hall and at the Alexandra Palace draw crowds. Moreover the clubs provide Sunday amusement for some thirty or forty thousand people in winter.

In the way of Sunday pleasuring much is spent on themselves alone by the men, who leave their wives and children at home. The thoughtless selfishness and indifference of men of all classes are denounced, and the consequent lack of home life is mentioned as a blot. The clergy hold the upper classes especially responsible for sapping the foundations of religion by making Sunday a day of pleasure. 'Sunday is becoming the great holiday,' said one of them, and mentioned the stream of bicyclists, but at the same time bore witness as to his own following that 'our faithful people are very faithful, and our earnest people very earnest'.

A more agreeable and perhaps quite as true a view of the life of the people is that 'Sunday is the great day for visiting; families go off to see their relations, whilst others are receiving theirs at home.' 'In the morning they do not get up in time for church; in the evening they receive or visit their friends, and in summer go to the park or the common.' With some of a different class we hear that 'Sunday is spent in lounging about or gardening, and in the evening you hear the tinkle of the piano and the mandoline.'

Holiday-making is spoken of as 'one of the most remarkable changes in habits in the last ten years', and the statement is applicable to all classes. 'The amount saved by working men is little compared to what is spent in this way' and yet, in the opinion of this witness (a superintendent of police), 'they save more than they used to'. 'The district' (says one of the Hackney clergy) 'is almost deserted on Bank Holiday. The women go off as well as the men.' 'A great change', says another witness, 'has come over the people'; instead of 'spending so much in the public houses', they go for 'excursions of all kinds' and the result is recognized as a distinct improvement. But it is partly in connection with this that the public houses have acquired a new use, it having become customary for young men to take young women there, when out on pleasure together. The change of habit in holiday-making has thus helped to introduce a practice that was formerly never thought of – a change in fashion as regards what it is proper to do corresponding to that as regards smoking in the streets, which fifty years ago was inadmissible. This use of the public houses has been fostered by the fact that other places of refreshment are usually closed on general holidays as well as on Sundays, but there are some signs that a change is coming in this matter; tea rooms having been opened, as many of them certainly should be.

Excursions in brakes are without end. One of these noted consisted of sixteen vehicles, containing all the girls from some large works with their young men, as to whom all that the milkman, who was looking on, could say, was, 'Well, they dress better, but their manners are about the same.' The manager of another large works at which many girls are employed, said: 'It is useless to open the works on the day after Bank Holiday, or even for two days.' Very rarely does one hear a good word for the Bank Holidays. The more common view is that they are a curse, and, as already stated, the mischievous results from a sexual point of view due to a general abandonment of restraint, are frequently noted in our evidence. But the rough crush must act as a safeguard of a kind, although 'nothing', says one witness, 'can surpass the scenes of depravity and indecency' that sometimes result. From other points of view, too, there is some reason to think that their establishment was a step in a wrong direction. The religious festivals at Christmas and Easter, with perhaps one national day (which among them all we have not got), make perhaps a sufficiency of fixed points. Beyond these it would certainly be far better that each trade, or each business establishment, should arrange holidays to suit its own convenience and the seasons of its work, and this freedom might even be extended to each individual. The spirit of pleasure in London does not appear to need fostering so much as wise guidance. It is only as enforcing holidays when otherwise they might not be taken at all, that the atmosphere of a general holiday may be accounted as good.

'To keep the Sabbath holy' is worth a great effort; and for this purpose Sunday labour should cease, so far as possible, but when this high reason does not apply it seems folly to plan that all, except those whose work is such that they are over pressed to meet the needs of the holiday-makers, should take holiday on the same day. Those who cater for amusements, and the sellers of drink, are busier than ever; but other shops are closed very inconveniently, and it is said that though drink is always obtainable, food, too often, is not.

The closing of banks on these fixed days is inconvenient and quite unnecessary. The staff of every bank is arranged on a scale which allows for holiday absences.

The convergence on Saturday as a weekly half-holiday is on another footing, and though it may be abused, as in the case of men who spend half their week's wages before coming home, it more properly and more generally enables the wife to do her week's marketing in good time and still have leisure and money left for the evening's enjoyment; shops and markets in the poor districts and places of amusement everywhere being in full train of activity. With a richer class this half-holiday is valued as making 'week-end' outings possible.

The demand for amusement is not less noticeable than that for holidays, and supply follows. To 'What shall we eat, what drink, and wherewithal shall we be clothed?' must now be added the question, 'How shall we be amused?' To this an answer has to be found. Even to the police it has presented a problem. 'What', they ask, 'is to be done with young fellows? Every evening crowds of them come back from their work and loaf about the streets; they join in with whatever is forward, and are an embarrassment if there are no places of amusement for them to go to.'

And from something more than the police point of view, what can be made of it? 'It is a good thing for people to clean themselves up and go out', says a vestryman of long standing, who holds that not half enough local amusement is provided, and who declines to accept as adequate the efforts of the religious bodies in this direction. Unmistakably, taste is more critical, and, beyond this, any attempt to 'improve the occasion' is resented. 'Concerts and entertainments given by the Church are poorly attended', said a North-West London vicar, but added that if let for some benefit, when a concert of the usual music-hall type would be given, the hall was always crammed.

Passing by the ordinary mission entertainment, of which the failure is patent, and considering only professional work, there has been a great development and improvement upon the usual public house sing-song, as to the low character and bad influence of which there are not two opinions. The story of progress in this respect may be traced in many of the existing places which, from a bar parlour and a piano, to an accompaniment on which friends 'obliged with a song', have passed through every stage to that of music hall; the presiding chairman being still occasionally, and the call for drinks in almost every case, retained. But the character of the songs on the whole is better, and other things are offered: it becomes a 'variety' entertainment. The audiences are prevailingly youthful. They seek amusement and are easily pleased. No encouragement to vice can be attributed to these local music halls. The increase in the number, as well as size of these halls, has been rapid. The profits made by the proprietors have been great, and the favourite performers, being able to appear before a succession of audiences, passing rapidly with their repertoire from hall to hall, can be and are very highly remunerated. The performers also can be continually varied, for the supply of artistes is without end. The taste becomes a habit, and new halls are opened every year: soon no district will be without one. Then theatres follow. But meanwhile, and especially in poor neighbourhoods, the old-fashioned style of sing-song still continues in force.

In the central districts all places of amusement are very largely supported by the rich or by strangers visiting London. People from the outskirts come occasionally, but it is the music hall or theatre of their own neighbourhood that they frequent, and of which the influence has mainly to be considered. It is, perhaps, too much to ask that the influence of music halls and theatres should be positively and entirely good; at any rate no one claims that it is so. If it is not directly, or on the whole, evil, or if one can hope that it takes the place of something worse, a measure of improvement may be indicated. This can, I think, be claimed. It is not very much. A tendency in the direction of the drama, which is certainly an advance, may be noticed in music-hall performances, and it is to be regretted that questions arising from the separate licensing of play-houses should check the freedom of development in this direction amongst the halls. Excluding the dramatic piece or 'sketches', the production of which is hampered in this way, the attractions most usually offered are those of a low form of art or of blatant national sentiment, neither of which can be carried further without becoming worse; or of displays of physical strength and skill on the part of acrobats and gymnasts, or of performing animals; all representing, indeed, a background of patient and unwearied effort, but involving, it cannot but be supposed, not a little cruelty in the training of children and animals necessary to secure the rewards of popularity. But the 'variety' of the entertainments increases. In addition to conjuring and ventriloquism, which are old-fashioned, we have now, for instance, the cinematograph and various forms of the phonograph, and there has been much development in the forms of stage dancing.

Limitations in the form of entertainment apply less to the halls in Central London, where, for instance, beautiful and elaborate ballets are produced. These fashionable resorts have the best of everything that can be offered, and the performances, consequently, reach a perfection which silences criticism in that respect, though in some cases there may remain ground for attack on the score of encouraging vice. In these palaces of amusement even music is not neglected. The orchestra at the Alhambra is very famous, whilst those at the Empire and the Palace are also excellent. But in the minor halls, development is never in the direction of music. Strange as it may sound, anything that can rightly be called music is seldom produced at a local music hall. The only exceptions I call to mind are a performance of Lancashire bell-ringers and the vagaries of a musical clown on his violin. In this respect, the efforts of negro minstrelsy have been far superior. Perhaps music might some day find its way in through operatic sketches, if these were encouraged.

The taste for music, and for good music, in all classes, is undoubted. 'People' (says a London County Councillor) 'will not put up with any sort of music; they appreciate good music, and insist on having it.' 'They appreciate the best music you can give them', remarks the Superintendent of a Wesleyan Mission. They may not be so ready to pay for it, but they find pleasure in hearing it, will take trouble to go where it is given, and will pay a little – will pay to enter the enclosure near the band-stand, or for a reserved seat when the rest are free. Good music would seem to be amongst the things which can with safety be supplied collectively, and in this matter, as in others, the London County Council are showing the way. Voluntary effort in the same direction is exemplified by the People's Concert Society and by the choral societies and orchestras connected with many of the churches, Polytechnics and Settlements.

Over this matter Sunday becomes the bone of contention. On the one side it is said that to supply such attractions outside tends to empty the churches, or if given inside to lower the flag of religion: and on the other that the churches can, without going beyond their role, 'hold their own', and never will do more, and that it is from the delights of the public houses and the charms of the streets, and from homes that fail to delight and lack all charm, that the people are drawn to Sunday concerts or to the parks when the band plays. In confirmation of the latter view we were told at Greenwich that at the outset publicans readily set forth in their windows the bills announcing the times at which the band performances took place, but that they do so no longer. One of them (it was added) had said that his takings had been reduced £7 or £8. But we have also heard much of the increasing difficulty of holding the young people at church or Bible-class when the band is playing, and some, no doubt, are drawn from both directions.

BETTING

'You must change the people a bit before you'll stop betting; police orders won't do it'; 'Impossible to stop it without changing the character of the working man, which in twenty-one years shows no change'; 'Betting goes on, and always will'; 'What is a fine of £5 to a bookmaker? He pays it, and goes on again' – such are samples of the opinions that have reached us from many sources. But the system adopted reflects the attacks made on the practice. 'It is not largely carried on in public houses. The betting men are known to the police, and the publican might lose his licence.' Tobacconists and newsvendors act as agents on the quiet, and so do barbers (always the confidants of their customers), and a great deal is still done in the streets, especially in the dinner-hour. The bookmakers move about and seek their clients in place of their clients seeking them, and are thus less open to interference. A magistrate can only impose a fine of £5, and that is not heavy enough to deter. An occasional fine is rather an advertisement than a hindrance. 'What's the good of carrying me off?' said one man, 'you know well enough that it's not me, but my guv'nor who pays'.

In spite of all attempted interference, there is no doubt that the habit is on the increase. 'Increasing beyond what you could imagine', says one of the clergy.

All must bet. Women as well as men. Bookies stand about and meet men as they come to and from their work. The police take no notice. See the sudden life in a street after a great race has been run and the newspaper is out: note the eagerness with which the papers are read. Boys on bicycles with reams of pink paper in a cloth bag on their back, scorching through the streets, tossing bundles to little boys waiting for them at street corners. Off rush the little boys shouting at the tops of their voices, doors and factory gates open, men and boys tumble out in their eagerness to read the latest 'speshul' and mark the winner.

Every day the sporting papers have a vast circulation; they are found in every public house and every coffee-shop. They are read, and the news and the tips given are discussed before the bets are placed. 'The more money there is to spend, the more betting is done.' 'Men, women, and children are all in it.'

The Jews especially, of all classes, are great gamblers. I have in my mind the picture of a little Jew boy in a very poor street, playing pitch-and-toss all by himself, studying the laws of chance in this humble fashion.

'Betting', said a police inspector, 'is increasing out of all proportion to other forms of vice', and he did not think it would ever be stopped. He himself has had 'one man up five times already in the month, each time convicted, each time fined £5, but beginning again at once', and he knew that if he went out at that very moment he would find him booking bets. 'Gambling', say the clergy (and by this betting is chiefly meant) 'presses drink hard as the greatest evil of the day'; 'all gamble more than they drink'; 'newspapers, knowledge of arithmetic, more holidays, all encourage it'.

Gambling clubs are equally irrepressible. They are raided, and perhaps closed, but are opened again, or make a fresh start in some way. One of our informants said he had heard the proprietor of one such place, after being fined, say to his friends, on leaving the Court, that the club would be open for play as usual that evening.

I offer these few quotations for what they are worth. They fairly reflect the opinions expressed to us. But the subject needs special study, as do some of the others treated in this volume.

I will conclude this section with an account of a night visit to a gambling and dancing club:

Our conductor, formerly a workman, but now an employer of labour, champion light-weight boxer of his local club, and best known by a fancy nickname which I need not divulge, is very well thought of in his own neighbourhood, where he acts as judge or referee in most pugilistic contests; but the club to which he took us is elsewhere. After changing his work-a-day dress for frock coat, top hat, and gloves, he first picked up a friend, who is a regular member of this club, so that there might be no trouble about getting in. We proceeded by cab, and arriving at about 12.45 found the place just beginning to fill, but not many people there. Entry from the street was through a curtain into a passage, where there was a porter, then through a door into a large dancing room; piano at one end, bar at the other, seats and small tables round the sides; about eight women and several young men clerks, and a few middle-aged tradesmen there. The women were of the 'unfortunate' class, but behaving very respectably. A lady at the piano strummed waltzes and there was some dancing. An introduction to the manager – a short thick-set man, professional in the boxing line – was followed by soda and whiskey and cigarettes and talk, in which the histories of the ladies present were retailed.

Then we proceeded upstairs to the gambling-room, where we found about sixty young and middle-aged men round a table playing *chemin de fer*, and betting with one another whether the banker or punter would win. While we were there, there was never more than £6 on the table at once. No sum staked was under one shilling, or, so far as we saw, over twenty shillings. The majority of the young men were markedly Jewish. The older men might have been artisans or shopkeepers, probably both were represented. At one side of the room was the tape machine, on the information from which at race times there is a good deal of betting during the day. There was no excitement at all about the gaming, and not the slightest interest shown at our entry. No drinks were served upstairs.

DRINK

IT is to the habit of drinking and its results that the following notes refer. Questions of remedy will be touched upon later. There is, as regards these habits, a consensus of opinion which to my mind carries conviction, that while there is more drinking there is less drunkenness than formerly, and that the increase in drinking is to be laid mainly to the account of the female sex. This latter phase seems to be one of the unexpected results of the emancipation of woman. On the one hand she has become more independent of man, industrially and financially, and on the other more of a comrade than before, and in neither capacity does she feel any shame at entering a public house. As a rule, when men and women drink together, the man stands treat, but women treat each other as much, and even more than, is the case with men. Thus the social side of the consumption of alcohol is emphasized, and to this may perhaps be ascribed very largely the combination of more drinking with less drunkenness, of which almost everyone speaks. Drunkenness, on the whole, is antisocial. 'A really heavy drinker, one who soaks for ten days or a fortnight, without eating any solids, does not sit long over it as a rule, but goes home to come back when ready for more.' Women are far more sociable in this matter. 'One drunken woman in a street will set all the women in it drinking. A woman is so often talking with her neighbours; if she drinks they go with her.' Moreover, for men, 'pony glasses' have been invented to meet the case of 'come and have something', when neither side wants to drink at all, and only does so as a step in some business transaction. Among men who drink more shame is felt than used to be the case at having been drunk. 'Much more is drunk than formerly,' says one witness, speaking of some of the rough Irish, 'but there is less drunkenness, partly because the beer is lighter, but more because of a change in manners; nowadays you drink, and the more you drink the better man you are, but you must not be visibly drunk. Outward drunkenness is an offence against the manners of all classes.' The ideal is to 'carry your drink like a gentleman'. Of women it is however said, that 'they let the whole world know if they have had too much'.

Such is the position, looked at in a very broad and general way, but there are diversities of opinion affected by the point of view of the observer, as well as by the class observed, and once more I offer my readers a patchwork of quotations. They are drawn from the police, from the clergy, ministers of religion, and missionaries, from schoolmasters and others. Drinking habits and the disorderliness resulting from them could not but be continually mentioned in the course of the long walks taken in all parts of London day after day with the picked police officers who were permitted to assist us during the revision of our maps; and we had the advantage of discussing these and other cognate subjects with their divisional superiors. For the rest, I, of course, attach no names to the opinions I quote, nor do I indicate the precise locality to which they bore reference, but only when needed indicate the class.

As regards women:

Many more women are seen in public-houses; the middle-aged are the drunkards, not the young. Young people do their courting in public houses, since both sides are rather ashamed of their homes, and like to make themselves out a class above what they are. The young men treat the girls to a glass of wine. No harm comes of it. It is not till they get older that women take to gin and ale and become regular soakers.

Again: 'Girls begin when they first go out "keeping company"; neither sex become confirmed soakers before twenty-five or thirty, or with women till after marriage. The drunkards are probably married women.' Another police officer said, 'Drunkenness among women is on the increase,' but added that he had never seen a girl under fifteen drunk, and that it was never common before marriage. 'They take too much at times, but are surprised at their own state. They do not drink for drinking's sake, and very little upsets them, especially on an empty stomach. That is why so many are noisy on Saturday, when they are paid and let out early, having had no lunch. They take a nip and become hilarious in no time.' And another says: 'Factory girls drink, but it is more often the young married women and the middle-aged who indulge too much. Men drink beer; women more often spirits. Women drink more than they used to, perhaps because they earn more.'

'There are various classes of women drinkers: the factory girl who drinks once in a way, the prostitute who drinks in the course of business and very seldom gets drunk, the laundry-woman who drinks by reason of the thirsty nature of her trade, and the married woman who drinks because her husband drinks.' 'Women have lost all shame about entering a public house, and as they never drink singly, the evil spreads.' 'Public houses are more attractive than they were; ladies' saloon bars are to be seen everywhere. Publicans tell you that it is in response to a demand, but it is difficult to distinguish between cause and effect.' Such are other police opinions.

The clergy of the Church of England, Nonconformist ministers, and schoolmasters may be quoted to the same effect, though perhaps in some cases with more of a teetotal bias, or with less sense of proportion. That 'drinking has increased enormously among women' is heard again and again, and very rarely anything to mitigate this opinion, only that it is added, 'Young women do not get drunk, unless on Bank Holidays or at marriages or funerals.' 'Drink worse than ever,' we are told, 'especially amongst women'; and this it is felt is 'a funny thing in face of all the agencies'. 'Women drink to excess more than men. They take to it largely to carry them through their work.' And again: 'The women are worse than the men, but their drinking is largely due to their slavery at the washtub.' Of the same class it is said, 'Nearly all get drunk on Monday. They say "we have our fling; we like to have a little fuddle on Monday"'. And of a yet lower class we hear that they 'live on four-ale and fried fish'.

The master of a poor school speaks of the habit of

drinking among the women being very general; 'even quite respectable mothers, when they come to see him in the morning, nearly always smell of drink'. Two other masters also mention the large proportion of mothers who smell of beer when they come to see them at the schools; while a schoolmistress, 'judging from the women who come to see her, infers that nearly all have a morning dram'. 'The poorest and most destitute seem', she says, 'to look upon drink as the first necessity of life.' A Board school teacher at school in a poor neighbourhood says that the attendance is worst early in the week, while the public houses are full of women; 'the children being at home while the mothers drink'.

The increase of the habit among women still applies as we pass slightly upwards in the social scale. It is said to be 'the regular thing for women to go in and have a drink when shopping', and another witness notices the 'marked increase in the number of respectably dressed young women who drink'. They may be respectable as well as respectably dressed. One of the East End clergy told how a woman who had been talking to him on the subject said that 'when she was young no one would have dreamt of going inside a public house. But things have altered. Her son is engaged, and the girl goes with him there sometimes. In earlier years you would have put her down as not respectable, but not so now.' A member of an Anglican Sisterhood put it that 'the time had long since gone by for regarding it as a scandal that a woman should drink at the public house'. And an 'old resident', speaking of the increase of drinking among women, says: 'You cannot but see it: respectable women go into public houses without any compunction, a sort of thing never seen until late years.'

Amongst the better-to-do, also, drinking is stated to be worse than it used to be, 'especially among women'. 'Every doctor will tell you that women have acquired the habit of "nipping".' Some (said this witness) accuse grocers' licences, but he did not himself attach much importance to them. The real reason was, he said, that the women had so little to do. 'All round London are growing up suburbs of small houses whose occupants have just enough to live on comfortably. Women left at home; small ailments; immediate stimulus of drink; that is how it begins.' Another agrees that 'the habit of drinking among women is most often contracted by young wives whose husbands are away all day'. 'Shop girls who marry find the loneliness in the suburbs unbearable after shop life.' Emphasis is also laid by many on the increasing amount of secret drinking among strictly middle-class women, and the taking of morphia and other drugs, as a result, perhaps, of home troubles, and medical men are blamed for not being careful enough when they prescribe stimulants. But the most objectionable drinking is described as being found among retired men of this class who have nothing to do and pass their time in going from saloon bar to saloon bar. Thus do 'City habits lead to disaster'.

Of the increased and respectable uses made of public houses by young women we have, as our quotations show, heard much; and it may be noted that the age of limitation, the age at which liquor may be supplied to the young, agrees with their natural tastes; indeed, sweets remain in the ascendant for some years longer with most young women. Alcohol is seldom any temptation to the young, but nevertheless, the habit may be acquired and become a temptation later. It is directly on this account and indirectly on others, that legislation has been introduced to check the practice of sending children to fetch the drink required by their parents. At the time of our inquiry this subject was before the public, the Bill had not yet passed through Parliament, and the *pros* and *cons* were in everyone's mouth. The matter is now settled; we have only to see how the law works in practice; and if I reproduce some of the statements and arguments connected with it, it is mainly on account of the light they throw on the habits of the people, but partly also as concerning the whole general policy of control of the liquor trade by licence.

A parish nurse, working in the East End, said that as to drink, there is more there among women than among men. They drink beer, or rather porter, not spirits, and always in company. When once inside a public house, they stay there. For this reason she believed that if a law were passed (she was speaking in 1898) prohibiting children from fetching the dinner and supper beer, it would do distinct harm to East London. It was to her a sad thing to see children going into the public house, but she could not honestly say that it did them any harm. She had never seen a child the worse for drink. They sip the beer, but only on the general principle that they take a little of everything they are sent to fetch; and if it were milk they would take a great deal more of it. Children of the rough class fetch the beer from the public bar because they are often given a penny by some of the men there; children of the better class go into the jug and bottle entrance, get their beer, and go away at once. Sweets are given, but not as a general thing. The giving of sweets by publicans is forbidden by law, with the idea that children will fetch drink with less alacrity if this encouragement is denied them, but to set against this, a child who is sucking a sweet will certainly not sip the beer. The object of giving the sweets was to induce the child to pass other public houses in order to reach one which was liberal in this respect. Many shops adopt the same plan to secure the patronage of child messengers. It is improbable that any more drink would be sent for because of the child's willingness to go, or that any greater familiarity with the public house would result.

The principal of a Ladies' Settlement (speaking in 1899) said she had only once seen a child the worse for drink, and that was from drink that had been given to it by its parents. She had often seen them sip, especially in hot weather, but children do not care for the taste of beer. They much prefer sweets. She herself used to be rather glad than otherwise when she saw that the beer was sent for, and that the woman did not go herself. The attractiveness of the public house to the child is not inside but outside. The lights are bright, the pavement is carefully mended and smoother for marbles and other games; organs and niggers come to play and sing there; and at night there is the sight of the drunken man being chucked out or trying to get home; sometimes he is hauled off by the policeman. Children spend their money on sweets, and some say that the habit of sucking induces a craving in the palate which later is satisfied by drink. In any case, more harm is done to children by sweets than by beer.

A police superintendent (from the same district as the nurse quoted above and speaking in 1897) said:

There is not much harm in sending children to fetch beer – absolutely none in this district; the language and atmosphere is no worse in a public house that what they hear at home. Besides, it would not prevent the children frequenting the houses which they look upon as a sort of paradise. It is always to them that they are taken by their parents for a cake or sweets. They go there from babyhood upwards. To send them there to fetch a pint of beer is no demoralization for them, or the introduction to anything new and harmful. In better-class districts, where the parents do not frequent the public house, it would probably be better not to send the children. They always sip the beer they are sent to fetch;

he has noticed it scores of times, but does not think they acquire their taste for beer in this way.

To the above I may add a picture from our own notes (1899) of the dinner-hour in a poor South London quarter:

Children going in large numbers to the public house at the corner with jugs for the dinner beer; no sipping; our companion, the police sergeant, knows it is not usual to think so, but has never been able to see any harm come of it himself. One child looked as though she were sucking a sweet as she came out, but the others did not: it was constant come and go, one moment to go in and get the jug filled, and out again the next; none of the children waited to talk or play with one another, but at once hurried home.

Of the police spoken to on the subject, some had, and some had not, noticed the children sipping the beer they carried. The question is not, perhaps, of great importance. The children could not take much without being detected. To drink out of a jug at all without spilling the contents, must be difficult for a small child; and if much were lost, there would be trouble. If, however, the mere tasting of the drink be the danger it was sought to avoid, is it to be supposed that opportunities for this would not have occurred in homes where beer was being constantly drunk? But, in fact, children do not really care for it, and with open heart are quite ready to join and faithfully obey the rules of their Bands of Hope.

The question of familiarity with the public house, engendered by being constantly sent there, is more serious. Even those who think no harm comes of it, would very likely not allow their own children to go, but if legislation can do nothing in this respect for the child whose home is on the level of the public house, neither is it required for those whose homes are superior. It might therefore seem to have been a waste of good effort to pass this particular restriction, when so many of greater importance are sadly required.

If we leave the children themselves out of account, it may however be argued that if they cannot be sent, it is tantamount to reducing the facilities for procuring drink, and that less will therefore be taken. It is likely that in some instances this would be so, but we have to consider the alternatives. Instead of a young child, a boy, or more probably a girl of over sixteen, may be sent. Would that be an improvement? The presence of a child, we are told, has often a marvellous effect. 'Consider the child' is a rebuke to which, thank God, no man refuses to listen. Behaviour at the public bar is more likely to gain, than the child to suffer. But with a young girl how would this stand? And it must be remembered that she *is* allowed to take a drink, and perhaps is beginning to have a taste for it. It is no question of sipping, but of some man standing treat. That the wife should herself fetch the beer is a better alternative, but if instead of taking it at home with their meal, those who want it adjourn to the public house to drink there, this plan is surely not to be desired, and is likely to lead to more rather than less being consumed.

To return to the more general aspect of the question. Whether the people drink less or not, the police are practically agreed in saying that they are much less rowdy than formerly: 'Totally different people to what they were thirty-three years ago', said one who joined the force then; an improvement which he claims has extended also to publicans and the police themselves, of whom the latter are now an almost entirely sober body of men, while the former are much more respectable and steady, and for the most part careful as to the conduct of their houses.

The modern publican is of a totally different type to the man of twenty years ago, with his white hat and black band, and his bull-dog: the decayed prize-fighter type. The publican now is usually well educated, respectable, and a keen man of business, who can keep his own accounts in proper order, and fully realizes that it is to his interest that the law should be strictly observed in his house.

As to drink, this last witness reiterated the opinion that there had been a great decrease, if not of drinking, certainly of drunkenness, and was one of the few who asserted that the alleged increase among women was not a fact, the true way of putting it being that drink had decreased among men, but not, or at all events not in the same degree, among women. As to drunkenness he said, 'Go and look at Hampstead Heath on Bank Holiday and compare it with what it was twenty years ago, or walk in the streets on Saturday night.'

The drunkenness that occurs is not held to be so serious an evil as the impoverishment that results from the habit of drinking. A schoolmaster, whose school is in North London, speaks of the enormous amount spent, though the district is not drunken; whilst amongst our extracts from the views of the clergy we find such opinions as, 'Not much drunkenness but an appalling amount spent in drink; out of all proportion to earnings'; and, 'Amazingly thrifty in many respects and not drunkards, but spend an enormous proportion of their earnings in drink.' A similar view is expressed by two medical officers connected with the Poor Law, one of whom, an out-door superintendent, speaks of 'drink as leading to pauperism, not because of actual drunkenness, but because of the habitual spending of so large a portion of their earnings in this way. Alcoholism', he adds, 'is a disease affecting all classes, but it is not this which is the prevailing mischief, but the general drinking habit. Insurance money, payable at death, apart from the extravagance in funeral trappings, goes largely in drink, and it is surprising how quickly widows who have had £20 insurance money find their way to the relief office.' The other medical officer said that many cases came into the infirmary through drink, but it was on account of the exhaustion of means which, otherwise, would have sufficed to pay for treatment outside.

'Drink is not conspicuous,' said a London City missionary working in Mile End, 'but the people drink enough to keep them poor. A man and wife earning twenty-four shillings would spend four shillings to six shillings in this way and be temperate.' It is a common thing, we hear from others, for labourers who are seldom, if ever, drunk to spend one-fourth of their earnings in drink. A temperance man might give his wife twenty-three shillings out of twenty-five shillings, a moderate drinker twenty shillings. 'When converted they give up drink and save five shillings a week', such is the simple arithmetic of this subject. But it is also said that the more money there is to spend amongst those not accustomed to having it in their possession the more of it goes in this way. The police couple increased drink with increased wages, averring that ' a great amount of drunkenness is still a sure sign of work being plentiful. It is then that the police are also busiest.' 'There is also increase of drunkenness at each holiday season, but this does not lead to a great increase on the charge sheet because the police are lenient at these times. If a man can get home anyhow he is allowed to do it, whereas on an ordinary day he would have been run in for a certainty.' Still 'Bank Holidays are the worst thing for the police.' 'Bank Holidays are a curse', at any rate from the police point of view.

'The tipple of the labourer (and for the most part that of the artisan) is beer. The class above more often take whisky.' 'A steady artisan will drink two quart pots (or 8d.) a day.' 'If you sweat you may drink with impunity.' The following we are told is a working man's account of how men of his class get drunk: 'We have a pint of beer and then "two" of rum; then another fellow asks you to have a whisky'; a very injudicious mixture.

Upon the connection of poverty, or at any rate the poverty that seeks charitable relief, with drink, the statements are uncompromising. A Wesleyan minister, referring to claims on their relief fund, stated that in almost every application the necessity was traced ultimately to drink on the part of man or wife 'or both'. A Congregationalist says that he came to London believing that the influence of drink was much exaggerated, but has been convinced that it is at the root of all the poverty and distress with which they come into contact; with every case of distress that is relieved they always find afterwards that drink has been the cause of leakage. A Church of England vicar speaks of it as 'the great trouble; the main cause of all the poverty. In almost every application for relief there is a history of drink.' He began with a determination not to help when either parent was a drunkard, but has found this impossible. Apart from drunkenness he emphasized the fearful extravagance in drink. A lay church worker, while agreeing that though there might be no actual decrease in drinking, 'there were fewer outward signs of drunkenness in the streets', said that 'in almost every case that came under his notice for assistance there was a history of drink, not necessarily in the life of the actual applicant, but at least somewhere in the background'. And a relieving officer of an adjoining Union confirms this, saying that 'though there is less rowdiness, the general habits of drinking have not decreased', and that in his experience 'in all applications for relief, except from widows, cripples, and the aged, the ultimate, if not immediate cause of poverty is drink'.

I could multiply evidence such as this; and the great part played by drink in the genesis of poverty cannot be denied. A leading member of the Charity Organization Society, for instance, states that 'they generally find that more or less directly drink comes in as an explanation of trouble in the home, drink taking a high place in the competing attractions of life'. It is this that makes it in his view so necessary that there should be a strong impulse competing with it and with correlative weaknesses, such as idleness, and cause him to advocate extreme severity in the administration of the Poor Law and great strictness in the distribution of charity.

But I think it will be seen even from these extracts that it is not really possible to isolate drink as a cause of poverty. It plays a part, and a great part, but it is only as the accompaniment of idleness, extravagance, incompetence, or ill-health that it is fatal. 'The tendency among church workers', says one of the clergy, 'is to be much harder on drink than they used to be. Everybody who takes a drop "drinks": "Mrs Smith," says the Scripture Reader; "oh, she's a boozer", when probably the luckless body only has her dinner beer.' To trace every misfortune to drink is a device similar to the 'Who is she?' of the Eastern despot.

In an early volume I attempted to give an arithmetical expression to the place occupied by drink in connection with poverty. I will not attempt the task again, but will merely conclude by quoting from my notes a few more pregnant remarks and telling one story.

The story is that of an unmitigated case mentioned by a London City missionary:

A family with four children occupying one room – the woman, a poor, wretched, ragged creature; the man, a drunkard, earning thirty shillings a week as a dustman, and probably making forty shillings a week in all. No furniture but the frame of a bedstead, an old straw palliasse, and one sheet. The baby lay covered with a jacket. The missionary saw the man helped indoors from the public house at the corner, and within an hour his wife helped him back again.

From this lowest depth we pass with a sense of relief to the 'hard-working set of people in Bethnal Green', mentioned by one of our police guides, 'who work honestly for their living, and only get drunk on Saturday nights', or even to the big-boned men of Bermondsey, 'whose sole idea it is to bury their nose in a quart pot'. 'The trade that drinks the most' (says another of our police guides) 'is that of the French-polishers', but it is added rather sweepingly that 'the whole furniture trade keeps "Saint Monday" and "works a ghost" on Friday night to make this possible'. A third officer gives the palm in the matter of drink to the building trade. Boot and shoe makers and others are also mentioned in the same connection, and coal-porters especially, but of none of these can it be said that they are more likely than most to ask charitable assistance, or to come upon the Poor Law. Compared to those who indulge in drink, the numbers who fall into destitution are small. Can it then reasonably be said to be caused by the drink? 'Where those upon whom the tower of Siloam fell guilty above all others?'

Then some excuses are offered: 'Much drinking', the out-door medical officer of one of the Unions believes, 'is due to poor victuals and bad cooking.' The matron of an East End Nursing Association thinks that the standard of cooking and domestic economy is lower than it was, due to the preference for factory life over domestic service, and connects increase in drinking habits with increase in the discomfort of the homes. She would have these household subjects taught more widely. 'It is no use preaching against drink; men must have somewhere to go in the evening.' The headmaster of a school, also in the East End, says the same: 'With such homes as they have, men must go out at night; there can be no improvement until the homes are better. In this matter we go round in a vicious circle, for if they earn more, they are so accustomed to bad homes, that the extra money goes not to the home, but to the pub.' Another medical officer is not at all surprised that drinking habits prevail, considering the conditions under which the people live: 'They must have some solace and amusement.' To the better home life of the Jews, based on their religious ceremonial and its solemn recognition of family duties, is attributed their greater sobriety. They are not teetotalers. 'The only thing which will decrease drunkenness', says one of the clergy, 'is the increase of self-respect.' All these happen to speak of East London; but what they say is true wherever poverty and drink are found together.

It is further pointed out that 'drink which is not drunkenness is the only mental stimulus the poor have: you or I take a book, and so get into a new world and change of thought; the poor have very little of this, therefore they drink. The cure,' added this witness, who is rector of a large North London parish, 'is not to forbid drinking, which at present is a necessity to them, but by degrees to supply a different sort of stimulus. With clerks the greatest preventive of drink has been the bicycle.' Another of the Church of England clergy, speaking of women, said, 'Worry is what they suffer from, rest and hope what they want. Drunkenness dulls the sense of present evil and gives a rosiness to what is to come. That is why they drink.'

From the religious point of view it is remarked that teetotalism is apt to become a cult of its own, of a rather narrow kind, and it is added that 'those who yield to the seductions of temperance are sometimes too much bitten by the idea of saving.' But carping such as this leaves untouched the great main fact to which we have endless testimony, that 'Christian people are nearly all temperate and thrifty', and the better in every way for being so.

MINOR NOTES

THERE are some points of interest concerning the habits of the people as to which I have gathered stray items of information, and in the following pages these are given haphazard, without comment. No attempt has been made to add to or complete them by special inquiry, but as illustrations they may be found suggestive.

1. MONEY MATTERS

(a) *Pawnbrokers.* It is, we are told, no good for an outsider to enter this trade. It is a 'father to son' business, needing special knowledge of the value of the things pledged, and still more of the people pledging them, their habits, and their motives. There are grades of pawnbrokers' shops as there are of other shops, but the grade depends more directly on the article to be pledged than on the class of the customer. That is, a poor man would not hesitate to enter an establishment in a principal street if he had anything of recognized value to dispose of, but if he has only clothes to 'put away' he goes to a shop where he is known, because he will get more there than elsewhere. Thus it is that local knowledge is of value. If the tradesman knows his customer, and knows that the things pledged are almost sure to be taken out again on Saturday for Sunday's use, he can afford to advance an extra sixpence. On such in and out business, recurring at short intervals, he makes his largest profit. Those who are ashamed of the transaction, and do not wish to be recognized, generally go to some place at a distance from where they live. Monday and Tuesday are the days on which most things are pledged, Wednesday and Thursday being quieter, but on Friday there is a slight increase again, due to those who find that they cannot last out the week without this resource.

Pawnbrokers, all of whom are licensed and most of whom are respectable tradesmen, are not receivers of goods stolen in their own district; nor 'receivers' at all in the technical sense of the word, though their shops may be used extensively for turning into cash things stolen some way off and not easily traced. Each district has its own 'fences', or professional receivers of stolen goods, and these are well known to all the thieves, so that when any stolen article is at all easily traceable it would go to the 'fence', and only if not traceable would it be likely to come to the pawnshop.

(b) *Money-lending*. The habit of pawning and the habit of borrowing are cognate difficulties. The facilities for borrowing are numberless, and the practice of money-lending prevails in all poor districts; in the poorest the most – 'in the shape of the man who will "sub" in the public house, in the man who will give "tick", and in every street and court in the person of some one who is prepared to make advances.' Even the church loan club may be abused by those who, taking advantage of the comparatively low rate of interest charged by it, can borrow to lend again in what may be called 'the open market'. 'Every street has its lender, often a woman', is reported from one very poor quarter; while from another we hear that 'there are women who make a trade of it, and who in order to increase their business tempt women, generally younger than themselves, first to drink, and then to borrow'. There is no legal protection to the lender; terrorism is relied on. 'Loaning is a curse.' 'The people, especially the costermongers, are in the grip of the money-lender, with his penny in the shilling per week interest.'

(c) *The Tallyman's* cajolery is almost equally dangerous, but applies to better neighbourhoods. Many of these men drive round with their wares in a smart trap, and their groom perhaps wears a cockade. They are peddlers on an extensive scale. 'Their power of talk does it. Wives left at home all day, dull; along comes a tallyman with an oily tongue; they like a gossip, and don't have the chance of seeing many men, so they talk, and then buy.' To match this in the supplying of the poor, the small shops give credit, and are dear compared to the costermongers who sell only for cash. In many better-to-do neighbourhoods the general prevalence of the credit system is noted. People not only buy their furniture, but also their clothing on credit, and even take a loan for a summer holiday. Everywhere, and with almost all classes, the most usual plan is to spend first and save afterwards to repay some form of loan.

(d) *Costermongers* are busiest on Sundays and Saturdays, and consequently these days are the quietest in the courts where they live. Things become lively there on Monday, and there are many charges for drunkenness and assaults amongst themselves. In their anger they summon one another freely, but in the end will often subscribe to help their assailant to pay his fine.

Some costermongers are well-to-do, but the majority live a hand-to-mouth existence, and like, it is said, to 'start fresh' (that is with a new loan to buy stock) on Monday.

2. INDUSTRIAL QUESTIONS

(a) A very close connection, it is remarked, can often be established between the system of employment and poverty. There are many trades that require boys and youths, and not men. The work can be done by very young hands, and consequently dismissal often comes at about eighteen years of age. Thus a crop of 'larrikins' are turned out every year, who have started life by earning fairly good wages, but who know no trade, and many of whom are bound to become loafers.

(b) On the other hand 'many men over fifty are always out of work. They get a little from one or another of their children; but these have been trained in the same school, and tend to the same end.'

(c) 'A large part of the "out of work" is through bad character, but there are a number of poor, helpless, incapable creatures, who just keep their heads above water in the summer, and are thrown out in the winter through no fault of their own.'

(d) A leading Congregationalist minister says:

'Of the type embruted by perpetual dependence on casual employment, it is hopeless to make *men*, while they remain in this condition; but give a man a uniform and a badge, any token that he is something more than a casual, and there will be a complete change in his moral character.'

(e) Speaking of the experience of the 'Abbey Mills' test, by which, in connection with a Mansion House 'Unemployed Committee', employment was provided for persons out of work, one of the local secretaries states that the majority of those dealt with were quite willing to work, but were hopeless, many of them demoralized by years of casual employment at the docks, the reorganization of which may, perhaps, have been the cause of their being finally thrown entirely out of work. The witness adds that, next to drink, casual labour is the most demoralizing influence in the part of London for which he speaks.

(f) A Roman Catholic priest, speaking also of dock labourers, asserted that, except for occasional 'bursts', his people were willing to work. The normal irregularity was greater than they desired. They were not loafers. And an Anglican curate, working in the same neighbourhood, describes casual labour as 'the curse of the parish'. The men earn good wages when paid by the piece, but probably cannot keep up the pace, and the result is that they work very hard for a short week; two days on and five days off being a very common thing.

(g) Another Catholic says:

'Men who are regularly employed get into regular ways, and attend to their regular duties. If not employed they tend to become irregular in all sorts of ways, and religion comes in for its share.'

(h) 'Women working at washing send their children to school in the morning, and do not themselves return home until 8 or 9 p.m. During the hours after school the children mix with other boys and girls in the streets, hearing and learning all kinds of evil talk and action. Their characters are ruined in those hours.' As an extension of the work of the Recreative Evening Schools Association, this witness (a Baptist minister) suggests that playing halls should be provided, where tea could be obtained at a small cost.

(i) 'The lowest class of women who work' (says a lady visitor) 'shell peas in the market; above them in the social scale are box-makers. Girls take employment as soon as they leave school, and for the first year or two work intermittently, but afterwards settle into regular factory employment.'

(j) 'On either side of the road' (runs one of our notes

on South London) 'lies the dust-yard of a contractor for several vestries, full of rough, dirty women from the surrounding streets: a disgusting occupation.'

(k) 'Nearly all the girls in Central London work at some trade or other. They would not make good servants, and it is a frequent argument of mothers that it is a good thing for them to have something to turn their hands to, so that if they marry and lose their husbands, they are independent. There is a terrible temptation to widows to lead an immoral life, more or less publicly, which may thus be, at least in part, avoided.'

(l) 'One of the managers of an Institute says that the girls who come to it are wage-earners, receiving from 7s. to 21s. a week at mantle and clothing factories. Numerous breaches of the Factory Acts seem to occur, for which the foremen are perhaps to blame, rather than the employers; but the girls are generally unwilling to talk of it.'

(m) 'Step-girls do nothing but clean steps, at 2d. or 3d. a house. They prefer the freedom they secure, to being general servants. In some districts they are numerous, and their presence throws light on the standard of the lower middle-class households for which they work.'

(n) 'Navvies' (says an employer of labour) 'generally work in gangs, and being often too uneducated to share out any odd money contrive to pool it by spending the money on beer.'

3. RESOURCES OF THE POOR

(a) 'Habits of thrift', it is said, 'must be improving. It would be impossible otherwise to explain the wonderful reserve power of the poor. The poor help each other more than any other class, and there must be resources to a greater extent than is realized.'

(b) 'How the poor live' (says a nurse) 'when they are helpless remains a mystery, save for their great kindness to each other, even to those who are strangers. This is the great explanation. It is nearly always the neighbours.'

(c) 'It is only the poor that really give' (says a Nonconformist witness). 'Personal help and timely relief are the keynotes of the charity of the poor. They know exactly the wants of one another and give when needed.'

(d) 'To each other' (says a Roman Catholic priest) 'their goodness is wonderful.'

(e) The headmaster of a poor Board school tells us that 'in many cases there is a bitter struggle to live. A good deal of kindness is shown by the poor to one another, but there is also a good deal of jealousy when assistance is given, and the begging spirit is apparent when the scent of gifts is in the air. This, however, is only natural. A mother whose man is out of work, or negligent – too often brutally so; and who has little ones needing food badly, and some sick and ailing – has no fine sense of independence.'

4. WAYS OF LIFE

(a) 'The men have' (says the vicar of a City parish) 'a good time compared to the women, who lead fearfully hard and almost slavish lives.'

(b) 'As a rule' (to quote another vicar) 'mothers of families are harder worked than their husbands or than their daughters "in business", although these work hard.'

(c) Again, we hear: 'It depends on the man.... Many of our widows are better off than the women with husbands.'

(d) 'A decent man earning 25s. a week will give 20s. to his wife. She ought to be able to, because in many cases she does, feed four children, dress them and herself, and pay rent out of this. The 5s. is kept by the man for his beer and tobacco, and sometimes he pays for his own dinner out of it. After a certain minimum it depends more on the wife than on the amount of money, whether the home is comfortable, and the children decently fed and dressed.' Our informant, a nurse, said she knew households where the wife was allowed 30s., which were not better off than those in which the woman only had 20s.

(e) 'Working men are very hard, and keep as much for themselves as they can. Boys living at home pay for their food, and if out of work cannot pay. Then they often enlist, which they seldom do willingly. "Father looks at every mouthful I eat," said one lad; and the question with their parents is, "How much can we get out of them?"' This our informant attributed to the selfishness of the men; the mothers have to concur, and get hardened to it.

(f) An intelligent police inspector thought that the granting of grocers' licences had nothing to do with the increase of drinking among women. Male heads of families allow their wives a fixed sum for household expenses; anything the wives can save out of this they can spend how and where they like. This, he pointed out, is true of both the working class and the middle class above them, so that in their case there is no need to ask the grocer to put down so many bottles of beer as so much coffee, in order to hoodwink the husband, as is sometimes asserted.

(g) 'The very poor' (remarks a medical witness) 'never seem to buy new clothing. If they are given good things they pawn them and put on their old, dirty clothes again. There are enormous sales of clothing which has been pawned and not redeemed.'

(h) 'Children' (said a schoolmaster, referring to a very poor and low district) 'are given food in a handkerchief, and live in the street, coming or not coming to school at will. Sometimes they are lost for a week or two, living meanwhile by begging or pilfering. It is useless to speak to the parents.'

(i) 'Bad language is reported as a growing evil.' 'Filthy language in the streets is getting worse.' 'Disgusting words are always in the air.' 'The language of the children is shocking, loose life and talk are increasing.' 'The behaviour of boys and girls is as coarse as possible.' Why it should be so bad, and, still more, why it should get worse, I do not know, nor can I affirm that it is so, but it is commonly so said. A Salvation Army captain, putting it at the best, says of the children, 'Their language is very bad – disgusting,' adding, 'I think some of them know the meaning of the words they use.' It is, however, remarkable that, 'degraded as their habits and filthy as the language they hear and use, obscene writing in the school-yards occupied by these children is rare, whereas it is a constant trouble at more respectable schools'.

(j) *Slang* – The word 'class' is used for what is superior. 'My father isn't class,' said a six-year-old, 'he's always boozing.' There is a constant change in the words used. For instance, 'pinch' was the last equivalent for 'steal', having at that time recently supplanted 'nick', which had succeeded 'sneak'.

(k) *Kindness to animals* – Moral improvement among the people is immense, owing mainly to education; shown amongst other ways in kindness to animals. The day was (says an old resident) when no cat could appear in the streets of Bethnal Green without being hunted and maltreated; now such conduct is rare.

(l) 'The people will put money away if the agencies are brought to their door, but not otherwise' (remarks a vicar). 'They will never take trouble about anything. This leads to much wastefulness in housekeeping and cooking, and to the constant purchase of cooked meat.'

(m) As showing the large sums which are often coming in, in apparently poor streets, a district visitor mentioned a family living in a cottage whose combined income for father, mother, son, and daughter was about 75s. a week; yet their home was always a den.

(n) 'Fever and ill-health, to a certain extent, may be attributed' (a relieving officer thought) 'to the amount of personal and domestic uncleanliness. There is not enough soap and water going, and dirty bedding is a special feature.' The quite unnecessary dirt and filth sometimes found are appalling. 'In hot weather there are plagues of flies, like nothing seen ordinarily. In one house, the table' (it is described) 'was fairly black with them, and the woman of the house was helpless; she did not know how to get rid of them. It had never occurred to her to wash the table.' 'Teach cleanliness, and we shall get rid of a lot of poverty.'

(o) Reluctance is found, at first, on the part of the poor to accept the services of a nurse, due, perhaps, to her insistence on method and cleanliness.

(p) 'Costers congregate in districts convenient for their markets, and prefer rough quarters.' They find their own level, and cannot live in a respectable building. This applies to others besides the hawkers. The case was mentioned of a cabinet-maker who had three rooms in the house next door to a mission-room, and whose family consisted of wife and two children. In a recent winter they moved the bed into the kitchen, and lived and slept there, leaving the other rooms empty. They did not like going to bed in the cold.

(q) A noticeable thing in poor streets is the mark left on the exterior of the houses. All along the front, about on a level with the hips, there is a broad dirty mark, showing where the men and lads are in the constant habit of standing, leaning a bit forward, as they smoke their pipes, and watch whatever may be going on in the street, while above and below the mortar is picked or kicked from between the bricks.

(r) The roughest lads will not mix with the more respectable, and, after they leave school, escape all civilizing influence. This difficulty affects all social work. 'The boys of one street' (says an East London vicar) 'won't associate with those of another.'

(s) Comparing the present time with 1866, an enormous improvement can be noted. That year was the time of the cholera epidemic, and our informant, in visiting, obtained an insight into the homes at that time, the memory of which, he says, has never left him. 'No doubt there are still slums, but the worst are gone, and the present state of things cannot be compared with the squalor, misery, and neglect which prevailed thirty years ago.'

(t) 'Since the Jubilee there has been a tendency to spend more on luxuries.' It was an awakening to luxury much to be regretted, thinks the Baptist minister who makes the observation.

(u) The usual position of a typical tenant of a house in an old-fashioned 'pink' street, paying £36 to £38 per annum rent, is thus sketched by a police inspector:

The tenant himself, with his family, would occupy two rooms and kitchen on ground floor and retain one upper room, and would let out the first floor, containing front and back room and box-room (which though very narrow, is often used as a bedroom) for 7s. a week; while above these would be one room, which may be let to a single old lady unfurnished for 4s., or perhaps to two single young men furnished at 5s. or 6s., according as they sleep in two single or one double bed. Thus, first floor at 7s. would pay £18 4s. per annum; second floor at 4s. would pay £10 8s. per annum, leaving £8 to £10, plus an equal [or more probably larger] amount for rates and taxes as the share of the tenant-in-chief, always supposing that the rooms let out are never vacant and the rents regularly paid.

The first-floor occupants make their front room their best room, using it as a bed-sitting room. For cooking they have a range in the back room. Where there are young men lodgers they usually take all their meals out, except Sunday dinner, paying a regular sum for eating this with their landlord. (As a rule the cook-shops are not open on Sunday.) If the top floor is taken by an old lady, she will cook all her meals over her own little fire; on the rare occasions when such a facility may be needed, she would have the use of the oven downstairs without charge.

(v) The evil of the necessity of 'speculating in lodgers' is spoken of. People take a house at a rent they could not themselves afford with the intention of letting half. Perhaps the lodgers do not come, or coming, do not pay their rent. The occupier gets £5 or £10 behind, loses heart in the struggle with debt, and goes under.

(w) 'It is common to abuse landlords as bloodsuckers, etc., but, on the whole, they treat their tenants with wonderful patience and forbearance,' says one of the clergy. He is convinced that in his district they do not receive more than two-thirds of their rent, and that the return on their investment is not large.

(x) Contents of a packet of papers (belonging to a late inmate) found in a Salvation Army shelter:

(1) Bailiff's business card, which announced, 'Undesirable tenants speedily ejected'.

(2) A 'hearty welcome' card to a free meal at a mission-hall.

(3) A Salvation Army *Soldier's Song-book*.

(4) The Gospel of St Luke.

(5) Four halves of four cancelled bank cheques.

(6) Three copies of *The Golden Grain Almanack and Christian Text-Book for 1898*.

(7) A book of miniature pictures of the *Daily Graphic*.

(8) A letter commencing 'My dear son', and ending 'Your affectionate mother'.

Institutions[9]

Working Men's Clubs. The 115 clubs in East London and Hackney may be primarily divided into those which can be entered by a stranger and those which cannot. Those which open their doors at all, do so very readily and very completely. They have not only nothing to hide, but are very generally proud of their position. They are moreover not infrequently linked by affiliation to the 'Working Men's Club and Institute Union', or the 'Federation of

9. First edition, Vol. I, pp. 94–124.

Working Men's Social Clubs', on terms which provide for the welcome of the members of any one club by any other club in the same association. Thus a very wide natural publicity is given to all their proceedings, and it is not difficult for the social inquirer to obtain trustworthy information about them and even himself to experience their hospitalities.

As to those which decline to open their doors to strangers, I can give no information except as to the reputation they enjoy, which, it must be said, is very bad. They are usually called 'Proprietary' clubs, and there can be no doubt that betting and various forms of gambling, but chiefly betting, are their main objects. On my list are thirty-two such clubs within the limits of the district. Some are dramatic and others make dancing a principal attraction, but in all cases their foundation and *raison d'être* is gambling in one form or other. Some of them are respectable, frequented by bookmakers of good repute. Others are very disreputable indeed, being, it is said, a combination of gambling hell with the lowest type of dancing saloon. All alike maintain a jealous privacy. An outer door labelled 'members only', an inner door of baize; a window with a sliding shutter, through which, as the visitor enters, appears promptly the face of the doorkeeper; an entire refusal to give any information or admit any strangers; such are their suggestive characteristics. Grave responsibility evidently attaches to their management, and police raids from time to time justify the precautions taken. These clubs seem to be short-lived, but die in one street only to spring up in the next. Shoreditch is the quarter in which most are found. Those in Whitechapel, of the same sort, but belonging to Jews and foreigners, are more permanent and probably more truly social in character. These clubs are of various grades and cater for every class from A to H; but not one of them can be properly called a working men's club. The total number of members will not be very large.

The clubs which live in the light of day may be conveniently considered in three divisions: (a) Philanthropic clubs in connection with churches or missions, started, supported, and managed by outside influence; of these there are thirty-three; (b) Social, numbering eighteen; and (c) Political, of which there are thirty-two.

The division between the Philanthropic and the true Working Men's club is not very clearly defined, for while many philanthropic clubs are merely adjuncts to missions, others, such as the 'University Club' in Victoria Park Square, and the 'United Brothers' in Commercial Street, are practically self-supporting and to a great extent self-managed. All, however, are *superintended*, and so are not as interesting a study as the spontaneous self-managed clubs. A practical distinction between the philanthropic and the self-supporting club is to be found in the question of drink. All the philanthropic clubs but one are teetotal; while, with the sole exception of the Jewish club in Great Alie Street, all the social and political clubs are not. To make a club self-supporting without the sale of beer is very difficult. The bar is the centre and support of a working man's club – the pole of the tent. The structure must be upheld in some way, and failing the profits from liquor sold, support must be found in subscriptions from outside; for in no other way but the paying for drinks will any of these clubs make sufficient effort to support itself – a rather striking proof of the preference for indirect taxation. Moreover, the clubs are not only run on the profits of the beer sold, but the prospects of these profits in very many cases raise the funds needed to make a start. Brewers find it to their interest to follow up their customers in this way, and lend money towards the fittings of the club. Repayment is not pressed, nor is the security scrutinized; for the lender is repaid by profit on the beer supplied.

The difference between the Social and Political clubs is slight, lying mainly in the mode in which they are started.

Social clubs in East London may or may not acquire a political tinge, but those intended to be political cannot stand unless social, and the social side tends to become more important than the political. For both, the friendly mug of beer – primordial cell of British social life – supplies the social bond, as well as the financial basis. There must be beer, but there is a good deal else. Almost every club has entertainments on Saturday and Monday, and a concert or discussion, lecture, or some other attraction, once or in some cases twice in the day, on Sunday; and billiards, bagatelle, and whist are greatly played. Whether from the publican or from the club, these are the things demanded by the people – beer, music, games, and discussion.

It is said by those hostile to clubs that they are mere drinking dens, sought because they remain open when the public house is shut. Or they are objected to in a general way as antagonistic to family life.

As to the first charge made, it has, with regard to the great majority of members, no foundation. As to the second, it is not so much the clubs which draw men, as their own restless spirits which drive them from home. In any case they would go out, and better as I think if they go to the club than elsewhere. Some competition is not amiss: the homes might easily be made more attractive than they are.

In considering these objections and the whole question whether clubs are on the whole an element of good, it would be unfair to take too high a standard. The leaders may consciously realize the higher ideas of the movement, but the rank and file are not above the average of their class, and usually join clubs with no higher motives than those which influence the ordinary club-goer of any class, or would otherwise take them to the public house. Looked at in this rather low way, clubs seem to me better than the licensed public houses they tend to replace. Nor do I see that they compare unfavourably, all things considered, with the majority of clubs in other places. The language one hears in them is the language of the streets; stuffed with oaths, used as mere adjectives; but in every class, oaths of one sort or other are pretty frequent on the tongues of men, and especially young men, who are numerous in every club. The fashion of the oath is not of much importance, whether beginning with a B or with a D.

Evidence of the spirit of self-sacrifice is not wanting. In many cases the members do all the repairs and alterations of the club after their own day's labour is done. In a new club in Bethnal Green the chairs and tables have been made, walls papered, and bars fitted up, stage erected, and scenes painted in this way. Many, too, are ardent politicians, and begrudge neither time nor money in advancing their political views.

And something more may be said. Coarse though the fabric be, it is shot through with golden threads of enthusiasm. Like Co-operation and like Socialism, though in a less pronounced way, the movement is a propaganda with its faith and hopes, its literature, and its leaders. This, it is true, applies to a few individuals only, but to many more club life is an education. If the leaders are few, those who belong or have belonged to the Committees of Management are numerous. It may perhaps be thought that enthusiasm might find some better aim, and citizenship some other field, than the management of bar-parlour and 'free-and-easy'; but taking things as they are, the working man's club is not a bad institution, and it is one with very strong roots.

To come to some sort of analysis of the clubs. There are among the Religious and Philanthropic sixteen, with about 2,600 members, named after the churches or missions with which they are connected. Most of these are intended for artisans and labourers. There are three belonging to the Y.M.C.A., mostly for clerks, etc., and some seven others, among which are the 'University Club' and the 'United Brothers', already mentioned as ranking more properly with the self-managed and self-supporting clubs. In addition to these, are six Boys' clubs, of which the Lads' Institute, in Whitechapel Road, and the Whittington Club are the most important, having between them about 500 members.

The Social clubs are, as a class, much older than the political clubs: one half of them date their foundation as far back as 1880, and two of them previous to 1870; and their growth has been steady, in marked contrast to the uneven rapidity with which the political clubs have sprung into existence during the last few years. There are in all eighteen social clubs, with about 5,530 members. Of these, four are Jewish, while in six the majority of members are foreigners; eight belong to the middle classes, and though the remainder may be, and are, called working men's clubs, they contain among their members a large sprinkling of the middle class. The subscription and entrance fee vary with the class of the club, but in most cases are higher than those of the political working man's club, and the financial position on the whole is stronger.

Of Political, or more strictly Politico-social clubs, there are thirty-two, of which twenty-two are Liberal and Radical, six Conservative, three Socialistic, and one Irish Home Rule. The Conservative clubs, with about 1,800 members, belong mainly to the upper or lower middle class; only one of them, with 200 members, is *called* a working man's club. Of the Liberal and Radical clubs, seven (with over 2,000 members) belong to the upper or lower middle class, six (with less than 1,000 members) to the working classes, while nine (with nearly 6,000 members) are mixed. The three Socialist clubs count only 200 members amongst them, and the Home Rule club has over 100.

Judging by the clubs there would seem to be no doubt of the political complexion of East London; and the weekly papers mostly taken – *Reynolds's* and the *Dispatch* – tell the same story. But the tone is not so much Liberal or even Radical as Republican outside of the lines, authorized or unauthorized, of English party politics, and thus very uncertain at the ballot box. There is also a good deal of vague unorganized Socialism.

It will be seen how large a part the lower middle class plays in East London club life, but it is not easy to draw the line between this class and so-called working men. 'What is a working man?' is a question to which no very clear answer can be given. In theory, dealers and small master men would be excluded, but in practice my classes E, F, and G, the central mass of the English people, consort together in a free and friendly way. Some of the clubs draw also from classes C and D. Class H has its own clubs apart, class B has only those provided for it philanthropically.

There are four clubs which from their size deserve special mention: the United Radical with 2,000 members; the Boro' of Hackney with 1,800; the Jews' Club and institute in Great Alie Street with 1,400 members; and the University Club with 700 members, besides about 400 belonging to the women's and children's sections. Any of these large clubs almost every evening is full of life, rising on occasion to the climax of a crush. All show what can be done with numbers, and point to the conclusion that in the enlargement of clubs rather than in their multiplication lies the road towards perfection. The possibilities in this direction amongst a dense population are almost unbounded; and it is found that men will come long distances to obtain the advantages which clubs on a large scale can offer.

The Jews' Club, though now ranking as a social club, was practically established on a philanthropic basis, its large and substantial premises having been built at the expense of Mr S. Montagu, M.P., and others. As a social club it is remarkable in three ways: (1) it is teetotal; (2)

it admits both sexes to membership; (3) it prohibits card-playing.

No club in East London is more ambitious than the University Club; nor any more strict in confining its membership to the working class. Helped at the start, it now pays its way, and this without the sale of beer. It owes its success to the direction of its President, Mr Buchanan, who hopes to show 'that a people's palace can be built out of the people's pence'.

The subscription to an ordinary working men's political club is 6d. per month with 6d. entrance fee. The club opens at 6.30 p.m. and closes at 12 or 12.30; on Sundays, 11 a.m. to 1 p.m. and 6.30 p.m. to 11.30 p.m. If the club remains open longer the bar is closed. Great care is taken not to serve beer to anyone not a member or entitled by affiliation to members' privileges. The ordinary number of members is from 300 to 400. The management is by committee, consisting of president, vice-president, treasurer, secretary, trustees, and a varying number of ordinary members. The duties of door-keeper and bar-tender are in some cases taken by members of the committee in turn. The clubs pay their way, but usually owe more than their assets, if sold up, would discharge. A monthly or weekly statement of accounts is usually posted in the doorway with other notices. Beer, spirits, tobacco, and teetotal drinks are supplied at the bar at a profit of 30 to 50 per cent. The games played are billiards, bagatelle, and cards (chiefly whist and cribbage), draughts, and dominoes. The rule against gambling is strict and is not infringed to any noticeable extent. Billiards are the principal attraction, and the standing of a club may be gauged by the number of its tables. There is usually a small library kept in a room used for committee meetings. Some evening papers are taken, perhaps two *Stars* and an *Evening Standard*; *Reynolds's* paper, the *Weekly Dispatch*, and some illustrated or comic papers, with a local print, complete the list. The club premises consist of a large room with billiard and bagatelle tables, a hall with small stage, bar-room and committee-room, library or reading-room. The club has a political council whose lead the members usually follow. Entertainments, lectures, and discussions for Saturday, Sunday, and Monday are arranged by the committee. To the entertainments ladies may be brought and do come in considerable numbers, and there will be dancing on special occasions. The entertainments are sometimes dramatic but more generally consist of a succession of songs, comic or sentimental, the comic songs being often sung in character with change of dress. A music-hall entertainment is the ideal aimed at. A chairman presides and keeps order, as at the free-and-easy or benefit performances held at public houses, and as till recently was invariably the practice at the public music halls. The chairman sits at a table with his back to the stage, flanked by his intimates, and sundry jugs or pots of ale which are passed from hand to hand. He alone of all the audience is uncovered and he is faultlessly dressed. At his right hand lies his hammer of authority, and sometimes a sort of wooden platter to receive the sharp blows with which he calls for silence or emphasizes the chorus. He does not spare this exercise of his authority, and gives out, before each song, the name of the singer, in the ordinary public house concert-room style; the formula being 'our friend so and so will now oblige'. The singers are sometimes professional, but more commonly semi-professional; those who do a good deal in this way and no doubt make money by it, but have other occupations. Others are purely amateur, members, or friends of members, who really perform to 'oblige' their brother members. Two or three songs may be expected from each singer. The more purely amateur, the more purely sentimental the song as a general rule. The performance, though poor enough, serves to amuse the audience, but except on great occasions does not empty the billiard-room. The entertainments are at times connected with some charitable object; a member has perhaps had an accident or suffered from illness, and a concert is got up and tickets sold for his benefit. A pleasing feature connected with the entertainments given is a practice recently adopted of having a children's Christmas party. It is now very general, the expense being mainly defrayed by voluntary subscriptions of members. The United Radical Club alone entertained 4,000 children this year.

On the whole these clubs are a bright and lively scene, and very attractive as compared to the ordinary homes of the classes from which the members are drawn...

Friendly Societies. East London has shared in the development of prudential thrift shown by the growth in recent years of the great Friendly Societies. One with another they have 50,000 members in the district, of whom 17,000 belong to the Ancient Order of Foresters, about the same number to the Loyal United Friends, 7,000 to the Hearts of Oak, 5,000 to the two orders of the Phoenix (Temperance), 3,000 to the Odd Fellows, and a few to the Rechabites and Sons of Temperance.

Of the 700,000 members belonging to the Foresters it is noticeable that 17,000, with 114 Courts, are in the district, while the Odd Fellows, an equally strong society, being located chiefly in the north of England, has here only 3,000 members and eighteen lodges. These are the premier societies. Similar in the principles on which they are conducted, with well-managed sick and death benefits, they are too widely known to need special description.

Of quite another kind is the Order of Loyal United Friends, which is so largely represented in East London. An unregistered society, its system of working is somewhat peculiar. Its lodges are amalgamated into districts, and have no separate purse, but each district manages its own affairs. There is no central fund, nor is any distinction made, as is insisted on with registered societies, between sick fund, burial fund, and management. Candidates for admission are not required to be medically examined, if under forty years of age, and the society has no doctors. In case of sickness two members are sent to report, followed up, if need be, by the secretary himself, who finally may call in a doctor at the expense of the society. On the other hand, this society is especially careful about occupations, a large number being interdicted. The society numbers, in all, some 50,000 members, and, so far as this country is concerned, is peculiarly a London society, its furthest lodge being at Gravesend. It has, however, a branch in New Zealand. The subscription is from 3s. 6d. to 4s. 6d. per quarter; the benefits are £10 at death, or £5 at death of wife, and in sickness 10s. a week for twelve weeks, and then 6s. for twelve more weeks.

The Hearts of Oak, a large society having in all 115,000 members, dates from 1842, and is registered. Its social level is somewhat above that of the other societies, and its entire management different. A centralized society, with neither lodges nor districts, it employs no collectors, all contributions being paid in, and claims met, at the office of the society. Consequently, it can boast of exceptionally small management expenses; but it is evident that part of the expense saved to the society is thrown on to the individual members. It has no doctors of its own, but has an arrangement with certain 'medical agencies' in London and the provinces, at which members, for a small subscription, can be attended. In East London there are no less than twenty-three of these agencies.

The contribution to the Hearts of Oak is 10s. per quarter, and the benefits are £20 and £10 severally for death of member or wife, and an allowance in sickness beginning at 18s. a week. In addition, to attract young married men, it gives 30s. for the lying-in of a member's wife, and to gratify the old, 4s. per week superannuation allowance. It also pays £15 in case of loss by fire, £5, if needed, to provide a substitute for the militia, and as a relic of a former state of things, 5s. a week in case of imprisonment for debt. The 7,000 East End members of the society are no doubt, all fairly well-to-do.

There are five total-abstinence benefit societies at work in East London, but the principal three are off-shoots of one stem, 'The Phoenix'. The bone of contention amongst them has been the question of consolidation, the wealthier branches not unnaturally objecting to pool their funds with the poorer ones. So far back as 1862 the present 'United Order of Total Abstinent Sons of the Phoenix' seceded from the 'Original Grand Order' of the same. The latter was opposed to consolidation, and until December 1887, employed instead a system of levies in favour of any lodge unable to meet its death payments. It has, however, now adopted consolidation at the cost of a further secession, which has founded a third order called 'The Amalgamated Independent Sons of the Phoenix'. The estimated deficiency by valuation of these orders is considerable, but their position is always better than would seem, as the failure to maintain the temperance pledge increases the ordinary proportion of lapsed membership. The figures so far bear this out as to make it appear that the societies live by their lapses, being able to trust with scientific certainty to a proportion of their members breaking the pledge.

The Original or 'Red' order, as it is called from the colour of its insignia, confines its benefits to the case of death, but the United or 'Blue' Order has introduced a separate sick contribution and benefit, which some of the lodges have taken up. The contributions vary with the different lodges, but are about 2s. 2d. per quarter; this provides £14 at death of member, and £7 at death of member's wife.

The Rechabites, an old-established Temperance Society (dating from 1835) with 75,000 members, has too few members in East London to be particularly noticed here. Its peculiarity is that sick as well as death funds are centralized. The Sons of Temperance are also very slightly represented in our district.

On the whole there is evidence of an effort towards prudent thrift, falling far short, no doubt, of what it might be, and not equal to what is being done by similar means elsewhere in England, but, in itself, very considerable, and from its growth, very hopeful. Nor does the work of these societies represent the full extent of the spread of this virtue, for the 'Prudential' and other companies do a very large business even amongst the quite poor. The system of agents and collectors employed by these companies is no doubt expensive, but pleads that justification which success rarely fails to command. The terms offered by Government are more liberal, but the methods employed do not suit the poor so well.

Besides the agencies already noticed, there are in East London a number of 'dividing societies', which, although they appear to partake of the advantages of benefit societies, cannot be included in the agencies which a sagaciously thrifty person would use. To these organizations young men will subscribe 6d. per week for benefits which, considering their age, might be provided at 3d. At the end of the year, the accumulated funds are divided amongst the members, all liabilities having been previously met. Of the 26s. paid into a new club, each member will often get 20s. back. This goes on, year after year, but as the members grow older the claims get larger, and the amount to be shared proportionately smaller. Efforts are made to introduce new blood, but the younger men refuse to bear the burdens of the older ones, and the society falls to pieces just at the time when its assistance is most needed.

Then the old members complain that the benefits of friendly societies are mythical, and so strong is this feeling in some quarters, that these 'dividing societies' are said to have done more harm to the Friendly Societies' movement than all other adverse influences put together.

Another form of thrift (of a sort), is to be found in what are called 'loan and investment societies'. These provide the commonest form of what may be called 'publican's thrift'. A number of men meeting weekly at some public house form a society with treasurer (usually the publican), trustee, check steward, and secretary; 3d. entrance fee is paid, and 3d. more for the book of rules, including a card on which loans and repayments are noted. Each share taken up involves a weekly subscription of 6d.; the number of shares that may be taken by one member is generally limited. There is also a small quarterly subscription for working expenses. The funds so subscribed, week by week, are available for loans to the members, who stand security for each other. The interest on the loan (5 per cent) is deducted when the amount is borrowed, and 1s. in the £1 is payable every week. The loan is thus repaid in twenty weeks, and a good interest is made by the common purse. Fines are levied if repayments and subscriptions are not punctually met week by week, and great care is exercised not to lend more than is safely secured. The result at the end of the year is a profit of 3s. or 4s. per share, and if not in debt to the society at the time, each member receives also the £1 6s. accumulated (6d. per week). The money is divided at Christmas, and comes in handy at that time for expenditure, which is doubtless greatly to the benefit of the house in which the society is held. Every member is expected to borrow to some extent, and may perhaps be obliged to do so or pay the interest, otherwise he would obtain what would be thought an unfair advantage in the division of profit. There is a jovial spirit about this sort of thrift, but it may be doubted whether a man's family will gain anything by it.

A still simpler plan, common among factory girls, is for a number to club together weekly 6d. or 1s. each, the whole sum being taken by one of the members in rotation by lot. The object is to get a large enough sum at once to make spending profitable: to buy a hat, or boots, or have a fling of some sort. It is perhaps hardly to be called thrift, and yet it comes very near it. I must confess to feeling great sympathy with this plan.

Co-operative Stores. In the East End is situated the London head-quarters of the Co-operative Wholesale Society, whose very handsome new building in Hooper Square, Whitechapel, bears testimony to the progress of the movement and is a centre of propaganda. London generally is still behind some other parts of the country as to co-operation, but has made a considerable advance in the last few years, and in our district there are some half-dozen distributive societies. Of these by far the most important is called the Tower Hamlets Co-operative Society, situated in Mile End, with branches at Poplar and Bow. It numbers 1,560 members, and has £5,000 capital; its sales for 1887 reached £24,000 and net profits were £1,400.

The next largest is the Borough of Hackney Co-operative Society, started in 1886 with 87 members, and having in September, 1888, about 400 members and a business of £5,000 in sales, with a profit of £250. It has just absorbed the South Hackney Society, an older but less successful concern. Two of the clubs have started co-operative societies – the United Radical about a year ago, and the University Club still more recently. This is a noteworthy extension of club possibilities.

Productive societies have been from time to time started in East London, but their career has been neither long nor brilliant. They have often had a semi-philanthropic basis, and have been well-meant but hopeless efforts to supersede 'sweating' by co-operation. None now working are of sufficient importance to be mentioned...

Public houses play a larger part in the lives of the people than clubs or friendly societies, churches or missions, or perhaps than all put together, and bad it would be if their action and influence were altogether evil. This is not so, though the bad side is very palpable and continually enforced upon our minds.

A most horrible and true picture may be drawn of the trade in drink, of the wickedness and misery that goes with it. So horrible that one cannot wonder that some eyes are blinded to all else, and there is a cry of away with this accursed abomination. There is, however, much more to be said. Anyone who frequents public houses knows that actual drunkenness is very much the exception. At the worst houses in the worst neighbourhoods many, or perhaps most, of those who stand at the bars, whether men or women, are stamped with the effects of drink, and, if orderly at the moment, are perhaps at other times mad or incapable under its influence; but at the hundreds of respectable public houses, scattered plentifully all through the district, this is not the case. It could not be. They live by supplying the wants of the bulk of the people, and it is not possible that they should be much worse than the people they serve. Go into any of these houses – the ordinary public house at the corner of any ordinary East End street – there, standing at the counter, or seated on the benches against wall or partition, will be perhaps half a dozen people, men and women, chatting together over their beer – more often beer than spirits – or you may see a few men come in with no time to lose, briskly drink their glass and go. Behind the bar will be a decent middle-aged woman, something above her customers in class, very neatly dressed, respecting herself and respected by them. The whole scene comfortable, quiet, and orderly. To these houses those who live near send their children with a jug as readily as they would send them to any other shop.

I do not want to press this more cheerful point of view further than is necessary to relieve the darker shades of the picture. I would rather admit the evils and try to show how they may be lessened and what the tendencies are that make for improvement.

It is evident that publicans, like all the rest of us, are feeling the stress of competition. Walk through the streets and everywhere it may be seen that the public houses are put to it to please their customers. Placards announcing change of management frequently meet the eye, while almost every house vigorously announces its reduced prices. 'So much the worse' some will say. But no! it is a good thing that they should be considering how to make themselves more attractive. Undermined by the increasing temperance of the people, and subject to direct attack from the cocoa rooms on the one side and the clubs on the other, the licensed victuallers begin to see that they cannot live by drink alone. Look more closely at the signs in their windows. There is hardly a window that does not show the necessity felt to cater for other wants besides drink. All sell tobacco, not a few sell tea. 'Bovril' (a well-advertised novelty) is to be had everywhere. Hot luncheons are offered, or a midday joint; or 'sausages and mashed' are suggested to the hungry passer-by; at all events there will be sandwiches, biscuits, and bread and cheese. Early coffee is frequently provided, and temperance drinks too have now a recognized place. Ginger beer is sold everywhere, and not infrequently kept on draught.[10] These things are new, and though trifles in themselves, they serve as straws to show the way of the wind. The public houses also connect themselves with benefit clubs, charitable concerts, and 'friendly draws'. No doubt in all these things there is an eye to the ultimate sale of drink, but every accessory

---

10. It is then called 'Brewed Ginger Beer' – a sort of sheep in wolf's clothing.

attraction of departure from the simple glare of the gin palace is an improvement. In order to succeed, each public house now finds itself impelled to become more of a music hall, more of a restaurant, or more of a club, or it must ally itself with thrift. The publican must consider other desires besides that for strong drink. Those that do not, will be beaten in the race.

In all these efforts there is bad as well as good, and a monstrous ingenuity may be exerted in tempting men to drink – gambling and other vices being used to draw people together and open their purses. As public servants, the licensed victuallers are on their trial. The field is still in their possession, but let them be warned; for if they would keep their place they must adapt themselves to the requirements of the times. If they should neglect the larger wants of the great mass of the people, content to find their principal customers amongst the depraved, they would deserve the ruin that would inevitably fall on them.

In such a situation it would be a fatal mistake to decrease the number of the houses in the cause of temperance. To encourage the decent and respectable publican by making existence difficult to the disreputable is the better policy, but let us on no account interfere with a natural development, which, if I am right, is making it every day more difficult to make a livelihood by the simple sale of drink.

Cocoa Rooms, and especially Lockhart's cocoa rooms, have become an important factor in the life of the people. At first cocoa rooms, or 'coffee palaces' as they were then called, were the result of philanthropic or religious effort. They were to pay their way; but they did not do it. They were to provide good refreshments; but tea, coffee, cocoa, and cakes were alike bad. It was not till the work was taken up as a business that any good was done with it. Now it strides forward, and though Lockhart's are the best and the most numerous, others are following and are bound to come up to, or excel, the standard so established. Very soon we shall have no length of principal street without such a place, and we shall wonder how we ever got on without them. In their rules they are wisely liberal: those who drink the cocoa may sit at the tables to eat the dinner or breakfast they have brought from home, or bringing the bread and butter from home they can add the sausage or whatever completes the meal.

Amusements. There are three theatres in the East End: the Standard in Norton Folgate, the Pavilion in the Mile End Road, and the Britannia in Hoxton; all homes of legitimate drama. Everywhere in England theatregoers are a special class. Those who care, go often; the rest seldom or not at all. The regular East End theatregoer even finds his way westwards, and in the sixpenny seats of the little house in Pitfield Street I have heard a discussion on Irving's representation of *Faust* at the Lyceum. The passion for the stage crops up also in the dramatic clubs, of which there are several. But by the mass of the people the music-hall entertainment is preferred to the drama. There are fully half a dozen music halls, great and small, in the district, and of all of them it must be said that the performances are unobjectionable – the keynote is a coarse, rough fun, and nothing is so much applauded as good step-dancing. Of questionable innuendo there is little, far less than at West End music halls, and less, I noticed, than at the small benefit concerts held at public houses. At one of these public houses a more than *risqué* song was received with loud laughter by the men and with sniggering by the married women, but by the girls present with a stony impenetrableness of demeanour, which I take to be the natural armour of the East End young women. The performances, whether at the music halls, or at the clubs, or at benefit concerts, all aim at the same kind of thing, and may be taken as supplying what the people demand in the way of amusement.

Music, moreover, of whatever sort, never comes amiss, and is a pleasure common to every class, for there seem to be as many in whom this faculty is highly developed in one class as another. Of dancing, too, all classes are very fond, but it seems not easy to arrange so as to avoid the scandal which surrounds all dancing saloons, and below class G there is not very much of it. The shilling balls of this class are eminently respectable and decorous so far as I have seen. In the streets the love of dancing bursts out whenever it has a chance; let a barrel organ strike up a valse at any corner and at once the girls who may be walking past, and the children out of the gutter, begin to foot it merrily. Men join in sometimes, two young men together as likely as not, and passers-by stand to enjoy the sight. A couple of ragged, perhaps even bare-footed children, dancing conscientiously the step of the latest *troistemps*, are a pleasant sight to see.

But the exercise in which the people most delight is discussion. The clubs provide for this on Sundays, but the custom flourishes yet more freely in the open air. Mile End Waste on Saturday night, Victoria Park on Sunday, are where the meetings are mostly gathered. It may be that those who make up the crowds who surround the speakers and who join in the wordy warfare, or split into groups of eager talkers, are the same individuals over and over again. But I do not think so. I believe keen dialectic to be the especial passion of the population at large. It is the fence, the cut and thrust, or skilful parry, that interests rather than the merits of the subject, and it is religious discussion which interests the people most.

The People's Palace, the idea of Mr Besant and the work of Sir Edmund Currie, aided by the liberality of the Company of Drapers, stands out conspicuously in East London, as an attempt to improve and brighten the lives of the people. The Queen's Hall and the

Library are fine buildings, the technical schools have suitable quarters, and there is a large swimming bath. The rest at present consists of 'Exhibition buildings' used (very successfully) for gymnasium purposes. The whole appearance is unfinished. On every feature is stamped 'we need more money'. The number of members is now 1,800 (two-thirds male, one-third female). There are also 2,250 students in the technical classes, 400 boys in the day-school, and 400 more in the junior section for gymnastic training, etc. So that in all about 5,000 young persons are connected with the Palace. The subscriptions run from 1s. to 10s. a quarter, but all the money obtained from subscriptions goes but a little way towards the expenses. Of endowment there is about £5,000 – (half from the Charity Commissioners and half from the Drapers' Company) – and beyond this the public must every year be appealed to for large sums to keep the Palace in full swing. The exhibitions and entertainments provided for the outside public at a small entrance charge have been without end, very interesting and extremely well attended. The following societies and clubs are held in connection with this institution: Choral, boxing, dramatic, literary, cycling, cricket, football, harriers, chess and draughts, orchestral, Parliament, ramblers, sick, photographic, sketching, ladies' social, shorthand, and military band, with others in course of formation. Each society is composed of members of the institute and managed by its own members.

Here then is a huge growth in the short time since the institute was opened. It must be said that there is about both method employed and results obtained a sort of inflation, unsound and dangerous. Hitherto success has justified the measures taken, but nevertheless a slower growth for such an institution is much to be preferred, and it has even yet to be proved whether the People's Palace is to be regarded as an example or as a warning...

Toynbee Hall and Oxford House are both efforts by

means of residential settlement to bring University culture into direct contact with the poorest of the people. Each connects its action with that of the parish in which it is situated, and each is the centre of a great amount of work of social organization. The amount of life which is thus set and kept in motion may be gathered from the actual bill of fare at Toynbee Hall for a single week, taken haphazard:

Sunday	7.30 p.m.	Ethical Lecture – "Socrates".
	9.0 p.m.	Popular Lecture, with magic lantern – "Normandy".
Monday	8.0 p.m.	Univer. Exten. Lecture – "Chemistry of Arts and Manufactures".
	8.0 p.m.	Reading party – Spinoza.
	8.0 p.m.	*Classes* – Elementary Shorthand. Carpentry. Beginners in Latin.
	7.30 to 9.45 p.m.	Three successive Singing Classes in connection with Popular Musical Union.
Tuesday	4.30 p.m.	Reading Party – English Literature.
	8.0 p.m.	Univer. Exten. Lecture – 'Age of Pope'.
	8.0 p.m.	Recreative School party (of those who attend East End Recreative Evening Classes).
	7.0 p.m.	*Classes* – Intermediate Shorthand. Intermediate Greek.
	8.0 p.m.	Advanced Shorthand.
	8.0 p.m.	Elementary Greek. Carpentry. Embriology (Advanced). Botany. Elementary French.
	8.30 p.m.	Physical Geography.
	7.30 to 9.45 p.m.	Three successive Violin Classes (Pop. Mus. Union).

Wednesday	4.30 p.m.	Reading Party – English Literature.
	6.0 p.m.	Reading Party – English Literature.
	8.0 p.m.	Univer. Exten. Lecture – 'English and European History (Stuart Period)'.
	8.0 p.m.	Reading Party – English Literature.
	8.0 p.m.	Elizabethan Society Meeting (monthly, to read paper).
	7.0 p.m.	*Classes* – Intermediate French for women.
	8.0 p.m.	Elementary French for women. Decoration.
	7.0 to 9.0 p.m.	Elementary Chemical Analysis.
	8.30 p.m.	Reading Party – Plato.
Thursday	8.0 p.m.	Popular Concert.
	8.0 p.m.	Boy Foresters' Party.
	8.0 p.m.	Toynbee Shakespeare Club.
	8.0 p.m.	Lecture – 'Political Economy and Trades Unionism'.
	8.30 p.m.	Lecture – 'Starfish', etc.
	7.30 p.m.	*Classes* – Venetian Art. Decoration (Boys).
	8.0 p.m.	Wood Carving and Clay Modelling (Boys). Advanced French.
	8.30 p.m.	Italian.
	7.0 to 9.0 p.m.	Elementary Chemistry.
Friday	8.0 p.m.	Univer. Exten. Lecture – 'Physiology of the Senses'.
	7.0 p.m.	Two reading parties in connection with above lecture.
	8.0 p.m.	Reading Party – Bacon.
	7.0 p.m.	*Classes* – Intermediate Latin.
	7.30 p.m.	Elementary German.
	8.0 p.m.	Mazzini. Intermediate French. Advanced French.
	8.15 p.m.	Advanced Latin.
	8.30 p.m.	Advanced German.

Saturday	8.0 p.m.	Lecture – 'The Saxon Chronicle'.
	8.0 p.m.	Lecture – 'Engraving'.
	8.0 p.m.	Annual Meeting Pupil Teachers' Assoc.

'Black and White' Exhibition open Saturday and Sunday of this week.

The Library is open all day on Sunday; 1.30 to 10.30 p.m. on Saturday; and 4.30 to 10.30 p.m. on other days.

Something of this kind goes on every week. There are over 600 members on the register of the classes, and 600 tickets were sold for the last course of University Extension lectures. In all about 1,000 people come weekly to Toynbee Hall for concerts, lectures, classes, etc. Outside of all this, the residents – 20 members of the Universities living in Toynbee Hall – do what is recognized as their chief work in forming friendships with the people, and coming into touch with their needs in connection with school management, co-operation, local government, charity organization, and children's country holidays. An excursion was arranged for a large party (many being school teachers) to Florence last Easter, and one to Venice is proposed for this year. The Lolesworth Club – a social, self-governing and self-supporting club on teetotal principles, whose members are a happy family drawn from the tenants of Lolesworth and other neighbouring blocks of buildings – provides an opening for, and is provided with, continual lectures and entertainments; and the United Brothers, another club, has been fostered, and the Whittington Club for boys very much helped from this centre.

The value direct and indirect of such work is very great – great to those for whose benefit it is done, and not less so in the education of the educators.

Oxford House is the centre of much social and religious effort, as well as of a ring of clubs, of which the University Club already described is the most important.

CHAPTER 5

ILLUSTRATIONS

RANDOM OBSERVATIONS FROM BOOTH'S NOTEBOOKS

At the end of each volume in the third series, Booth included random jottings from his notebooks which he called 'illustrations'. These were mainly personal experiences and confrontations which he felt should be recorded and preserved, but from which he was not able to draw any systematic inferences. The illustrations provide a uniquely candid glimpse of London life in Booth's era and of the extent of his curiosities and wanderings.

Missions, Etc.[1]

(3) *A Mission to the Jews*

We had received a postcard asking us to call on Saturday afternoon, from 3.30 to 5, when 'we should find a full room, and be able to talk after'. The door was opened by a matronly-looking Jewess, who proved to be the wife of the missionary. The room into which I was ushered was a small one, and was, as had been claimed, full, with twenty-five Jewesses and five Jews. I was given a seat at the top of the room, next to a strange-looking individual with a black beard, who is the most important person in this story. The missionary and another man, who acted as a chairman, sat also at the upper end of the room. On his legs was a German, who was addressing those present in Yiddish. He spoke fluently, and with a good

---

1. Third edition, third series, Vol. II, pp. 231-3.

deal of gesture; but, with the exception of two Jewesses in the front row, all seemed to hear him with complete apathy, mingled with unconcealed signs of boredom. But the two women were evidently following the speaker closely, and constantly nodded their heads, apparently in consent to his arguments. The German having finished, the black-bearded man was asked to say a few words. He was a most extraordinarily grotesque person, and it is not easy to give any, even the most remote, conception of his appearance, his speech, his manner, his gestures. He spoke in English, with a voice something between a rook and a corn-crake; but even more astounding than his voice was his accent, which, if reproduced on the stage, would be described as an absurd burlesque of the vilest type of modern cockney speech. The matter was of the usual street-preaching kind, on the lowest level. The Jews probably did not understand a word of it, and they mainly looked profoundly bored. At the end, we Christians sang a hymn in English, out of Moody and Sankey's collection: 'I am trusting, I am trusting, Sweetly trusting in His blood'. The Jews had no hymn-books, and showed no signs of being able to follow. The proceedings closed with a prayer in Yiddish from the missionary, and the audience trooped out, leaving me with the missionary and his wife, and the bearded man. From the conversation that ensued, I gathered that this man was in truth the founder of the mission, twenty-six years ago, and that the present missionary and his wife were his converts, having 'loved their Saviour', respectively, twenty-six and twenty-two years. As to present conversions, they said that all those in the front rows at the meeting were really converts; though owing to persecution, they were not all 'professing Christians'. 'The persecution is terrible,' said the missionary's wife, adding, 'I have been through it, and know what it is.' Asked about relief, she said they were 'very poor, and that what God sends us we give them'. The mission, being in financial difficulties, was about to be transferred to a larger organization. The bearded man said he saw signs of a great movement among the Jews, and asserted that this mission had converted thousands! 'You may report', he said, at the end, 'that they are coming over in thousands.'

(4) *A Quaker Adult School Meeting on Sunday Morning*

... There were thirty-five or forty men in the Class at the commencement, and these numbers were fully doubled by the end. The men seemed to have their accustomed places, and vacant seats were left to some extent for absentees. The chapter to be read was the 55th of Isaiah: 'Ho, everyone that thirsteth', etc. We read the whole of this, and most of the 56th chapter, and went twice over the first portion, so that everyone present might read a verse. I gathered that the 54th and 55th chapters had been read last Sunday, so that each verse would be read over several times before it was done with. Perhaps the pace depends on the inherent interest of the passage, and in this case every word was of great value. No remarks were made during the reading, which went verse after verse from man to man, in the order in which we sat. When the reading was finished, and after a short prayer, the man who had promised to open the debate being absent, it was left to any one to take up some verse, or any subject suggested by what we had read, and several spoke in turn – none spoke for long, the president's *only-three-minutes-more* bell never had to be brought into requisition. The remarks were homely expressions of the feelings roused by the language of the texts, continued sometimes so as to drag in the drink question, or the poverty question, or whatever the man's mind was full of; and, in some cases, showed that his mind was chiefly full of himself. The only lengthy exhortation was that of a man who told us that the reading of the words just heard had helped him to win, in a battle with self, as to forgiving his 'own flesh and blood', by which or by whom he had evidently felt deeply aggrieved. He slowly ground this out. He told us how this person and that had urged this duty upon him, and how he had met their honest and kind advice with refusal and insult, but how at last he had been broken down. I suppose the man's mind was eased by making a clean breast of it all, even in public; but yet the confession seemed out of its proper place, and with a very slight twist might be regarded as self-congratulation, rather than self-condemnation; and that it was in any way the result of our Bible reading was not to be supposed, thought, doubtless, the meeting and its customary proceedings gave him an opportunity.

Notes of a Walk on New Year's Eve[2]

I STARTED at about 11.15 p.m., intending to make my way to Somers Town, but looked in at two or three places of worship on my way. At a Baptist chapel I found a congregation of sixty or seventy people, and a young man speaking on the vicarious nature of Christ's sacrifice, with tone and gesture that would have been well suited to a vestry election meeting. It was not very edifying, but the effect was improved by the quiet singing of a hymn. The minister presided. The congregation was mostly composed of those who looked like regular worshippers, but scattered among them were some who had strayed in to bid good-bye to the Old Year in what was evidently a strange environment. Passing onwards, I called in at the chapel of a Boys' Home. Here, too, there was a service, but only twenty or thirty had come to it —

2. Third edition, third series, Vol. III, pp. 210–14.

a quiet little middle-class gathering. In the road outside a well-dressed woman, quite drunk, disappeared in the distance, and I imagined that in her I had a premonition of the scenes of excess that I expected awaited me in the more disreputable quarter of Somers Town.

At the Salvation Army Hall, to which I had gone on Christmas Day, I found a congregation of very much the same size and character as had gathered then, but there were many fewer soldiers on the platform and the people looked very tired. A Sister was speaking – she to whose urgent prayer I had listened a few days before. The address was a pleading and an invitation, and held me as well as her hearers. It was not until the end that the fire blazed up, but at that point, when addressing herself especially to young men, she told them with simple directness that if they rejected Christ and did evil, hell would await them. The same officer was presiding as on Sunday, but he, poor fellow, looked as tired as the rest, and I could not wait to see if he introduced the brighter touch into the service that he had certainly done on Christmas Day. While the Sister was speaking an almost painful eagerness and strain pervaded the meeting, but I was left with the impression, which Salvation Army gatherings have always given me, that they are centres of much earnestness of purpose and goodness of life. From here I got as quickly as possible to Somers Town, so as to reach St Mary's if possible before midnight, which I succeeded in doing; but the church was closed and dark: there had been no service. At the Roman Catholic Church in Clarendon Square, where there had been a midnight service on Christmas Eve, I thought I might find the typical New Year's congregation that I had still to seek; but here again I found an empty building.

I went on into Chalton Street, arriving there just about 12 o'clock. The street market was only lingering on, but there were many people about, and, at the moment, 1899 was being vociferously welcomed with shouts and cries, with cheers, and the singing of Auld Lang Syne, and above all, perhaps, by the clanging of tins and the loud striking of the butchers' barrows and boards. Altogether, it was a most extraordinary din, but it was all very uproarious and very good-natured, with much hand-shaking and wishing of a Happy New Year and not many signs of excessive drinking.

I looked in for a minute at Christ Church to find a small congregation – perhaps eighty to one hundred; the general effect dull and depressing, especially so perhaps by way of contrast with the hearty, noisy scene outside. By Chapel Street I passed into Ossulston Street and went down the entrance to York Place to see if chronic squalor relieved itself on this night of the year with a debauch. But the court was in complete silence; lights at a few of the windows alone telling that it was occupied. At a few minutes after twelve I reached the Presbyterian Church, and here at last found the crowded New Year's congregation of my imagination. But even here, although a number of people were standing near the doors, there were a good many seats in the gallery not occupied. At first I went in downstairs, and the impression given was of an orderly and ordinary congregation. Later I proceeded upstairs and found myself at once in the motley group that the occasion is reputed to attract to the sanctuary. The crowd was a strangely mixed one, many being the regular folk that one might expect to find there any Sunday. But many others were obviously strangers, and some were those whose church-goings were probably not more than events of annual occurrence. There were noisy girls who found the occasion amusing, but there were others, both men and women, of the poorer and more miserable type – evidently:

> From a certain squalid knot of alleys
> Where the town's bad blood [still] slept corruptly.

And some of these were inclined to take their unwonted experience with a certain touch of resentment and ribaldry. One couple were especially noticeable, the husband, somewhat in liquor, accompanying the preacher's remarks with a running commentary of his own, not very complimentary or choice in phrasing. One thing alone seemed to satisfy him, and that was the preacher's remark that at no future time was he likely to be face to face with his present audience. 'That is b— certain,' said the man, 'you spoke a true word that time.' But a few minutes later, when the people were singing, and we stood side by side, he was conscious of his past indecorous conduct, and shook me by the hand, with the promise that he would be there on the following evening 'with my Bible under my arm and my hymn-book in my pocket'. He was a muscular, full-blooded ruffian of thirty-five or forty. His wife, during the little outbreaks, was half angry, half fearful lest he should be turned out. She was conscious of the occasion, and in her badly scarred face it was easy to detect the desire for the moment to be quiet and subdued.

The address consisted largely of exhortations to live a better life in the coming year, to come to chapel again that same evening (it was now Sunday morning), etc.: every single sentence plain, if disconnected, and every word could be heard. Towards the close of his remarks the minister asked the people to say after him the words: 'Lord Jesus, I promise that henceforth I will love and follow Thee.' There was a murmur of response through the chapel, but it was by no means general. I watched most of the people leaving and they appeared to be largely representative of the regular *habitués*; perhaps one-fourth were quite poor and essentially strangers within the gate. The regular people could be recognized by the greetings that were exchanged. Perfect order prevailed; and the large crowd rapidly scattered homewards. Tracts were being given away, and a beautiful illuminated card bearing the text of the evening was being sold for a penny.

On my way home, although I met two or three groups of young fellows a little gay and noisy, I saw no one really drunk, and the only approach to bad temper was in a group of four women at the corner of a street, two of whom were spitting at each other and threatening blows. But they parted with nothing worse than angry and unpleasant words. For the rest, if there were any noise, it was just singing and good wishes. The worst sight I saw was the well-dressed woman who staggered away in the better class road.

The small proportion of the people of Somers Town who appeared to be attending any religious service was striking. It does not appear that attendance at these New Year's services is by any means the almost universal custom we have been led to suppose.

"Men's Own" Services[3]

(1) At the East London Tabernacle the afternoon service for men is in effect a Bible-class. It is held in the 'young men's room'. At Edinburgh Castle, though quite religious in character, the service is made pleasant with orchestral music and solo singing, and evidently attracts young fellows. In all there were 500 or 600 present, mostly young, and some quite lads, all of lower middle and working class. The orchestra and chorus number about 100, and include female voices. At the Great Assembly Hall there is also a meeting, but of a different character. It is held in the small hall, which looked quite full with perhaps 300 men. The men were on the average ten years older, and quite a degree, or a class, poorer than the audience

3. ' "Men's Own" Services', 'The Salvation Army', 'A Sunday Walk',' and 'Other Extracts' (pages 321–34) are taken from Vol. I of the third edition, third series, pp. 239–51.

at Edinburgh Castle. Some did not wear collars and the atmosphere testified that many were unwashed. They were in hearty accord with the speaker, whose address was very effective – on Zaccheus, the little man who climbed up into a tree to see Jesus – so disadvantages might stimulate to higher things. The service included and closed with a performance of 'religious minstrelsy' by blind singers. At the back of the hall were clerks at tables to enrol new members – a special effort in this direction made for the new year, it being early in January. On the following Sunday I attended a similar service at the Bow and Bromley Institute, and arriving at 3.30 I found the hall ringing with the first hymn. There were then fully 300 men present and more were streaming in every minute, so that the total might probably reach 400. The hall is a large place and looked dishevelled and almost dissolute with the traces and debris of the Saturday night's entertainment, which had consisted of gramophone and magic-lantern displays interspersed with songs and dances 'intended' (as the advertisement claimed) 'to elevate as well as amuse'. This entertainment had been largely attended – admission 3d. and 6d. The Sunday afternoon meeting consisted very largely of working men of all kinds and ages. They showed genuine religious feeling, and the leader held their attention with ease. There was a large orchestra, vocal and instrumental, and the singing was strong.

(2) I have twice attended Mr Watts Ditchfield's Sunday afternoon men's service at St James-the-Less. On the first occasion it was 'Question Sunday'. The body of the church was full of men, not less than 500, I thought. Looking at them from my seat at the back I took them to be mostly above working-class level, but studying them later as they left the building one could see that a large proportion were either artisans or the sons of working men employed as clerks. The answering of the questions

is very popular and the service draws the largest congregation. A sheaf of posers are sent in every month, of which some are dealt with and the rest postponed. On this occasion the first was 'Is it wrong to smoke?' and the reply in effect was 'according to circumstances': don't annoy others; don't become a slave to a habit; don't overdo it; don't begin too young. Then followed six questions suggested by the Book of Job as to Satan and God's relations with him (according to this authority), which were very difficult to answer from a simple ordinary biblical point of view. Other questions succeeded, and finally a series concerning the present state of the Church of England and the responsibility of the clergy for her doctrines as embodied in the Thirty-nine Articles were considered. The audience was keenly interested in all these points, and the way in which some words of high respect for the late Mr Spurgeon, and others animadverting against High Church doings were received, showed the general religious complexion of those present; and certainly suggested that even if they are non-churchgoers (as is claimed) their minds are fully awake on religious subjects.

On the occasion of the second visit, made a year later, the men only loosely filled the body of the church, which might mean 300. All ages were represented, inclining to young, and there were some possibly of middle class; but the general bulk were lower middle and upper working class, with no very wide divergence amongst them, It is a regular religious service beginning with a specially selected liturgy, the book being provided, followed by hymns and lesson before the sermon. The service was conducted by a very quiet earnest type of curate, and a young layman, who had evidently been schooled to speak up, read the lesson. The vicar came in before the last hymn and at once mounted the pulpit. Without perhaps much spirituality, he has power and simplicity, and goes straight at his object. The (advertised) subject of his sermon was 'The first prayer', and his opening words on the lasting memory of the prayer learnt at a mother's knee were very beautiful. He pursued his subject on the need for and efficacy of prayer, and of becoming what he termed 'a praying man', without very much subtlety of thought, but ended with a genuine appeal made with confidence, and therefore effective and touching.

The church is stamped with the same spirit as the services held in it. It is a wide building, with a fine open roof, painted white, and deep high-pitched galleries; decorated in white and gold.

(3) An earlier and practically pioneer attempt of the same kind, of which we have received an interesting account, is that called the Men's Social Union in connection with the Stepney Meeting House of the Congregationalists. It was founded by the son of a previous minister who, returning to England, desired 'to do something for the old place', and this took the form of a Sunday afternoon meeting of men not exactly evangelical, nor simply social in character, but definitely aimed at the advancement of religious and social reform. The combination requires management. Some men boggle at the discussion of social subjects as being 'politics', others, if religious subjects are chosen, 'can hear a sermon any day', but by sandwiching the two both sets are retained. The attendance is not what it was in the earlier and more enthusiastic days, but for some years past there has been no change, and 120 remain members. Once a month, when women are admitted and a special musical programme arranged, the audiences are large. The members pay 1d. per week, and the money is partly returned in books, a plan, now usually adopted, which came (as did the whole suggestion of the Pleasant Sunday Afternoon movement) from the Midlands. Amongst the members there is a nucleus of men who are very keen, upon whose devotion the whole thing really rests.

There is a week-day meeting place, constituting a club on purely social lines. The need of this was early felt, and a room in the old schools was provided; but money to make the necessary alterations lacked; whereon the men buckled to and did the work themselves, about twenty-five giving in their names, plumbers, painters, carpenters, etc., and for some three months gave their leisure, so that the room was prepared without one penny being spent in wages.

The Salvation Army

(1) ... Opposite the churchyard gates is a Salvation Army Citadel, and as I came by the Salvationists marched up, a very small group with noisy instruments. It was just 11 o'clock on Sunday morning, and I entered after them. A few women and children and some lads were already there, and perhaps all told, after the marching party arrived, there would be ten to fifteen adults and twenty children. The soldiers' first duty was to look to the fires, and soon a hymn was started and sung to a lively ballad tune. I did not make any stay. In the evening, after 8 o'clock, I found a larger gathering, which kept increasing by late arrivals of those who had evidently been attending services elsewhere, and finally the total numbers would be forty to fifty, all adults. The service flagged. The conductor started verse after verse of the hymn 'Come to Jesus', and he and some others sang at the top of their voices, but order was badly kept, and a great deal of talking was going on behind me and all round. Then a young woman, with an excited face, poured forth a prayer, which the leader accompanied by a running fire of ejaculations, as did also some of the others. After her a pale-faced, earnest young man, hardly more than a boy, prayed in the usual simple salvationist fashion – from his heart, I thought. The male conductor now gave up his

place to a woman, and when I left I found him outside. He bade me 'good night and God bless you'.

(2) I entered a Salvation Army barrack one Sunday morning, attracted by the sound of the music, and found there a very energetic little party of people, some twenty or thirty adult Salvationists, and at least an equal number of children. The women all wore the bonnet, but only the men on the platform were in the soldier's garb. The leader, a forcible young man, shouted and waved his arms, and the trumpets brayed, and prayers of the usual kind were poured forth, interspersed with the verses of a hymn. The leader was very professional in all he did, turning to talk and even laugh with those behind him, while his arm still worked and his hand thumped to emphasize the tune.

(3) One Sunday evening I came across a corps of the Salvation Army which was just opening new premises. They were in great force, with brass instruments and white helmets for the bandsmen, and the women and officers in regulation dress. They were thirty or forty in all and capable of producing a prodigious noise as they marched along, with a following of ragged children, to a street corner, where they formed up and held a rather emotional service, attracting absolutely no attention; except indeed for a moment from the lighted windows of a house opposite, where some one raising the blind disclosed a tea party and a curate in the act of lifting his cup to his mouth, and then the blind fell again. I stayed on. One of the Salvationists, an educated woman, threw out a passionate appeal into the darkness; vaguely addressing bystanders or the world at large, for she could not see us; and the fierce threats she launched against those who disregarded her words – a bitter outburst of her soul – seemed to pass us by. She was succeeded by the leader of the party, a German, who raved and ranted and excited

his followers till they almost danced. And then back they went, the ragged children and I still in attendance, till they reached their new hall, where doubtless they would have a 'full meeting and much saving of souls'. This was their opening Sunday. I did not go in.

(4) ... Congress Hall is a curious cockpit of a place, like Edinburgh Castle, but looked even larger. It must hold 2,000 to 3,000 easily and was gradually filling. The preaching was the same as always. That Christ by His blood has saved us and that He stands ready to receive us NOW. No other ideas at all are offered, nothing but the passionate appeals and expositions and prayers of the soldiers who conduct, mingled with the singing of the hymns. These last were not well given here, there being too much brass band and drum, and too little congregational singing. But the leader was an excellent type of soldier. I was struck with his taking off his tunic and throwing it behind him; stripping to his red shirt as he found conducting hot work. The action was very typical.

A Sunday Walk

It was a foggy Sunday morning, gradually clearing. A proper day, one should suppose, for church-going. From King's Cross I went on foot up the Caledonian Road to Charlotte Street, and looked in on the King's Cross Mission to the Masses. I ascended to the gallery and found myself among some Sunday-school children. It was about 11.15, and a hymn was being sung energetically by the choir to an orchestral accompaniment. In the body of the church there were only a few people scattered about. The masses certainly do not come in the morning nor, I found later, do any very large numbers come in the evening. I did not stay. Thence through the fog to Copenhagen Street, and through the dark blue and black patch to the east of Half Moon Crescent, of which the worst part is empty of inhabitants and undergoing renovation. Then by Barnsbury Road and Penton Street to the corner of Chapel Street, opposite which stands St Silas's Church. Here, too, I went in. The church has a good interior, and the service is well appointed, but there was hardly any congregation, not more than fifty people at most. Inscribed in large letters could be read, 'This is the House of the Lord. This is the Gate of Heaven,' and it seems to be only too true that few there be who enter therein.

Then I passed along Chapel Street, where were many poor women standing round the cheap auctions of second-hand clothing. At each there is a great pile of old garments, and two women, one at each side, who sell. They pick up piece after piece, display it, name three times as much as they propose to sell it for; then successively mention lower prices one after another with hardly a pause; then fold it up as though the figure last named was in truth the final bottom price; but invariably open it out once more and then come rapidly down to real business: 1s. 6d., 1s., and 9d., following in quick succession for an article that had been opened at 2s. 6d.; or 4d., 3d., 2d., for one which began at 6d. Then, if no sale is made, the garment is thrown aside and another taken up. I saw nothing sold, but the women went on displaying their goods, and their customers waited, and no doubt knew that what they looked for would come sooner or later; for I think they had special wants, rather than any sporting idea of picking up 'something' cheap. There were half a dozen of these clothes sales in Chapel Street, and the usual Sunday market stalls for meat, vegetables, and odds and ends, all of the poorest description.

From Chapel Street by Liverpool Street to Trinity Church, Cloudesley Square. Again a large church fully appointed, and just a few people scattered about among the seats. In Upper Street I entered Unity Church, a large and handsome building belonging to the Unitarians, with hardly any people in it. Also in Upper Street is St Mary's, a fine old-fashioned building, well arranged for a large congregation, but again a mere handful of people. The Islington Chapel, belonging to the Congregationalists, which also I entered during this walk, was a little less empty than the rest – perhaps one-quarter full, and here, as I stood at the back, I heard a portion of an eloquent and remarkable sermon, delivered in a voice with a strong north-country burr to it. The subject fell in with my thoughts. It was on the disappointments of religious effort: the discontent with Christ. Our feelings today were compared to those of the disciples who laid the dead Christ in the tomb, from which His Spirit, in ways unforeseen by them, was to burst forth and flood the world.

In a corner behind St Mary's Church is a little Temperance Hall, on the wall of which hangs a board with the following inscription:

The Christadelphians meeting in this hall believe in the divine inspiration of the Bible, and look for the second appearing of Jesus Christ, to give immortality to the righteous and to rule the nations for a thousand years.

Then followed notices of the services, and elsewhere there was a placard stating that the subject of the evening's discourse that Sunday would be the coming destruction of the Devil. A young man approached and, after listening awhile, pushed the door open, and entered, and I went in with him. He was evidently at home there. I, fearing to intrude further, stood still, and looked on for a moment. It was a small place, arranged like a lecture-hall. Near the entrance was a table loaded with books and pamphlets. The preacher or lecturer was speaking in a low voice, audible no doubt to all near him, as there was perfect stillness. Here was one of the little communities which continue to bubble up from the great fountain of

Christianity. Here, at any rate, there was earnestness. Here two or three were gathered together, and one could not doubt that Christ was in their midst.

Other Extracts

(1) *Opium Smoking*

... We knocked, and our conductor inquired, 'Are you at home, mother, may we come in?' 'Come in, come in, my dear,' answered a woman's voice from an inner room, and we passed through a small dark room into another rather less dark, but smaller. The greater part of it was taken up by a large square low bed or couch with curtains at the two sides. In the centre of this bed was set a tray with a small lamp under a glass shade, round the lamp three or four little boxes or bottles, and at the back of the bed four small square pillows. Reclining on either side of the lamp were a man and a woman, both fully dressed, except that the man was in his shirt sleeves. The trousers he wore hung loosely on him, showing an outline of bones and joints which had evidently not been born to wear trousers. The man was a Hindoo, the woman English, or perhaps Irish. They were man and wife, and kept the opium den. As we entered they were just about to start smoking. They complained that business was bad. Ships now insist on their crews being on board at 7 p.m., which interferes with smoking at night.

Another den was found behind a Chinese general shop. It was a back room, only about six feet square, with a low bed like the other, and on it two Chinamen, one happy and jolly, wreathed with smiles, who *had* smoked, and a very sour-looking pigtailed heathen who was just *starting* his pipe. Business was bad, we again heard, in spite of the fact that a rival, who had three dens on the other side of the street, is dead and his place turned into a laundry.

The proprietor in this case did not himself smoke. He does business of all kinds for the Chinese here, and is very prosperous...

(2) *A Double Funeral*

... The two funerals were dealt with in a single service. The graves lay side by side, and round each the particular mourners pressed closely, the chaplain standing somewhere in the middle of them, and a small crowd collecting round about. In two or three minutes all was over. The mourners seemed hardly to realize it, and the parson slipped unobserved away.

The forlornness and the very impersonal character of the whole proceeding was its most marked feature. Death the Comforter seemed far away. The chief female mourner of one of the funerals had been sobbing loudly, even from the moment she left the chapel door, and when the time came to leave the graveside she broke out into violent hysterical grief. She was carried away, and both parties soon after drove off. A little later, when I left the cemetery, I saw the coaches of her party drawn up at a public house at the corner of the street.

I found the chaplain in the chapel, with five minutes to spare before his next funeral. He had seemed to be pretty busily occupied, but really it was a quiet day for Monday, with only five funerals, whereas there are generally about fifteen. Saturday and Monday are the busiest times, and on these days a crowd collects. 'It is one of their sights.' Just before I left, the bell began to toll; a warning that the next cortège was approaching. Of the general public there were only some forty or fifty present, mostly women. As I walked down the drive I met two additional onlookers, young fellows, arm-in-arm and both drunk.

Funerals, said the chaplain on another occasion, are still very extravagant, especially in the case of the poorest people, flowers being one of the chief items of expenditure. Plumes on the horses' heads are quite commonly used, but the panoply of ostrich feathers carried in front of the procession is only occasionally seen now. It costs £1 1s. to hire. Fish and cats'-meat dealers and costermongers are the people most addicted to showy funerals. A large proportion of the elaborate tombstones facing the main drive belong to these people. There is a feeling among the poor that when a man dies if he has saved money it is his: 'he made the money, poor fellow, and he shall have it'. The people are by habit 'noisy in their grief', sometimes with little basis of real feeling. A woman, who from the chapel to the grave had repeated in perfectly unbroken sequence the words 'Ay! But what shall oi do without my poor Moike – God rest his soul', on reaching the place and looking down, interrupted this formula with the involuntary ejaculation, 'Good God, what a hole.'...

(3) ... A tradesman, who has a shop nearly opposite a public house much frequented by women, said that 11 a.m. and between 6 and 7 p.m. were the great hours for women's drinking. All classes of women go in, and no one seems to mind in the least being seen. The favourite tipple is gin. There is a butcher's stall close by, and those who buy a joint are treated to a drink. Drinking among women has certainly increased. Factory girls drink, but it is the young married or middle-aged women who take too much. The increase is not among the poor only...

(4) ... Friday is the most remarkable day at the cattle market. Ponies, horses, carts, donkeys, and goats for sale, as well as a miscellaneous rag fair, where nearly everything is offered and nearly everything finds a purchaser. Books by the hundredweight, old pictures, clothes, vegetables, toys, hot drinks, stewed eels, furs, harness, rusty nails, locks, chains, rubbish that one would think would not pay to move a yard. But good things turn up occa-

(5) ... We went to see Charlie, a man who keeps a rough coffee-shop. The shop was apparently empty, except for Mrs Charlie and her child of about five, the shop girl, and one customer. There was a long counter, on which were piled, in rude plenty, many loaves of bread, flitches of bacon, a quantity of butter, two tea-urns (unpolished and out of use), three beer-pumps for Kop's ale, and a glass jar filled with pickled onions, together with a great debris of mustard pots, glasses, knives and forks, ginger-beer bottles, and a knuckle of ham. In an open space, where a bagatelle board once had stood, was a perambulator and a heap of old boots and other rubbish. We were told that everyone was downstairs watching a skittle match. A staircase led down from the far end of the shop to a cellar, which had been converted into a skittle alley, and here there was a thick crowd of a rough class: young lads of sixteen to eighteen and men of twenty-five to forty, labourers in corduroys tied round the knee: in nearly every case a neckerchief took the place of collar. Several of the men were half drunk. 'All the greatest blackguards about,' said the friendly proprietor. The final round was in progress. Forty entries, at 6d. a head, for a silver watch (cost 6s. 6d.). But for the proprietor's command of language (he is also known to be ready with his fists if need be), there were many moments when a row seemed imminent, but the strongest and noisiest withered away when addressed by him. After the watch was won a match for a leg of mutton was to follow. There were about sixty or eighty persons crowded down in the cellar on either side of the skittle run; no women. After the first match a number came upstairs and partook of a ham sandwich and glass of ginger beer or a cup of tea. The demand was brisk, and Mrs Charlie, in order to be free to cut sandwiches, gave over her child to the care of the

noisiest and roughest man, who became tame and quiet in a moment. Charlie himself sat in a corner counting his takings, and no one was paying much attention to the counter, when a navvy who entered seized the great pickle jar and, conveying it to where some boys were eating, invited them to help themselves – all this being done to start Charlie's tongue, which it did very successfully.

(6)[4] *Saturday Night in Bromley and Bow – Perambulation on Bicycle (Summer-time)*

11 o'clock. Men and women buying, no shop shut, a few children about: more men than women seen through the open doors of the public houses, all of which were full, but not filled to overflowing; pawnshops full of women: a few common prostitutes trying to induce young men to accompany them: no street rows or brawling.

11.45. Shops – butchers, grocers, etc. – begin to put up shutters. Solitary women making bargains for the last joint.

Across the bridge into Stratford the scene was altogether different: shops nearly all shut; public houses shut, the closing hour being earlier; all quiet. Several women sitting on their doorsteps.

Between 12.15 and 12.30 in roads between Bow and Victoria Park, shops with shutters up, but doors generally open; shopkeepers taking a breath of air before closing up for the night. One or two men the worse for drink, but none incapable.

(7) *Note by Daylight*

... One public house in Ford Street (North Bow), situated close to a dark blue patch, has a flag-staff on an adjoining piece of ground, and half-way up this a board is nailed, with the following legend in rough characters: 'No more starvation. Mild Ale, 2d. per pot.'...

4. We have taken the liberty of correcting Booth's numbering in these observations. – EDS

Sundry Notes[5]

(1) A Salvation Army After-service

It is a big, barn-like building. In the front row some twenty to thirty Salvationists were singing, shouting, and gesticulating, their leader pacing up and down like one possessed. At times he seized hold of a concertina, and almost danced as he played. Scattered about the hall were sixty or seventy other people, taking apparently but small interest in the proceedings, but probably at home there and well used to them. Some were talking in groups, others walked in and out with clattering noise, whilst, in contrast to this, two or three Salvation Army officers passed quietly, almost stealthily, from one person to another endeavouring to obtain converts. At one time two male Salvationists and one female were all at the same man – a quiet-looking young fellow – who seemed to have enough of it and passed out. I was myself approached by a middle-aged man of some education. He spoke of death, and what was to happen after to those not prepared. He told me he had been the means of bringing many to Christ.

(2) Simple Faith and Prayer

Having no fixed salary, the minister depends on the voluntary contributions of the congregation, but 'God is the same yesterday, today, and for ever, and never allows His ministers to want.' 'When things reach a low ebb,' he says, 'I pray, and never without response.' Only last Friday – he and his wife and children being in the last stage of shabbiness as regards clothing – he prayed over the matter, and on Saturday morning a parcel arrived containing clothes for all of them, and all fitted exactly.

---

5. 'Sundry Notes', 'The London City Mission', 'Salvation Army', and ' "Unity Sunday" on Peckham Rye' (pages 335–64) are taken from Vol. VI of the third edition, third series, pp. 170–95.

The things had come from a complete stranger, a lady who had heard of him, but had never seen him, but who had felt an irresistible prompting to send him the things. If, said the minister, this was not an answer to prayer, what was it?

(3) *The Passion for Betting*

Gambling is increasing beyond what you could imagine. 'Pitch-and-toss' is too dull: all must bet; women as well as men. Bookies stand about and meet men as they go to and from their work. The police take no notice. See the sudden life in a street after a great race has been run, and the newspaper is out: note the eagerness with which the papers are read. Boys on bicycles, with reams of pink paper in a cloth bag on their back, come scorching through the streets, tossing minor bundles to smaller boys, who wait for them at street corners. Off rush the little boys, shouting at the top of their voices: doors open; factory gates part; men and boys tumble out in their eagerness to read, and it is the betting news alone that they are eager about.

(4) ****** *Place*

Several women came out to see what our business might be, and began to complain of the drains. There appeared to be some special grievance at one of the houses, inside which was an agitated group. At their request, we went in and looked at the closet in the little yard behind. Whether from want of flushing or from stoppage, it was hopelessly blocked, and in a most filthy condition. One stalwart woman said that things had been as we saw them for months, and that complaint to the landlord was met with the reply, that if they did not like the houses they could leave them and let someone come in who would pay 7s. instead of 6s., the present rental. We were told of the numbers who had been made ill by the drains, and one poor thing was pointed out who had just returned from hospital. The sadness of the scene culminated in a small coffin of a child that stood on a table at one side of the room in which we all were. When we asked who the owner was, the rent book was shown, and later in the day, when we reported the state of things at the office of the local medical officer, we gathered that the name was familiar, but the man spoken to committed himself to no opinion. He was silent.

(5) *In a Poor Suburb – Sunday Night*

Inside they were singing Sankey's hymn, 'Safe in the arms of Jesus'; outside, as I stood in the lighted porch, I heard childish voices shouting from the darkness, 'Let's come in, Guv'nor, we won't make no noise; we'll behive ourselves.' Going towards them, I made out several small, rough-looking children peering through the railings from an adjoining field. I suggested they would be better at home and in bed at this time of night; to which a girl of about eight (and little at that) replied in saucily precocious style, speaking for herself and a companion, 'Garn, we're ahrt wiv ahr blokes; that's my bloke.' 'Yus,' said the other girl, 'and that's mine' (they pointing to two boys about their own size). At this there was a general shout of laughter; and then came a plaintive plea from the first child, 'Give us a penny, will you, Guv'nor?' Regular cockney arabs these.

The London City Mission

Instructions to Missionaries

The annual report made by each missionary is written in a prescribed form according to printed instructions. In these instructions the Committee earnestly desire that the strictest accuracy should be observed and no overstatements made, and impress on the missionaries the importance of their bestowing pains in faithfully reporting their work. They point out that the interest of the public in the Society is kept up chiefly by these reports and that subscribers are entitled to expect some information as to the operations of the missionaries, and in order to guard against reporting cases too generally or too briefly, and probably also to ensure definiteness, the following suggestions are made:

1. Give a description of the houses and the social conditions of the people in your district. If the district be a bad one, describe the worst street or court.

2. Are infidelity and drunkenness on the increase or decrease among the people in your district? What do you believe to be the cause of the increase or decrease of each respectively?

3. To what extent are the people in your district influenced by socialistic or revolutionary doctrines?

4. Mention as nearly as possible the number of *men* you visit periodically or in the course of the year, in factories, public houses, and other places.

5. Report any social benefits which arise from your spiritual work. Mention individual cases.

6. In cases of blessing, when individuals are Scotch, Irish, or of any other nationality than English, mention the fact in the heading and in the index on the back of wrapper.

The following report made by one of the missionaries, serves as an illustration:

A case of interest is that of a man and wife named —, the former a dustman, the latter working in a market garden. I knew nothing of this family till after the husband's professed conversion. I then discovered them living in my district. The family history was the sad, but oft-repeated story of trouble through drink, the husband losing both situation and character through it. It appeared that the man had gone out with not a thought of religion in his mind, but dejected and despondent owing to his folly. Whilst passing along the street he stopped at an open-air meeting, and there heard the hymn, 'What a Friend we have in Jesus'. He went home and told his wife that there was still a friend who he had heard would never leave them. From that time he began to pray and earnestly seek the Lord, and it was in this state of mind I found and at once set to work to help and encourage him. My first thought was to get his wife converted, but I found the poor woman very dark, and neither of them could read or write.... I got them both to attend the House of God, and they both of them testify, and indeed, by their conduct exemplify, a complete change of heart and life.... I promised to get him re-instated if possible.... The surveyor gave him another trial, at first as scavenger, and now he is restored to his old position, proving the truth of the Scripture, 'Godliness is profitable unto all things, having promise of the life that now is and of that which is to come.'

Salvation Army

(1) *Salvation Army Shelter in Blackfriars Road*

I called without notice in the morning, with an order from headquarters, which, however, I did not need to use as I was readily received and shown round. The place had appeared empty when I arrived, and I penetrated through corridors and some out-buildings and even to the kitchens before I encountered anyone. At last I came to the large room of the shelter around which the berths are placed, and in which the religious meetings are held and which forms at other times a central lounge. Scrubbing was going on, a daily operation which the condition of the uncleaned part showed to be very necessary, and which was completely carried out. This shelter is said to be the largest in the country, accommodating between 500 and 600, being 42 places at 3d., 472 at 2d., and 48 at 1d., and is generally about full. Half of the lodgers are regular, but do not here get the seventh day thrown in as is done at the S. A. metropoles and in many common lodging-houses. There is no free accommodation, except that at 4 in the morning the doors are opened and any who may then be in waiting are admitted without payment, it being assumed that if out at that time of night they must be in great need. They are provided neither with bed nor food, obtaining nothing but warmth and shelter. The penny lodgers receive six ounces of bread. The 2d. and 3d. payments are for the sleeping accommodation only. Our conductor thought the place about paid its way, which could not be said of many other branches of the social wing. The buildings are an extensive block and were once a forage depot. There is abundance of space, but it is not well used. The bunks seemed to be ill-arranged; the old-fashioned ones, shallow boxes resting on the floor, being set too near together, while those of newer pattern in the large hall, placed in two tiers and at the same time two abreast, are hardly, if at all, more desirable. The 3d. lodgers have cubicles. The bunks of the 1d. lodgers are in a corridor.

The shelter is opened at 4 in the afternoon, at which time lodgers can occupy the 1d. places; at 5 the whole place is open. At 7.45 in the morning the signal for clearing out is given, and by 8 all have to leave, except on Sunday, when the arrangements are different. The class of men that comes appears to be, as usual, a very mixed one, but none are young. A limit is set at about twenty-five, and if any come who are under that age they are sent to another place. It does not answer to mix the young and the old, the former annoying the latter with noise or ragging. The occupations mentioned were sandwich-men, bill-stickers, and, our attendant added, a good many who could be called 'mouchers'. There are also many helpless old men. Nearly all come on their own account and pay for themselves, but some are sent by one or other of the Salvation Army corps of the district and in these cases, which are not numerous, the lodging money is paid by the senders.

Besides the two officers, there are twenty men employed for scrubbing, or in the kitchen, or as watchers. The bar provides tea, cocoa, rashers, bread, jam, etc., at very low prices. The men employed are sent from the 'elevators', to which places they may possibly have been forwarded from the shelter itself. In addition to any influence that may be brought to bear on the lodgers by personal contact with the officers, or through the religious meetings held, the Army is able to help those who find their way to the shelter by sending on a certain number to headquarters with a view to their being passed on to one of the elevators. About twenty or thirty are found suitable and sent on in this way every week, a small proportion of the whole – for most of the men either have their own work or would shun the discipline of the elevators and simply use the shelter as a common lodging-house.

Some light is thrown on the manner of life of at least some of the lodgers at such shelters, by the remark that on Sunday morning there are a number of places to which the men can go and get food for nothing, as we know is the case, and it is clear that many prowl for the poor pickings of religion and charity, and that the whole system makes existence at a low level more possible, enabling those who do any work to get along on a lower wage than would otherwise be possible, and certainly doing nothing to raise the standard of requirement.

For hot baths and for the 'cremation' of verminous clothing a small charge is made to cover the cost of heating. The arrangements generally are as they have been for some years, the indecision of the Courts as to liability to inspection having checked voluntary improvement.

No trouble occurs in regard to discipline; the matter was fought out early, and it is now recognized that rules have to be observed and decent order kept. The religious meetings, which are for the lodgers only, are fairly well attended. The men are on the spot.

(2) Salvation Army Metropole, 'The Ark', Southwark Street

I called at about 6 in the evening, in driving wind and snow, when everyone was under shelter that could manage it, and the place was at its fullest: the kitchen crowded with men. I went without notice, armed with an order, and again found it not needed. The officer in charge and the cashier were busy giving out checks and doing the ordinary business of a common lodging-house, but the latter volunteered to show me round the place, which presented the ordinary common lodging-house features: kitchen; lavatories, for washing both person and clothes; baths; bar, with food at cost price; dormitories and cubicles; lockers practically free, since of the 6d. key-money, 5d. is repaid on return of the key, without limit of time. Arrangements something better than those of any shelter or of most common lodging-houses, something worse than of the Rowton Houses or the best portions of the Victoria Homes in Whitechapel; on the whole, convenient, clean, sanitary, and well suited to the purpose. The chief difference from the S.A. shelter was to be found in the sleeping accommodation, which was better in every respect and more roomy. Behind the kitchen was an extra room to be used as reading-room, but at the moment under repair.

The men in the kitchen, or rather in the public room where the bar is and in which they can if they like cook their own food, looked like an ordinary lodging-house group, not of the lowest kind. They were listless and quiet. Very little talking was going on. Many were comparatively young. The charges are 4d. and 6d. a night, and the seventh night is thrown in free. There is accommodation for two hundred lodgers. The greater proportion are regular and most are newspaper-sellers. Some had already gone to bed and were fast asleep; the men can be called at any hour, and at 1, 2, and 3 in the morning the outward movement begins. All must be out between 11 a.m. and 1 p.m. for cleaning. Religious meetings are held on three week-nights, and there is a special meeting on Sunday afternoon.

As at the shelters, likely cases are sent on to headquarters with a view to trial at one of the elevators, but, unless special interest is felt, nothing either here or at the shelters is known as to what afterwards happens to them. Only if they came back, it would be known. The captain in charge thought 10 per cent might perhaps be dealt with in this way; but the place seems first and foremost to be a well-managed common lodging-house.

The men who come to the Salvation Army shelters and metropoles do not seem to differ in class from those frequenting other common lodging-houses, and it is said that a large proportion are Roman Catholics, from whom at any rate it is useless for the Army to expect any religious response. As a rule the men attend the meetings and, even if they do not respond, are quiet. One night, however, a man came and claimed his money back. 'I don't want any of your b— Gospel', said he; to which the officer unhesitatingly replied, 'Very well, but remember it is by the b— Gospel that you will be damned; here is your fourpence; good night.' The man was taken aback, being answered in his own vernacular, but pocketed his money and went. There may, perhaps, be more to be hoped for from this man than from many who sit unmoved in stolid listlessness.

(3) *Salvation Army Elevator and Home in Bermondsey*

Again I went without notice, but at the address given us found a deserted building. The work had been removed to new quarters. On reaching these I entered a very muddy yard, which was surrounded on two sides by buildings, old and new, and on the third by the unimaginable litter of a paper-sorting establishment. Directed to the captain in charge, I passed through a group of sorry-looking men and caught a glimpse of a large sorting-room in which a much greater number were at work. The captain, without being keen or sanguine, was interested in his work, but explained that with the moving and rebuilding all was in confusion and that the work dragged for lack of funds.

As we have been told, the men are sent to the elevator from headquarters, and when discharged they are returned to headquarters for the next step, the elevator captain as a rule knowing nothing of what happens to them, except that if they turned out badly complaints would be made. We gather that the first berths given to those who have served a probationary term in an elevator are those of cleaners, etc., at one or other of the shelters or metropoles. From there a man might get promotion to the ranks of the Army itself, or he might return to the world and get work on his own account in the open market. This plunge many are afraid to make, preferring to continue to serve the Army for small pay.

The length of time that men stay in the elevator itself varies according to their inclination or capacities, but appears rarely to exceed about six months. The hours of work are 6.45 to 8.15, 9 to 1, and 2 to 6, stopping on Saturdays at 1.30, or $53\frac{1}{2}$ per week. Men may go out in the evening till 8 o'clock, but not later without special leave. The religious services are for the inmates only, and they, it is said, respond heartily; but watching them at work it was hard to imagine it. The system of sorting and packing the paper was very methodical; the men working with a subdued air and giving an impression, not of blackguardism but of degeneracy; a sad scene of human wreckage. All the paper comes from other parts of London; it is hoped that a collecting station may be started in Bermondsey and provide another branch of work.

(4) *Salvation Army Farm Colony in Essex*

The estate was bought when land was at its lowest figure in Essex some years ago, and the value per acre is now considerably higher than it was at the time of purchase. In other respects also, the site appears to have been well selected. It covers about three thousand acres, running down from the high ground where Hadleigh village stands, and where all the dwellings used by the Salvation Army are, across the low level stretch of land that borders the river, to the Thames itself. A railway traverses the estate; a wharf has been built, and cheap carriage on the tideway thus secured for the produce of the colony, this being of special importance in handling the bricks, of which large numbers are made. Much of the land in this lower part is of poor quality, somewhat marshy, and only good enough for rough grazing. The brickfields and kilns which constitute the most important industrial undertaking are near the bottom of the slope, and for some kinds of bricks the clays and sand are well suited.

On one hill-side, beautifully placed, is the poultry farm with over 1,500 head of poultry, some of them prize birds; for the Army is getting a name at the shows, and for some strains can command high prices.

In other parts of the estate are the fruit gardens and orchards, the vegetable grounds, and the ordinary farming lands. The industrial buildings include a well-appointed cow-shed with accommodation for 100 head, piggeries, and stores. Other buildings are the 'Citadel' – a hall with room for 500 people where the larger meetings are held – and the men's dormitories, dining-room, etc.

There were in residence 250 colonists, and employment could be found for fifty more without further outlay. The chief control is vested in a 'Governor' who, in the case of the present holder of the office, seems to be given a very free hand. There are various departmental officers, not all of them belonging to the Army, but the manager of the dormitories, who is in special charge of the meetings and the spiritual welfare of the men, is naturally always a Salvationist.

Newcomers are first put to work in a kind of apprentice ground, to be tried and trained, and even nursed, into fitness for the regular colonist life. Some may get no further, but in most sufficient adaptability is found to carry them forward into one industrial branch or other. A considerable and increasing number find their own way to the colony, and these, being a natural selection, provide the most hopeful cases; others (and the bulk) are in effect selected by the Army from those who come to their night shelters, and in addition a few are sent (and paid for) by the Guardians, these yielding the smallest percentage of success.

In its way the colony is a very complete and remarkable undertaking, and very nearly self-contained, so far as current requirements are concerned, except for groceries and clothing, and these can be bought on the premises. No intoxicating liquors are allowed, but tobacco is. No Salvationist officer is allowed to smoke, though soldiers of the Army may. The colonists are of course, as a rule, neither one nor the other.

The weather was brilliantly fine when we visited the farm, and it was seen under very favourable circumstances; many of the views are even beautiful, the most striking feature being the river in the distance, almost an estuary here, with great ships passing up and down the highway to London. The Governor took us round the place.

Passing by the poultry farm we came to the brickfields, upon which much more capital has been spent than upon any other section; and a considerable portion of the colonists (though the number varies with the season) are always employed in it. The men engaged were not all colonists, though the unskilled mostly were. The gangs are made up of skilled and unskilled, graded to the task and all paid by the piece; the work was partly in the hands of local contractors. The blending of what may be termed independent outside labour, with that of the regular colonists, is necessary for efficiency in every part of the work. Going on from the brickfields we came to the dormitories, which are arranged in three classes; the main difference being in the number of those who sleep in a single compartment, the better class sleeping only about three together. All places looked clean. The accommodation as regards bedding, etc., was roughly that of a London elevator or metropole.

On some of the walls of the public rooms notices were hung, recapitulating the promises that each colonist makes on admission, as regards drinking, trespassing (a man may go to no section except the one to which his work takes him), attendance at the special Saturday meeting, and at *some* religious service on Sunday (be it Protestant or Catholic). Not knowing what they had promised had been made a frequent excuse for default. The obligatory Salvation meeting on Saturday is made as bright as possible, though the religious tone is preserved. The Governor attaches much importance to attendance at this meeting, finding in it an opportunity, if he wishes to use it, of addressing every one. Meetings of one kind or other (addresses, concerts, etc.), at which attendance is optional, are held every evening in a smaller room. Discipline in the colony (as in the shelters, etc., in London) is easily preserved, and dirty or unpleasant conduct, in the dormitories or elsewhere, is said to give no trouble. With drinking it is otherwise; some of the men being apt to procure it, in spite of promises, when in the village. But even this trouble appears to be exceptional. (Part of what they earn comes to the men as pocket-money.)

It is not to be supposed that an establishment of this kind can be made profitable. The property, with the buildings, improvements, and machinery on it, stands in the books at over £100,000, and the stock at over £10,000. Leaving interest on this capital sum out of account, there was still for many years a heavy loss; but lessons in the art of management have been learnt, and, at the time of our visit, something approaching an equipoise between incomings and outgoings had been established. A judicious combination between the two classes of labour – outside, independent; and inside, colonial – is necessary if loss is to be avoided; and yet more necessary is the permission to retain for a while as colonists those who have learnt to be useful, instead of sending them away into the world in order to make room for new broken-down men. The Governor put it tersely as an alternative between 'making money and making men'. But on the other side it may be said that men may be very satisfactory while at the colony, and yet be quite unfit to face the temptations of the world; and strange though it may seem, the limit of numbers lies not with the capacity of the farm and its industries to employ labour, but with the applicants. There is no rush. The difficulty rather is to find amongst the derelict classes even three hundred men who are willing to accept this life of discipline and labour, with such future chances as it offers. The colony is a very useful institution, and as an experiment its value has been even greater, justifying all the money and zeal expended on it; but as a solution of the 'employment' question in London, even if multiplied ten-fold, it would be of no account.

(5) *A Night in a Salvation Army Shelter*

[The following account appeared in the *Western Mercury* newspaper on 29 July 1902, and reached me through a Press Cutting Agency. I know nothing of the writer, but the description he gives bears the unmistakable stamp of truth.]

The Salvation Army, despite their host of detractors,

are no doubt doing no small amount of good. To get at the bottom mass of this world it is certainly necessary to use unusual means, and the fanaticism of the Army services is one way in which to reach the soul of the godless. Scattered about the great metropolis, they have established a number of night shelters. The awful, ever-increasing number of homeless and shelterless seen in the streets of London at night is confounding in this so-called civilized England, and it is to counteract this that these shelters have been erected.

'No man need go without food', 'No man need be without a bed', 'No man need commit suicide', says the Salvation Army, and, in a measure, this is quite true; but – and there is a big but in it – the character of a night shelter is often distressing to anyone of a sensitive mind.

Finding myself one evening with the magnificent sum of fourpence in my possession, I set out to seek a shelter for the night. The sun was just setting, and as I stood on Blackfriars Bridge, and watched its last yellow glow tinge tower and steeple, and kiss Old Father Thames until his waters were as molten gold, I wondered why a city so favoured should hold so much that was evil.

But weariness was creeping over me, so I wended my way down the broad thoroughfare, with people jostling me on every side, until at length I came to a building over which was the sign 'Salvation Army Shelter, for Men Only'.

A long line of close on three hundred souls extended up a passage-way, at the end of which was an office, and, being ignorant of the exact price of the night's shelter, I turned and inquired of one of the men.

He seemed surprised at my query, for though I had little money I was fairly respectably dressed.

'Yer doan't want to go in 'ere, do you?' he asked.

I nodded.

'Well, yer pays twopence fer yer "doss"; and if yer wants any "scrag" two more "steevers".'

Privation had taught me that a 'doss' was a bed, 'scrag' was food, and a 'steever' a penny. So I fell in behind him.

'Ne'er bin in 'ere 'afore?' he asked, as the line began to move forward.

'Never', I replied.

'Ay, well, they're rum viles; but keep wi' me, I'll see yer reight.'

The pressure behind kept us from further conversation. Oaths rippled from one end of the line to the other. One who attempted to force his way into the line was knocked back, and cleared off to the rear, nursing a fast-closing eye. At last I reached the office, where for the sum of fourpence I received a ticket, after the style of a railway ticket. On it, at the top and at the bottom, was stamped 'One Penny.'

I followed the old fellow who had given me the information along a passage that seemed at one time to have formed part of a cellar. Here were seated two officials, who, after taking my name and age, informed me that my bed was numbered 219; so, turning to the right, I entered my bed-chamber.

The sight and stench that met me almost turned me sick. Seated on long rows of wooden benches were several hundred men in all degrees of wretchedness. There was a dull rumble of conversation, but most of them seemed engaged in eating – eating as if the food before them were the first morsel they had had for days...

'Nar then, come an' get some scrag,' urged my companion, as I hesitated; so I followed him.

'Wad yer fancy? Bread and jam; bread and burrer, soaup, tea, corfee – give it a name. It's a fine hotel, this 'ere is.'

At a kind of bar two men served out, in return for a portion of the ticket, a certain amount of food. I invested half my ticket, and secured about a pint of tea, served in a tin can, and half a slice of thick bread and butter. My companion preferred to have soup with his bread, and together we took our seats on one of the hard benches amidst the motley crowd.

Round the room were bunks, in tiers of three. This room would hold about two hundred dossers. In another room were rows of coffin-shaped boxes on the floor. These were the beds of late-comers. The mattress was an oil-cloth sheet, the covering 'ditto'. This is necessary, for were cloth coverings to be used the place would soon be uninhabitable because of vermin.

The crowd around me were engaged in many ways. Some produced needle and thread and endeavoured to patch up their tattered clothing; one man did a small trade, and earned several sundries and ha'pence, by patching up worn boots; another sorted and set straight a few wares for the coming day's trade. Many leant their heads on the rail of the seat in front, and fell either into thought or slumber. Many a murder and many a robbery has been planned in a Salvation Army Shelter. A few related stories of the road, others recounted escapades in prison.

'Two threes, eh?'

'No, twelve months' hard.'

'Seen Nockie lately?'

'He's agon fer 'is 'olidays ter Portland.'

'W'er' did yer swing yer kip larst night?'

'Runs up agenst a drunk an' nicks 'im fer a bob.'

And so the talk goes on until a bell rings out for silence. Very little heed is taken of it.

'Order!' cries one; his friend curses him.

'What yer pulling that face for, black-mug?'

'Go it, De Wet!'

'Hallelujah. Go to blazes!'

This directed to the Salvationist who conducts a short service every night in the place.

'Bring out the hymn-books!' yells another; but there are none, so the hymn draggles on to the end, and with another prayer the red-tuniced captain disappears.

Then preparations are made for bed. I climbed up to my bunk, which fortunately was a top one, and watched the scene. It was like one of Dante's Infernos. The lights had been lowered, and most of the 'dossers' stripped to the 'buff' – that is, they took off all their clothes and lay down naked.

I could not sleep. Throughout the night the heat and stench were choking.

Some snored, others groaned in anguish of mind. Some babbled of bygone days, and others cursed their birth. Never did daylight come more welcome to me. I rose, and washed in the lavatory, and after exchanging the other portion of my ticket for a pint of tea, I emerged into the streets; and seldom before had the air seemed sweeter to me than that morning when I came out of a Salvation Army Shelter.

'Unity Sunday' on Peckham Rye

'UNITY Sunday' is celebrated annually on the first Sunday in July, and the meeting in 1901 was the fourth occasion of the kind. On this day all, or nearly all, the religious bodies that carry on open-air work in this part of London combine to show that, although they may differ in some matters of opinion or of method, they are working in the same cause and are all good friends. It was with this demonstration in view that the visit was especially paid, but it proved to be but one point of interest among many, and not the greatest.

The day was superb, perfectly fine, and not too hot, just the day for successful open-air demonstrations. I got to the north end of the Rye at about 3.30 p.m., and at first thought I must have mistaken the day, or time, for there was nothing to be seen but the open stretch of grass with a few people dotted here and there, and no sign of a crowd or banners or bands. Walking on further, the points of meeting came in view, but in the distance they merely formed little clusters of people in a great expanse of green. It is only an exaggerated view that suggests that the Rye as a whole is noisy and crowded. Over by far the greater part lovers could spoon or philosophers meditate undisturbed. In only one corner, near the bandstand, is the Common strident.

Nearing this corner, a loud voice reached the ear, and I joined the crowd it had attracted. The speaker was plainly recognizable as one of those of whom we had heard, but a query made sure that it was indeed the redoubtable preaching bookseller of Paternoster Row. A couple of hundred yards further on was the audience that the demonstration of the Christian Union had attracted, differentiated even in the distance by its colours, not of banners, but of the sunshades and dresses of the women, of whom it was mostly composed. In this respect it differed from almost every other group on the Rye. The bookseller had practically none but men around him, some of them being working men, but hardly any rough, and most seemingly of the lower middle class. I went back to him several times, and, in the whole course of the afternoon, only noticed one woman really in the ring and listening, although at times there were a few standing on the outskirts. It was clear that the speaker, whatever else he might be, was a man's man. Round the Unity Sunday platform, not only was the female element large, but it was clearly a much more religious crowd. In the other groups there was no singing; here, when hymns were sung, many joined in; they had brought hymn-books with them. The people gave one the impression of being what, if members of the Union, they would be, a selection from all the Noncomformist churches of the neighbourhood, and that this was so was borne out towards the end by an urgent request from the chairman that the regular services should not be allowed to suffer because of this demonstration, but that all should make a point of being in their own places at chapel or hall in the evening.

There may have been an attendance of a thousand or so. The platform was formed of two vans placed together; at each end was a flag, in the middle a harmonium, and near by a band. On the plaform were some twenty-five people, including a well-known South London L.C.C. member and several mission preachers and local ministers, the best known of whom was chairman. A lady in the dress of a Sister of the People sang, and there were several speakers. The last of these, an Evangelist of some kind, wound up by asking all who felt that they had had a message from Christ that day to hold up the right hand. A considerable number did so, and to these he returned his thanks, much as an auctioneer does for a bid, and then thanked God in a sentence or two of prayer. Next he asked all who had some unsaved friend for whom they desired prayer to be offered to hold up their hands, and fifteen or twenty hands went up. Lastly, he asked the unsaved and backsliders to hold up the right hand in token of their new sense of sin and their desire to lead a new life, and one hand went up. Then the speaker angled for others, but no fish rose. So after a minute or so of not very impressive invitation, he gave it up, and sat down, leaving an impression that neither he himself nor those around him on the platform thought he had done very well. Soon after five the meeting came to an end, and the people drifted away. At no time did the meeting seem a success as an expression of religious feeling. Its significance lies in the proof it affords to the public that the different denominations are in sympathy with one another.

There were several other centres of interest: secularist and spiritualists, temperance advocates and a political partisan, and a strange creature, locally well known, whom, towards the end of the afternoon, I found sitting on the ground, chanting hymns and rhapsodizing incoherently in the intervals. Twenty years ago he was a 'sound Gospel preacher', but now on matters of religion he is a little off his head. He turned up again later.

The secularist was a very fair speaker, with perhaps as good a brain as any of the Rye orators. He was speaking of evidence and belief, and it was noticeable that nearly all who were listening to him were men. He was often smart, and some of his points the orthodox people at other circles would have found it difficult to deal with; but he was not impressive, because he tended constantly to become either shallow, profane, or vulgar. Referring to the incredulity of Thomas, and quoting the sentence, 'Unless I put my finger', etc., he exclaimed, 'That was all very well for Thomas, but it won't do for me.' And then, after a moment's pause, and apparently yielding to a low inspiration of the moment, added, 'It's all Thomas-rot.' The speaker lacked all reverence. It was a narrow Christianity that he attacked, and his criticisms of the Bible were of the old-fashioned type, for which the doctrine of literal inspiration alone affords any excuse. But round him on neighbouring platforms were plenty of speakers whose views are sure to be met in this way, one, for example, on the Unity platform, who, holding up the Bible, said, 'I believe every word in this book; I believe in the cover too, for it keeps all the rest together.'

The spiritualists were not uninteresting. The keynote of their gospel seemed to be individualism. Spiritualism, said a Welsh coalminer (who had gone down the pit to work at eight years of age), had taught him that what a man meant to be he would have to become by his own efforts and by the working of his own spirit. It was useless, he said, to think that this or that outside agency could relieve him of his own responsibility. In politics this belief led him to give up looking to Parliament for help; and in religion it had undermined the doctrine of the vicarious sacrifice of Christ.

There is little that need be said about the temperance

speakers or the political partisan. The opening speaker on temperance, who had to create his circle of listeners, began in a voice of extraordinary animation, betraying intense excitement; shouting as it were to the Rye at large, for he had no group round him. I was attracted by the noise, and asked a police inspector who he was. 'Another lunatic', was the laconic answer, reflecting, perhaps, the police point of view on the local proceedings. The spiritualists, I was informed by the same man, had appeared that day for the first time.

The political orator had a fair number round him the whole time, but his audience was divided in opinion and the balance appeared to be against the speaker. There was a good deal of interruption, but no excitement and no rough play. The ball was taken up by a local man on what one might call the Government side, again with some interruptions, but with the majority, as it seemed, backing him. In this circle again nearly all were men. The numbers varied from about eighty to one hundred and fifty.

After all, the bookseller was perhaps the most interesting person on the ground. He is a man of about fifty, dark, robust in build and in manner. He was speaking when I arrived at 3.30, and he went on till about a quarter past five, with no break, save from the interruptions of his hearers. These interruptions are clearly a recognized part of the proceedings and do much to make the success of the meetings, for this man is a master of rough repartee. This gift, honesty of tone, a good temper and a strong voice seem to be the secrets of the success he secures.

I joined his group several times in the course of the afternoon (there were always one hundred and fifty to two hundred round him) and never without being interested and entertained. The interruptions, generally inaudible to the crowd at large, were frequent, but the speaker was always ready with a swift retort and remained easily master of the situation. Sometimes he professed to be wearied with the persistent stupidity of the people, but he never lost his temper and was practically always able to turn the laugh against the person who ventured to interpose. Such repartee affords much of the amusement of these talks, but the interest comes in mainly when the orator is allowed to get on with his discourse, for which he had prepared notes and in which he was apparently working through some definite theme. There was a good deal of broad liberality in his teaching, and it is noteworthy that he had not joined in the Unity Sunday demonstration, but whatever his doctrinal position may be, he is a very practical Christian. All I heard him say was very sagacious and wholesome, and for all his roughness and uncouthness he must exercise a really good influence. He spoke of the envious man who can never look on the best side of other people. 'Yes,' says such a one, 'Yes, Dr —, a very clever man; I dare say he is all right, but he makes a rare good living out of it, eh?' Or of Dr —, 'Oh, yes, —, he's a good preacher, but he has gone dotty on the South African war.'

Yet more striking and significant were his remarks about attendance at church or chapel. He did not know, he said, what those around him might be going to do that evening, but don't let them make the mistake of thinking that they could get to heaven by going to a prayer meeting with a Bible under their arm. Then he broke out (he had a huge voice at times): 'Go to the friend you've played false to, and ask his forgiveness,' and then, in subdued accents, 'It'll be better than going to church or chapel.' Again, with a roar, 'Go and take back that hammer you've sneaked': (and quietly) 'It will be better than going to church or chapel.' (Another roar): 'Go to the woman you've deceived or been hard on, and tell her you've been a miserable cur, and ask her to give you another chance'; (once more) 'It will be better than going to church or chapel.' At such moments there were no interruptions. There was stuff in the words and a man behind them, and the people felt it.

Towards 5.30, when I left, the secularist was still answering a critic, one or two small groups were still discussing the South African war, and a knot of little children surrounded the poor eccentric. But there were not two hundred people left on the ground; all had gone home to tea, and comparative quiet reigned. One small group, that had formed on the outskirts of the secularist crowd, had its centre in two men, one of thirty-five or so, and the other some ten years younger. They were a striking contrast: the former thin and tall, with the far-away look of a religious enthusiast, somewhat shaken and troubled by the shock of opinion vented on the Rye; the younger man, who looked like a German, short and broad-shouldered, very quiet, but also in dead earnest. As I came up the young fellow was saying: 'You have just mentioned Strauss. Well, I have some quotations from Strauss, if you would like to have them.' With the word he took a paper out of his pocket and unfolded two or three pages of type-written matter. Looking over his shoulder I could read the headings. I think the extracts were from the *Leben Jesu*. Then, as I went away, I wondered how many other people on the Rye had come with their pockets full of arguments in favour of this or that religious position. The indifference of which we have been told so often is clearly far from universal.

My intention in the evening had been to find out what kind of a crowd the band drew and then go, but there was much more to see, and I stayed on. There was now a really great concourse of people, and up to half-past eight, when I left, the numbers were still increasing, streams of people still making their way towards the music. But even so, with perhaps ten thousand people present, the Rye itself is only crowded in one corner, the same corner where I had found the people in the afternoon, with the addition, of course, of the great throng round the bandstand. The stand is on some rising ground about three hundred yards or more from the roadway, and it is still nearer this road that the various meetings take place. When I arrived in the evening some five or six meetings were in progress – mostly for some form of Christian propaganda, held by mission-bands from this or that religious centre. Neither the bookseller, nor the spiritualists, nor the temperance advocate were there. One of the missionaries, who had been present also in the afternoon, was the well-known 'converted sweep' referred to in a previous chapter, and of all the men I came across during the day I should be ready to give the palm to him for simplicity of faith and honesty of purpose. In the evening he was conducting a very lively meeting with, apparently, much more music and singing than speaking. As I came near, a tall Irishman dressed in a frock coat and wearing a tall hat, was singing a solo with chorus about 'Taking off the old coat and putting on the new', and he complimented the audience on joining in so well. It showed that they had a good ear for music, and that was well, for when we 'get up there' singing will be our chief occupation: what a good thing, therefore, to begin down below. 'That's true,' said the sweep, 'now chorus again, "Take off the old coat, put on the new",' and so on, with great fervour. Here, at any rate, was a man who was not only sincere, but perfectly self-forgetful, and, for the time at least, perfectly happy.

The Irishman followed with an address. He did not seem to have contemplated speaking, but, although apparently called upon quite unexpectedly, in thirty seconds he was raging in a torrent of words. Two things, above all others, seemed to stir him; firstly the 'deliberate lies' that were uttered Sunday after Sunday from the secularist platform; and, secondly, the apathy of the people, whom he charged with coming week after week, just as idle listeners, and responding not at all. 'The fact is,' he shouted, 'you don't want Christ,' and he repeated the terrible indictment, 'you don't want Christ.' 'But', he added a threatening undertone, 'you need Him, you need Him.' The sweep lost his look of happiness, and the contrast of the furious energy and terrible voice with the pleasant hymn-tune that the speaker had been singing a few minutes before drove me away. I came back, however, more than once, always to find the Irishman there, six feet two of fierce Ulster Protestantism – even when silent the most conspicuous figure in the ring and a standby whenever they sang.

The general behaviour of the crowd was quiet and orderly, perhaps the chief exception finding its centre in the poor eccentric whom I had seen first in the afternoon. I came across him in the evening, not with little children or well-disposed people round him, as before, but pursued by a crowd of mischievous urchins to whom he was just a source of amusement and of baiting. At times he would take up some position of vantage, often standing on a bench, with his enormous Bible slung round his shoulders. But he was never in one place for long. The boys would get bolder, and often a push would bring things to a crisis. The poor fellow's patience would give way, and, with a rush and an objurgation, he would chase the offender, and there would be a stampede, the element of disorder spreading through the general crowd in the immediate neighbourhood. But after a minute or two, he could be again heard incoherently addressing the people from a bench. Sometimes he was more patient than at others, and I came across him once being hustled along unresistingly by a throng of youngsters. As he passed close by he was saying, half in speech to his tormentors, half in soliloquy, 'What do I care for you pack of boys! My God is stronger than the whole of you put together; you are only a lot of little specks of clay.' But he was for the moment helpless. Probably he ought not to be allowed to come on the Rye at all, and perhaps before long the police will think so too, and prevent him. A lady begged him to go home, but he paid no attention, and a gentleman did the same, with the like result.

But, after all, the eccentric, the sweep, and the rest are only minor attractions in the evening; the band's the thing; it is the music that has attracted the vast majority of the people. Not that all who are not listening to one or another of the various speakers are paying any attention to the music: hundreds, perhaps thousands, are listening to nothing at all, unless it be the voices of the friends with whom they are chatting. The spot is a pleasant lounge, not simply in the more immediate neighbourhood of the bandstand, but all round.

The Peckham Rye Band has a long record, and, as a steward informed me, was the first to give Sunday music in a public open space in London. It started in the days of the Metropolitan Board of Works, getting the necessary permission from that body, and making a beginning 'with four performers, who played standing on four pieces of wood'. Now, the band consists of forty performers. All wear black coats and tall hats, and make an imposing show, the array, forty strong, seeming to set a seal of respectability on the whole proceedings.

When the County Council took up the question of music in the parks, the Peckham Rye Band was unwilling to give up the Sunday playing, and now, with the sanction of the L.C.C., uses the excellent stand that the Council has built. This is the explanation of the words on the penny programmes: 'By authority of the London County Council'.

Immediately round the bandstand is the customary enclosure, asphalted and filled with chairs, with room for one thousand five hundred people. Admission here, including the use of a chair, costs a penny, and practically every seat was taken. The crowd is estimated to reach a maximum of about twenty thousand persons, and it is noticed that the greatest numbers come each year at about the third Sunday in the season. Many of those who come are young people, and the general behaviour is very good.

When the music stopped at nine o'clock the great mass of the people drifted slowly away, but for a quarter of an hour or so a certain amount of noisy play was noticeable in the immediate vicinity of the stand, the noise invariably coming from young men and young women or boys or girls. The proceedings were very juvenile: there was a good deal of running and squealing; some embracing and kissing; but not very much excitement, and the girls who were run after seemed to have come for the purpose. Some were too young, both boys and girls, to be allowed to go loose in this way. Others were 'grown up'. One of the latter, a girl of perhaps twenty, was caught in a momentary whirl of the crowd, and seized by a man to be embraced roughly and kissed. No sooner was she released, than another man, apparently thinking that she was fair game, repeated the process, and then, hot, flushed, but hardly disconcerted, the girl rejoined her proper companions, consisting of a second girl and two young men. She had, apparently, some words of protest on her lips, but all the consolation she received from her swain, who seemed to have accepted the proceedings with a kind of grumpy calmness, was the remark: 'You shouldn't be so d—d saucy.' He seemed to have hit off the situation, not only as it affected his own companion, but a good many others round about: on the one side, d—d sauciness; on the other, responsive rudeness.

The more serious question was as to the real character of the Rye in the growing darkness. People were dotted about everywhere, occasionally in little groups of friends of both sexes, sometimes two or three boys or young men together, but in the great majority of cases couples. For some the conditions were probably dangerously risky, but there appeared to be no grounds for thinking that the Rye on a band night, at any rate up to half-past ten, is a centre of vicious resort. For this, there are, for one thing, too many people moving about, often roughish boys, the debris of the band crowd, and the fact that the band has collected thousands of people, many of whom linger in the neighbourhood, in itself does much to protect the place from becoming, in any case up to the time mentioned, a place of evil resort. There were no signs of professionalism: there were no women walking about alone on the outskirts of the Rye, nor, so far as I could observe, on the adjacent roads.

The experiences of the afternoon and evening, taken as a whole, were full of interest, and are made more so by the reflection that they are typical of what occurs in several other similar centres in the Metropolis, notably in Victoria Park in East London (with the important difference, however, that the parks are closed at nightfall, whereas the Rye is not). Thus, the medley of interests that the Rye presents on these occasions, although, perhaps, unequalled in variety, is by no means unique: the propaganda carried on by enthusiasts or charlatans on behalf of temperance or spiritualism, political reform, secularism, or some other cause, may be found on all sides of London; open-air evangelistic effort is almost ubiquitous, and other instances are not wanting of the attempt to secure at least a momentary union of divided sects; music is provided now in many parts, and with it is sure to come the concourse of people, the quiet enjoyment, and the meeting of friends. Add to the picture presented some glimpses of the Sunday life of most of the people seen – their later rising in the morning, the doing little things about the house, the Sunday newspaper, the important midday meal, perhaps a visit to the public house; and, for a much smaller number, their attendance at some church or chapel; and the Rye will then, except for those who do not stay in London on fine summer days, be found to suggest fairly completely the ways in which Sunday is spent by scores, perhaps by hundreds of thousands of Londoners – the things they do, the interests that can rouse them, and the pleasures they enjoy. On the whole, the impression left is a favourable one. Not wholly bright, for what picture of the multitude ever can be? but the prevailing tones are those of quiet orderliness and increasing capacity for rational enjoyment that are characteristic of what appears to be a steadily-increasing section of the people.

Street Scenes[6]

(1) *Sleeping in the Open Air*

... Sleeping out of doors is one of the features of Whitechapel. It is a centre for common lodging-houses and shelters. Destitutes from all sides are drawn there. Many would rather sleep out of doors than indoors in the warm weather. If they are without visible means of subsistence the police can charge them; if they have a few pence, as they generally have, they can only be moved on from door to door, and finally will move no further and are left sleeping on the doorstep. They also sleep during the day on such seats as are provided. These people are covered with vermin and cannot be touched with impunity.

(2) *Description of a Low Bit in Stepney*

... We went East along Brook Street, colour dark blue; rough, poor, many common lodging-houses, but no brothels. Then further East past the Friends' Meeting House to Cosh's Buildings, which fill the space between School-house Street and Collingwood Street, where Dunstan's Place used to be, and where that saint might well have seized the Devil by the nose. Here there are now

6. Third edition, third series, Vol. II, pp. 244–6.

three four-storeyed blocks. The centre one is very bad. Shrieks of a woman, who was being ill-treated, resounded as we passed through, and there was much excitement, all the women looking out of their houses; ragged, dirty, square-jawed women, and one was saying, 'She deserved a good deal, but I hope he won't go too far.'

Further on comes Causeway Court, a place not marked on the map, with drains choked, everything overflowing into the court, and all windows broken — and so on and so on. But all is not bad; in Weston Place – a cul-de-sac of three-storeyed houses, rough and dismal-looking, with ragged children playing about – a mite of eight or nine years was on her knees scrubbing the steps and the flags in front of the house. Dipping a rag and brush into the pail beside her as if she were fifteen, she called out, 'Look, mother, ain't I getting it clean?'

(3) *Prostitution in Whitechapel*

... Many of the women are from a distance and come and go a good deal. After being herself absent for a few weeks the mission woman was struck by the number of new faces. Not a little 'poncing' is done. The bully follows closely on the heels of the pair, and asks what the stranger is doing in his room – a row, with robbery, follows, and the stranger is kicked out; or, the man having parted with some money in advance, finds himself 'bilked' and left alone and is hustled out by the neighbours. Those who enter rarely leave with money or valuables upon them...

(4) *A Friend to the Cats*

... A woman came along with a basket on her arm full of cats' meat, which she distributed to the cats as she passed. 'Do you see that woman?' said our companion. 'She was a prostitute and still lives in a brothel, but she goes daily round the district feeding the cats.' In appearance she was a frowsy, debauched, drunken-looking creature...

(5) *The Pleasure of a Funeral*

There had been a fire with terrible loss of life: mother and eight children burnt, and the same day the husband had died in the infirmary of consumption. The funeral was by public subscription and was just starting. The band was playing the 'Dead March', and was preceded by a number of men and children. The roads were blocked with people, the day being observed as a holiday; falling in with the usual habits of the people on a Monday in these parts. There were four hearses with the coffins, four mourning carriages, plumed horses, and mutes on foot with flowing crape bands, and handkerchiefs with deep black borders were conspicuous in the hands of the mourners. There were also three omnibuses prepared to take passengers to Plaistow (the burial place) and back for 1s., and each was crammed with women, and there were two hansom cabs and a few carts, and a respectful crowd of people looking on, with thirty policemen to keep order. But all was very orderly. Everybody on their best behaviour, in their Sunday clothes, washed and dressed for the occasion.

'It is wonderful how much they think of a funeral', said our conductor. 'There will be many wishing they too had been burnt, to have such a turn-out as this.' 'A man may beat his wife, and ill-treat her so that she dies of it, but if he gives her a good funeral he will be forgiven by the women of the neighbourhood, who say, "but he can't have been so bad, poor man, look what a handsome burial he gave her."' Even the poorest will pay £8 or £10 for a burial and then starve the week after.

[We may insert here the story of a dying girl who belonged to a club at Millwall. Her friends in the club, who were told that there was no hope of her recovery, joined together before her death to buy a wreath for her coffin; they were exceedingly anxious that she should live long

(6) *The Market of the Fancy*

... Passing along Bethnal Green Road in an omnibus, coming home on Sunday morning after attending service further East, I stumbled on the 'Fancy Market' of Sclater Street at its height. Not only was Sclater Street itself blocked full with men, but there were thousands in Bethnal Green Road: a great crowd. Here were the men. I got off the bus and walked among them, listened to the harangues of the bookies, bought a racing tip for 3d., and watched a corn-cutter operate on the foot of a young man laid out on the box of his vehicle, while all around were the buyers and sellers of dogs, fowls, pigeons, and other pets...

(7) *Part of Soho*

... The west end of Broad Street might be part of Whitechapel. Jewish faces and shops; hatless children; touslehaired women; men with bundles of trousers wrapped in cloths, and hands of tailors as they draw the thread seen above the window curtains; sense of crowding and dirt. Workshops and living rooms built up behind the houses...

CHAPTER 6

RECOMMENDATIONS

In separate sections of each of his series, Booth presented his piecemeal recommendations for dealing with the poverty he had described in all its aspects. The excerpts that make up this chapter will give some idea of the distance that separated the two sides of Booth: the impartial investigator who followed his material wherever it led him, and the conservative businessman who sought to impose solutions that reflected his class interests.

Economic Conditions of Life[1]

WORK and leisure, earning and saving, spending and sparing – such are the necessary elements of economic life, and on the maintenance of a due balance between them does its success depend.

Every civilization demands the provision of a certain amount of capital, or, as the word perhaps implies, a quota of possessions per head. The existing type of what has been termed 'Western' civilization requires a great deal of these things, and its advance is based on their increase. The ideal expressed in the words 'rich not in the greatness of my wealth but in the fewness of my wants,' is far removed from us. To us Diogenes would have appealed in vain. We may regret it, but it is so. The poor may scoff at luxury, but they are more self-indulgent than the rich; and the rich may sigh for simplicity, but even when they really wish for it, find it unattainable, and, if it were attainable, would probably not like it.

1. Third edition, third series, Vol. III, pp. 92–6.

It is said that if none were wealthy there would be no poor; but it does not at all follow that the poor would gain by the impoverishment of others, or by any form of redistribution. In some hands, or in some form, increase and accumulation of property are necessary to our civilization. Those who accumulate it serve the rest; and no radical change in the resultant economic balance could be maintained without a complete alteration in the motives that actuate mankind.

In this indirect manner every child is born to a share in the common inheritance. On this provision its actual home and its future chances depend. The measure of this potential share in the capital stock of the nation cannot, perhaps, be exactly calculated, or apportioned; but at the lowest estimate it is a substantial amount. It must, moreover, be by some means provided, if the work of the country is to be carried on, and labour enabled to secure its due reward. In this necessity is found the fundamental connection which exists between saving and earning.

That the function of replenishing and increasing the common stock should be widely spread, and shared by many, is doubtless desirable, but it is so mainly because to the individual holder his own savings have a special value. To those, and they are the majority, who, being practically without capital themselves, lean on the common stock, it matters not who provides it. It is the part of some not only to earn but also to spare, while the function of others is to earn and spend. All ought to earn; for earnings are the basis of the whole; but to spend is as essential as to spare, and that the two functions should be to a great extent distinct is in itself no evil.

The view which I put forward as theory is instinctive in the people, and is reflected in their habits. The working classes regard as their capital the labour they have to offer. Out of what they receive for its use, they may pay the cost of an insurance against sickness and debility, but they spend the rest. The very prudent set aside a little cash against emergency, but the more usual plan is to trust, if thrown back, to obtain temporary credit. On either plan, what is aimed at is an average subsistence. To this, standard rates of wages and habits of life adjust themselves. The labour given might be more valuable, the wages earned might be higher, the insurance more complete, the savings against emergency more substantial, but the principle adopted is right. It is better for themselves, and for others too, that these classes should spend freely. The question at stake for themselves, and for others also, is how they spend their money. On a wise expenditure both their welfare and their higher social value depend. This is the economic problem of their lives, and amongst the penalties of a false solution lurks ruin.

With those on whom misfortune or incapacity or moral weakness has already impressed the seal of poverty, a further and special difficulty arises, when the savings necessary to establish an average spending income may bring the level of that income below that of subsistence. Those who are so situated become inevitably an economic burthen upon the self-supporting. The less they have of prudence, energy, and other virtues and the fewer their advantages, the more they need them; out of this strait they must by some means be dragged.

The settled rich are the holders and trustees of wealth, but, as with the working classes, their true function is to spend wisely rather than to save. The more solid their position, the more exacting do the claims on their purses become. And thus they, too, must learn to spare as well as spend; but, except to a quite limited extent with regard to the establishment of children, it is not for the sake of accumulation, but to maintain an average. The welfare of others, even more than their own, depends on this economic exercise, and the ruin of others, as well as of themselves, may be the penalty of failure. With the working classes the object is to render irregularity of income equal to the calls of a regular expenditure; with the rich this is reversed, and the aim is rather to make a comparatively fixed income meet the claims of a varying expenditure. In place of saving, many, or perhaps most, will trench for a time on their capital by selling out stock, or by borrowing what they immediately need. Again, while the theory may not be recognized, this course of action is instinctively pursued. And the principle is right. In detail much improvement is again possible. Lives might be made more useful; duties better performed; money better spent; but on the whole the course pursued by this class is as well adapted as that of the working classes to the place it fills, and its functions are no less essential to the social structure.

It is on the class between that the real task of accumulation devolves. Excluding a section of professional men whose savings (like those of the working classes) are mainly a matter of insurance, the main object of the lives of the members of this class is money-making, and in doing so, even when they are narrowly self-seeking and indifferent to the welfare of others, they must, to a great extent, serve the public. They include both rich and poor. Many of them are hard pinched by poverty; others may be multi-millionaires, but all alike are chained to the oar. The motives of this slavery are manifold and mostly good; but are greatly misunderstood, and strangely misrepresented as 'the worship of Mammon'.

The origin of this devotion to money-making is found in individual desire for advancement, and this motive runs through the whole; but it widens as it goes and assumes many secondary forms: as for the sake of wife or of children, or personal ambition, which is seldom sordid; 'goals for the eager' of many kinds, which may never be reached. The life is strenuous, and soon the curtain falls.

The faculty needed is far-sightedness, and the qualities required to attain success are patience and persistence in working for a distant object, coupled with a readiness to make the present sacrifices that this entails. A new value is discovered in savings, and a new form of expenditure instituted. Others save in order to consume, but those whose economic position we are now considering, make use of savings in order to produce. Whatever delinquencies may result from their over-eagerness in the pursuit of money, the service rendered to the community is great. The whole present social structure depends on it; without this service we should starve. It is no poetic exaggeration to say 'it would have been better if we had not been born', for without the efforts of this class the country would not support one-tenth of its present population.

Fortunately the passion for acquisition and advancement is strong. It does not even depend upon the motives that first call it forth, but comes to have a life of its own. A man will often sacrifice everything; his own life, his family, and his home; to satisfy its claims. No mistress is more exacting. But on the other side it tends also to be hard upon others; grinding those whose service it employs, unless restrained by some means; and relentless in competition; save for an occasional truce between exhausted opponents. It needs the curb, but is a strong beast and it pulls our wagon.

Though the functions are distinct, no such exact division can be made amongst individuals. Not a few try to combine them; but the more distinct they are kept the better. An artist, for instance, may imagine that business management is 'as easy as lying', but will probably lose his money if he abandon his true position, perhaps the noblest of all, as highest in degree among the working classes. Or a man living upon a settled income from property may think to increase it by speculation, which will benefit no one: himself, probably, least of all. The soul which gives life to trade is not in either bosom. And if, on his side, the trader, abandoning the sound foundations of business, grasps at immediate advantage, urged on by greediness to make and eagerness to spend, he too, sacrifices his own true dignity without attaining that of either of the other two classes.

Various Methods of Inquiry[2]

THE root idea with which I began the work that has taken shape in the series of volumes of which this is the last, was that every fact I needed was known to some one and that the information had simply to be collected and put together. But it was necessary that in the process of collection the facts should be reduced to some common measure of validity by being passed, as it were, through a sieve which should make it possible not only to reject the false and hold back the improbable, but also to tone down exaggeration, or, reading between the lines, to find and add the requisite emphasis to an understated truth. To do this has been a difficult task, in which success could only be partial. I have relied first and chiefly on mere average and consensus resulting from the great number and variety of my sources of information. Statements on which reliance could be placed would tend to enforce themselves, and errors balance each other and drop out of count. But looking at the matter in this rather wholesale way, it was all the more necessary that there should be no persistent bias at the centre at which all this varied information was assorted and assimilated. On this the entire value of the work depended, and I can only hope that genuine impartiality has been maintained.

I have been fortunate in having had for the most part the same co-workers throughout; thus general uniformity has been secured. We have co-operated as men of various views, working to the common end of unbiased exposition. Anticipations as to the outcome (perhaps the most subtle form of bias) have differed greatly amongst us, and

2. Third edition, *Final Volume*, pp. 32-8.

have changed from time to time as the work proceeded. Of any other bias I am certainly unconscious. That the honesty of the attempt has been so widely and generously recognized has been a source of the highest gratification.

Most of such work as this of mine could not, as I think, be advantageously attempted officially; nor is it so well suited for voluntary association as for the enterprise of a single person. The appropriate agency varies with the subject of investigation, as do the methods to be adopted; and while comparing these methods we may also consider the part in social research best taken by the central or by local authorities, by voluntary associations, or by private individuals.

If I do not discuss the advantage of such inquiries, it is not because I think that this can be assumed as a matter of course, but because their value will be found to depend so very much on the temper in which the information is sought, and the spirit in which it is received, as well as on its accuracy, and because these things in their turn depend in great measure on the agency employed and on the methods adopted.

In a general way it may be said that the more public the character of the inquiry, the more impersonal should be the information aimed at. The enumeration of the people is a good example of what I mean. The particulars obtained concern many of the most intimate facts of family life. From the aggregate of these facts conclusions may be drawn of the greatest social value. But neither in their collection, nor in the public use made of these facts, is the veil of privacy ever practically set aside; nor ought it to be. Such work must be done by the Central Government. Only so could it be carried out in the right spirit, and only so obtain the requisite sanction and breadth of application.

A question then arises as to the manner in which the material collected should be tabulated. Should the aim be to produce what may be called finished statistics, intended to throw definite light on definite points of interest; or merely to evolve general tables which will be raw material for further manipulation? Again, the more public the character of the inquiry, the more general should be the immediate arrangement of the facts. To produce pabulum for others is the right plan. Any special aim is likely to distort or circumscribe the published information. The national census (to revert to our example) has undoubtedly suffered in general utility by being made a branch of the Registrar-General's work. But it is nevertheless necessary that the uses to be made of the material should as far as possible be foreseen and carefully considered and provided for. Other Government departments, local bodies and private statisticians may be trusted to put forward their claims, as I have myself done again and again, being met at all times most kindly. It should be for the central authority to meet these various wishes, so far as practicable, and this course would be all the more easy for it to pursue if it had no special axe of its own to grind.

Each Government department necessarily accumulates statistics, and in addition to those which it needs for itself might make some contribution for general use. In this, as between department and department, there would be reciprocity, and the same rule of having in the records they keep, one eye on their own purposes and one on general utility, should hold good for local authorities also. If collected in this spirit, the value of public statistics would be very great and their cost extremely small.

So far I speak only of impersonal statistics, which will very largely be drawn from the current facts of administration. They may sometimes involve special first-hand inquiry, but are not the result of investigation levelled at any particular social abuses or difficulties. Investigations such as these last, if undertaken by some Governmental department or local body, aimed at the improvement of their own administration, may be placed in the next category. It does not follow that the results of the investigations are ever published, and it may be better they should not be; if published it will probably be in self-justification, or (more rarely) to rouse public opinion. In such matters voluntary effort is almost useless, for unless the inquiries spring from genuine energy of administration grounded in goodwill, no benefit can result.

The Board of Trade has taken action of this kind more than once in connection with the enforcing or amendment of the Factory Acts. The methods adopted have been to supplement by special investigation the reports of their own inspectors, and it has been the business of the appointed investigator to invite informal evidence from any one likely to be able to supply information. The method could hardly be improved. It lacks something of the freedom of private work, being necessarily very closely restricted in aim; but for an immediate practical purpose this is hardly a disadvantage, and, with the power and prestige of a great Government department behind it, the work done is very effective. But the more common examples of such work are those afforded by local bodies in their inquiries into the conditions of life as to crowding and sanitation, having for immediate aim the discovery of the extent to which breaches of the laws or by-laws on these subjects prevail, and as ultimate object the raising of the standard of health and decency. These are questions on which the rousing of public opinion may be essential to action. Or it may be that the Medical Officer of Health needs the evidence to convince his superiors in authority. To this end he works out the death-rate as it applies to selected areas, and tabulates the cases of illness, the houses are inspected, their condition and the state of the drains are described, and finally the difficulty of enforcing the laws when both landlord and tenant wish to evade them is explained. All this is done in order to impress upon the authorities the necessity of some sweeping change, and, again, the methods adopted could hardly be improved. It is the inspector's business to inspect; there is official sanction for all that is done; and, strange as it may appear, the action taken raises no false hopes, nor indeed any hopes at all, in the minds of the poor, but rather some fear of disturbance. In this class of investigation, too, there is not much room for volunteer effort, unless, indeed, there is scandalous official indifference. If undertaken privately, the avowed aim is to stimulate the authorities to action, and that action if taken necessarily includes a public investigation covering the same ground.

It is, however, in this way, by directing public attention to the existence of evils, that much can be done by voluntary associations of those whose feelings have already been aroused. Full of burning zeal, they are the best possible medium for work of this kind, and simple methods of inquiry which seek solely the evidence they need, are the most applicable. These methods waste no time and no force but go straight to the point, and if honestly conducted are often very effective.

Finally, there is the work of the private individual, who, impressed by the thought that about so many matters upon which most people (including himself) talk freely, so very little is really known, and believing that with better information ways may be found towards many needed improvements, sets deliberately to work to obtain the knowledge and secure the benefit. I suppose that I am myself a character of this kind, and Mr Rowntree is another instance.[3]

I have already described my own method, into which I was drawn by the task of attempting the social and industrial analysis and classification of more than four million people. Mr Rowntree at York, with less than one-fiftieth of that number, had a different task, and was able to apply other methods, but the spirit was the same. In his case one lady was able to visit every house, and at

3. B. S. Rowntree had recently published the results of an intensive study of poverty in York (*Poverty: A Study of Town Life*). – EDS.

many of them, as he says, even to make repeated calls. In her notebooks were recorded many facts about each poor family and its way of life. Under Mr Rowntree's guidance, the even measure and the pitch and tone of the social gamut used in the inquiry depend on this lady. But the details are a great help. The facts speak. And in every direction old and new clues were followed. Not only were family budgets – a method of intensive investigation deserving a much wider recognition in this country than it has yet received – not only were such budgets obtained to show the actual expenses of living in various classes, and the cost of food per man (each woman and child figuring from this point of view as certain agreed fractions of a man); but this food was again set out as containing so much of this or that necessary constituent of human life and energy according to the latest scientific pronouncement; while the conclusion that not enough proper food was taken to furnish growth and maintain full vigour was held to be borne out by the comparative analyses given of prison and workhouse dietaries. A very important sidelight, too, was sought by comparing the height, weight, and general condition of school children of the same age belonging to different social classes. In its way the picture given is complete, and it is consistent in its different parts.

It is to be noted that such investigations as these last, into food stuffs and nutrition in connection with growth and development, or with labour of varying severity, are not well suited for individual work, but ought to be undertaken either by bodies of recognized experts, on their own initiative as a pure question of science, or by some responsible association as a matter of philanthropy, or by Government as affecting national welfare generally; for it is not a subject on which there should be left any doubt which scientific research and authority can remove.

In recent years much use has been made of various forms of Governmental inquiry: by Committees of either House of Parliament and by Joint Committees; by Departmental Committees of many kinds; and by Royal Commissions. Any of these may be turned towards social subjects, and each has its appropriate sphere of utility, though it may not keep strictly to it; and if the parts are exchanged each will probably fail. The first paves the way for, or decides on the practicability or impracticability of legislation; the second is the handmaid of immediate action, whether legislative or administrative; while the last is incomparable for discussion. The great Royal Commissions of our day on Housing, Sweating, Old Age Pensions, The Depression of Trade, Labour, and Local Taxation, though unwieldy as the instruments of inquiry into fact, and unsatisfactory as direct aids either to legislation or administration, are each admirable in the dialectical treatment of opposing suggestions and theories.

Eliminating Poverty[4]

IT is not easy for any outsider to gain a sufficient insight into the lives of these people. The descriptions of them in the books we read are for the most part as unlike the truth as are descriptions of aristocratic life in the books they read. Those who know, think it a matter without interest, so that again and again in my inquiries, when some touch of colour has been given illuminating the ways of life among the people who are above the need for help, it has been cut short by a semi-apology: 'But that is not what you want to know about.' Something may be gleaned from a few books, such for instance as *Demos*; something perhaps may be learnt from the accounts of household expenditure in the preceding chapter. Of personal knowledge I have not much. I have no doubt that many other men possess twenty or a hundred times as much experience of East End people and their lives. Yet

4. First edition, Vol. I. pp. 157–71.

such as it is, what I have witnessed has been enough to throw a strong light on the materials I have used, and, for me, has made the dry bones live. For three separate periods I have taken up quarters, each time for several weeks, where I was not known, and as a lodger have shared the lives of people who would figure in my schedules as belonging to classes C, D, and E. Being more or less boarded, as well as lodged, I became intimately acquainted with some of those I met, and the lives and habits of many others came naturally under observation. My object, which I trust was a fair one, was never suspected, my position never questioned. The people with whom I lived became, and are still, my friends. I may have been exceptionally fortunate, and three families are not many, but I can only speak as I have found: wholesome, pleasant family life, very simple food, very regular habits, healthy bodies and healthy minds; affectionate relations of husbands and wives, mothers and sons, of elders with children, of friend with friend – all these things I found, and amongst those with whom I lodged I saw little to mar a very agreeable picture, fairly representative of class E, and applicable to some at least of classes C and D. Of others, belonging to the lower of these classes, who came under my observation, I cannot give so good an account. In the room above mine at one of the houses, a room about nine feet square, lived a car-man and his wife and their two children, girls of seven and thirteen. The man, though a heavy drinker, was not a bad fellow, and steady enough over his work. It was the wife who was bad. She also drank, and as to work, 'never did a thing'. Late to bed and late to rise was her rule. The father went out early and returned to breakfast, which was prepared for him by the child of thirteen, who made the tea and toast and cooked the herring at a fire in the washhouse, which, the weather being warm, served for the cookery of the entire household. She also made ready her own and her sister's breakfast, left the tea for her mother (who was too lazy to make it even for herself), and then proceeded with her sister to school. The little sister was the pretty one and the pet of her parents; the elder one was the drudge, and twice this child had run away and stayed out all night before or after a beating. What chance of respectable life had she? This is an example of class D, with bad wife and bad mother. No less disreputable was a woman of the same class or lower, who with her daughter lived in another room of the same house. She had a small allowance from her husband, which went mainly in drink. He lived elsewhere. The daughter earned a trifle and tried vainly to keep her mother sober.

I do not mean to suggest that such specimens predominate in class D, or that they are never to be found in E or F, with which we are more particularly dealing. There is no gulf set between adjoining classes; E passes imperceptibly into either the irregular position of C or the bare remuneration of D, but from each of these there is another step as wide to reach the wretched casual character of class B. I watched with much interest the relations existing between classes E and D in the persons of my landlady and her other tenants. *Mutatis mutandis*, they were not very different from those which exist in the country between hall and village. There was the present of a dress altered to suit the hard-worked, ill-dressed child (it was forthwith pawned, the poor girl never wore it); the rebuke, dignified, well-timed, and, as it appeared, efficacious, of the father's drunken ways; amounting in the end to 'amend your ways or go'; and the word in season to the little girl whose 'tongue was too long and must have a bit cut off' (she having told some tale about her sister); the women met over their washing in the yard, and the children were allowed to play together – play at house, or plant a garden with cut flowers stuck in the earth, or swing, or dress their dolls, but if there were sweets to be eaten it was my landlady's little girl who paid for them. In short, there was evinced a keen sense of social responsibility, not unaccompanied by a sense of social superiority.

The children in class E, and still more in class D, have when young less chance of surviving than those of the rich, but I certainly think their lives are happier, free from the paraphernalia of servants, nurses, and governesses, always provided they have decent parents. They are more likely to suffer from spoiling than from harshness, for they are made much of, being commonly the pride of their mother, who will sacrifice much to see them prettily dressed, and the delight of their father's heart. This makes the home, and the happiness of the parents; but it is not this, it is the constant occupation, which makes the children's lives so happy. They have their regular school hours, and when at home, as soon as they are old enough, there is 'mother' to help, and they have numbers of little friends. In class E they have for playground the back yard, in class D the even greater delights of the street. With really bad parents the story would be different, but men and women may be very bad, and yet love their children and make them happy. In the summer holidays, when my car-man had a load to carry for some building in the country, he would take two of the children with him. Supplied with bread and butter and 2d. to buy fruit, they would start off early and come home in the evening happy, tired, and dirty, to tell of all the sights they had seen.

I perhaps build too much on my slight experience, but I see nothing improbable in the general view that the simple natural lives of working-class people tend to their own and their children's happiness more than the artificial complicated existence of the rich. Let it not be supposed, however, that on this I propose to base any argument against the desire of this class to better its position. Very far from it. Their class ambition as well as their efforts to raise themselves as individuals deserves the greatest sympathy. They might possess and spend a good deal more than they now do without seriously endangering the simplicity of their lives or their chances of happiness, and it would be well if their lot included the expenditure of a larger proportion of our surplus wealth than is now the case. Moreover, the uncertainty of their lot, whether or not felt as an anxiety, is ever present as a danger. The position of the class may be secure – some set of men and their families must hold it – but that of the individual is precarious. For the wife and family it will depend on the health, or habits, or character of the man. He drinks or he falls ill; he loses his job; some other man takes his place. His employment becomes irregular and he and they fall into class C, happy if they stop there and do not drop at low as B. Or it may be the woman who drags her family down. Marriage is a lottery, and childbearing often leads to drink. What chance for a man to maintain respectability and hold up his head among his neighbours if he has a drunken wife at home, who sells the furniture and pawns his clothes? What possibility of being beforehand and prepared to meet the waves of fortune? Or it may be that trade shrinks, so that for a while one man in ten or perhaps one in seven is not wanted. Some must be thrown out of work. The lot falls partly according to merit and partly according to chance, but whatever the merit or the lack of it, the same number will be thrown out of work. Thus we see that the 'common lot of humanity', even though not much amiss in itself, is cursed by insecurity against which it is not easy for any prudence to guard...

It is class B that is *de trop*. The competition of B drags down C and D, and that of C and D hangs heavily upon E. I have already said, and I repeat, that industrially we gain nothing from B. All that B does could be done by C and D in their now idle hours. Nor is this so impracticable as it might at first seem. At least, we might move in that direction. What I above all desire is to arouse the interest and ingenuity of the classes who are themselves so vitally concerned in this matter, as not till then shall we approach with any chance of success the solution of the problem of poverty as it is presented in England today.

In the meantime we are face to face with the immediate difficulty of the relief of indigence, and with the fact that mere giving as a remedy for poverty no longer holds the field. That the rich of their abundance should humbly, and in the name of God, give to the poor, help the unfortunate, and succour the distressed, was the solution of religion, but in these latter days the efficacy and even the virtue of mere giving has been denied, and, on the other hand, our faith in the new doctrine, lacking somewhat on the positive side, is not very firmly established. Of the change of feeling, however, there is no question. Although a certain stimulus has been given in late years to mendicity by sentimental appeals and such efforts as the Mansion House Relief Fund, no student of the history of England can fail to see that begging, though it still exists among us, is falling into discredit; that as a profession its palmy days are over, its great prizes things of the past. It is driven to assume new shapes to lull suspicion. Even in the tales of Miss Edgeworth, who in her time occupied the van of enlightenment, we find the good ladies recommending their children to give their pennies to the hungry with an indiscriminateness to which even the most unenlightened mother of our own days would impose some limits; whilst among the number of those who have thought seriously about the matter at all – and the number who think seriously about it is a constantly increasing figure – it has become a sort of commonplace to hold that almsgiving without inquiry, method, or personal labour serves only to intensify and perpetuate the evil it desires to relieve. In this respect, and in the growing intelligence and care with which the Poor Law is administered, we tend towards firmness, even hardness, of treatment of each individual case, and yet I can assert without fear of contradiction that towards ephemeral or even deserved suffering greater general tenderness is felt than ever, so that to support us in our principles, and confirm us in our resolution to abstain from the enticements of personal almsgiving, we need to be assured that in some way suffering is really relieved. If we lay aside personal giving, we are constrained to employ professional almoners; we no sooner limit the action of the Poor Law in one direction than we begin to consider its extension in another. It is this condition of the public mind which might I think be taken advantage of to get rid of class B, or at least to mitigate the harm which their unregulated existence does to others as well as to themselves.

Already several ingenious and thoughtful schemes for dealing with the unemployed are before us. The leading idea is to provide the labourer with land on which to work and so find his own living. Unoccupied or ill-occupied land in England, says one; unoccupied land in our colonies, says another; a temporary occupation in England to lead to a permanent occupation in the colonies, says a third, seeking in this way to obviate the rather evident difficulties in the way of the first two. The ingenuity of this last scheme, which combines training with relief, must be admitted; yet it no less than its cruder companions fails to satisfy the broader conditions of the problem of poverty. All these schemes profess to deal with the unemployed – an imaginary army of men; they would really deal with a very limited number of picked out-of-work cases. Such may doubtless be found, and when found deserve the utmost consideration, but they do not really touch the problem of poverty which is wrapped up in the whole of class B, employed, partially employed, or unemployed, as the case may be, but rarely to be described correctly as 'out of work'.

My own ideas on this subject have taken shape

gradually in the course of my work. In beginning my inquiry I had no preconceived ideas, no theory to work up to, no pet scheme into agreement with which the facts collected were to be twisted or to which they would have to be squared. At the same time the consideration and the hope of remedies have never been out of my mind. In laying my ideas before my readers, I trust that if they are considered futile and visionary, the facts I have brought to light may not be discredited by being brought into company with theories from which I can honestly say they have taken no colour, but that out of the same material some other hand may be able to build a more stable structure.

The state of things which I describe in these pages, though not so appalling as sensational writers would have us believe, is still bad enough to make us feel that we ought not to tolerate it in our midst if we can think of any feasible remedy. To effectually deal with the whole of class B – for the State to nurse the helpless and incompetent as we in our own families nurse the old, the young, and the sick, and provide for those who are not competent to provide for themselves – may seem an impossible undertaking, but nothing less than this will enable self-respecting labour to obtain its full remuneration and the nation its raised standard of life. The difficulties, which are certainly great, do not lie in the cost. As it is, these unfortunate people cost the community one way or another considerably more than they contribute. I do not refer solely to the fact that they cost the State more than they pay directly or indirectly in taxes. I mean that altogether, ill-paid and half-starved as they are, they consume or waste or have expended on them more wealth than they create. If they were ruled out we should be much better off than we now are; and if this class were under State tutelage – say at once under State slavery – the balance-sheet would be more favourable to the community. They would consume more, but the amount they produced would be increased in greater proportion by State organization of their labour and their lives. It is not in the cost that the difficulty lies, but in the question of individual liberty, for it is as freemen, and not as slaves, that we must deal with them. The only form compulsion could assume would be that of making life otherwise impossible; an enforcement of the standard of life which would oblige every one of us to accept the relief of the State in the manner prescribed by the State, unless we were able and willing to conform to this standard. The life offered would not be attractive. Some might be glad to exchange their half-fed and half-idle and wholly unregulated life for a disciplined existence, with regular meals and fixed hours of work (which would not be short); many, even, might be willing to try it; but there would be few who would not tire of it and long for the old life of hardship and vicissitude, saying

> Give me again my hollow tree,
> A crust of bread and liberty.

If we could adopt this plan, there is no cause for fearing that it would encourage idleness or weaken the springs of energy. No! the difficulty lies solely in inducing or driving these people to accept a regulated life.

To bring class B under State regulation would be to control the springs of pauperism; hence what I have to propose may be considered as an extension of the Poor Law. What is the Poor Law system? It is a limited form of Socialism – a Socialistic community (aided from outside) living in the midst of an Individualist nation. Socialistic also to a great extent are our Board schools, hospitals, and charitable institutions, where the conditions of relief are not the services which the applicant can render in return, but the services of which he stands in need. My idea is to make the dual system, Socialism in the arms of Individualism, under which we already live, more efficient by extending somewhat the sphere of the former and making the division of function more distinct. Our Individualism fails because our Socialism is incomplete. In taking charge of the lives of the incapable, State Socialism finds its proper work, and by doing it completely, would relieve us of a serious danger. The Individualist system breaks down as things are, and is invaded on every side by Socialistic innovations, but its hardy doctrines would have a far better chance in a society purged of those who cannot stand alone. Thorough interference on the part of the State with the lives of a small fraction of the population would tend to make it possible, ultimately, to dispense with any Socialistic interference in the lives of all the rest.

This, in rough outline and divested of all detail, is my theory. It is rather with a view to discussion that I put it forward; and save in a very guarded and tentative way I shall not venture to base upon it any suggestions for immediate action.

Put practically, but shortly, my idea is that these people should be allowed to live as families in industrial groups, planted wherever land and building materials were cheap; being well housed, well fed, and well warmed; and taught, trained, and employed from morning to night on work, indoors or out, for themselves or on Government account; in the building of their own dwellings, in the cultivation of the land, in the making of clothes, or in the making of furniture. That in exchange for the work done the Government should supply materials and whatever else was needed. On this footing it is probable that the State would find the work done very dear, and by so much would lose. How much the loss would be could only be told by trying the system experimentally. There would be no competition with the outside world. It would be merely that the State, having these people on its hands, obtained whatever value it could out of their work. They would become servants of the State. Accounts would have to be kept, however, and for this purpose the work done would have to be priced at the market rate. It would even be well that wages should be charged and credited each person at the fair proportionate rate, so that the working of one community could be compared with another, and the earnings of one man or one family with others in the same community. The deficiency could then be allotted in the accounts proportionately to each, or if the State made no claim for interest or management, there might be a surplus to allot, opening out a road back to the outside world. It would, moreover, be necessary to set a limit to the current deficiency submitted to by the State, and when the account of any family reached this point to move them on to the poorhouse, where they would live as a family no longer. The Socialistic side of life as it is includes the poorhouse and the prison, and the whole system, as I conceive it, would provide within itself motives in favour of prudence, and a sufficient pressure to stimulate industry. Nor would hope be wanting to those who were ambitious to face the world again.

As I reject any form of compulsion, save the gradual pressure of a rising standard of life, so too, I suggest no form of restraint beyond the natural difficulty of finding a fresh opening in an ever hardening world. The only desirable return to the individualist life (except in the case of children) would be with funds in hand earned by hard work and good conduct, saved within the cost the State was prepared to bear. For the future of the children careful provision would be made. Incompetence need not be hereditary; it should, on the contrary, become less so than is now the case.

It is not possible that action of this kind could be rapid. To open a little the portals of the Poor Law or its administration, making within its courts a working guild under suitable discipline; to check charitable gifts, except to those who from age or infirmity are unfit for any work; to insist upon sanitation and to suppress overcrowding; to await and watch the results, ready to push forward as occasion served – this is all that could be done. Much would be learnt from an experiment. It might be tried in some selected district – for instance, in part of Stepney, where official relief already works hand in hand with organized charity. The law as it stands would, I believe, admit of this; the cost, if shared between private and public sources, need not deter. Such an experiment is what I venture to suggest.

The good results to be hoped for from such an extension of 'limited Socialism' as I have suggested would be manifold. Class A, no longer confounded with 'the unemployed', could be gradually harried out of existence. The present class B would be cared for, and its children given fair chances. The change could only come in a very gradual way; a part, sharing the improved chances of classes C and D, would be pushed upward into self-supporting habits, and another part, failing to keep itself even when helped by the State, would pass into the ranks of paupers, so that the total numbers to whom the proposed State organization would ultimately apply would be very much less than the present numbers of class B. Class C would then have more work, class D more pay, and both be able to join hands with the social policy of classes E and F. Trades unions and co-operative societies would be able to build from the bottom, instead of floating, as now, on the top of their world. Great friendly societies might hope to include the mass of the population in their beneficent net. Improved morale of labour would go hand in hand with better organization of industry. The whole standard of life would rise, and with its rise the population difficulties, whether of internal increase or of immigration, would become more manageable.

What should we lose by such a change? We are always losing something of the poetry and picturesqueness of the past. The rags of the beggar, his rare orgies, his snatches of song and merriment, his moments of despair, his devil-may-care indifference to the decencies of civilized life – all these touch the imagination and lend themselves to art; they are excellent theatrical properties, less imposing but not less attractive than the personal state and impulsive changes of feeling of the absolute monarch, or the loyal devotion of the feudal dependant, and a hundred characteristics of a fallen society – gone, never to return. Yet audacity, daring, generosity, devotion, impulsive affection, still exist and flourish among us; the setting alone is changed. In the same way, there would be no less room than now or than always for charity, whether the stately generosity of endowment or self-sacrificing service of man, or pity which seeks its exercise in the relief of suffering; all these would find their place in softening the inevitably hard action of the State, but would be required to fall into line with it.

And what of the position of the rich? It is difficult to say whether, at the end of all – when poverty no longer drags down industry, and industry itself controls the profits of production and distribution – whether even then there will be in England less wealth accumulated in individual hands or handed down by inheritance than is now the case. Whether or no matters very little, and any change would come slowly. It is, however, by no means true that 'by no conceivable plan can the poor become less poor unless the rich become less rich'. It may be expected that the rate of interest (as distinguished from profit) would continue to fall. It has fallen in no long period from 5 per cent to 3 per cent, and might well reach the true 'simplicity' of 1 per cent. But the less the capital of the rich is needed at home, being driven out by the savings of the mass of the people, the more it would seek investment abroad in the service of less advanced communities, and its profits would return, through the channels provided by the rich, to the continual benefit of home industry. Similarly as to profits: extraordinary achievements in industrial management might meet, as now, with extraordinary and sometimes enormous rewards, but the field at home for such efforts would become more and more restricted, and the ordinary level of profit would be very low. Those bent on winning wealth would increasingly seek their fortunes abroad, and it would be through their hands that the surplus wealth of the rich would seek new fields of operation. Rich people would doubtless continue to be; they would only be less rich by contrast with the common lot of humanity. Their social functions would remain what they are now, and they would fill their place more usefully and profitably, and above all more happily, under a state of things which would secure the final divorce of poverty from labour.

Industrial Remedies[5]

1

THE industrial evils for which remedies are sought are infinitely various in nature. We think of the chemical worker earning fairly good wages, but ruining his health by the wilful neglect of reasonable precautions; of the half-skilled plumber; of the bricklayer on strike, or the bootmaker locked out; of the housewife shopping unnecessarily late on Saturday night; of the tailoress losing time through waiting at her employer's door for a retarded task; of the pressure in the West End during the busy weeks of the London season; of the long hours and insanitary conditions of small workshops; of the discomfort and unhealthiness of the home of the domestic fur-worker; of the young mother returning to the factory; or of the boy of twelve selling papers in the street. Very

5. Second edition, Vol. IX, pp. 294–7, 308–18.

many needs are suggested, and the remedies considered in detail are inter-connected in various ways. The most certain method, for instance, of securing better health may be by shorter hours of work, or the only way of obtaining higher wages may be through increased efficiency.

Or, if we consider the principal objects which remedies have in view – higher wages, more regular work, shorter hours, better health and longer life, greater personal safety, proper training and increased efficiency, and the maintenance of industrial peace – it is clear that the pursuit of all these objects is not equally reasonable or requisite in every field of employment. To some they do not apply at all.

The appropriate instrument of remedial action will vary with the object aimed at. Sometimes we may find the instrument within the borders of the trade concerned. To employers and foremen, for instance, we may look for better management and more thoughtful distribution of work, by which the maximum of regularity may be secured, not only from week to week but also from day to day; or to the wage-earner for greater care in using the safeguards prescribed for health; or to employers and employed alike for the frankness and consideration which conduce to the maintenance of satisfactory relations.

Or we may have to look outside the borders of the particular trade: to Parliament for legislation or to local authorities for bylaws; to the central or local government for better administration; to the consumer for some discrimination as to what is purchased, that it be not 'cheap and nasty', and for some regard as to when purchases are made or orders given, so that undue pressure or excessive hours of work may be avoided. Or finally, when those within the trade are either apathetic or helpless, we may find in an aroused and enlightened public opinion the main lever by which the tardy wheels of reform may be quickened.

There is thus no single panacea, no philosopher's stone

by which economists or statesmen can touch the surging life of London, even with the glint of an age of gold. It is, indeed, not this or that particular remedy that is the most essential need, but rather a vital movement; not laws or regulations, but the creation of a quiet determination on the part of men and women, rich and poor alike, to do their individual share.

2

Industrial remedies must not be curative, only, of existing evils; they must be preventive also; and prepared to meet new evils as they arise. Again the same large principles apply; foresight and adaptability are demanded from the individual to take advantage of the cushion of continuous expansion, and in the facts as to declining and expanding trades we have evidence of the remarkable, and for the most part unobserved, processes of industrial adaptation and elasticity. But important as are the facts of these changes, far more so are those brought about by death. If only we could apply effective remedial action to the young, in a generation the evil conditions which seem so unchangeable would be swept away. Thus it is that education comes to be of the first importance.

What we seek from education is not simply, nor perhaps even primarily, economic in character, but the best hope of economic improvement is ensured by this foundation; and on this basis the adoption of other remedies becomes more possible. Few of these have an entirely external source; and, even when authority steps in, there is nearly always need for the intelligent co-operation of the individuals affected. Factory legislation and sanitary measures, for instance, are more easily administered for those who can understand and appreciate the regulations by which they benefit.

The most valuable external influences, however, are not those which control the individual, but those which enable him to act more freely and more intelligently for himself. In this respect above all, we recognize the fundamental importance of education as an instrument of industrial reform. For some, the advantages secured by a complete scientific training may be the first consideration; and for others a sufficient though more limited technical training. But for all, the 'education of the citizen' will be calculated to have solid and beneficial results, and the extent to which the advantages of technical education in particular, and of improved industrial training generally, will be used, is largely determined by the thoroughness of the preliminary teaching. From this consideration the proposal to raise the age of legal employment derives its great practical importance. At present it is often just the quickest children who, because they are able to pass the prescribed standards at the earliest age, are most liable to be withdrawn from the school influences from which they, especially, are able to benefit. Still further restrictions on the employment of the young would be desirable, but may not be practicable.

The thousand opportunities for earning precarious livelihoods presented by great centres of population are an evil peculiarity; a source of demoralization for all who come within their influence, and most especially for the young. It may be that this does not apply to London to any disproportionate extent when compared with its vast population, but in a village or small town, those who gain a subsistence in this way are merely a few, or it may even be only isolated members of society; whereas, in London they form a large class, exerting the influence of a class, and affording day by day a deplorable and seductive demonstration of the possibility of scraping through life without knowledge of any trade, without discipline, and without even the elements of an orderly industrial life. If it were possible by stricter police regulations against loafing and cadging, no less than against begging, to check the manufacture of this class, it would be desirable by these means to weaken the harmful influence of the school of irregularity which some of our public thoroughfares present.

The immense London demand for boy labour, at high rates of wages, but for employments which have no future, is, from many points of view, a matter for regret, but errand boys, messenger boys, van boys, and those employed on mechanical tasks in excessively specialized trades, have at any rate a better chance than those who find their living in the streets, and the fact that there is this demand for young labour facilitates the absorption of wastrel boys into industry...

3

It cannot but be admitted that the industrial conditions under which we live lead to poverty, or at least that poverty follows in their train. The immediate explanation of poverty is usually very simple: No savings; no opportunity of remunerative work; inadequate pay; inability or unwillingness to do the work that offers; reckless expenditure – such are the causes of which one thinks. But in seeking remedies it is rather for *causae causarum* that we must look. We ask why pay is insufficient, how it is that work cannot be had, by what chance the sufferer has no share of accumulated wealth; or we may seek to explain incapacity or to analyze sloth. Finally, in the attempt to reach the very root of things, we are driven to turn these questions another way, and to inquire why work should be remunerated at all; how there comes to be any accumulated wealth, or what claim any one in particular has to its enjoyment. I do not wish to pursue abstract reasoning of this kind, but when, as is sometimes the case in socio-economic discussion, it seems to be assumed that those who lack work or money are on that account wrongfully treated, it is desirable to ask what it is that entitles men to either – not in any spirit of cynicism, but rather in that of the scientific dictum, 'A nihilo nihil fit.'

Remunerative work with payment by results is the basis of the industrial order on which our civilized life rests. When men earn largely the world has usually benefited in proportion; and, similarly, when they are paid very little or are unable to earn anything at all, it is fully probable that what they contribute to the service of the world is no less insignificant. Opportunities might very well be more equal, but it may be questioned whether under any different industrial system they would, on the whole, be as great; and whatever the system – whether individualist or socialist, competitive or paternal – the final cure of poverty must lie either in increasing the serviceableness of the work done, or in securing for the less capable a sufficient share of that which is produced by the more capable members of society, or most likely in a combination of these two.

Social remedies are all concerned with securing advantages for the less capable. Industrial remedies, while using both methods, are more particularly directed to the widening of opportunity and the increase of serviceableness.

Let us first take the case of insufficient pay.

At the outset, it may be observed that the employments in which a low rate of pay is found are those which almost anyone can undertake at short notice, as needing neither special training nor special powers of any kind. Under such conditions the rate of remuneration naturally falls to the bottom level, whatever that may be, and poverty is then not far off. For this state of things the most certain cure lies in improving the character of the work done or the service rendered. If this can be accomplished the worker will assuredly be lifted out of the slough in which he is now sunk. Nor is this all: for by the decrease in the numbers of those who are only fit for the lowest class of work, the value of even their poor services will be enhanced. It may perhaps be objected, that the over-plus of labour would in that case be merely transferred; and that any gain to the lowest would be illusory, since the class above would be dragged down by the excessive competition. This objection assumes an economic rigidity very far from the truth. The wants and activities of men rise with the average of capacity, and the amount of work to be done is accordingly increased. Thus, more than in anything else, the way of improvement lies in the increase of the numbers of the capable and willing, and the decrease of the incapable or the shirkers. The industrial activity of capable men makes opportunities for all the world. In no other way can permanent advancement be attained. Acts of Parliament may do something to raise and protect the standard of life; combination among the workers be useful in fighting their battle; and public opinion have effect in strengthening, or even in creating, a sense of responsibility amongst employers; but unless the final result is to add to the utility and serviceableness of the work done, improvements have little chance of lasting.

This doctrine is applicable as much to the employer as to the employed, or even more so; in their case on the largest scale may be seen 'the making of opportunities for all the world'. But if they fail...

Unfortunately the inherent differences in the potentialities and value of human effort are imperfectly apprehended, and attention is chiefly directed to the terms on which the product, treated as a fixed quantity, shall be divided. The notion of 'undifferentiated labour' is the basis of theoretic Socialism, and is more or less involved in all schemes for bringing industry under State control. Socialistic calculations and plans of action almost depend upon a simple labour unit. The extraordinary diversity of powers and conditions, to which every line of our inquiry bears witness, is constantly ignored, and the economic value, whether positive or negative, of the

RECOMMENDATIONS

employer is scouted. Trade unionists, the working classes generally, and even a wider public, are to a considerable extent under the influence of these ideas.

They affect the relations of capital and labour in a somewhat one-sided way. The employer is for ever seeking to utilize to the utmost the labour of those who work for him, and if he fails in economic virtue it will usually be on other ground than this; but on the part of the men thought is seldom given to the necessity of adapting the work done to the employers' needs. An attempt on his part to reduce wages, or the refusal to raise them, is never met by seeking to increase the utility of the services offered, but always and solely by a refusal to render them at all, or the threat of this; or occasionally, if the employer persists and a strike is inconvenient, by the opposite plan of giving as little utility as possible in exchange for the wages paid; that is by the fatal resource of giving slow work to match small pay, known as the 'ca' canny' policy.

To fight is often strictly necessary, and the power to fight efficiently can never be dispensed with, but such action as this, unless of the most temporary character, appears to me to be bad generalship on the part of the union leaders, as well as bad economics, and only to be accounted for by misconception on their part as to the permanent basis of industrial value. To seek to make a bargain more equal by decreasing the utility of what you have to sell is surely suicidal. If you give less (the Sybilline Books notwithstanding), you cannot reasonably hope to receive more. It will, perhaps, be said that to give less, either in quantity or quality, is the bottom fact in every rise of price, the method invariably adopted; but the parallel does not exactly hold. As regards quantity the portion of the product withheld remains in stock: it is not so as to labour which passeth with the day. As regards quality, if the quality be that of intensity, there is something to be said. Intensity implies exhaustion, and a man may as reasonably measure his services by units of effort as units of time; to do so is the basis of all piecework remuneration. It may suit one man to work six or eight hours intensely and then stop for the day, while another gives ten or twelve hours to his task. Or the character of the work may decide the intensity of the strain it involves on nerve or muscle and the pay will rightly be proportionate (amongst other things) to the energy expended. No employer can reasonably ask for more effort without offering more pay, unless the change is to be regarded as reducing the remuneration, and no employee can be expected to strain himself to the point of exhaustion, unless remunerated accordingly (only what he has agreed to do that he must honourably perform); but in the shape the bargain takes he will do well to consider the convenience of the employer and the success of the work.

Moreover, 'quality' in work is by no means confined to intensity, or even skill, but includes conscientious care of every kind, and in this every man has much to give for which he ought and would be paid, did he know how to play his cards aright. The results are often attained. A good master will not fail to recognize such men, and in fixity of tenure, if in no other way, they reap what they have sown. But they play no game. It is part of their virtue that they are unconscious of it. It is only as an instance that I refer to their case. It is not of individual success that I am thinking, but of the policy and methods of action open to united bodies of men consciously seeking their own advantage and deliberately playing their own game. To them I would offer '*do ut des*' as a motto. The threat, 'pay us well or we will serve you ill', cannot compare in effectiveness with the demand 'pay us well because we serve you well'. If wages are to be raised to the utmost and then maintained at the top level, it is essential that the wage-earner should consider first the interests of the employer.

It will, perhaps, again be hinted that 'sauce for the goose is sauce for the gander'. Why, it may be asked, should the generosity of the opening, the present tense of 'I give', be expected from the men rather than the masters? why should not the masters leave the subjunctive 'that thou mayst give' (involving something also of a future tense) to the men? But it is not a practical suggestion. It is always for the seller to show his wares and satisfy the buyer of their value. The buyer must be won. He stands on guard. *Caveat emptor*. In this case buyers and sellers have a common interest more than usually direct, and were mutual suspicions at rest agreement ought not to be difficult. Moreover, no transaction stands alone. Every industrial bargain is based on the result of previous bargains and is the link which connects them with those which come after. To be jealous of the success of one's opponent in any transaction is short-sighted. His advantage today becomes the sure basis of your own success another time.

A margin of profit to the employer is necessary to continuity of employment; in this sense it is his security. The more certain and safe it is the less this margin needs to be, and the less it will inevitably tend to become. By this means, in the end the wage-earner and the consumer together share a permanent benefit, and it must never be forgotten that the consumer is largely the wage-earner over again.

We have seen how various are the elements of utility. Men do not know the possibilities of their own value. Such virtues as truthfulness, honesty, and loyalty might seem smirched if appraised, though they are the most valuable of all commodities. Others, such as trustworthiness, promptitude, punctuality, and sobriety are more freely recognized as merchantable qualities, and find a place wherever characters are asked and given. It is all these, no less than skill and strength, that make the value of a man's work; and to bring them to market, while it honours him, does not degrade them.

It is only by giving his best services that any man is in a position to insist upon a full reward. In this way each individual must seek industrial salvation. For low wages there is no other cure, and what is true of the one man is true also of the mass. Underlying all that may be done for him by combination or by legislation or by public sentiment, the individual, in asserting his claim to a living wage, needs to base his action on a sounder philosophy and a firmer faith than that which usually prevails. To be as useful as possible – such is the Gospel of industry; and there is no one, high or low, rich or poor, to whom it does not apply.

4

The poverty that is due to low wages is, in London, less in volume as well as less acute than that which is consequent on some form of lack of work. The causes of this industrial failure and consequent irregularity of employment are many and complicated. Socialism boldly offers a solution, and to this owes its influence over the minds and hearts of men. But the ideal it holds out has no solidity of structure and no firm basis. This is shown by the splitting into different camps of those who are thus associated which is invariably experienced when the moment of action is even approached. Connected with this natural cleavage is the throwing off of the more violent elements under free discussion, the abandonment by the majority of extreme views, and the acceptance of legality of action. Amelioration of existing conditions, rather than radical change, then becomes the aim. Revolutionary ideas are discarded, and the whole subject falls into the lines of ordinary democratic government. Finally, it is found that the solution is not there. The dream has faded and is gone.

Even if there is agreement as to the ends in view, the means to be adopted under law and constitution to secure more equal conditions still leave room for much difference of opinion, and the widest divergence appertains to the part which the central authority is expected to play in improving the conditions of life. This action may be brought to bear on any of the troubles of the poor, but it is especially with regard to lack of work that its possibilities need now to be considered. For questions of public health and education are already fully recognized as being within the province of the State, and on the other hand, if the Socialistic idea yields so far as to admit wages at all, the rates will generally still be recognized as remaining within the scope of individual action, limited and controlled by voluntary combination. There then remains the questions of finding employment when needed, of savings, and of care for the future, as to all of which the proper sphere of the State is disputed, although with a general admission that interference with private initiative may, within certain limits, be desirable.

To be able and willing to work, and yet to be unable to obtain work, seems a hard fate, and singularly unnecessary in a world where the welfare of all might surely be capable of increase in some degree by the work of each. It would appear to be a mere question of the application of work to useful ends, but, however simple this may sound, it is fraught with great difficulties. The doubt that faces us is whether it is possible for the State by special action to start or stimulate work in one direction, without checking it, or taking away some other stimulus, in some other direction.

We may say with some confidence that the volume of employment depends on the relation which the amount of enterprise bears to the numbers seeking employment. But enterprise itself depends on many things: on the pressure of capital seeking investment; on the presence of unemployed (and therefore cheap) labour; on the demand of consumers for the things or services they require; and finally on the hope of gain, the spirit of adventure, and the pushing of inventive genius, and all these interact, employing each other as well as hiring labour. They are also all subject to two forms of exhaustion, being liable to repletion or collapse. The play of these forces is apt to result in cyclical alternations of good and bad times, and in a competitive struggle for success in which the weakest go to the wall. The question then is – Can the central action of the State or the interference of local government either increase the total volume of enterprise or beneficially regulate its flow?

It is evident that any operation undertaken by the State must adversely affect some, if not all, of the sources of private enterprise. It will withdraw capital and so decrease the pressure exercised by the amount seeking investment. It will absorb labour and tend to raise its price. It will satisfy needs that would otherwise seek other methods of satisfaction. So far as it competes with private enterprise it will reduce the chances of profit, and may thus damp the spirit of adventure. Public action may indeed forestall the natural flow of enterprise, but if this is all it can do, and if we suffer a permanent loss of spontaneity, we might find we had paid very dearly for the temporary advantage. In spite of this, so far as such action does not come into immediate competition with possible or probable private enterprise, there would still be some field for it. Within the limits of moderation there would be no serious objection to the absorption of labour and capital in this way. Neither capital nor labour are fixed and rigid in amount or in efficiency. Their elasticity in response to demand is great. Moreover, it is rare for either to be fully employed at any one time.

The limits to the desirability of such action depend on the nature of the government and also on the character of the people governed. With an absolute government and a dependent people, State enterprise may be desirable, whilst where there is freedom and industrial energy it would do more harm than good. The class of work, too, that it may be desirable to undertake varies according to the prevailing conditions of life; for instance, railways may be a more fitting national work where population is sparse, and the rebuilding of cities where it is crowded. In a general way it is desirable that the wants supplied by these means should be such as are widely felt, and at the same time more easily catered for by public than by private effort. In such cases, public action, if cautiously and carefully undertaken, may increase the total volume of enterprise and add greatly to the general prosperity.

Such operations, however, would not be aimed at, and would not particularly touch, the case of the unemployed, who are so, while others find work, mainly because of some personal disability under which they suffer. With greater general prosperity there might, indeed, be fewer of those who suffer in this way, but even that is not certain, and at any rate the class would not cease to exist.

To organize systematically the labour of those who are incapable of finding a living for themselves would be an entirely different undertaking. The Socialists think it can be done by self-devotion on the part of the capable, and a final sternness which shall enforce obedience by the threat of starvation. The practical difficulties in the way are perhaps overwhelming, but in theory I see no objection to the assumption by the State of this responsibility; and the very close limits within which alone such a course is possible are due, not to fear of injury to independent lives nor to the danger of perpetuating or increasing the assisted class, as might at first be supposed, but arise solely because the incapable would refuse to submit to the discipline which alone would give any value either industrial or educational to their work. If attempted, it would be of the nature of a State charity, and socialistic in the sense of the Poor Law rather than as involving any change in the economics of industry.

It is to other quite as much as to industrial remedies that we must look for the cure or relief of poverty. We have to consider what the State or private effort does or might do in London for the young and for the old, for the morally weak and for the sick, as well as for the unemployed; and what religion and philanthropy are doing or might do to form public opinion, to supplement or modify the influence of legislation, and to disseminate wholesome views of human life; or what other action, public or private, may assist in eradicating the causes or softening the hardships of poverty.

The Organization of Charity[6]

OUR general review of the local conditions of life, contained in the volumes describing the religious influences, includes a short account of the administration of the Poor Law in each union. From these it may be noted that the principles and practices adopted vary widely; more so than seems reasonable in a matter which is not only of common interest, but of which the charge is largely met out of a common purse, and as to which there has accumulated the experience of more than half a century. There are also other reasons for thinking that the time is ripe for the unification of Poor Law administration, not only in London but throughout the country. But it is only as regards London that I now speak.

Where great aggregations of population are brought together there is (as we have found in London, and it is equally true elsewhere) a tendency towards uniformity

6. Third edition, third series, Vol. III, pp. 142–50.

of class in each section. Poor districts become more uniformly poor, because the better off leave, and betake themselves to the parts they prefer. If therefore, under these conditions the cost of the poor under the Poor Law is to be borne locally, it necessarily presses unjustly. On the other hand, if the community as a whole bears the cost, it must control the management; and yet the administration, in order that it may have any real life, must be local. Amongst these rocks the path of compromise, by means of partial equalization of charges, is not entirely satisfactory.

The divergence of view as to what are the best principles of administration is really less than it appears to be under the magnifying glass of democratic ideas. Those who administer the law differ among themselves far less than do those who elect them, experience of the work tending to bring together those whose views were at the outset perhaps far apart. It would, therefore, seem possible to agree upon general rules of action to which the whole administration should conform, in connection with which the charges might be further, if not completely, unified, and greater practical efficiency be combined with many economies.

The Poor Law is the foundation of organized charitable relief. The next step demands the limitation of its field by the recognition and, so far as need be, the organization, of voluntary effort; a recognition which should be mutual, and thus lead to a clear understanding of the part to be played by each in dealing with poverty and its troubles. In London I believe that a practical agreement on this subject could be reached. An immense amount of experience has been accumulated by unions adopting quite different lines of action in perfect good faith and with an equal desire to assist the poor; and the general drift of this experience is in the direction of co-ordinating the efforts of official and voluntary relief.

I myself advocate as a third element the introduction of Old Age Pensions, contributed directly from the national purse, not so much in aid of poverty as of thrift; but acting directly and indirectly in relief of the Poor Law and of private charity; simplifying the problems which each has to treat; and making concerted action on their part in dealing with destitution and distress more practicable and more efficacious.

To this end the recipient of a pension must have kept in the main clear of poor relief; otherwise the fewer the conditions imposed the better. The coming of the pension at a fixed age must be certain, provided independence has been maintained before. Under these two fundamental conditions the expectation of the pension will surely stimulate individual effort to hold out till it comes and to add something to its meagre provision. Thrift tests are unnecessary and delusive. To adopt them is to drop the reality in catching at the apparent, like the dog in the fable.

As my plan bears closely on the administration both of the Poor Law and of private charity, I will venture to recapitulate it.[7] I would make seventy the age at which a free and honourable pension should be granted to everyone who up to then had not received poor relief (other than medical), and I put the amount at seven shillings per week, in place of the more generally adopted proposal of five shillings a week at sixty-five. Proof of age, nationality, and residence in England during the working years of life would be required. There would be no restriction as to earnings (if at seventy any are still possible); nor as to amount of savings: the seven shillings would be in addition to whatever the recipient had or might earn, but would be drawn weekly by personal application, or in cases of debility or illness by some accredited relative or friend. If on this system any who

---

7. *Old Age Pensions and the Aged Poor – a proposal.* Macmillan, 1899.

did not exactly need the money, should still collect it, so much the better for maintaining the dignity of the rest; as one may welcome a bishop or a lord who deigns to travel third class.

At and after seventy most of the difficulties and, I think, all the dangers of a universal pension system melt away. Its cost is no longer prohibitive, while the coming of the pension would be of untold value in limiting the liabilities which prolonged life entails, not only on the individual, but on thrift agencies and on charitable funds, and would lift from very many old hearts the fear of the workhouse at the last.

It is, however, before seventy, and mainly between sixty and seventy, that the battle of independence has to be fought; and it is to the beneficial effect of a coming pension on the lives of the people, especially during this period, that I attach especial importance. It is this effect, moreover, which brings the subject definitely within the range of the subject I am now discussing.

To those who demand that the State pension should begin at sixty, and who claim that it is impossible for working men to save enough for maintenance in old age, I would say that most could provide enough to eke out the earnings which are still possible between sixty and seventy; and that their clubs could more easily assist them in this if relieved of all liability for those whose lives are prolonged. To those again who take their stand on sixty-five as the right pension age, with five shillings as the amount, I can only say that in my view, seven shillings at seventy provides a more practical scheme. The cost would be substantially less, and the difficulties, both economic and administrative, very much so. The future seven shillings coming at the age of seventy would, perhaps, loom as large in the imagination of a man of fifty or sixty, as would five shillings accruing at sixty-five. Up to seventy he would have to provide for his life; beyond that age he need not worry, though few who save at all would limit their action so closely or be content when seventy was at last reached, if they had not some funds in hand to help out the pension allowance. The motive to save up to the time of the pension and beyond it would be strong; as also, too, would be the motive with those living nearer the line of pauperism, to avoid application to the Poor Law. The effect of looking forward to a pension would be the exact opposite to that of the anticipation of Poor Law relief, any claim to which must rest upon absolute destitution.

It is a mistake to suppose that no advantage would come except to those who live beyond seventy. The provident would feel the benefit at once through the decreased rate of contribution for remote benefits, which would be possible if their clubs could omit old age in their calculations, while the effective value of any other savings they are able to make will be immediately increased, in so far as the possible years of extreme old age can be dropped out of financial count. For very many, the one doubt as to being able to escape the workhouse would be removed. And even those who largely trust to others to do their saving for them would find it far easier to obtain aid from some old employer, or friend, or relative, or even child, if the liability were limited to a definite term. Those of the improvident class who lived past seventy might still find themselves stranded, without friends, in their old age; but, to parody an old rhyme –

> When friends are gone, and money spent,
> Then Pensions are most excellent.

and the certainty of a pension accruing would often bridge the gulf, enabling those who might otherwise have been abandoned to the Poor Law, to maintain a decent home outside.

My plan goes still a little further, and it is at this point particularly that united action between the Poor Law and private charity becomes essential. There will be cases unsuited for the Poor Law, for which it may be nevertheless difficult to secure sufficient private assistance; cases in which a small pension is clearly the form in which assistance could be given most judiciously. Such may occur at almost any age, but it is more usually after sixty that, failing other help, the workhouse comes so near. It would then seem very hard that the pension assured to any who live till seventy should not in some way be made available; and I suggest that with the co-operation of the Guardians, who are directly interested in keeping people off the rates, a case might be made out for an *immediate pension at a permanently lower rate*, which would be actuarially equivalent to the value of the deferred pension, provided the recipient can by some means be assured a total income from all sources sufficient for independent maintenance. The object would be to prevent the dissipation of savings, and to rouse in time the effort that is needed to secure an adequate provision for life. Practically no one would be likely to ask this accommodation who would not otherwise become a pauper; charity would find its opportunity, and while the national exchequer would hardly suffer at all, the rates would profit.

If the separate spheres of Poor Law and charity were distinctly recognized, and pensions, thus adapted, were available to assist voluntary effort of all kinds, out-relief could and should be abolished. With its abolition all difficulty of deciding what agency ought to be employed in the relief of poverty would pass away. Evidently no case ought to be relegated to the workhouse which could be satisfactorily dealt with outside. Those who are abandoned to that last resource, because from sickness or infirmity they are unfitted for any home that is open to them, would be cared for in one building, while the destitute who come upon the Poor Law from any other cause would be accommodated in another building and altogether differently regarded.

It is commonly said that few of the old who are now inmates of workhouses could, if a pension were granted, find any home outside. That may be so, but it hardly affects the question. The object of the pension, actual or prospective, is to *maintain* a home, which is a very different thing from suddenly *finding* one. The pension itself is only one factor out of many that would be found working with it in this direction. The preservation of the homes would exercise a constant wholesome influence on family relations as well as on thrift. The young would look to the old, instead of only the old looking to the young. Some, doubtless, might be completely stranded in old age, and might be glad to abandon their pension for the haven of the workhouse, and there would be others whose tempers made home life impossible; but I cannot doubt that if they were no longer a financial burthen, most old people whose health permitted it would remain outside. For the most part they do so now where out-relief is given, though the amount allowed them is very small. It is only those whose infirmities are such that they require a nurse's care who ought to be recommended to give up home and pension in favour of the workhouse infirmary. Such as these should, indeed, be encouraged to do so, but it would be the work of charitable and friendly kindness to minister to the comfort and happiness of all such as can remain in the world outside.

The abolition of out-relief is, I think, essential, and at the same time quite possible, if Poor Law and organized private effort will work hand in hand, and if the pension, which becomes in itself a great motive to thrift, is assured in the future. The difficulty as to widows, though great, is not insuperable. Even now, most men's lives are insured to some extent; the immediately forlorn position of the wife and children they will leave behind readily fills their imagination. A distinct tendency towards the increase of this provision is shown by the readiness to join temporary 'sharing-out' societies, as well as, and often in addition to, the permanent friendly societies, and by the increase of insurance for small sums in the Prudential and other companies. But whatever the amount be, it comes in a lump, and is in danger of being rapidly disbursed, so that the woman is destitute before she has had time to rearrange her life. It would be far better if, beyond the actual sum needed for funeral and mourning, which is generally much less than is actually spent, the money should be made payable in weekly instalments spread over twelve months. Thrift agencies might do something to encourage a provision of this kind. But even if the widow should be left entirely without resources, it would ordinarily be far better for her if assistance from the rates in the form of out-relief were not available. For the immediate needs of the widow and the orphan left without support, collections are commonly made among the deceased man's working mates, or his neighbours institute a 'friendly lead', or money is raised by an effort of some other kind; and for her future, and that of her children, established forms of charity can always be relied on to some extent. No class of case (except sudden sickness or accident) obtains assistance so readily, for the simple reason that the stress is usually of a temporary nature. It is thus a form of charitable action which has satisfactory results to show: from dire want, with the future trembling in the balance, the recipients may pass to independence and a happy home. Not only can money be found, but friendly assistance and kindly personal relations. As things are, such aid as if forthcoming is too often speedily spent, and so soon as exhausted the Guardians are appealed to. To abolish out-relief would both strengthen these resources and cause a better use to be made of them; so that the Guardians need not be applied to at all, unless it be necessary in some cases to relieve the mother by taking charge of some of her children of school age; or, in others, when from any circumstances the case cannot be helped to independence, it will evidently be better treated in the workhouse.

These, then, are the suggestions I would make towards the better organization of charitable relief in London:

(1) An extension of the system of a common Poor Fund, subject to agreement as to the principles of administration;
(2) Consultations between Boards of Guardians and charitable agencies as to relief, and a distinct recognition of their respective spheres;

and, as applicable to the whole country as well as London,

(3) Old age pensions, coupled with the then practicable abolition of out-relief.

By these means most of the difficulties, both of Poor Law administration and charity organization, would be removed or lightened.

Housing[8]

IN considering this subject I shall first enumerate the evils and try to allocate responsibility, and then indicate the efforts that are being made to improve matters, and their results.

Undesirable housing conditions may be classified under some twelve heads: (1) Old property in bad condition; (2) Comparatively new houses badly built; (3) Property neglected by the owner; (4) Property abused by the occupier; (5) Houses built upon insufficient space; (6) Houses erected on damp or rubbish-filled ground; (7) Houses occupied by families of a class for which they were not designed and are not suited; (8) Insanitary houses; (9) Badly arranged block dwellings; (10) Badly managed blocks; (11) Excessive rents; (12) Crowded homes.

8. Third edition, third series, Vol. III, pp. 158, 170–8.

All these overlap to some extent. The bad condition of old property may have been aggravated by neglect, and neglect have been followed by abuse; good houses would be wasted on ground which must render them unhealthy; and inconsiderate management follows naturally on inconsiderate construction; while bad sanitation and high rentals for the accommodation supplied are features common to all.

Apart from economic causes, for which no one can be held especially accountable, and administrative legal enactments by which for the moment all are bound, the responsibility for these evils rests either (1) with the owner and his agents, or (2) with the occupier, or (3) with the local authority (including magistrates), or is shared among them...

Of the evils which we began by enumerating we have now considered all except the more general ones of excessive rents and crowding. In allotting responsibility, we have spoken of owner and occupier, and there remains the local authority with its duties of inspection and interference according to law, and beyond these, optional powers of clearing congested sites, and itself undertaking building on the vacated ground or elsewhere. We will now take up these remaining points:

... There are few parts of London, especially of those occupied by the working and lower middle classes, in which rents are not rising. The needs of the people for houses are not adequately met. From Outer-South London we have such statements as 'High and rising rent, a rise at each fresh tenancy'; 'Rents have risen from 7s. 6d. to 9s. 6d. in the last five years'; and 'Peckham is becoming poorer owing to increased rents driving better class workers away.' From a more central part comes, 'Housing difficulty insuperable, rents enormous, large single rooms 15s. to 17s.,' but it is said that 'high rents are due partly to the non-payment of arrears'. 'Foreigners', it is asserted, 'will pay anything to get in', and 'bad folk are crowding the good out'. 'Rents not low, but collection irregular,' comes from further north. In East London, where there is little migration and steadily increasing pressure, houses are said to be 'let before they are empty, and people daren't move'; while in the extension of West London, 'notwithstanding all the building, the poorer streets are becoming crowded,' and in South-West London it is again said, 'none dare quit'. It may happen that a couple begin comfortably with two rooms, and then, as children come, cannot afford to move or cannot mend matters by moving. In another part of London the increase of rents since the enforcement of the Health Acts is specially noted, and the consequent driving of the people into cheaper districts. It is hardly necessary to trouble the reader with more quotations on this subject. The conditions may be slowly changing for the better, but at present the difficulty is extreme and insistent. Those who can afford it move out, and those who cannot escape, crowd in. 'Property becomes more profitable in a working-class than in a middle-class district,' and even more profitable still when none but the poor are left as residents. By a strange perversion, as rents rise in the more central districts, the better off are more likely to be driven away, while the poor remain.

... The pressure falls particularly heavily on families where there are many children. Such often 'cannot obtain respectable quarters, and then become degraded by their surroundings'. This is mentioned often. 'It is almost impossible to find room, and when people have to move they roam about like hunted dogs.' The Guardians are often appealed to for accommodation. Special instances of overcrowding appear frequently on our notes, such as 'Father, mother, and eight children in one room.' In another instance, 'Man and wife, two sons, ages twenty-seven and twenty-one, and two daughters, ages twenty-one and eighteen,' all living in one room. Again, an old woman, her daughter and grandson, and in two other cases, man, wife, and five children occupied one room. Such instances are by no means extreme or unusual.

With single people 'Box and Cox' arrangements are not unheard of. 'Is it right', a decent woman said (speaking to a deaconess), 'that I should have to sleep in a bed that a man sleeps in during the day?' 'Crowding', says one of the clergy, 'is the chief obstacle to spiritual influence. Decency, modesty, cleanliness, etc., are made impossible, but', he adds, 'so full are the people of natural virtue, that with better housing there would be no difficulty.' 'Drink is fostered by bad houses.' 'Crowded homes send men to the public house.' 'Crowding the main cause of drink and vice.' 'Incest is common resulting from overcrowding.' 'Religion has failed, education has done something, but good homes lack.' 'The root of evil is deficient house accommodation.' These are but a few out of many expressions of opinion that could be cited.

We have ourselves seen 'little one-room domiciles fitted up in out-houses' and, the smallest abode of all, an eight-foot square tin shanty occupied by a coster. 'Cellars, too, are used as sleeping-rooms, despite the law,' which it is alleged is the more difficult to enforce because it is frequently broken by the rich in the accommodation of their servants.

Foreigners, it is said, 'minimize crowding so far as possible, by living in the street', and most poor children eat their food as well as play their games there. Not infrequently those whose rooms are stifling and uncleanly practically live out of doors in hot weather, in out-of-the-way streets and courts, and excepting in very cold or wet weather, the destitute class, covered with vermin, prefer to sleep out, even though they may have the price of a night's lodging on them. If without any means, they are liable to be 'run in', but if they possess the requisite pence they can only be 'moved on' by the police from doorstep to doorstep, and finally are often left in peace in some obscure spot till morning. More horrible still, it is said that people will take refuge for the night in, and even make a dwelling-place of, caverns hollowed in the dust-heaps. Those who roam the streets at night get their sleep in the parks or elsewhere during the day.

Passing now to the local authority, the first point to notice is the remarkable development that has taken place during the period of our inquiry. The London County Council, established in 1888, has deservedly won the great position it now holds; and many of the separate boroughs into which the same area is divided and which were constituted ten years later, already show considerable vitality; while the old vestries, which have been turned into or absorbed by the Borough Councils, have experienced a double transformation, having previously been democratized out of all recognition.

The history of Local Government in London promises to make an interesting chapter of some future book, but it cannot be written yet. In the preceding volumes I have merely tried to reflect current opinion as expressed to us by those who looked to the local authority with hope or fear, regarding its action with approval or with condemnation. And as to the larger sphere of action of the London County Council, hardly anything has been said. But in what I have yet to say the versatile energy of this central power in London life will be freely assumed.

It is hardly necessary to discriminate between this and that local authority. All stand upon a democratic basis. The people are practically their own masters, free to tax and free to spend. It would be folly to suppose that the powers that have been given will not be exercised. It is probable that a good deal of money will be spent, and that experiments of all kinds will be tried; but it would also seem almost certain that high rates will still prove an effective drag; that after any fit of extravagance, or yet more of incompetence or folly, those who can promise the rate-payer 'retrenchment and economy' will succeed at the polls, and that the social balance between progress and reaction, or recklessness and prudence will be maintained.

Municipalities and other local bodies will have to learn by experience the limits of successful action, and it may be hoped that rules of general application will gradually emerge. Meanwhile, the fetters in which they have to dance, of Parliamentary sanction and the control of the Local Government Board, are by them found heavy enough.

Something has been done by more effective administration to introduce a higher standard of life, especially as regards crowding. 'Overcrowding', says one of our witnesses, 'is the great cause of degeneracy, but there is less of it than formerly, owing to a higher standard of requirement,' and we have seen that this is borne out by the census statistics. . . . But in spite of this general improvement the evil has become worse in places, and of these, naturally, one hears most. In one street in Southwark where there are 'many single-room tenements', it is said that there are eight hundred people living in thirty-six houses. 'There is a tendency, in this neighbourhood' (we are told) 'to subdivide two-room holdings into single rooms, under a resident landlady.' And throughout London, wherever clearances have been made, things become worse in the surrounding streets. This difficulty is inherent in the whole problem.

Manifestly there can be no cure that does not include expansion. Given freedom to expand, there would quickly be a great change. The local bodies do not lack energy; their medical officers are keen on their work, taking a professional pride in it; public opinion is fairly aroused. But the difficulties in the way are insurmountable, or at any rate the road has not been found. Sanitary authorities dare not enforce the law stringently, knowing that if they evicted the people, many could not obtain house room. 'Much agitation about housing, but appear helpless. Find they could not build to let cottages probably under three shillings a room, nor any cheaper in blocks', was said of one of the vestries. When rebuilding is undertaken 'the public are told that the class turned out will be re-housed, but the authorities know perfectly well that they will not be. They don't want such accommodation, and would not take it if offered, and, if they did, it would only end in the new buildings being spoiled.' In another quarter it is said, 'the displaced people have the first offer, but are got rid of as soon as may be'. And again, 'the people turned out did not come; their places were filled by railway men and police.' Still, the evicted find new quarters somewhere, and even if they tend to make a new slum there, may gain something: 'The forcible process of scattering is salutary'; 'Those that come are bettered by the mere fact of change'; 'Bring the poor to the light and you improve them.' I fear, however, that the remark it is also true that 'it is harder for bad to become better than for good to become worse,' and, in any case, 'housing is not solved by moving people on.' Moreover, the people most concerned are ill-pleased. It is regarded as 'a — shame to pull down the houses of the poor'. 'Going to turn us out of our houses, are you? You'll have to find us some others if you do'; but it is just this that it is so difficult to compass.

Thus the benefit of such improvements is indirect and uncertain, while the cost is enormous. Schemes are made and laid aside, or hung up during discussions between the Borough Councils and the L.C.C. as to sharing the cost, or with the Local Government Board on the numbers to be re-housed and where. Years perhaps elapse, and meanwhile every evil is aggravated; a fresh excuse is provided for postponing all repairs, and speculation is rife, 'much money being invested in such sites in anticipation of clearance', since compulsory powers of purchase are held even in these cases to call for the fullest compensation. Clearly the way out of this difficulty has not been found...

The demand is for new houses, not old. There are those who will only live in new houses, and move when the street becomes 'old' – move 'simply to change their house and start fresh painted'. 'Young married people, who, as soon as the brass handle is tarnished, move elsewhere.' From one district we hear that 'tenants come from all parts of London, drawn by the fact that suitable houses are to be had', these being 'two-storeyed houses of newest style arranged for two families'; affording 'small flats of four rooms fitted up with all conveniences'. 'All my young people are taking these', says a Congregationalist minister, and adds that they are 'lighted up by the new surroundings'; and even themselves 'acquire a dainty look'.

Put baldly, 'lower buildings and wider streets' are the things needed, and instead the people are offered 'depressing streets, dark and narrow', or 'tall, prison-like dwellings'. But their tastes carry them on a good deal further. Not only is much more expected from the builder than formerly in house fittings, but the demand for 'artistic cottages' is noted, and gardens are the pride of those who possess them: 'houses blessed with gardens – a wonderful influence'. 'Houses with good gardens at back; seldom empty, and hard to get': 'Houses with porches creeper-covered eagerly tenanted'. There are, however, limitations; prudence and the pressure of city life step in. Gardens must not be larger than can be tended without hired help, or, if the rent that can be afforded is insufficient for both, an extra room may be preferred.

I wish I could rouse in the minds of speculative builders a sense of the money value that lies in individuality, with its power of attracting the eye, rooting the affections, and arousing pride in house and home.

Then would they seek to use, in place of sedulously destroying, every natural feature of beauty, and take thought to add others. A slightly greater width of garden on the sunny side, whether front or back, may make all the difference; a single tree left standing can glorify a whole street. Fresh painting and papering within, is not the highest ideal; its charm passes; the other gathers force as the years go by.

Expansion[9]

IN our survey of London we have watched the forces which, through increasing pressure at the centre, and in other ways, tend to drive or draw the resident population outwards in every direction, and have found curious resemblances between opposite sides or corners of the social map. In some places this centrifugal action has seemed to proceed by bounds, overleaping the intervening space; but this is rarely the case except with the rich, who when they move are not deterred by distance from seeking the most advantageous spot for a new home, or with the very lowest class who, ejected and rejected, sometimes make one flight to some outlying district where, in the disadvantages it offers to others, they can find their miserable advantage: happy if permitted to create a new slum undisturbed. More generally the movement takes place gradually from ring to ring, accompanied by a slow change of class. But the advance on new ground shows a noticeable tendency to shoot out tongues, like the sun's corona; the intervals between being filled up later. These tongues follow the 'lie of the land' and the facilities offered for speculation in building; but the more important cause and key of explanaation is always found in the available means of communication, be it tramcar or a good highway adapted

9. Third edition, third series, Vol. III, pp. 182-6, 198-9.

as an omnibus road, or the local service of a railway line. It is this fact, coupled with the present palpable inadequacy of facilities of locomotion in London, that leads me to look to their extension, and to improvement in the speed and cheapening in the cost of travel, as a first and essential step towards the solution of the housing problem in London. I am glad to know that public opinion is now roused on this subject, and I hope that we may shortly see the establishment of an authority competent to deal with this matter, as an outcome of the Royal Commission recently appointed. The object of this authority, I conceive, will be to study and report to Parliament on the needs of the public, and on all proposals made to meet these needs, whether by municipalities or by private capitalists; so that if possible a complete and harmonious scheme may be framed, from which all districts and all classes alike may benefit. I do not anticipate that such an authority, if appointed, would be empowered to take action itself, since that, I assume (apart from private enterprise), would lie with the rating authorities; but it would be in a position to advise Parliament on the subject; paving the way for such action as was needed. Holding a quasi-judicial position, it would take account and give due weight to the sectional views of different localities; and finally, after endeavouring to harmonize them, would report when and where sectional interests must be compelled to give way. For some such authoritative guidance there is pressing need.

Before further considering this question of locomotion, let us first glance again at the other more direct methods of dealing with the difficulties of housing to which reference has been made in the preceding section. They are:

(1) Regulations against overcrowding, etc.

(2) The acquisition by the authorities of special areas for demolition and reconstruction.

(3) The obligation enforced upon those who obtain

Parliamentary powers for acquiring sites for industrial, municipal, or other private or public purpose (even if it be for the destruction of overcrowded and insanitary property), to 're-house' those whose homes are disturbed, or at any rate a proportionate number of people, in or near the same neighbourhood.

(4) The acquisition by municipalities or County Council of vacant land for the construction of suitable dwellings.

It is not too much to say that the action taken so far in London in any of these directions has been very half-hearted. Confidence is lacking; public opinion unconvinced. It is felt to be impossible to press regulations against overcrowding when other house room is not available, and very difficult to reform sanitary conditions when landlord and tenant are in league to 'let well alone' (as they regard it). Thus it is just where things are worst that it is most difficult to amend them by direct attack. Schemes for demolition and reconstruction, great and small, have proved, as we have seen, in many ways unsatisfactory. A nuisance is indeed removed, but at a very great cost, largely owing to the terms of compensation for compulsory purchase, and to the obligation to re-house. Good houses are built only to be occupied by a superior class; the evicted poor crowd in elsewhere. Though formulated with the best intentions, the re-housing clauses attached to Parliamentary powers of purchase have proved of doubtful benefit, or rather in some respects certainly injurious. It rarely happens that such powers are needed, except for general public purposes, or for railway extensions which, if the opportunity were seized to stipulate for an improved local service of trains, ought rather to be encouraged than hampered. Moreover, it is to be noted that so far as new dwellings are provided, the legal obligation is generally, and perhaps unavoidably, met by building high blocks, an evasion rather than a cure of the problem at issue.

Finally, the public acquisition of land, beyond the London boundary, for the purpose of supplying working-class houses at reasonable rents, almost necessitates the provision of improved means of communication with what becomes a kind of city colony. The alternative, and as I think, better plan would be to improve the facilities of locomotion generally, or wherever likely to be most useful, without entering upon any public speculation in land or houses.

In support of the policy of purchase, it is pointed out that with better means of communication, and as the population spreads, the value of the ground will certainly rise; and that to provide solely the means of communication is to throw away this advantage. But a far wider policy is called for. The rise in value will not be limited to the patch bought, nor can the aims of improved locomotion consider anything less than the wants of the whole community...

The present system is full of inequalities. These, as well as those which the proposed re-adjustment would bring, would tend to be lessened in succeeding years by the substitution of a well for an ill-balanced system, and meanwhile the immediate sacrifices called for would fall almost entirely on the centres best able to bear them.

The suggestion is of general application, and if adopted at all would hardly be confined to London, but it is for the sake of London that I now ask consideration for it. The needs are pressing; some dislocation may be faced, and some sacrifices may be asked, if by these means the evils of crowded urban life can be mitigated.

I have painted these evils as they are, having first sought to trace their origin or their causes, and to study the efforts made to deal both with these causes and with their effects. At every turn I have been forced to recognize that evils driven under or driven out at one place, reappear at another, and are barely kept at bay by all our efforts. I have seen, too, how the causes and consequences of poverty hang together and interact for evil, and how at the root of all that is both best and worst, lies home life. To improve these conditions, engrained as they are in character, every effort of every agency will still be needed, but the task will become more possible if the standard of the home rises.

It may perhaps be objected that the effect of providing better and more rapid communication would be to foster centralization, and so increase the evil we are trying to amend. But in many ways it would have the opposite result. Wherever a man may go to find his work, it is near home that he will seek his pleasure, and his wife will find her shopping, and thus a local centre is formed. Such centres are to be found now all round London, with brilliant shops, streets full of people, churches, and chapels certainly, perhaps a Town Hall, and probably a theatre. The growth of such local life in London during the past decade is very noticeable, and would undoubtedly play an increasing part in the greater and happier London I desire to see.

Another very reasonable fear is that all there is of natural beauty in the neighbourhood of London will be swamped by the advancing streets, and that whereas we now have open spaces, of a kind, because held in this condition speculatively for a rise in value, we shall then have none; since the owners, it may be thought, will be almost obliged to make their market. The process will really be gradual. It is not possible that all the vacant land around London can find its ultimate use at once, but as large quantities will come into the market, real and not speculative values will prevail, and the rates to be paid will not be very high. Nevertheless there are dangers in the rapid extension of streets and houses, only to be met by the setting apart in advance of sufficient ground for parks and open spaces, carefully, and if possible nobly planned, for the needs of the coming people.

This will be a necessary expense, but the land will be available at a moderate price, and part at least of the cost will be found again in the rateable value of the remainder.

Thus I note these objections only to rule them out, but in conclusion I would emphasize once more the point to which they lead: the crying necessity for forethought and plan in the arrangement of our metropolis, with its great past and, I hope, still greater future.

Conclusion[10]

THINGS AS THEY ARE AND AS THEY MOVE

SEVENTEEN years and an equal number of volumes have been occupied with this inquiry. In as many pages I must now try to sum up the results: seventeen words would doubtless suffice did I know how to choose them aright. But the subjects covered offer a wide range; being no less than life and industry as they exist in London at the end of the nineteenth century under the influences of education, religion, and administration.

We see life cursed by drink, brutality, and vice, and loaded down with ignorance and poverty, while industry is choked by its own blind struggles, and education is still painfully mounting, and too often slipping back from, the first rungs of its ladder. We see religion paralyzed by its own inconsistencies, and administration wrapped in the swaddling clothes of indecision and mutual distrust. Such is the dark side of the picture, which, perhaps, looks the more black to our eyes owing to the heightened demands of a rising standard of life, and the expectancy of better things; as it is said that the greatest darkness precedes the dawn.

Improvement certainly there has been at every point.

---

10. Third edition, *Final Volume*, pp. 200–4, 210–16.

As to drink, although teetotalism no longer arouses the enthusiasm of early days, yet those who abjure alcohol exercise a great and increasing influence; whether it be in the army, or in the police, or in civil employment of every kind, responsibility largely devolves upon them, while with those who take alcohol, though there may be more drinking, there is, undoubtedly, less drunken rowdiness. So, too, in spite of outbursts of 'hooliganism', there is much less street violence; and such scenes of open depravity as occurred in years gone by do not happen now. There is greater intelligence, even though it be largely devoted to betting, and wider interests prevail, even if they be too much absorbed in pleasure-seeking. Side by side with these improvements the whole level of poverty has been pressed upwards by increasing demands on life – demands which were unthought of forty, thirty, or even twenty years ago. But the gulf is still wide which separates the poor from such a degree of confident comfort as civilization calls for, and as we should wish all men to enjoy.

While the whole of life might well be lifted on to a higher plane, we cannot dare to wish that the struggle should be avoided. And light breaks through the darkness. Destitution degrades, but poverty is certainly no bar to happiness. If we permit our minds to dwell upon the masses in London who exist under its disabilities, we may think also of thousands of poor but wholesome homes; of husbands and wives happy in working for each other and rejoicing in their children – of whom it may in this world be said, 'of such are the kingdom of home'.

Thus in regarding the conditions of life at their worst, and in seeking to improve them, there are two distinct tasks: to raise the general level of existence, but especially the bottom level, is one; to increase the proportion of those who know how to use aright the means they have is another and even a greater. But each effort should aid the other.

RECOMMENDATIONS

Among ameliorative agencies, very high hopes were placed upon the benefits of compulsory school teaching, and in spite of palpable failure to secure the results anticipated, these ideas still run riot in our imaginations. A whole generation has been through the schools, but in scholarship there is not much to show for it. Almost all can, indeed, read, though with some effort; and write, after a fashion; but those who can do either the one or the other with the facility that comes of constant practice are comparatively few. Nevertheless, popular education has been far from wasted even in the case of those who may seem to have learnt but very little. Obedience to discipline and rules of proper behaviour have been inculcated; habits of order and cleanliness have been acquired; and from these habits self-respect arises. Thus the boys who have experienced school life, however rudimentary their knowledge of the most elementary subjects, and although they may remember nothing else that has been taught, may yet be better fitted to take up the duties of adult life. The same is true of girls, whose teaching moreover seems to be more directly useful as well as more successful than that of boys; while with regard to the parents, the fathers and mothers who have experienced school life are no longer unfriendly to education. They do, indeed, nearly always take their children away from school at the earliest possible age, but are nevertheless far more anxious that they should benefit by the advantages offered than were their own parents. The old attitude of suspicion, often amounting to hostility, has almost passed away.

And again, brighter light breaks through when we pass from the general to the particular. If we think of the overwhelming mass of ignorance that still persists, we must not forget the case of boys and girls who eagerly grasp every opportunity and, even if by units, justify the perfecting of the ladder of learning now reaching from elementary school to university. Once more two tasks lie before us: to lift the whole level by recognizing the part which elementary education can really play, and then adapting it for that part; and also to increase the number and the opportunities of those who are capable of profiting more fully by the training they receive.

As with the total abstinence movement on the social, and with compulsory schooling on the educational, side, so too, religious work suffers under great disappointments, though they are as yet far from being acknowledged or even fully felt, many of the efforts made being so recent and so much buoyed up by enthusiastic faith. The religious bodies will, I think, incline more and more to intensive work, but they, too, need to recognize that they have a double task: in the raising of the human ideal, which applies to all, as well as the gathering in of the few who respond fully to any particular doctrines taught.

With regard to progressive administration, still shaping its ideals and fretting against restraints, the day of reckoning and disappointment is not now, and though it will surely come, there is in that no reason for holding our hands. The failures may be many, and the success that can be won may take some unexpected shape, but at least the effort to attain it must be good in stimulating the consciousness and vigour of common life.

And if we turn to industry, the Atlas on whose broad shoulders our world rests, though we have to face disappointment at the failure of trade union organization to fill the place expected of it, and though public opinion, backed up by law, still struggles vainly to check abuses and prevent or punish fraud, we are conscious of a power and vigour in the impulses of trade, which can wipe out mistakes.

Closely connected with the vitality and expansion of industry, we trace the advancement of the individual which in the aggregate is represented by the vitality and expansion of London. This it is that draws from the Provinces their best blood, and amongst Londoners selects the most fit. Amongst such it is common for the children to aim at a higher position than their parents held; and for the young people when they marry to move to a new house in a better district. A new middle class is thus forming, which will, perhaps, hold the future in its grasp. Its advent seems to me the great social fact of today. Those who constitute this class are the especial product of the push of industry; within their circle religion and education find the greatest response; amongst them all popular movements take their rise, and from them draw their leaders. To them, in proportion as they have ideas, political power will pass. . . .

THE ROAD AND ITS DIFFICULTIES

IMPROVEMENT must be sought, first of all, in the deepening of the sentiment of individual responsibility. This sentiment rests no doubt upon right feeling, but is subject to stimulation by the opinion of others, and may finally be enforced by law. Of these three, public opinion seems to me to be the most lax. The expectation of evil, the attributing of bad motives, and the ready acceptance of a low standard constitute the first difficulty we have to meet. Cynicism is accounted so clever that men pretend to be worse than they are rather than be thought fools. Clear views of right and wrong in matters of daily action, however firmly they may be rooted in the hearts of men, seldom find utterance; and when this polite rule is broken some surprise is always felt. It is no question of charitable construction of the acts of our neighbours, on the ground that, not knowing all, we hesitate to judge; an attitude for which, though it may be weak, something might be said; but it is that we deliberately refuse to know, in order that we may not need to judge. And this is not the worst, for without knowing or judging, or seeming to care at all, many, if not most men, in order to be safely sensible, indiscriminately assume rascality everywhere. This moral laxity applies to all classes, with some divergence as to the subjects on which the point of honour stands out and cannot be ignored; and by none is it exhibited more widely than by the great masses of respectable working men.

It would seem inevitable that the sense of duty must be weakened by the loss of the habit of judging and of the experience of being judged, as well as by laxity, but nevertheless I venture to assert that it is maintained at a far higher level than is generally thought or claimed. Thus legal enactment, if carefully aimed and measured, becomes doubly and trebly valuable, serving first to check the evil-doer, and secondly to awaken the individual conscience, while it also, by impressing an undeniable seal of condemnation, crystallizes the looseness of public opinion as to any particular offence. Legislation can never go far beyond the sanction of existing public opinion, but may yet lead the way, and in many cases has done so.

The owner of a house, if he be given, and if he accept, his proper place, will be but the medium by which punishment will fall on the evil-doer and order be enforced; and by the performance of this service he will acquire a new and noble title to his property. By this means, and by this means alone, can houses of ill-fame be suppressed or controlled, and the difficulties of enforcing the Factory and Workshop Acts in minor establishments be overcome. It is not the ultimate owner and immediate landlord alone whose sense of responsibility may be strengthened, and upon whom new duties and new liabilities may justly be thrown: against others, too, besides the holders of licences, penalties for breach of social regulation or moral order may wisely be enforced. In proportion to the degree of effective liability maintained in this respect do we see a rising standard of public judgement and expectation; and it would be the same throughout if responsibility could be enforced. The attempts made by special legal enactment to stamp their true character on unscrupulous money-lending, on secret commissions, and on fraud in company promotion, though very difficult of execution, have undoubtedly had a considerable effect on public opinion. In addition, the giving or receiving of bribes in connection with the work of public officials deserves some special stigma of disgrace, and a public recognition of this would probably be welcomed by all well-meaning officials.

It is in such ways that the sense of individual responsibility may be strengthened and used.

Private corporations and associations for the advancement or protection of acquired interests are more frankly selfish than individuals. They provide a conservative element of the utmost value in the social structure, and may be expected to act up to the letter of the law. But even more than individuals, they need to be humanized by the influence of public opinion, or their giant strength may be abused. They constitute our second difficulty.

We then pass to political, philanthropic, and religious associations, which in their efforts to enlighten and advance mankind are the most zealous of all agencies. To them even more than to the direct working of public spirit in administration do we look for the methods of improvements; but their zeal itself brings its difficulty. Each is too apt to cry 'I am the way', and to be unable to admit any other possible salvation. It is not jealousy, for jealousy, like imitation, is a manifest form of approval, but positive hostility, due, it may be, to the feeling that one proposal traverses another; but far more to actual condemnation of the efforts made by others, however well-intentioned they may be. And from this feeling of antagonism it is that each effort is apt to draw its greatest strength. To find a fulcrum which shall neither be nor involve hate is the third and greatest difficulty of all.

As to administration, this is at present in a highly experimental stage, particularly in London, and needs encouragement fully as much as criticism. It has to form its own experience, and to stand or fall, or change its ways, according to the results. Vast powers have been most deliberately conceded to local authorities, and these powers are increased every year. To suppose that they will not be used is to assume the ridiculous position of a father who, after giving a young man a latchkey and money to spend, expects him to be at home every evening by ten o'clock. It is not one experiment, but hundreds or thousands that are being made, by local bodies, large and small, all over the country, with varying aims and under varying auspices. The Local Government Board may cluck from its coop, but the young birds will run far, and, if they are ducklings, will take to the water. London differs only because of its size. It is the 'ugly duckling' of this story.

In 1888 the Conservative Government, by establishing the London County Council, took a great step in the development of the sense of local responsibility, relying for its success on the good sense of the people; and on this same foundation our hopes for the future rest. It is probable that the sphere of collective municipal action will gradually be defined, though it may be too soon yet to lay down rules. As trenching on the sphere of industry, one theory would confine it to necessary monopolies, another would extend it to all monopolies, while a third would create monopolies on purpose. Probably only experience can decide as to what shapes collective action, whether monopolistic or not, may wisely take. Democratic local government is at present in the making, but it is one of the points (for of these there are still several) in which I believe our country to be in advance of all others, and if we can keep the lead in this particular, we shall not fail to hold our great place in the economy of the world.

Finally, facts are still needed. But the spirit of patient inquiry is abroad; my attempt is only one of its children. Every year that passes produces valuable work in this direction, both official and voluntary. The various 'settlements' are all centres of research, and the work often carries a small endowment. Moreover, the London County Council has in nothing shown a higher sense of its position or a more truly progressive spirit, than in the careful collection and liberal publication of statistical and social information.

These considerations have reconciled me to the incompleteness of my own work. At the best speed possible to me, it would have taken three more years, and I suppose three more volumes, to have dealt adequately with the new subjects touched upon in the preceding pages; an extension which the limits of my readers' patience (to say nothing of my own) absolutely forbade.

At this point, therefore, my work ends. I have not attempted to make any direct inquiry into the habits of the people in their various classes, nor made any detailed study of administration as conducted by the various local authorities. But these subjects have naturally been continually before me, and a good deal of information has been gathered concerning them. Placed between saying nothing and saying what I could, I have chosen the latter alternative, and can only beg the indulgence of the reader for the presumption with which I have put forward my views on subjects so debatable and difficult.

Further than this it will be remarked that some subjects of extreme importance in connection with the life of London are hardly mentioned at all. The great Friendly Societies have been barely alluded to, and the system of popular life insurance has been neglected. Of Co-operative Distribution, whether on its wholesale or retail side, little has been said, whilst the great question of Co-operative Production has been but incidentally spoken of. More noteworthy still is the omission of any reference to the influence on London life of art and literature, and especially to that branch of literature which is termed *par excellence* 'The Press'. With regard to all these subjects I can only plead that in the absence of the body of special information needed, I could have offered but a few general and perhaps obvious remarks. There will doubtless be other subjects or points of view, the neglect of which may strike the reader, though perhaps none of quite equal importance, or so likely to be involved in future developments, as those I have mentioned. But besides any of which we may now be conscious, there will be others which coming years will unfold, when if this book should be consulted as a record of the past it will surely be with amazement at the failure to remark, or give their true significance to, the tendencies that will then appear to have been so evident; the stirrings of mighty movements, or the shooting of new life. How, it will inevitably be asked, is it possible that any one could have been so blind?

The last word I would add is this: the object of the sixteen volumes has been to describe London as it appeared in the last decade of the nineteenth century. Beyond this I have sought, however imperfectly, to show what is being done to ameliorate its conditions, and have suggested some directions in which advance might be made; but this last was no part of the original design, which was, solely, to observe and chronicle the actual, leaving remedies to others. To this attitude I would now revert. For the treatment of disease, it is first necessary to establish the facts as to its character, extent and symptoms. Perhaps the qualities of mind which enable a man to make this inquiry are the least of all likely to give him that elevation of soul, sympathetic insight, and sublime confidence which must go to the making of a great regenerating teacher. I have made no attempt to teach; at the most I have ventured on an appeal to those whose part it is. Some individual views and convictions have been intentionally allowed to show themselves here and there in comments made, but no body of doctrine is submitted.

The dry bones that lie scattered over the long valley that we have traversed together lie before my reader. May some great soul, master of a subtler and nobler alchemy than mine, disentangle the confused issues, reconcile the apparent contradictions in aim, melt and commingle the various influences for good into one divine uniformity of effort, and make these dry bones live, so that the streets of our Jerusalem may sing with joy.

Bibliography

Following is a list of books and pamphlets published by Booth

Life and Labour of the People, 1st ed., Vol. I. Williams & Norgate, 1889.

Labour and Life of the People, 1st ed., Vol. II. Williams & Norgate, 1891.

Pauperism, a Picture, and the Endowment of Old Age, an Argument, Macmillan, 1892.

Life and Labour of the People in London, 2nd ed., Macmillan, 1892–7. 9 vols.

The Aged Poor in England and Wales, Macmillan, 1899.

Old Age Pensions and the Aged Poor: A Proposal, Macmillan, 1899.

Improved Means of Locomotion as a First Step towards the Cure for the Housing Difficulties of London, Macmillan, 1901.

Life and Labour of the People in London, 3rd ed., Macmillan, 1902–3. 17 vols. First Series: *Poverty* (1902) Vols. I–IV. Second Series: *Industry* (1903) Vols. I–V. Third Series: *Religious Influences* (1902–3) Vols. I–VII. *Final Volume: Notes on Social Influences and Conclusion* (1903).

Poor Law Reform, Macmillan, 1910.

Reform of the Poor Law by the Adaptation of the Existing Poor Law Areas, and their Administration, Macmillan, 1910.

Comments on Proposals for the Reform of the Poor Laws, Macmillan, 1911.

Industrial Unrest and Trade Union Policy, Macmillan, 1913.

We found the study by T. S. Simey and M. B. Simey, *Charles Booth, Social Scientist* (Oxford University Press, 1960), indispensable in tracing the genesis and development of Booth's investigation. Booth's wife, Mary Booth, wrote a brief memoir, *Charles Booth* (Macmillan, 1918), which contains a number of his interesting letters.

Finally, we recommend the following works on the period

which proved useful to us. A fine brief history is David Thomson, *England in the Nineteenth Century: 1815–1914* (Jonathan Cape, 1964; Penguin Books, 1950). Much more detailed, especially on political matters, is R. C. K. Ensor, *England, 1870–1914* (Oxford, Clarendon Press, 1936), a volume in the Oxford History of England series. G. M. Young, *Victorian England; Portrait of an Age*, 2nd ed. (Oxford University Press, 1953), is a classic study of Victorian England. J. H. Clapham, *Machines and National Rivalries (1887–1914)*, Vol. III of *An Economic History of Modern Britain*, 2nd ed. (Cambridge University Press, 1930–8), exhaustively covers the years between 1886 and 1914. Administrative and political changes in Britain are clearly set forth in K. B. S. Smellie, *A Hundred Years of English Government* (Duckworth, 1950). And D. C. Somervell, *English Thought in the Nineteenth Century*, 2nd ed. (Longmans, 1947), provides decent summaries on prominent social reformers.

MORE ABOUT PENGUINS
AND PELICANS

Penguinews, which appears every month, contains details of all the new books issued by Penguins as they are published. From time to time it is supplemented by *Penguins in Print*, which is a complete list of all books published by Penguins which are in print. (There are well over three thousand of these.)

A specimen copy of *Penguinews* will be sent to you free on request, and you can become a subscriber for the price of the postage. For a year's issues (including the complete lists) please send 20p if you live in the United Kingdom, or 40p if you live elsewhere. Just write to Dept EP, Penguin Books Ltd, Harmondsworth, Middlesex, enclosing a cheque or postal order, and your name will be added to the mailing list.

Some other books published by Penguins are described on the following pages.

Note: *Penguinews* and *Penguins in Print* are not available in the U.S.A. or Canada

Penguin Modern Classics

MY APPRENTICESHIP

BEATRICE WEBB

Beatrice Webb, though for years she professed anti-feminism, might be termed the prototype of the intelligent and emancipated women of this century. The story of her work for Charles Booth and of her long partnership in the 'firm' of Sidney and Beatrice Webb is inseparable from the history of the Labour Movement and the Fabian Society.

In this brilliant account of her Victorian upbringing and early life she reveals the origins of her philosophy and method in social investigation and private life. Characteristically George Bernard Shaw wrote of the book:

'The treatise on method holds us as a unique volume of confessions, to say nothing of its record of contacts with all sorts and conditions of men, from the most comfortably corrupt and reactionary functionaries to the most devoted revolutionists of the gutter, or from Herbert Spencer, whom her genial unmetaphysical father entertained much as he might have kept a pet elephant, to all the parliamentary figures who passed as great, from Joseph Chamberlain to – well, to the present moment. And these are no mere staring and gabbling reminiscences, but judgments and generalisations which give depth to the narrative and value to the time spent in conning it.'

a Pelican Book

VICTORIAN PEOPLE

ASA BRIGGS

'With this book Asa Briggs makes good his right to be regarded and respected as one of the leading historians of the Victorian Age' – G. M. Young, author of *Victorian England*.

That 'Victorian' need no longer be considered a derogatory word is made very plain by Professor Briggs's reassessments of people, ideas, and events between the Great Exhibition of 1851 and the Second Reform Act of 1867.

A few of his chapter headings indicate the type of personality on whom the author has based a fresh viewpoint of the period: 'John Arthur Roebuck and the Crimean War', 'Samuel Smiles and the Gospel of Work', 'Thomas Hughes and the Public Schools', 'Robert Applegarth and the Trade Unions', 'John Bright and the Creed of Reform', 'Benjamin Disraeli and the Leap in the Dark'.

Recounted with unusual clarity and humour, the story of their achievements conjures up an enviable picture of progress and independence and adds substantially to the ordinary reader's knowledge of the last century.

'A warm and vivid book, as readable as it is well informed' – *New York Herald Tribune*

Not for sale in the U.S.A.

a Pelican Book

A HISTORY OF LONDON LIFE

R. J. MITCHELL AND M. D. R. LEYS

We have all heard of the Great Fire of 1666, but how many of us know of the Great Stink of 1858? The 'Blind Beak', Bartholomew Fair, public executions, the street vendors of birds' nests, groundsel, and lavender – these and many other curiosities are all described in this intriguing chronicle of the lives of London's inhabitants, ranging in time from pre-Roman days to the formation of the L.C.C. The authors, both distinguished historians, have drawn on varied contemporary sources such as unpublished letters, official documents, cartoons, and advertisements, to present an unusual and entertaining survey. Each of the chapters is linked with the name of a famous Londoner representative of his age, and through the eyes of such as Chaucer, the Chippendales, and Charles Dickens a fascinating composite picture of the metropolis emerges.

'Provides much welcome information, and is equipped with model footnotes to indicate sources. Sections cover every possible interest' – *Daily Telegraph*

a Pelican Book

VICTORIAN CITIES

ASA BRIGGS

'Our age is pre-eminently the age of great cities' – Robert Vaughan (1843).

In 1837 England and Wales boasted only five provincial cities of more than 100,000 inhabitants; by 1891 there were twenty-three and they housed nearly a third of the nation. Meantime London had expanded two and a third times.

Neither were these Victorian cities 'insensate' antheaps, as Lewis Mumford has called them. As this century progresses we can better appreciate the energy and civic purpose which created the cities of the nineteenth century.

In this revised and augmented edition of his companion to *Victorian People*, Professor Asa Briggs concentrates his inquiry on Manchester, Leeds, Birmingham, Middlesbrough, Melbourne (representing Victorian communities overseas), and London, the world city. Between these cities of the age of railways, trams, drains, and gas there are superficial resemblances in their problems of housing and sanitation, location of suburbs, schools, town halls, and churches: but Professor Briggs points up the differences too, and he provides us with a fascinating contrast between Manchester and Birmingham, as their civic courses diverged economically, socially and politically.

Not for sale in the U.S.A.

a Pelican Classic

REPORT TO THE COUNTY OF LANARK

A NEW VIEW OF SOCIETY

ROBERT OWEN

Robert Owen, the New Lanark mill-owner and social philosopher, was one of the first to stress the influence of environment upon character. His rationalistic belief in human perfectibility, and his unbounded faith in education to bring about a new moral order without class conflict led the Fabians to revere him as the father of English socialism. But his influence, V. A. C. Gatrell argues, was even wider; for although 'Owenism' as a cooperative movement soon dated, his belief in a harmonious organic community in contrast to unrestrained capitalism also inspired a Tory tradition. Owen's ideas and practice have entered our cultural bloodstream through many different channels.

ALSO IN THE PELICAN CLASSICS

Owen: *A New View of Society*
Edited by V. A. C. Gatrell

J. F. Cooper: *The American Democrat*
Edited by George Dekker and Larry Johnston

Adam Smith: *The Wealth of Nations*
Edited by Andrew Skinner

Hume: *The History of Great Britain*
Edited by Duncan Forbes

Mandeville: *The Fable of the Bees*
Edited by Phillip Harth

Mill: *The Principles of Political Economy*
Edited by Donald Winch

Jevons: *Theory of Political Economy*
Edited by R. D. C. Black

Ricardo: *Principles of Political Economy and Taxation*
Edited by Max Hartwell

Malthus: *Essay on the Principle of Population*
Edited by Anthony Flew

Machiavelli: *The Discourses*
Edited by Bernard Crick